BELIEFS IN GOVERNMENT

Volumes of a Research Programme of the European Science Foundation

Series Editors: Max Kaase, Kenneth Newton, and Elinor Scarbrough

PUBLIC OPINION AND INTERNATIONALIZED GOVERNANCE

This set of five volumes is an exhaustive study of beliefs in government in post-war Europe. Based upon an extensive collection of survey evidence, the results challenge widely argued theories of mass opinion, and much scholarly writing about citizen attitudes towards government and politics.

The **European Science Foundation** is an association of its fifty-six member research councils, academies, and institutions devoted to basic scientific research in twenty countries. The ESF assists its Member Organizations in two main ways: by bringing scientists together in its Scientific Programmes, Networks, and European Research Conferences to work on topics of common concern; and through the joint study of issues of strategic importance in European science policy.

The scientific work sponsored by ESF includes basic research in the natural and technical sciences, the medical and biosciences, the humanities, and the social sciences.

The ESF maintains close relations with other scientific institutions within and outside Europe. By its activities, ESF adds value by co-operation and co-ordination across national frontiers, offers expert scientific advice on strategic issues, and provides the European forum for fundamental science.

This volume arises from the work of the ESF Scientific Programme on Beliefs in Government (BiG).

Further information on ESF activities can be obtained from:

European Science Foundation
1, quai Lezay-Marnésia
F-67080 Strasbourg Cedex
France

Tel. (+33) 88 76 71 00
Fax (+33) 88 37 05 32

BELIEFS IN GOVERNMENT   VOLUME TWO

PUBLIC OPINION
AND
INTERNATIONALIZED
GOVERNANCE

❖

Edited by
OSKAR NIEDERMAYER
and
RICHARD SINNOTT

OXFORD UNIVERSITY PRESS

Oxford University Press, Great Clarendon Street, Oxford OX2 6DP

Oxford New York
Athens Auckland Bangkok Bogota Buenos Aires Calcutta
Cape Town Chennai Dar es Salaam Delhi Florence Hong Kong Istanbul
Karachi Kuala Lumpur Madrid Melbourne Mexico City Mumbai
Nairobi Paris São Paolo Singapore Taipei Tokyo Toronto Warsaw
and associated companies in
Berlin Ibadan

Oxford is a registered trade mark of Oxford University Press

Published in the United States by
Oxford University Press Inc., New York

First published 1995
First issued as paperback 1998

British Library Cataloguing in Publication Data
Data available

Library of Congress Cataloging in Publication Data
European publics and the internationalization of governance / edited by
Oskar Niedermayer and Richard Sinnott.
—(Beliefs in government ; v. 2)
Includes bibliographical references and index.
1. European Union—Public opinion.   2. United Nations—Public
opinion.   3. North Atlantic Treaty Organization—Public opinion.
4. Public opinion—Europe.   I. Niedermayer, Oskar.   II. Sinnott, R. (Richard)
III. Series.
JN30.E93   1995   337.1'42—dc20   95-633
ISBN 0-19-827958-2
ISBN 0-19-829476-X(Pbk.)

Printed in Great Britain
on acid-free paper by
Biddles Ltd, Guildford and King's Lynn

FOREWORD

This is one of five volumes in a series produced by the Beliefs in Government research programme of the European Science Foundation. The volumes, all published by Oxford University Press in 1995, are as follows:

i *Citizens and the State*, edited by Hans-Dieter Klingemann and Dieter Fuchs
ii *Public Opinion and Internationalized Governance*, edited by Oskar Niedermayer and Richard Sinnott
iii *The Scope of Government*, edited by Ole Borre and Elinor Scarbrough
iv *The Impact of Values*, edited by Jan van Deth and Elinor Scarbrough
v *Beliefs in Government*, authored by Max Kaase and Kenneth Newton

The first chapter of *Beliefs in Government* presents a brief history of the research project, its general concerns, approach and methods, and an outline of the relationship of each volume to the project as a whole.

All five books share a debt of gratitude which we would like to acknowledge on their behalf. The European Science Foundation (ESF) supported and funded the research programme throughout its five long and arduous years. Eleven of the research councils and academies which are members of the ESF have made a financial contribution to the overall costs of the project—Belgium, Denmark, Finland, France, the Federal Republic of Germany, Ireland, Italy, the Netherlands, Norway, Sweden, and the United Kingdom. We would like to thank the ESF and these member organizations five times over—once for each book.

All five volumes were copy-edited by Heather Bliss, whose eagle eye and endless patience are unrivalled in the Western world. At Oxford University Press we were lucky indeed to have two understanding editors in Tim Barton and Dominic Byatt.

In particular, John Smith, the Secretary of the ESF's Standing Committee for the Social Sciences, and his staff put in huge efforts and gave us encouragement at every stage of the project. Having gone through the process with other ESF research programmes a few times before, they knew when we started what an immense task lay in wait for us all, but were not daunted. We cannot lay claim to any such bravery, and have only our innocence as an excuse.

Max Kaase
Kenneth Newton
Elinor Scarbrough

December 1994

PREFACE

This volume is the second in the series of five volumes resulting from the *Beliefs in Government* programme directed by Max Kaase and Kenneth Newton. It is the joint product of a research group of fifteen scholars from twelve European countries who worked together for nearly five years, meeting in Paris, Milan, Colchester, Sintra, Dublin, and Berlin.

This period was professionally fruitful and socially enjoyable. We therefore thank our colleagues in the research group not only for their contributions to this volume but also for the good times we had together. Our one regret is that Annick Percheron's last illness prevented her from joining the group; our work would have benefited from her wisdom and experience.

We wish also to thank several people and institutions for their assistance in various aspects of our work. We are grateful to the European Science Foundation for initiating the project and supporting it throughout. Special thanks go to Dr John Smith whose remarkable skills and flexibility in the administration of the project made our lives so much easier.

The success of our work very much depended on the availability of cross-national survey data. We are therefore particularly indebted to the Zentralarchiv in Cologne, especially to Ekkehard Mochmann, for providing us with the data we needed.

Our work benefited from the advice and criticism of many colleagues both from within and outside the BiG project. Particularly valuable were the contributions of Beate Kohler-Koch and Richard Eichenberg, presented at the Strasbourg conference held in June 1993. Their constructive comments on the draft manuscript helped us greatly when it came to finalizing our work.

For tremendous help in all stages of the project, including the editorial work for this volume, we thank Elinor Scarbrough, the research co-ordinator for the BiG project. We are also grateful for the secretarial assistance provided at different stages of the project by Christine Wilkinson, Helen Sibley, and Sharon Duthie.

Oskar Niedermayer
Richard Sinnott

February 1995

CONTENTS

LIST OF FIGURES

LIST OF TABLES

ABBREVIATIONS

AIDS	Acquired immune deficiency syndrome
CIS	Commonwealth of Independent States
CSCE	Conference on Security and Co-operation in Europe
EC	European Community
ECSC	European Coal and Steel Community
EEC	European Economic Community
EFTA	European Free Trade Association
EPC	European Political Co-operation
EU	European Union
EURATOM	European Atomic Energy Community
NATO	North Atlantic Treaty Organization
PASOK	Panhellenic Socialist Movement
SEA	Single European Act
SEM	Single European Market
TEEPS	European Élite Panel Survey
UN	United Nations
ZEUS	Zentrum für Europäische Umfrageanalysen und Studien

Standard country abbreviations used in the tables and figures

AU	Austria
BE	Belgium
BUL	Bulgaria
CZ	Czechoslovakia
DK	Denmark
FI	Finland
FR	France
GB	Britain
GE	Germany
GR	Greece
HUN	Hungary
IC	Iceland
IR	Ireland
IT	Italy
LU	Luxembourg
NL	Netherlands
NO	Norway
POL	Poland
PO	Portugal
SP	Spain
SV	Sweden
SW	Switzerland

LIST OF CONTRIBUTORS

FRANK AAREBROT, Associate Professor, Department of Comparative Politics, University of Bergen.

STEN BERGLUND, Professor of Political Science, Åbo Academy, University of Finland.

AGUSTI BOSCH, Lecturer, Faculty of Political Science and Sociology, Automona University of Barcelona.

SOPHIE DUCHESNE, Associate Professor, Centre d'Étude de la Vie Politique Française, Fondation Nationale des Sciences Politiques, Paris.

PHILIP EVERTS, Director of the Institute for International Studies, University of Leiden.

ANDRÉ-PAUL FROGNIER, Professor of Political Science, Catholic University of Louvain.

JADWIGA KORALEWICZ, Professor at the Institute of Political Studies, Polish Academy of Sciences.

GUIDO MARTINOTTI, Professor of Urban Sociology, University of Milan, Chairman of the Committee for the Social Sciences, European Science Foundation.

OSKAR NIEDERMAYER, Professor of Political Science, Free University of Berlin.

KENNETH NEWTON, Professor of Government, University of Essex.

RICHARD SINNOTT, Lecturer in Politics and Director of the Centre for European Economic and Public Affairs, University College Dublin.

SONIA STEFFANIZZI, Researcher, Istituto Superiore di Sociologie, Università L. Bocconi, Milan.

THOMAS WENINGER, Lecturer, Institute of Political Science, University of Vienna.

BERNHARD WESSELS, Senior Fellow, Wissenschaftszentrum, Berlin.

BETTINA WESTLE, Researcher, Zentrum für Umfragen, Methoden, und Analysen, Mannheim.

1

Introduction

OSKAR NIEDERMAYER AND RICHARD SINNOTT

The second half of the twentieth century has been marked by a continuing transformation in the role of the state. One of the most potent sources of this on-going transformation has been a series of developments in the international system. These include: the intensification of economic interdependence; the need, which was especially evident in Europe after the Second World War, to find an alternative means of managing the security aspect of inter-state relations; the increasing inability of the nation state to solve a range of problems that transcend national boundaries and, finally, the emergence of a variety of transnational actors. The response to these pressures has taken the form of a growing internationalization of governance.

In seeking to clarify this term, we must emphasize that we are dealing with an analogy. In some cases, the analogy to governance in domestic political systems, defined as the 'authoritative allocation of values' (Easton 1965: 50), is quite close. In other cases, in which states merely accept some minimal institutionalized constraints on their behaviour, it is more tenuous. This latter category consists of a set of institutions for the management of interdependence. In the international relations literature, such institutions are referred to as 'international regimes', defined by Keohane and Nye as 'the sets of governing arrangements that affect relationships of interdependence' (1977: 19) We may put the matter another way by saying that we think of internationalized governance as spanning a continuum from a fully fledged international governmental system (political union) through a more rudimentary system (the European Community, or latterly the European Union)[1] to the weaker forms of internationalized governance comprising a variety of 'international regimes'.[2]

Theory and Data

The subject matter of this volume is the attitudes and orientations of European publics towards the continuum of internationalized governance.[3] Of necessity, the institutions and processes of the European Community have constituted the main focus of our work. This is so, primarily, because the European Community has long been the main embodiment of internationalized governance in Europe. Secondly, the bulk of the available public opinion data relates to the European Community. Where possible, however, we have expanded our inquiry to other forms of internationalized governance, and throughout the enterprise we have sought to frame our research in such a way as to draw out the significance of the findings for the process as such rather than just for a particular instance of internationalized governance.

What is there to suggest that there is such a phenomenon as mass orientations towards internationalized governance? Several years ago, that question might have caused a hiccup in a programme of research of this sort and doubts would not have been quelled by the images derived from the version of neo-functionalist integration theory then current. However, the events of the year 1992, especially the Danish rejection of the Maastricht Treaty in June, the close call in France in September, and the rejection by the Swiss of the European Economic Area Agreement in December put paid to any such doubts. More importantly, the review of theories of integration in Chapter 2 shows that the emphasis on élites in integration theory was more apparent than real. Over and above establishing the relevance of public opinion to internationalized governance and identifying the circumstances in which public opinion becomes relevant, the theories of regional integration and international regimes reviewed there throw considerable light on the range of attitudes involved. But the range of attitudes also needs to be spelled out systematically. This task of classifying the modes and objects of orientations towards internationalized governance is tackled in Chapter 3, in which, following a discussion of various approaches to categorizing orientations and attitudes, an analytical scheme adapting aspects of Easton's systems framework is put forward. This provided a common vocabulary for the volume and served as a check-list to guide the research.

Before previewing the research agenda, we should emphasize that given the available data and the general approach of the Beliefs in Government programme, our research focuses exclusively on mass attitudes. We are interested, primarily, in the dimensions and in the sources and correlates of attitudes, while making assumptions about their impact and consequences. A further important aspect of the design underlying the Beliefs in Government project is that the research is based on secondary analysis of existing data. This design feature opens up considerable possibilities but also carries with it certain limitations, which may be particularly acute in the study of attitudes towards integration. In discussing the impact of cultural variables on integration, Wallace noted that while they are essential elements in political integration, they are 'the most contested because the most difficult to measure' (1990a: 9).

Having painstakingly picked our way through a thicket of operationalization issues, we can only agree that measuring such things as diffuse and specific orientations towards internationalized governance, sense of community and European identity, democratic values, and policy orientations is problematic. Some of these problems are inherent in research on mass culture and public opinion; for example, problems arising from the artificiality of the interview situation. In cases where the issues concerned are of low salience, there is always the danger that the interaction involved in the interview situation generates an attitude which would not otherwise have existed. Over and above this, there is the general problem of validity: do the data tell us what we want to know? Are the answers to particular questions valid indicators of the particular attitude we want to measure? As noted elsewhere in the companion volumes, the problem of validity presents a particular challenge in studies which are systematically cross-cultural. Furthermore, the freedom of manœuvre that a researcher has in dealing with the problem of validity is particularly limited when the approach is based on secondary analysis of available data. In this regard, it should be noted that our study relies heavily on data from a single source—the long series of Eurobarometer surveys. The time span covered and the wealth of data contained in the series make it by far the best source of evidence available for our purposes. This is not to say that it is a perfect source.

The Eurobarometer surveys are conducted on behalf of the Commission of the European Communities. This programme started in 1970 with the first European Community Study, followed by a second in

1971, and a third in 1973. In 1974, the Eurobarometer surveys were launched as a regular programme to monitor public opinion in the Community. Since then, representative national samples of the public in each member state have been interviewed in the spring and autumn of each year.[4] Eurobarometer surveys are omnibus surveys consisting of a standard part and supplementary studies. The standard part includes questions on orientations towards the European Community as well as towards other social and political objects. There is also a standard series of demographic questions. The aims of these surveys are to provide information for the Commission and other Community institutions and to inform the public.

Some of the issues and themes pursued by the Eurobarometer studies over the years have arisen from purely scientific concerns. The sustained preoccupation with the measurement of materialism and post-materialism is a good example. However, many of the Eurobarometer questions are driven by policy concerns rather than scientific considerations. These policy concerns limit the choice of topics covered and may affect the wording of questions. While this is a benefit in terms of the policy relevance of the indicators, there may not, at times, be enough distance from the immediate issues to provide the kind of data we would ideally like to have. Moreover, changes in the wording of questions dictated by changing policy considerations face us with difficulties in the construction of time series. When we note discontinuities in trends, we sometimes do not know whether these are due to changes in the questions or to other factors.

Set against these limitations, there are also advantages attached to the Eurobarometer data, provided the indicators are carefully handled and evaluated. These advantages derive from the purchase the Eurobarometer data provides on two aspects of variation in attitudes—systemic variation and variation over time. The existence of comparable measures over a long period of time and across a large number of political systems allows us to pursue two types of analysis at different levels: cross-sectional and longitudinal analysis—that is, analysis at a single point in time and analysis of change over time. The different levels are the micro-level analysis of individuals, without reference to the system in which they are located, and the macro-level analysis of differences between countries and the systemic properties which give rise to them. Combining the distinctions between types and levels of analysis clarifies the range of analytic possibilities. These are set out schematically in Table 1.1. In common with the other volumes in this series, this volume

TABLE 1.1. *Types and levels of analysis and corresponding variables*

Type of analysis	Level of analysis	
	Micro level	Macro level
Cross-sectional	Socio-structural position; political involvement; values/norms/ideology	Political/cultural heritage; position in the international division of labour
Longitudinal	Modernization; value change	Societal learning; economic development

focuses primarily on the micro level of analysis. However, where possible, we also present macro-level analyses tracing differences in the orientations of the citizenry of various countries to variations in the characteristics of those countries.

The Research Agenda

With these distinctions and qualifications in mind, we can go on to outline the structure of the volume and the themes taken up in the individual chapters. Following a review of the theoretical background to our research in Part I, and drawing in particular on the analytic scheme developed in Chapter 3, Part II focuses on the development and sources of support for European integration in general. The first chapter in this part, Chapter 4, presents a descriptive overview of attitudes towards the EC during the last two decades, and also discusses possible explanations for country variations in terms of geo-political and historical links between countries and the political heritage of individual countries. The longitudinal nature of the analysis allows a preliminary exploration of the societal learning hypothesis and the impact of short-term factors (in this case, a particular political event) on attitudes towards the EC. The event in question is the signing of the Maastricht Treaty.[5]

Chapter 5 focuses on economic explanations of support for integration, pursuing the theme at both the macro and the micro level. The macro-level analysis examines the impact of variables such as net budgetary transfers between the Community and individual member states, each country's position in the international division of labour, as well as several indicators of economic development. At the micro level, the chapter analyses the influence of individual economic circumstances, perceptions, and expectations on their attitudes and orientations.

In the contemporary world, the common feature of a range of micro-level variables which have a potential impact on attitudes is change—the changing nature and salience of occupational class, rising educational levels, changes in the significance of generation and gender, ideological and value change, changes in levels of political involvement. Accordingly, the impact of such variables over time has to be considered. Chapter 6 tackles this question, focusing on the issue of whether change in attitudes towards European integration are characterized by a process of replacement or by a process of diffusion. Whatever the processes affecting changes in attitudes at the individual level, they do not function in isolation from the institutional context and the political process. The role of élites is particularly important and Chapter 7 sets out to examine 'mass-push' versus 'élite-pull' interpretations of the relationship between élite action and public opinion. This leads on to an examination of a cascade model of opinion formation and to consideration of the impact of party manifestos in the periods running up to and immediately after national elections. It is important to bear in mind, however, that the arena within which party competition and party mobilization takes place is also an object of attitudes, sometimes an object of intense attachment. Chapter 8 examines the relationship between attitudes towards the national political system on the one hand and attitudes towards the EC on the other and develops a fourfold typology of attitudes towards national and internationalized governance.

The classification developed in Chapter 3 highlights the importance of dealing with orientations towards the different components of internationalized governance. The implication is that legitimacy may be a highly differentiated phenomenon, depending on which aspect is being considered; that is, whether one is dealing with, in the terminology developed in Chapter 3, orientations towards the political collectivity (for example, identity and trust), towards the functional scope of internationalized governance (policy orientations), or towards the political order (orientations towards democracy at the international level). Following up these distinctions, Part III considers the empirical evidence relating to each of these dimensions of internationalized governance.[6]

Chapter 9 focuses on the question of European identity, asking whether there is any evidence that such an identity exists at all at the mass level. Chapter 10 tackles the question of trust and sense of community between the peoples of the member states. However, establishing legitimacy requires more than just a sense of community and mutual identification. Chapter 11 deals with the functional scope of internationalized governance, focusing in particular on attitudes towards the allocation of policy competences between the national and international level. The analysis seeks to tease out the implications for legitimacy of possible discrepancies between mass orientations, the actual allocation of competences, and the principle of subsidiarity. Finally, since progress along the continuum of internationalized governance quickly encounters issues to do with the political order, particularly the problems of democratic accountability, access, and participation, Chapter 12 examines the 'democratic deficit' from a public opinion perspective.

In Part IV, our perspective is broadened to consider attitudes towards the extension of internationalized governance. Extension can take three forms: extension of the territorial scope of the European Community or Union through successive waves of enlargement; extension of the functional scope of the Community through the inclusion of a wider range of issues within its ambit; and extension of internationalized governance through other institutional frameworks. Chapter 13 examines the question of EC enlargement as seen from within the Community, beginning with attitudes towards the first round of enlargement in 1973 and bringing the story up to the point at which enlargement has become one of the principal issues on the internationalization agenda. Chapter 14 examines attitudes towards the European Community in five EFTA countries (the Nordic countries, Austria, and Switzerland) while Chapter 15 analyses attitudes in the countries of Central and Eastern Europe towards various forms of European integration and co-operation. Both chapters emphasize the need to take account of the macro-level context in attempting to explain the attitudes in question. Chapter 16 deals with the second and third aspects of extension, examining attitudes towards the North Atlantic Treaty Organization (NATO) and also considering how such attitudes relate to attitudes towards European integration and the role of the European Union in the area of security and defence. In so far as the limited data permit, the chapter also looks at attitudes towards a third relevant institution in this area of internationalization—the United Nations. Finally, Chapter 17 draws together the different threads of our research and offers some concluding reflections on the legitimacy of internationalized governance in Europe.

NOTES

1. As this volume largely focuses on longitudinal analysis over the past two decades, we use the term 'European Community' as the general designation, resorting to the specific terms 'European Economic Communities' or 'European Union' only when the context requires it.
2. There is some dispute in the international relations literature as to whether the term 'internationalized governance' or 'global governance' should include international regimes. Rosenau (1992a: 9), for example, explicitly excludes them. Our usage is in line with that of Kratochwil and Ruggie (1986: 759), who argue that 'international regimes were thought to express both the parameters and the perimeters of international governance'.
3. Definitions of the terms 'attitudes' and 'orientations', and related terms are considered in Ch. 3. Where precision is essential to the argument the terms are used in the technical sense defined there. In this introduction and in the broad discussion elsewhere in this volume, the terms are used together or separately simply to denote public opinion in general.
4. The standard sample size of these surveys is approximately 1,000 per country of the population aged 15 years and older. A smaller sample of 300 was taken in Luxembourg until 1990, but since then the sample size has been 500. Since 1975, a sample of 300 for Northern Ireland has been added to the sample for Great Britain to constitute the United Kingdom sample. Since autumn 1990, an additional sample of 1,000 has been interviewed in East Germany resulting in a total sample size of 2,000 for Germany. As most of the analyses in this volume focus on long-term trends, the German data refer to West Germany unless otherwise stated.
5. International political events usually influence the attitudes of citizens via the mass media. Thus, we have to distinguish between the political events themselves and their interpretation by the media. A systematic analysis of the relationship between events and orientations would require not only several measurement points on the dependent variable in a specific time period but also an independent measurement of media coverage. Unfortunately, we lack cross-nationally comparable data on the media coverage of events. The only study we know of in this field is the analysis of British data by Dalton and Duval (1986). Accordingly, systematic analysis of the impact of events on mass attitudes is not included in this volume.
6. Empirical analysis of a fourth category of orientations—orientations towards the political authorities—is not possible because there are virtually no data relating to attitudes towards the major political actors at the EC level.

PART I

Theoretical Perspectives

2

Bringing Public Opinion Back In

RICHARD SINNOTT

In the light of events since 1989, it is now a common assumption that public opinion must be taken into account in any analysis of the increasingly complex and dense network of inter-state relations in Europe and, by implication, elsewhere. The purpose of this chapter is to go beyond *ad hoc* observations about the relevance of public opinion to explore what international relations theory, specifically the theory of political integration and regime theory, tells us about the relationship between public opinion and internationalized governance. The aim is to specify if, when, and how, public opinion might be expected to play a role, and what elements of public opinion are most likely to have an impact on the legitimacy of internationalized governance. Together with the detailed classification of orientations developed in Chapter 3, the discussion is designed to provide a focus and a context for the empirical chapters that follow.

One invests effort in integration theory with some trepidation. In the first place, it has been suggested that in the end it will be consigned to 'a rather long but not very prominent footnote in the intellectual history of twentieth century social science' (Puchala 1984: 198). Equally off-putting is the title of a book by one of the originators of the theory— *The Obsolescence of Regional Integration Theory* (Haas 1976). Finally, one quickly becomes aware that more is at stake than just explaining political integration; the underlying issues relate to intellectual battles between realism, neo-realism, liberalism, and idealism as contending schools of international relations theory (Nye 1987: 5–9; Puchala 1984: 206–12). This chapter is not the place to attempt to resolve such issues.

But encouragement can be derived from recent indications of a

revival of interest in the problems of theorizing about integration
(Keohane and Hoffmann 1990; Wallace 1990*a*; Caporaso and Keeler
1993). It can be argued that this renewed attention represents a third
phase in the development of the theory of political integration. In this
perspective, the first phase consisted of two ambitious initial formulations (transactionalism and neo-functionalism) in the late 1950s and
early 1960s.[1] A second short-lived phase, characterized by an intense
revisionism, can be identified in the late 1960s. However, despite the
theoretical progress made in this second phase, afterwards integration
theory suffered near fatal asphyxia in the Euro-stagnation of the late
1970s. The third, contemporary phase is therefore a revival, if not a
resurrection.[2] This chapter considers these three phases of integration
theory, with brief digressions to deal with the related theories of
disintegration and diversity.[3] We then broaden out the discussion to
incorporate insights from the theory of international regimes and to
review theoretical constructs used in previous empirical work on
attitudes towards integration.

Transactionalism: The Centrality of Sentiment

Although labelled transactionalism because it accords a prominent role
to the frequency of intra-group and inter-group transactions (Puchala
1984: 199), Deutsch's theory is far removed from communications
determinism. In fact, Deutsch *et al.* (1957: 22) specifically reject the
widespread belief that 'modern life, with rapid transportation, mass
communications, and literacy, tends to be more international . . . and
hence more conducive to the growth of international or supranational
institutions'. They begin with a definition. Integration is 'the attainment, within a territory, of a "sense of community" and of institutions
and practices strong enough and widespread enough to assure, for a
"long" time, dependable expectations of peaceful change' (1957: 5).
Such integration produces a 'security community' which may then
proceed to amalgamation (full political union or merger) or may not.
In the latter case it is referred to as a 'pluralistic security community'.
The prominence of 'sense of community' in the definition is particularly
interesting. Sense of community is 'a matter of mutual sympathies and
loyalty; of "we-feeling", trust, and mutual consideration; of partial
identification in terms of self-images and interests; of mutually successful predictions of behaviour, and of co-operative action in accordance

with it . . .' (1957: 36). From this it is clear that cultural variables are central to Deutsch's concept of integration. Such variables are equally prominent in the list of conditions conducive to integration, shown in Figure 2.1.

Even a glance at the figure indicates that the first three and the last three conditions are measurable at the level of the mass public by means of survey data (as well as by other means). In addition, items 7–9 (broadening the political élite, mobility of persons, and a multiplicity of ranges of communication) have implied cultural effects. Only items 3 and 4 bear no relationship to political culture and mass orientations. It may be countered that the conditions are required to exist in the 'politically relevant strata'. This reflects the fact that the investigation was based in many instances on pre-democratic societies. It is a matter for decision as to how one operationalizes 'politically relevant strata'. A narrow operationalization would confine measurement of the conditions in Figure 2.1 to some segment of the political elite, thus depriving the theory of relevance to mass public opinion. This would be unduly restrictive when, in the latter half of the twentieth century, a strong case

---

Essential conditions

1. Mutual compatibility of main values
2. Distinctive way of life: values, institutions, and habits of action which mark the area off from major neighbours
3. Expectations of stronger economic ties or gains
4. Increase in administrative and political capability in at least some of the units
5. Superior economic growth of at least some of the units
6. Unbroken social communication both across territories and across strata
7. Broadening of the political élite, both in regard to recruitment from wider strata and in regard to connections between strata
8. Mobility of persons
9. A multiplicity of ranges of communication and transaction

Possibly essential conditions

10. A compensation or balance of flows of communication, transaction, and rewards between units
11. Interchange of unit roles as contributor–recipient, initiator–follower, majority–minority
12. Mutual predictability of behaviour

FIGURE 2.1. *Conditions for an amalgamated security community*

Source: constructed from Deutsch *et al.* (1957: 46–58).

can be made that the politically relevant strata includes a sizeable section of the mass public. Moreover, a narrow interpretation would not be consistent with the references Deutsch *et al.* make to contemporary society or, indeed, with the inclusion of 'the broadening of the political élite' as one of the essential conditions. In sum, this first major statement of integration theory accords what is perhaps a surprisingly prominent role to public opinion and political culture.

Although a rich source of relevant concepts and hypotheses, Deutsch's theory has been criticized for failing to spell out the process which leads to integration. As Puchala (1984: 203) puts it, the theory is 'incomplete, not inaccurate'. Puchala argues that the necessary complement to transactionalism may be found in neo-functionalism. When the original formulation of neo-functionalism is examined, however, the proposed complementarity appears problematic, since that formulation specifically excludes mass opinion.

Neo-Functionalism: The Dominance of the Élite

Haas and Schmitter (1964: 707) begin by advancing the core neo-functionalist thesis: 'under modern conditions the relationship between economic and political union had best be treated as a continuum. Hence definite political implications can be associated with most movements toward economic integration even when the chief actors themselves do not entertain such notions at the time of adopting their new constitutive charter.' Political union is defined as 'any arrangement under which existing nation-states cease to act as autonomous decision-making units with respect to an important range of policies' (1964: 709). Haas (1958: 16) had earlier given a fuller definition of political integration as 'the process whereby political actors in several distinct national settings are persuaded to shift loyalties, expectations and political activities toward a new centre, whose institutions possess or demand jurisdiction over the pre-existing national states'. The theory goes on to specify the conditions which characterize this process on the eve of economic union, as the union is negotiated, and after it becomes operative. These conditions are set out in Figure 2.2.

The distinctive neo-functionalist elements in Figure 2.2 relate to the role and activities of integrationist élites and the significance of the policy process in which they are involved: that is, the mechanisms of supranational bureaucratic problem-solving (condition 7) and spillover

---

Background conditions

1. Size of units; approximate functional equality seen as desirable
2. Transaction rates: trade figures, labour mobility, capital movements, professional establishment, student exchange
3. Pluralism within units and in the area as a whole; group conduct should be functionally specific, universalistic, and achievement-orientated
4. Complementarity of élite values

Conditions at a time of economic union

5. Governmental purposes; presence or absence of strong commitment to political union with identical versus converging economic aims
6. Powers of union; built-in or automatic integration with independent regional bureaucrats versus negotiated integration

Process conditions

7. Decision-making style; supra-national bureaucratic problem-solving versus diplomatic bargaining
8. Transaction rates; item 2 above re-examined after economic union
9. Adaptability of governments; a combination of 'spillover' and the overcoming of crises by the manipulation and negotiation of new functions from obsolete purposes

---

FIGURE 2.2. *Neo-functionalist conditions of integration*

Source: constructed from Haas and Schmitter (1964: 705–37).

(condition 9). Although the other variables in Figure 2.2 parallel some of the 'essential conditions' in the Deutsch scheme, in this case they refer exclusively to élite, group, or institutional characteristics and patterns. Denial of the relevance of mass attitudes in the integration process is made quite explicit by Haas (1958: 16) when he elaborates on his definition of political integration. He explains at some length that the 'political actors' in the definition are 'elites': 'the leaders of all relevant political groups who habitually participate in the making of public decisions, whether as policy-makers in government, as lobbyists or as spokesmen of political parties'. Consistent with this, he argues that 'it is as impracticable as it is unnecessary to have recourse to general public opinion and attitude surveys'. All of this underlines the point that the original formulation of the neo-functionalist perspective provides little encouragement or guidance regarding the analysis of public orientations towards internationalized governance.

As the classic statement of neo-functionalism, the Haas–Schmitter formulation has been highly influential. It has entrenched the view that public opinion, political culture, and the mass of the citizenry are largely irrelevant to the integration process. However, as we shall see, one of the major changes in neo-functionalism in its revisionist phase relates precisely to the role ascribed to public opinion. But before turning to this, it is necessary to look at the other side of the coin, to consider theories which seek to explain the many manifestations of disintegration within states and of persistent diversity between them.

Disintegration Theory: Core versus Periphery

Core–periphery theory sees division rather than integration as the most likely effect of the increase in communication and interaction which accompanies modernization. Industrialization, the engine of moderniza-tion, is compared to a wave which hits different areas at different times. Industrialization is therefore inherently uneven. Unevenness leads to inequality between the geographically defined units; that is, between core and periphery. At this stage, however, conflict is not inevitable. The outcome depends on certain pre-existing cultural conditions. On the one hand, if the populations of the geographical units are culturally homogeneous, the population of the subordinate unit will gradually become incorporated and the region or territorial unit will become either depopulated or depressed as it awaits, perhaps vainly, perhaps not, the coming of the wave of industrialization. On the other hand, if the units are culturally heterogeneous, then the cultural differences provide the means to remedy the inequitable situation through a strategy of national secession (Gellner 1964: 171–2).

Hechter presents a very similar theory, but cast in the language of 'internal colonialism'. According to Hechter, where cultural markers differentiate a subordinate from a superordinate population the result is 'a cultural division of labour' (Hechter 1975: 39). This cultural division of labour contributes to the development of distinctive ethnic identities, greatly increasing the probability that conflict and secession rather than integration will be the outcome. In the case of core–periphery conflict theory, then, there is just one key proposition: uneven industrialization produces core–periphery inequalities, which, if allied to significant cultural differences, produce secessionist tendencies.

We saw in Figure 2.1 (items 4 and 5) that Deutsch postulates both political and economic inequality between amalgamating units as a condition of integration. Deutsch's theory even uses the language of core and periphery: 'Larger, stronger, more politically, administratively, economically, and educationally advanced political units were found to form the cores of strength around which in most cases the integrative process developed' (Deutsch 1957: 38). Given the prominence of the core–periphery distinction in both theories, what leads to different outcomes for Deutsch and Gellner? The difference occurs because, in the Deutsch model, inequalities are offset by a balance over a period of time in 'the flow of rewards, of initiatives, or of respect' (1957: 55). In other words, item 10 in Figure 2.1 is the factor in Deutsch's theory which makes for core–periphery integration rather than core–periphery conflict and disintegration. Entirely consistent with this, perceptions of group inequality based on a sense of cultural distinctiveness are crucial in explaining conflict and disintegration in the core–periphery theory. Thus both theories lead to the conclusion that students of integration should take careful account of cultural identities and of perceptions of equality and inequality among the mass of the population.

A Theory of Diversity: The Obstinate Nation State

Hoffmann's (1966) article 'Obstinate or Obsolete? The Fate of the Nation State and the Case of Western Europe' was probably the most formidable intellectual challenge to the integration theorists. Re-reading Hoffmann from the perspective of what integration theory has to say about public opinion is instructive. Much of the emphasis is on national interests and on the activities and importance of political élites, yet the argument frequently refers to the popular basis of élite action and to 'national consciousness'.

Focusing on what he calls the 'national situations' of individual states, Hoffmann rejects the neo-functionalist process approach, criticizing it from the point of view of its goals, its methods, and its putative results. He argues that it is not so much that neo-functionalism has no impact, but that it has a limit, the limit being the point at which different perceptions of national interest are encountered. From Hoffmann's discussion of this limit and of the obstacles to integration involved, it is possible to draw out an implicit theory of political diversity and, by implication, of political integration. At the risk of doing violence to the flow of Hoffmann's argument, several propositions can be extracted— as specified in Figure 2.3.

The first two items in this list, referring to national consciousness and

Conditions conducive to obstinacy

1. A negative, non-purposive national consciousness
2. A national conscience which is too strong or too weak
3. The comprehensiveness of the modern state (in the sense of its broad functional scope, well-established authority, and popular basis)
4. The enjoyment by states of an autonomous existence on the world scene for a long time
5. A high degree of involvement of the political units in the international system

Conditions conducive to obsolescence

6. An intense and positive general will or enlightened national patriotism capable of prodding leaders into political integration
7. Transnational political issues of interest to all political forces and publics across boundary communities
8. Integrating units which are themselves integrated political communities
9. Domination of the executives of integrating units by pro-integration leaders
10. Statesmen holding similar interpretations of their own historical experience and geopolitical position
11. A compellingness in the international system, i.e. a perceived external threat
12. The expansion of the popular basis of the new European political system, i.e. that parties and pressure groups should prevail over executives
13. A new central bureaucracy with self-sustaining and expanding capacity of scope

FIGURE 2.3. *Conditions conducive to the obstinacy and obsolescence of the nation state*

Source: constructed from Hoffmann (1966: 862–915).

national conscience are, by definition, cultural variables. It is true that the role of these variables is circumscribed; as Hoffmann puts it, the state of national consciousness is not the main obstacle to political integration. However, no such qualification applies to item 7 (transnational issues of interest to all political forces and publics across boundaries). This is clearly a public opinion variable; so is the notion of a general will prodding leaders towards political integration (item 5). In addition, items 8, 11, and 12 (that the integrating units be political communities, that there be some perceived external threat, and that the popular basis of the new European political system be expanded) have a significant public opinion dimension. Moreover, it is scarcely conceivable that item 9 (that executives be dominated by pro-integration leaders) could obtain without having a significant effect on public opinion or being influenced by it. Finally, there is item 3—the comprehensiveness of the modern state. Defined in terms of the extent of 'the functional scope, authority, and popular basis' of the state (Hoffmann 1966: 892), this has a clear public opinion referent both in terms of the popular basis of the state, which rests on 'socially mobilized and mobilizing political parties', and in terms of the public's attitude to the functional scope of the state and to its authority. This leaves only four of the thirteen variables extracted from Hoffmann's discussion—three relating to the international role of the state (items 4, 5, and 10) and one relating to the supranational bureaucracy (item 13)—which bear no relationship at all to political culture or public opinion.

Thus, contrary to what is often assumed, Hoffmann's critique did not argue that integration could never happen or that the obstinate nation state would inevitably triumph. Rather, he argued that integration is contingent. And it is contingent to a remarkable extent on developments in political culture and public opinion. Indeed, looking at Gellner and Hoffmann together, what is striking is that the critics of integration theory appear to have had a more profound grasp of the significance of political culture variables than the early neo-functionalists. In this respect, they had more in common with the transactionalist version of integration theory, although, obviously, the emphasis and the conclusions drawn were different.

Public Opinion Rediscovered

In introducing the revisionist phase of integration theory, Haas (1971: 26–30) explicitly withdrew his earlier exclusion of public opinion. This is particularly evident in his new 'master concept' of authority legitimacy transfer or sharing: 'a formulation I would myself prefer to the stress put on elite loyalties in my own earlier formulations'. Indicators of this concept are observable in activity 'in specific functional and organizational sectors and . . . in elite *and mass perceptions*' (emphasis added). This acceptance of the role of mass attitudes is confirmed when Haas addresses the problem of linking 'variables that describe the rate of transaction between units with variables that describe the attitudes of masses and members of the elites'. He suggests focusing on the notion of social learning as a major link, speculating on the various elements that might be involved; for example, increased contact and familiarity, growing complexity in the pattern of inter-group loyalties and social roles, education and informal socialization practices and progressively rewarding experiences derived from the activities of common markets. All this is a far cry from Haas's earlier rejection of the relevance of public opinion.

Schmitter (1971: 233) is quite explicit about his revisionist intentions, offering 'a revised formalization of the neo-functionalist or structuralist theory of the political consequences of regional integration with pretensions to general comparative relevance.' What is significant, for this chapter, is that several of the variables and hypotheses in this theory relate to the perceptions and attitudes of a segment of the population variously designated as 'national participant political groups', 'national elites attentive to integration issues', 'relevant elites', and 'participants or observers in regional processes'. It all depends, therefore, on whether one takes a broad or narrow definition of these groups. Schmitter does not explicitly address this question but a broad definition is clearly implied by his operationalization of the variables in question. Thus the variable 'elite value complementarity', is operationalized by reference to 'panel type survey data on the nature and intensity of commitment to similar goals within and across integrating units'. That the operationalization includes public opinion data is clear from the accompanying footnote which includes reference to Inglehart's work on public opinion and European integration. Similarly, regional identity is operationalized by reference to 'panel survey research on selected samples exposed to intensive regional socialization; inference from single surveys on the residual importance of regional contacts/level of information when controlled for other variables', and Inglehart's work is again cited (Schmitter 1971: 252). It is clear, then, that this major restatement of neo-functionalism explicitly assigns a substantial role to public opinion.

'Attitudinal integration' is actually singled out as a separate dimension of the integration process in the third of the revisionist contributions reviewed here. Nye (1971) argues that the concept of integration must be disaggregated into economic, social, and political dimensions. Each of these dimensions is further subdivided: economic integration into trade and common services; social integration into mass and élite level; and political integration into institutional, policy, security-community, and attitudinal (1971: 24–48). Although the notion of attitudinal integration is particularly interesting, Nye is cautious about the role of attitudes. He argues that while scepticism about the predictive value of regional attitudes may be understandable, it does not follow that they have no role. In order to decide the issue, it would be useful to have a 'separate index to determine the extent to which different levels of attitudinal integration lead or lag behind other types' (1971: 44). He goes further in spelling this out: 'Ideally we would like to have polls taken at different times to follow up on questions of identity and general preference, while others probed for a sense of urgency or imminence of expectations. Then we could construct scales of attitudinal integration, ideally for elites and general opinion both' (1971: 45).

In the development of Nye's revised neo-functionalist model, public opinion enters the scheme at two points. First, attitudinal integration— described as 'identitive appeal'—figures in an expanded list of 'process mechanisms'. In addition to determining whether or not a regional identity exists, Nye argues that it is necessary to assess the degree of salience and urgency attached to it and whether or not it is accompanied by a 'myth of permanence and inevitability' (1971: 73). The other side of this variable is the persistence of competing national identities. Secondly, public opinion enters as a variable in the domestic arena influencing the actions of national political leaders. Actors in the original neo-functionalist model—mainly the integrationist technocrats and interest group representatives—need to be supplemented by 'electoral or support politicians' whose primary function is to legitimize the actions involved in regional integration. This implies a very clear role for public opinion in the process of integration, which is reinforced by the inclusion of 'the category of mass opinion, or more accurately of opinion leaders, who create broad or narrow limits for the legitimacy of integrationist programs' (1971: 63).

Public opinion also figures in the four conditions which, Nye postulates, are likely to characterize the integration process over time: politicization, redistribution, reduction of alternatives, and externalization. This is particularly so for politicization, which involves a 'broadening of the arena of participants' in which 'political legitimizing decision-makers and broad political opinion become more heavily involved as integration decisions make heavier incursions upon national sovereignty and the identitive functions of the states' (1971: 89). Discussion of the impact of politicization on the prospects for integration leads to the hypothesis that such prospects may be imperilled by premature politicization before supportive attitudes have become intense and structured.

Figure 2.4 presents a set of public opinion variables which figure prominently in the revised approaches put forward by Haas, Schmitter, and Nye. This both underlines the fundamental change in

1. Increased contact and familiarity (Haas)
2. Growing complexity in the pattern of inter-group loyalties and social roles (Haas)
3. Education and informal socialization practices (Haas)
4. Progressively rewarding experiences derived from the activities of common markets (Haas)
5. Similarity in the distribution of the values held by respective national élites attentive to integration issues (Schmitter)
6. Changes in national values brought about by initial broad scope and high level of regional institutions (Schmitter)
7. Development of a distinctive regional identity and its wide distribution across classes and corporate groups (Schmitter)
8. Perception that enhanced international status is due to participation in a regional organization (Schmitter)
9. Perception that relative status and influence in domestic politics (e.g. an increase in votes) is affected by the redefined scope/level of regional institutions (Schmitter)
10. Regional party formation as a permanent intermediary focus for the diffuse sense of regional loyalty and identity (Schmitter)
11. Regional party formation as a means of linking the crisis issues to the broader concerns of the citizenry on a territorial, not functional, basis (Schmitter)
12. Regional identity accompanied by a 'myth of permanence and inevitability' (Nye)
13. Legitimization of the actions involved in regional integration by 'electoral or support politicians' (Nye)
14. Broad limits for the legitimacy of integrationist programmes created by opinion leaders (Nye)
15. Involvement of broad public opinion through heavier incursions upon national sovereignty and the identitive functions of the states (Nye)
16. Premature politicization before supportive attitudes have become intense and structured (Nye)
17. Group benefit or disadvantage in the redistributive process (Nye)
18. The development of regional identity in public opinion, leading to externalization (i.e. raising the issue of relations with third countries) (Nye)
19. Externalization (see item 18) leading to opposition and politicization through the involvement of political leaders and mass opinion in sensitive areas at too early a stage (Nye)

FIGURE 2.4. *Political culture and public opinion variables conducive to integration in revisionist neo-functionalism*

Sources: constructed from Haas (1971); Nye (1971); Schmitter (1971).

the neo-functionalist approach to the role of public opinion and summarizes the suggestions made regarding the particular aspects of public opinion which matter. It is abundantly clear that the revised versions accord a role to public opinion which is far removed from the exclusive emphasis on élites in the original theory.

The obvious question which then arises is why the new emphasis did not make an immediate impact on the research agenda. The problem was that, almost as soon as this broadening occurred and before it could really take hold, the theory itself seemed to be bypassed by events and treated by its authors, either explicitly or implicitly, as obsolescent. As noted earlier, it was rescued from oblivion by the resurgence of European integration in the mid-1980s.

Integration Theory Revived

Just as the debate about integration theory in the late 1960s was consciously revisionist, the debate which emerged in the late 1980s was consciously revivalist, the intention being to 'to rebuild the conceptual debate on European integration' (Wallace 1990*a*: 4). Likewise, Keohane and Hoffmann (1990: 284) argue for a re-examination of theories of integration, particularly neo-functionalism:

It seems unfortunate to us that many of the accounts of European Community politics have discarded older theories, such as neofunctionalism, without putting anything theoretical in their place. . . . Attempts to avoid theory, however, not only miss interesting questions but rely on a framework for analysis that remains unexamined precisely because it is implicit.

Deutsch rather than Haas is the source of theoretical inspiration for Wallace. Hence, sentiment and culture play a prominent role in the discussion. However, that role is repeatedly qualified by acknowledging the difficulties encountered in dealing with such variables. Expectations, common identity or consciousness, and a 'sense of community' are acknowledged to be essential elements of political integration but, as noted earlier, they are 'the most contested, because the most difficult to measure' (Wallace 1990*a*: 9). One cannot dissent from the view that measurement in this area is problematic. What is interesting is confirmation that the undertaking is theoretically worthwhile.

The core of the Keohane and Hoffmann position is a synthesis of neo-functionalist and inter-governmental perspectives: 'successful spillover requires prior programmatic agreement among governments, expressed in an intergovernmental bargain' (Keohane and Hoffmann 1990: 287). Acknowledging that this only pushes the question back further to what accounts for intergovernmental bargains or agreements, they analyse domestic and international events in the early 1980s, drawing the tentative conclusion that the existence of a 'regime'—in this case the EC—affected these states' calculations of incentives, and made it possible for them to see a policy of European *relance* as advantageous' (1990: 289). Keohane and Hoffmann's emphasis on the compatibility of neo-functionalist and 'statist' approaches to explaining integration, and their complaint that this compatibility had been overlooked by the stereotyping of the debate of the late 1960s (1990: 299 n. 39), is in line with the account given above of the evolution of theory and especially of the significance of revisionist neo-functionalism. That public opinion must figure in any such synthesis is confirmed by Keohane and Hoffmann's reference to 'domestic backlashes' or 'revolts' against the economic hardships the single market might impose on certain sectors, professions, or regions. It is echoed in their concern about the democratic deficit, and their reference to the paradox of 'integrated economies and separate politics, the paradox of an elaborate process of multinational bargaining coexisting with an obstinately national process of political life and elections, the paradox of the emergence of a European identity on the world scene coexisting with continuing national loyalties' (1990: 294–5).

Precisely this issue of loyalty is identified by Caporaso and Keeler (1993: 49) as one of the six principal directions of theoretically interesting research: 'To what extent will further integration necessitate the sort of shift in mass loyalties with which Deutsch and Haas were both concerned, if from very different perspectives, decades ago?' The point is reinforced by the renewed emphasis placed by Schmitter (1992) on the importance of politicization as one of the key factors which will determine the future development of the Euro-polity.

These examples are not put forward to suggest that the primary cause of integration, or the lack of it, is public opinion or political culture. The focus of explanation remains on élites, and on structures and processes, both at the international and national level. The point is that even those contributions which focus most on élites and on structural change tend to allow a role for public opinion. In summary, these various examples of renewed interest in integration theory contain repeated references to the role of public opinion which confirm the underlying trend in integration theory: that the emphasis on élites was too narrow and that the admittedly dominant role of élites needs to be incorporated in a broader perspective which gives adequate attention to public opinion and political culture.

Political Culture, Public Opinion, and Regimes

Turning to regime theory does not in fact involve a major break with the issues dealt with so far. Discussions of European integration made considerable use of interdependence and regime theory following the apparent failure of traditional integration theory in the late 1970s (see Webb 1983: 32–9). As we have seen, Keohane and Hoffmann also make reference to the EC as a regime, and in a particular sector of EC activity, Weiler and Wessels (1988) analyse the possibility of applying regime theory to European Political Co-operation. Indeed, continuities and connections between theories of integration and regime theory could be seen as reflecting the continuum of internationalized govern-ance posited in Chapter 1.

According to the most widely cited definition, international regimes are 'sets of implicit or explicit principles, norms, rules, and decision making procedures around which actors' expectations converge in a given area of international relations' (Krasner 1983: 2). In this defini-tion, principles are 'beliefs of fact, causation, and rectitude', and norms are 'standards of behaviour defined in terms of rights and obligations'. Of course, as Strange (1983: 345) argues, regimes do not deal with the whole range of issues or values of concern to society. It may be that they do not deal with the most important ones. They do, however, impose authoritative constraints on state behaviour in limited areas, and as such can be thought of as forms of internationalized governance.

At first sight, it seems highly unlikely that public opinion or political culture would have any relevance to the formation or maintenance of international regimes. The Law of the Sea, the International Food Regime, or the Nuclear Non-proliferation Regime are not household concepts. Regimes are the creation of élites. Indeed, Puchala and Hopkins (1983: 63) note this as one of their characteristic features: 'each regime has a set of elites who are the practical actors within it . . . regime participants are most often bureaucratic units or individuals who operate as part of the "government" of an international subsystem by creating, enforcing or otherwise acting in compliance with norms.'

Faced with the *prima facie* case that public opinion is remote from and irrelevant to international regimes, it should be noted, first, that regimes are defined in terms of attitudes; that is, attitudes held by élites (see Krasner's definition above). Then the question must be asked: are the principles and norms adopted by élites impervious to trends in public opinion and the broader political culture? Krasner (1983: 16) distinguishes between, on the one hand, endogenous norms and principles which are 'the critical defining characteristics of any given regime' and, on the other, 'norms and principles that influence the regime in a particular issue area but are not directly related to that issue area'. He refers to the latter as 'diffuse values' and argues that they can be regarded as explanations for the creation, persistence, and dissipation of regimes. A somewhat similar point is made by Puchala and Hopkins (1983: 64–5), who distinguish between superstructure and substructure or between diffuse and specific regimes. Both Krasner and Puchala and Hopkins identify a very similar set of diffuse values which currently condition the formation of international regimes. According to Krasner (1983: 18), this set includes the principle of sovereignty and the related notions of 'exclusive control within a delimited geographic area and the untrammelled right to self-help internationally'. Similarly, Puchala and Hopkins (1983: 64–5) argue that the 'current norms that legitimize national self-determination, sanctify sovereign equality, proscribe international intervention in domestic affairs, and permit international coercion, are all general principles of our world order.'

The main repository of diffuse values such as these may be various international institutions and traditional procedures, and the élites who operate them. There is no denying this, but some qualification is called for; in particular, that such traditions and values exist in a broad cultural milieu of which public opinion is a part. Take, for example, the norms of sovereign equality and the proscription of international intervention in domestic affairs cited above. In November 1991, *The Economist*, while cautioning against the temptation to exaggerate a tendency or extrapolate a trend, suggested that there was a new development in international affairs involving co-operation between states for agreed ends 'on a scale that hitherto only idealists have even dreamed about'. A significant part of the impetus to such co-operation, it was claimed, is 'world opinion', which, 'when confronted by television pictures of genocide or starvation, is unimpressed by those who say, "We cannot get involved. National sovereignty must be respected". National sovereignty be damned: the UN is already involved in Iraq' (*The Economist*,

1991). The UN, it was argued, is just one example of 'the new interference', which goes well beyond events related to the Gulf War. It was also argued that the democratic legitimacy of the trend is vital to its success.

A leading article in *The Economist* proves nothing; it could be regarded merely as the clever but ephemeral speculation typical of many leading articles. Indeed, in the wake of the subsequent vicissitudes of international intervention in Somalia, Yugoslavia, and Rwanda, some might argue that *The Economist* was suffering from an unwonted bout of premature optimism. But this would be to miss the point. The current debate about international intervention, and the often tragic situations which create a demand for such intervention, is not about questions of sovereignty but about the practicalities and modalities of intervention. From a theoretical point of view, what the debate illustrates is that the current set of values which condition the formation of regimes may be undergoing change. Moreover, in line with the argument that diffuse regime values are embedded in a wider culture, the debate suggests that public opinion may be a factor in the process. It thus suggests that consideration of the role of political culture and public opinion may be required in a comprehensive answer to Puchala and Hopkins's (1983: 65) questions: 'What . . . explains the origin of the normative superstructures that exist and persist at given periods in history? Why and how do the principles of such diffuse regimes—the superstructures—change over time?'

The distinction between issue-specific regimes and something broader and more diffuse which underpins them is also urged by Rosenau. He identifies this 'more encompassing concept' in terms of 'the governance that is inherent in a global order' (Rosenau 1992*a*: 9). From the point of view of this chapter, what is remarkable is the explicitness and robustness of his argument: 'the micro level of individuals has to be integrated into the analysis [of the emerging global order] because structures at the macro level seem increasingly vulnerable to shifts in the skills and orientations of the publics they encompass'; we must proceed 'as if citizens at the micro level are variables relevant to the emergent global order' (Rosenau 1992*b*: 274). These propositions are defended on several grounds; the power of states and governments has been dispersed and eroded; due to the revolution in communications and education, individuals have considerably enhanced analytic skills; there is an array of new issues which are characterized above all by interdependence; individuals can now observe the aggregation of micro-level actions into macro-level out-comes; and, finally, organization and leadership are considerably less important in the mobilization of publics (Rosenau 1992*b*: 274–6).

The mention by Rosenau of 'interdependence issues' emphasizes that, over and above contributing to the creation and maintenance of the underlying diffuse values and the cultural context of regimes and internationalized governance, there is a second, more concrete, sense in which public opinion may feed into regime formation. Mass publics may not know much about the Non-proliferation Treaty, the International Food Regime, or the Law of the Sea, but they do have attitudes towards nuclear weapons, world hunger, and the 200-mile limit. Policy concerns and preferences of this kind among the mass public are an indirect rather than a direct input into regime formation. The public is unlikely to have an attitude as to whether a regime does or should exist; it may not even be aware of the full international ramifications of a particular problem. However, by demanding solutions to problems which can only be resolved through concerted and sustained interna-tional co-operation, public opinion may create a demand for interna-tional regimes. The inclusion of this category of indirect demand for regimes gives added force and scope to Hoffmann's view that 'transna-tional political issues of interest to all political forces and publics across boundary lines are a prerequisite to political integration'.[4]

It has to be acknowledged that this notion of indirect input, via domestic politics, into the construction or destruction of regimes sits rather uneasily with the original version of regime theory. The early development of regime theory had a clear systemic bias. The view was that theorizing which focused on the systemic level of analysis had the merit of parsimony. More recently, however, there have been signs of a concerted rethink regarding this strategy. Thus, in a ten-year retro-spective on *Power and Interdependence*, Keohane and Nye (1987: 753) acknowledge that 'The need for more attention to domestic politics, and its links to international politics, leads us to believe that research at the systemic level alone may have reached a point of diminishing returns.' In the same year, a broad-ranging review of regime theory argued: 'Current theories of international regimes have ignored domestic political processes, in part because of the lure of parsimonious systemic theory . . . there have been few studies of the domestic political determinants of international co-operation. There are both methodological and theoretical reasons to open the black box of domestic politics' (Haggard and Simmons 1987: 513). A substantial part of the lure of the systemic level of theorising was, and still is, the compelling logic of game theory. But, for all its necessary simplifying assumptions, game theory need not, as so often taken for granted, limit analysis to the systemic level. In fact, Putnam (1988: 432) has suggested the notion of two-level games as a metaphor for domestic–international interactions. Public opinion figures explicitly in the second-level, domestic game:

A more adequate account of the domestic determinants of foreign policy and international relations must stress politics: parties, social classes, interest groups (both economic and non-economic), legislators, and even public opinion and elections, not simply executive officials and institutional arrangements.

In summary, far from regarding public opinion as something remote and irrelevant, regime theory, particulary in its more recent manifestations, strongly implies that domestic public opinion may impel or constrain moves towards internationalized governance, whether those moves are comprehensive and robust, as in the case of European integration, or partial and tentative, as is the case with most international regimes.

Empirical Models of Relevance

While, in the late 1960s and early 1970s, theory was inching its way towards the (re)inclusion of public opinion in the integration process, only to be made redundant almost as soon as this had been accomplished, scholars of a more empirical bent were analysing public opinion on the assumption that it mattered. Nor was the assumption arbitrary. From the beginning, such research has worked with either explicit or implicit models of the relevance of public opinion. We consider two such models.

Perhaps the most frequently cited is Lindberg and Scheingold's model of 'permissive consensus'. Originating in V. O. Key's (1961) notion of a permissive opinion distribution, this concept implies that data on public opinion cannot be taken as providing a reliable guide to the future of the Community. As Lindberg and Scheingold (1970: 41–2) put it:

Positive indicators simply suggest to us that policy makers can probably move in an integrative direction without significant opposition . . . conversely significant opposition and persistent social cleavage do not necessarily mean that integrative steps cannot be taken, but rather that the opportunities for blocking them are greater. Once again, then, we are discussing the problem of the hostile or congenial context as constraining or facilitating but not determining the growth of the Community system.

This model ascribes to public opinion a role which does not amount to much. Depending on whether it is positive or negative, public opinion will ultimately either passively accept élite initiatives or provide material for counter élites to work on. It does not allow for any impetus towards integration, or disintegration, to come from public opinion, nor is public opinion, whether positive or negative, ever regarded as decisive. In terms of ascribing a role to public opinion, therefore, it lags far behind many of the suggestions and assumptions in the broader theoretical literature. More importantly, treating the notion of a permissive consensus as a general model risks oversimplifying Key's argument. Key was arguing for taking into account the degree of attachment to an opinion, the intensity with which it is held, and the extent to which those who hold it include 'driving clusters of deter-mined leadership'. Thus, only if the plurality holding a particular view is an unstratified mass, with no perception of differential salience, and no variation in degrees of intensity, does one have a 'permissive opinion distribution'. On any particular issue, this may or may not be the case. Consequently, the notion of a permissive consensus should be treated as a hypothesis to be empirically verified in particular instances rather than a general model of the (very marginal) relevance of attitudes.

In contrast to the sweeping assumption of the permissive consensus notion, Inglehart argues that one must take account of differences of stratification within an opinion distribution, differences in the value correlates of an opinion, and differences in the macro-political context. Thus, three categories of variables—skills, values, and structure—have a bearing on the relevance of public opinion (Inglehart 1977a). In terms of skills, what is crucial is the balance of 'inert parochials' and 'skilled participants' in the population. The process of cognitive mobilization produces skilled participants and increases the relevance of public opinion to foreign policy. This is in fact an operationalization of a concept we have already encountered in Deutsch's notion of a politi-cally relevant stratum and in Rosenau's point about the enhancement of analytic skills due to the communication and education revolutions. Its relevance has undoubtedly increased since it was first raised by Deutsch and then by Inglehart.

The second conditioning factor identified by Inglehart is whether an issue touches deeply held values.[5] If it does, then the impact on élite action is more likely to be manifest and, conversely, élites are less likely to be able to lead public opinion in a particular direction. These first two points go a long way towards meeting Key's stipulations regarding the interpretation of any given opinion distribution. Finally, according to Inglehart, the relevance of public opinion depends on structural factors—or the macro-political context. One example is the competitive context; the more EC issues are entangled in the competitive struggle between political parties, the greater the relevance of public opinion. Another example is the difference between political systems which provide for referendums and those which do not.

This kind of conditionally positive assessment of the relevance of public opinion continued to inform empirical work in this area for the next two decades (Shepherd 1975; Inglehart and Rabier 1978; Dalton and Duval 1986; Inglehart, Rabier, and Reif 1987; Inglehart and Reif 1991). Of course, assumptions about the impact of skills, values, and structures are relevant to any opinion distribution on any political issue or process. They are not specific to integration. The force of the assumptions is, therefore, considerably strengthened when they are combined with arguments about the relevance of public opinion which we have identified as a recurring thread in theories of political integration and international regimes.

Conclusion

In seeking to understand the process of the internationalization of governance and its prospects, political culture, public opinion, and political legitimacy can neither be taken for granted nor ignored. It is clear that the exclusive emphasis on élites and the dismissal of public opinion associated with early neo-functionalist theory does not reflect the real thrust of integration theory as it developed from the early formulations through various revisions to recent efforts at revival. Moreover, the relevance of public opinion applies not just to formal processes of regional integration or specifically to the development of the European Community but applies right along the continuum of internationalized governance. Thirdly, the dimensions of public opinion which matter are evidently manifold. They include those attitudes which have some institutional or policy aspect of internationalized governance as their direct object. They also include attitudes which are indirectly related to internationalized governance, either as demands for solutions to problems requiring an internationalized response, or as constraints on such response.

In short, theoretical work on political integration and internationalized governance has been surprisingly rich in insights relating to the role of political culture and public opinion. These insights go a considerable way towards setting the agenda for the empirical analysis of the nature and the determinants of the orientations of European publics towards internationalized governance. This is the challenge taken up in this volume. Before proceeding to the main task, Chapter 3 sets out a classification of the dimensions of orientation involved.

NOTES

1. Mitrany's functionalism (Mitrany 1943) is another early strand of integration theory. However, this has tended to be as much normative as analytical, and has failed to generate a substantial research agenda (see Lodge 1978).
2. Using quantitative indicators, Caporaso and Keeler (1993, 16–25) demonstrate the decline in 'theory-driven scholarship' in 'the doldrum years' (c.1975–86). However, they also argue that research in that period should not be neglected and that it did contribute, mostly indirectly, to theory-building. But such research was only implicitly theoretical and did not address either the kinds of issues posed in this chapter or follow up on the theoretical insights of the revisionist period.
3. This chapter is not intended as a comprehensive review of a voluminous literature. It concentrates on key theorists, especially those who have had something specific to say, positive or negative, about the role of public opinion. For a useful introduction to the literature up to the early 1980s, see Lodge (1983: 6–23); thereafter see Michelmann and Soldatos (1994).
4. The notion of transnational or internationalized issues is further examined in Ch. 11.
5. In terms of getting at 'deeply held values', note the application of social psychological theory and methods to the study of attitudes towards integration by Hewstone (1986). However, the complexity of the data required by this approach restricted its application to a pilot study of a sample of 545 university students from four countries.

3

A Typology of Orientations

OSKAR NIEDERMAYER AND BETTINA WESTLE

If the analogy between internationalized governance and governance in domestic political systems is valid, there should be some parallels between the types or dimensions of orientations at the international and national level. Accordingly, in this chapter we approach the task of developing a typology of orientations towards internationalized governance by way of a critical review of the two main classifications of the dimensions of attitudes towards political systems. We then extend this review to examine a classification which deals specifically with orientations towards the European Community.

Classifying Orientations towards Political Systems

The first approach is that underlying *The Civic Culture* (Almond and Verba 1963). This study provided both a model for imitation and a valuable source of data for further research. It has also provided grounds for critical debate within the field. As a result, its methodology and findings have been systematically reappraised by the original authors, leading to a reformulation of the overall theoretical approach (Almond and Verba 1980).

Almond and Verba defined political culture as 'the particular distribution of patterns of orientation toward political objects among the members of a nation' (1963: 14–15). They then distinguished between objects and modes of orientation, the latter comprising three modes: cognitions, affects, and evaluations. In classifying political objects, they distinguished between the political system in general, input objects, output objects, and the self as a political actor. The combination of modes and objects resulted in a matrix of dimensions of political orientation (see Figure 3.1). Different combinations of orientation towards the four classes of objects were then used to define different types of political cultures—for example, the parochial, the subject, and the participant.

In returning to the concept of political culture more than a decade later, Almond (1980) reaffirmed the distinction between cognition, affect, and evaluation. However, these are no longer seen as different modes of orientation which are independent from each other at the individual level. On the contrary, in the revised concept Almond depicts cognition, affect, and evaluation as interrelated aspects—components, dimensions—of one and the same attitude. This means that cognition, affect, and evaluation—what we term the 'varieties of orientation' in Figure 3.2—are the closely linked dimensions of one and the same phenomenon. The other dimension of the matrix shown in Figure 3.2 (the objects of orientation) is reconceptualized under the general heading of substantive content, which includes system culture, process culture, and policy culture.

Referring to Easton's (1965) systems analysis, Almond (1980: 28) defines the system culture as 'the distributions of attitudes toward the national community, the regime and the authorities', which includes 'the sense of national identity, attitudes toward the legitimacy of the regime and its various institutions, and attitudes toward the legitimacy and effectiveness of the incumbents of the various political roles'. In this way, he combines, differentiates, and extends parts of the former categories of 'system as a general object' and 'output objects', because

MODES	OBJECTS			
	System as general object	Input objects	Output objects	Self as object
Cognition				
Affect				
Evaluation				

FIGURE 3.1. *Dimensions of political orientation according to Almond and Verba (1963)*

Source: reproduced from Almond and Verba (1963: 16).

MODES	OBJECTS (Substantive content)		
(Varieties of orientation)	System culture	Process culture	Policy culture
Cognition			
Affect			
Evaluation			

FIGURE 3.2. *Dimensions of political orientation according to Almond (1980)*
Source: constructed from text in Almond (1980: 28).

the effectiveness of incumbents is now included in the definition of the system culture.

The process culture is thought to include 'attitudes toward the self in politics (including the original parochial–subject–participant distinction) and attitudes toward other political actors (such as trust, co-operative competence, hostility)' (Almond 1980: 28). Thus the process culture refers mainly to the category of 'self as object'. It is not entirely clear, however, whether this definition really excludes all elements of the former 'input objects', which, according to his adoption of Easton's categories, should now belong to the 'system culture'.

The policy culture is defined as 'the distribution of preferences regarding the outputs and outcomes of politics, the ordering among different groupings in the population of such political values as welfare, security, and liberty' (Almond 1980: 28). Therefore, evaluations are no longer part of the policy culture. This gives rise to two problems. First, there is an overlap with orientations towards the legitimacy of the regime, which, according to Easton, includes such political values. Secondly, the policy culture cannot be systematically related to the varieties of orientation, because, on the one hand, the latter includes cognitions, affects, and evaluations, but not preferences. Preferences may be included in the variety of orientations only indirectly, in the way that evaluations are a consequence of the comparison between preferences and perceived outputs. On the other hand, the policy culture is defined as preferences regarding outputs. Thus, the definition of the policy culture is not restricted exclusively to an object but combines an object with a mode of orientation. None the less, in studying political cultures, and especially in studying orientations towards the internationalization of governance, preferences are a suggestive addition. The

policy dimension looms large in any discussion of the internationalization of governance, and output preferences might affect the prospects
for further development of international systems at least as strongly as
output evaluations.

Finally, adopting Converse's (1964) concept of constraint, Almond
states that political cultures may be distinguished according to the
relatedness of their components. This is an important new aspect,
although Almond seems to use Converse's concept in a broader sense
to include not only the relationship between orientations towards different objects but also the relationship between the three components—
or dimensions—of an orientation towards one and the same object.

The second main approach to classifying orientations towards political systems is drawn from Easton's (1965, 1975a) systems analysis.
Although Easton himself did not use his concept in an empirical study,
his ideas have encouraged many theoretical and empirical studies on
political legitimacy (see Westle 1989: 91–168). However, although
Easton refers to both demands and support as inputs to political systems, it is only his concept of political support which has been widely
adopted.

Easton distinguishes three main elements of political systems, which
can become the objects of support: the political community, the regime,
and the political authorities. The political community is defined as 'that
aspect of a political system that consists of its members seen as a group
of persons bound together by a political division of labor' (Easton 1965:
177). The regime is characterized by its general political philosophy
and consists of three hierarchical elements: the values of the political
philosophy, the norms of the political order, and the structures of
authority roles. The political authorities are defined as the occupants
of authority roles.

In addition, Easton distinguishes between diffuse and specific support. Diffuse support denotes a generalized evaluation, whereas specific
support means an output-directed evaluation. In his 1975 re-assessment
of the concept, Easton illustrates the distinction between the two modes:
'the uniqueness of specific support lies in its relationship to the satisfac-
tions that members of a system feel they obtain from the perceived
outputs and performance of the political authorities', whereas diffuse
support 'refers to the evaluation of what an object is or represents—to
the general meaning it has for a person—not of what it does' (Easton
1975: 437, 444). Because Easton links outputs directly to the political
authorities, he tends to restrict specific support exclusively to political

authorities, whereas diffuse support is directed towards all the objects (see Figure 3.3).

The general idea behind this classification is a hierarchy of elements which contribute to the stability of political systems. Specific support for the political authorities may vary in the short term, may even be lacking altogether or be negative, without affecting the political system as a whole. This can happen without undue effects for political stability provided there is stable long-term diffuse support for the higher ranking and more enduring objects—the political regime and the political community.

Whereas the distinction between political objects in Easton's classification seems quite clear, the distinction between modes of support is somewhat problematic. Specific support is conceptualized as one-dimensional whereas diffuse support is conceptualized as two-dimensional. Moreover, diffuse support takes different forms depending on the object. With respect to the political community, diffuse support is thought of as a primarily affective feeling of identity or loyalty. With respect to the regime, diffuse support is sub-divided into two dimensions: (i) ideological and value-oriented beliefs concerning the institutional structure; (ii) trust or sympathy as a spillover from ideological or even instrumental evaluations of outputs. Because the second dimension (which is normally restricted to the authorities as objects) includes output evaluations, it overlaps somewhat with specific support for political authorities. Thus, diffuse support for political authorities can be thought of as an ideologically based trust. Specific support for political authorities, however, is conceptualized in three rather different ways: as an instrumental evaluation of outputs which is directed towards political action; as an extraneous evaluation of personal competences or characteristics; and as an expressive evaluation of the outputs as a whole.

If we compare the two classification schemes, it is apparent that the

	OBJECTS		
MODES	Political community	Political regime	Political authorities
Diffuse	X	X	X
Specific			X

FIGURE 3.3. *Support for the political system according to Easton (1965)*
Source: constructed from text in Easton (1965: 153–340).

concept of support of Easton is more or less identical to Almond's 'system culture'. The 'policy culture' category, which has been defined as output and outcome preferences, is not included in Easton's concept of political support, but an analogous concept can be seen in Easton's somewhat neglected notion of political demands. A demand is defined as 'an expression of opinion that an authoritative allocation with regard to a particular subject matter should or should not be made by those responsible for doing so' (Easton 1965: 38). Easton explicitly excludes wants, expectations, motivations, ideology, interests, and diffuse preferences from this concept of demands, seeing them as exclusively directed towards the political authorities. He distinguishes two types of stress on the political system caused by demands: 'volume stress', which refers to the amount of demands, and 'content stress', which refers to the kind of demands. Demands are mainly integrated into the concept as 'a potential danger to the persistence of any kind of system' (Easton 1965: 37).

The inclusion of demands as possible counterparts of support is a theoretically more appropriate addition than Almond's concept of policy culture, because of its greater conceptual clarity. However, with respect to the development of international political systems, especially in a dynamic perspective, the role of ideologies, expectations, policy preferences, and so on may have an even more important impact than the sharply restricted category of demands in Easton's sense. Moreover, these factors may not only represent a possible danger to the system, but may also creatively and positively influence its further development. Therefore, it has to be asked whether the influence of these factors should be restricted to political authorities or should be seen as directed also towards other elements of the political system.

This brings us to an approach which was developed explicitly to conceptualize orientations towards a (rudimentary) international political system, the European Community, based mainly on Easton's model. In their conceptualization of political support for European integration, Lindberg and Scheingold (1970) differentiate, first, between identitive and systemic support (see Figure 3.4). Identitive support 'gauges what might be termed "horizontal" interaction among the broader publics of the system, while systemic support probes "vertical" relations between the system and these publics' (Lindberg and Scheingold 1970: 40). Referring to Easton, they further subdivide systemic support between community and regime. Due to the lack of data, they do not deal with the political authorities. In their view, the

	BASIS OF RESPONSE	
LEVELS OF INTERACTION	Utilitarian	Affective
Identitive		
Systemic Community regime		

FIGURE 3.4. *Support for the EC according to Lindberg and Scheingold (1970)*
Source: reproduced from Lindberg and Scheingold (1970: 40).

political community 'refers to the division of political labor and in the context of European Community directs us to questions concerning the scope of the system'. The regime 'refers to the nature of the political system and, therefore, directs us to such issues as the extent of supranational authority and the division of power among the institutions of the Community' (Lindberg and Scheingold 1970: 40).

Concerning modes of orientation, Lindberg and Scheingold distinguish between utilitarian and affective support. The utilitarian mode, which comes very close to Easton's concept of specific support, is 'based on some perceived and relatively concrete interest', whilst the affective mode, which is nearly identical to Easton's concept of diffuse support, indicates 'a diffuse and perhaps emotional response to some of the vague ideals embodied in the notion of European unity' (Lindberg and Scheingold 1970: 40). This model, too, is restricted to the support dimension of orientations towards political systems. In contrast to Easton, however, it extends the utilitarian mode of support to all objects.

The distinction between systemic and identitive support seems, at first sight, to be an improvement. However, in Easton's concept, horizontal interactions are included in orientations towards the political community in so far as they are political. His notion of political community comprises not only the territorial but also the personal element; the latter includes the individual's own identities and orientations towards other members of the political community. Because Easton deals exclusively with political support, only political orientations towards the political community are included in his concept. Non-political, social orientations are excluded.

However, Lindberg and Scheingold's operationalization of identitive support shows that they focus on social orientations. For our purposes, the inclusion of social orientations is a valuable addition. However, we see no need to extract social orientations from the other horizontal orientations or for treating them as a separate level of interaction. Such a separation would mean that some elements of the horizontal interactions—the political ones—are included in the systemic level of interaction, while the social ones would form a different level of interaction. Lindberg and Scheingold themselves give no theoretical reason for the usefulness of this distinction, and we think that both kinds of horizontal interactions should be included in orientations towards the political community. In addition, the term 'identitive' seems to denote a mode of orientation rather than an object. It has no clearly defined object, whereas 'systemic' orientations have two objects: the regime and the community. Thus, we find that Lindberg and Scheingold's classification does not separate the dimensions of objects and modes of orientation in a systematic way.

It will be apparent from this discussion that each of the three classifications we have examined is, in one way or another, problematic. We have explored these problems in detail elsewhere (Westle 1989; Niedermayer 1991). In what follows, we draw on these discussions to build a classification which is suited to our particular purpose of analysing orientations towards internationalized governance.

A Classification of Orientations

In developing our own classification of orientations towards internationalized governance we adopt the basic structure of objects and modes of orientations. With regard to the objects, we try to identify core characteristics of internationalized governance which were not taken into account in the models considered above. With regard to the modes of orientation we do not restrict ourselves to the concept of political support because our research interests and analytical perspective are broader. Moreover, in classifying the objects of orientation, we want to lean on Easton's model. It is posed at a relatively high level of abstraction, which allows us to cover the different (potential) stages of development in the internationalization of governance. However, several modifications of Easton's model are necessary.

Orientations can be directed towards a specific form of internationalized governance—such as NATO, EFTA, the EC—as a whole, or towards its components. With respect to the components, we propose distinguishing between the political collectivity, the political order, the political authorities, and policies. The 'political collectivity' can be defined as that aspect of internationalized governance which consists of its members seen as a group of countries and their peoples, bound together by a political division of labour. It denotes those entities which participate in a common political structure and a common set of political processes within a common territory. This definition clearly follows Easton's concept of a political community. However, we replace the term 'community' by the term 'collectivity'. Although it might seem as if this hints at a different meaning of community, denoting something 'natural', whereas collectivity denotes something 'artificial', we emphasize that it has nothing to do with the different meanings of the terms *Gemeinschaft* and *Gesellschaft* as used by Tönnies (1922) or Weber (1968). On the contrary, we consider it an open question whether people feel a sense of belonging and how important are 'value rationality' and 'instrumental rationality'. The reason for replacing the term 'community' by 'collectivity' is simply that 'community' has a concrete meaning in discussing international co-operation, interdependence, and integration—simply because of the existence of the European Community and the debates about its character as an economic or a political community.

There are some specific characteristics associated with international political collectivities. First, as with Easton's category of the political community, the definition and operationalization of the political collectivity depends on the unit of analysis. Everyone is a member of more than one political community; for example, there are multiple memberships at the subnational, the national, and the supranational level. Whereas, nowadays, the national level still can be defined as the political collectivity which covers the largest part of a common and sovereign political division of labour, existing forms of internationalized governance do not comprise the totality of the political process but only smaller parts of it and are in many ways not sovereign.

Secondly, we have to be aware of the problem of different kinds of membership. Whereas in the national context, individuals are the members of the political system, the corresponding elements in the international context are nation states. Nevertheless, the peoples of these nation states—the individual citizens—could be seen as members, too. We handle this problem by adopting the different elements of the political collectivity in Westle's (1989) concept: the territorial and the personal. The territorial element refers to the physical borders of a political system and its political sub-units. These sub-units are those political entities which carry semi-sovereignty with respect to the entire political collectivity; for example, the nation states in an international system of governance. The personal element refers to the peoples of these nation states, as groups or as individuals.

Thirdly, whereas the territorial element can be described as primarily a political factor, the personal element of the political collectivity in our concept can be described in terms of the 'social' or 'socio-political system'. In contrast to Easton, we do not want to exclude non-political, social orientations towards the collectivity. Whereas an individual's political and non-political roles can be separated analytically, in reality they often seem to be combined in a way which makes them difficult to separate empirically when studying attitudes (see Westle 1990). Moreover, orientations towards the social characteristics of a collectivity—such as images of the peoples of other countries—might have more impact on orientations towards common membership in a system of internationalized governance than orientations towards its political characteristics. In our conceptualization, orientations towards the political collectivity include orientations towards one's own nation and its people, as well as towards the other member countries and their people.

In line with this reasoning, we define the personal element of the political collectivity as including not only 'others' but also 'the self' as an object. Here, the self includes responding individuals and the people of their own country. This avoids the overlap between Lindberg and Scheingold's categories in so far as 'vertical' orientations might be thought of as including identification with the collectivity as a whole and yet would be categorized by them as 'systemic' rather than 'identitive'.

Moreover, whereas Lindberg and Scheingold place the personal elements outside the community, our concept of the political collectivity includes the personal element. This allows us to arrive at a more systematic classification of the object elements. At the national level, both the territory and the people are constitutional components of a state. They are only analytically separable. Therefore, with respect to internationalized governance, ascribing both the territorial and the personal element to the political collectivity seems more appropriate than separating them and ascribing them to different objects—as happens with Lindberg and Scheingold's identitive/systemic distinction. In addition, this conceptualization allows a more systematic classification of the modes of orientation in relation to the object dimension, as we noted earlier.

The second component of internationalized governance, the political order, refers to the organization of the political division of labour within the collectivity. This consists of two main elements: its political philosophy and its institutional structure. Both elements are conceptualized in a way similar to Easton's 'regime' category, but we avoid this term because it might be confused with the notion of regime in the international relations literature. The political philosophy element refers to the values and norms connected with internationalized governance in general. These values and norms might be specific to the international level or they might be identical to values at other political levels. This would be the case, for example, with the democratic values of freedom and equality. The second element of the political order, the institutional structure, comprises the horizontal and the vertical power structure. The horizontal power structure denotes the institutions of the international system of governance and the distribution of power between them. The vertical power structure is defined as the distribution of power between the international and the national level; for example, the right of nations to exercise a veto in the decision-making processes of rudimentary international systems of governance.

The third component of any specific form of internationalized governance consists of the political authorities, defined as the occupants of political roles at the international level. These incumbents are to be distinguished from the institutions and roles themselves. The latter elements belong to the political order and are intended to be enduring. The incumbents of particular roles, by contrast, may change or—at least in a democratic political system—should change periodically. We do not separate the political authorities into different elements, because the criteria we might use are not abstract enough to serve different analytical interests. For example, a distinction according to membership in institutions may be adequate for one purpose, whereas a distinction according to personal characteristics and role performance, or according to parties or countries, may serve other purposes.

The fourth component, the policy component, consists of the substantive dimension of internationalized governance. In his concept of support, Easton links outputs directly to the political authorities. We doubt that this corresponds to people's perceptions, especially in the international context. However, we do not separate the substantive dimension from the authorities just on account of speculations about perceptions. More to the point, our aim it not to restrict our research to political support, but to include other orientations—such as psychological involvement, preferences, and other forms of evaluation. Hence, we cannot concentrate exclusively on concrete outputs, but have to attend to policy plans and outcomes as well. In this sense, we go beyond Almond's concept of 'policy culture', which is restricted to outputs and outcomes. However, since there is only a very loose link between values and policies, or between institutions and policies, we would not feel comfortable attributing policies to the political order. Therefore, we deal with policies as a separate component. In addition to policy plans, outputs, and outcomes, this component includes orientations towards the functional scope of a specific form of internationalized governance; that is, the range of substantive policies to be dealt with at the international level.

Modes of Orientation

We define orientations as anything people have in mind with respect to a specific object. As to the emergence of an orientation, we think of the moment when a person turns towards the object, because the first condition for having any kind of orientation towards an object is to be aware of its existence. Thus, the development of orientations begins with an awareness of the object and ends with behavioural intentions towards the object. But how might this broad range of orientations be internally structured?

Returning to the studies discussed earlier, Almond's distinction between cognitions, affects, and evaluations on the one hand, and Easton's distinction between demands and support on the other, represent very different approaches to the internal structure of orientations. Whereas Easton's classification is specifically related to political science, Almond and Verba's classification is based on a socio-psychological approach. Let us, first, consider how far a socio-psychological approach to examining attitudes might be useful for our purpose.

Two different views on attitudes can be found in social psychology (see, for example, Silberer 1983; Dawes and Smith 1985; Stroebe *et al.* 1990). However, they have in common a concept of attitudes as a hypothetical construct, forming an enduring predisposition to respond in a consistently positive or negative way to a given object. The first view, the multi-component view, is closely connected with a whole string of theories such as cognitive-consistency theory (Rosenberg and Hovland 1960), or the theory of cognitive dissonance (Festinger 1957). In this view, attitudes are seen as comprising three components: cognitive, affective, and behavioural. An underlying attitude is indicated when these components show some consistency. Empirically, the difficulty is in determining the appropriate strength of correlations between these components. They should be positively correlated to indicate consistency, but if the correlation is very high, it is unclear whether this indicates high consistency or a failure to separate the components theoretically.

The alternative approach is a one-dimensional definition of attitudes. Here, attitudes are narrowly defined as categorizations of an object along an evaluative and/or affective dimension which should be measured on a bi-polar scale of affect. One prominent approach to systematizing the whole range of orientations with a one-dimensional conceptualization of attitudes is Fishbein and Ajzen's (1975) distinction between beliefs, attitudes, behavioural intentions, and behaviour. They define beliefs as probabilistic judgements about whether a particular object has a particular characteristic. Linking an attribute to an object in this way should be based on some information about the object and should be rational rather than evaluative or affective. Beliefs may differ in their strength, they may be held with varying degrees of certainty, and they may differ with respect to their subjective relevance. They should be measured on a dimension of subjective probability in an attribute–object relationship. Taking a person's different beliefs about an object all together and ordering them with respect to their degree of subjective certainty and salience is thought to enable one to predict some kind of a general attitude, attitude change, or behaviour related to that particular object. Finally, the concept of behavioural intention refers to a person's purposive design to act in some way with respect to a particular object. It should be measured, according to Fishbein and Ajzen, on a scale of subjective probability to perform a particular action which relates to the particular object in question.

This approach to attitudes has been used in the analysis of attitudes towards the EC (Hewstone 1986), and is potentially useful for our purposes. Nevertheless, we see severe difficulties in adopting it. At first sight, it provides useful categories of orientations and does not require a necessary structure of connections between them. A closer look, however, reveals the problem of insufficient distinctiveness between the categories 'beliefs' and 'attitudes'. The problem is whether the main difference between attitudes and beliefs is (i) the evaluative nature of attitudes and the non-evaluative, rather rational and neutral character of beliefs, which simply represent subjective knowledge of an object; or (ii) the affective, generalized, and enduring nature of an attitude and the singular, (potentially) evaluative character of a belief. Depending on which position one takes, different implications follow for operationalizing the concept of attitudes.

Let us first consider the position that beliefs are non-evaluative attributions to an object. This restricts the term 'beliefs' to just descriptive attributions to an object—to knowledge of an object, and a specific kind of knowledge about an object. We can illustrate this point with an example. A positive answer to the question 'Have you heard about the EC?' clearly represents knowledge of the EC. Answers to the question 'Which countries belong to the EC?' are a form of knowledge about the object which can be seen as a non-evaluative attribution to the object. This attribution can be objectively right or wrong, but whether it is right or wrong it is likely to have—if any—identical subjective consequences. Both types of knowledge can be defined as non-evaluative and thereby represent beliefs in the sense of the first position.

However, there is another type of attribution to an object which involves an evaluational component. For example, answers to the question 'Is the EC functioning in a democratic way?' are less easy to categorize than the previous examples. It is at least debatable whether answers to this question reveal only a 'neutral' knowledge about the object or whether this attribution carries an evaluational component and therefore should be categorized as an attitude. This problem is likely to be caused by many attributions of characteristics and by many typical survey questions—for two reasons. First, the characteristics or properties of an object are usually not neutral in themselves but carry an evaluative component, because they are either positively or negatively viewed by respondents. To say someone is competent, honest, fair, well organized, and creative represent attributions to an object which are clearly evaluative judgements. Secondly, survey questions referring to that kind of attribution are different in their syntactic and their semantic structure. Syntactically, the examples do not have an evaluative component, but semantically they do. To come back to our example: given that democracy has a positive connotation, that democratic politics is a precondition for EC membership, that democracy is the EC norm, and that the great majority of people in the EC countries favour a democratic political system, the ascription to the EC that it functions in a democratic or non-democratic way clearly represents an evaluation. Consequently, there is a wide continuum of beliefs about the EC, ranging from purely neutral knowledge of its existence through to attributions which include an evaluative element. As these beliefs constitute a continuum, we have severe problems in distinguishing between beliefs and evaluations in the multi-dimensional view of attitudes, and between beliefs and attitudes in the uni-dimensional view of attitudes.

Intuitively, these considerations support the second position, namely that beliefs are singular (potentially) evaluative statements about an object. Here, the term 'attitude' refers to an overall assessment of the object, whereas the term 'belief' refers to single elements of that object which might be judged as positive, negative, or neutral, and does not imply a generalized and enduring character. For example, knowledge of a politician and the attribution of a variety of positive as well as negative characteristics to him would be seen as beliefs, but a general sympathy for that politician would be defined as an attitude. However, whereas in the uni-dimensional concept of attitudes, beliefs may have no effect on attitudes or may combine to form an attitude, the concept of an attitude as a generalized affective evaluation involves a reverse relationship between attitudes and beliefs. In this case, attitudes serve as a filter for beliefs.

This position comes rather close to the multi-dimensional concept of attitudes as a hypothetical construct, separated into cognitive, evaluative, and affective (and sometimes behavioural) components. With respect to operationalization, this interpretation carries all the difficulties of measurement already mentioned, especially the problems of distinguishing between short-term and enduring evaluations and between rational and affective evaluations. The two interpretations of the uni-dimensional concept of attitudes differ in their notion of attitudes as having a primarily evaluative character or primarily an affective character, but they agree in defining attitudes as a generalized and enduring position towards an object. It follows that short-term evaluations of an object are either totally excluded or conceptualized within the category of beliefs, mixed with neutral knowledge.

This last point, however, leads to problems with the extension of the object of the two concepts we are dealing with. We think both concepts are too narrow to cover all the relevant aspects of our research. In particular, they do not deal with a mode of orientation towards an object which gains particular importance in the political context: the mode referred to as 'demands' in Easton's concept. In summary, for all these reasons, we depart from the models discussed above and conceptualize modes of orientation in a way which is more suitable to our research purposes.

A Conceptualization of Modes of Orientation

Our notion of orientations comprises all the positions an individual can take with respect to a particular object. Within this wide definition, we distinguish three modes of orientation according to the strength of their behavioural relevance: psychological involvement, evaluations, and behavioural intentions.

Usually, the weakest or most passive form of being concerned with an object is 'psychological involvement'. It comprises neutral knowledge of and about an object, interest in it, the salience of it, and non-normative expectations related to it. Typical of this mode of orientation is its non-evaluative character. Thus, we exclude knowledge as well as expectations with a clear evaluative component from this mode of orientation. Certainly, this raises some problems with respect to knowledge or expectations which cannot be classified, *a priori*, as either neutral or evaluative. However, we regard it as an empirical question whether, for individuals, these forms of knowledge and expectations have an exclusively neutral or an evaluative character, and, thereby, whether or not they belong to 'psychological involvement'. We can operationalize psychological involvement either directly, by examining self-reported interest, or indirectly by examining responses to questions about, for example, whether respondents want more or better information about the object.

The second mode of orientation towards an object, characterized by some degree of engagement and behavioural relevance, is 'evaluations'. We conceptualize an evaluation as any position a person has regarding a particular object in terms of a positive/negative continuum. An evaluation may be long term and enduring or short term and changeable. An evaluation is the result of a normative idea about how an object should be or should act and perceptions of how the object really is or acts. Evaluations may vary in their degree of subjective certainty. They can take the form of a direct positive or negative judgement about an object, or they can be expressed in an indirect form—that is, as a demand, because any demand regarding an object is implicitly an evaluation of the object.

To give an example of these distinctions, we take the European Parliament as the object of an orientation. First, there may be the normative idea that the Parliament should play an important role in the life of the European Community. Secondly, there is the perception that the Parliament plays an unimportant role in the life of the Community. Combining the normative idea and the specific perception of reality should lead to either a direct form of evaluation, that the role of the EP is not important enough, or to an evaluation in the form of the demand that the Parliament should play a more important role.

Our concept of evaluations, therefore, is broader than Easton's categories of demand and support. A positive or negative evaluation of an object with respect to any criterion can be interpreted as support only when that criterion is the same as the respondent's own criterion. For example, answers to the question 'Do you think that the Common Agricultural Policy of the EC is good or bad for the farmers?' is an evaluation, but it can only be interpreted as support if the respondent is a farmer. This kind of consideration applies to almost all the survey questions examined in this volume, hence the term 'support' is widely used in later chapters.

Since the normative ideas which guide evaluations can be based on very different criteria, we can subdivide the resulting evaluations according to classes of these criteria. As we have already shown, both Easton and Lindberg and Scheingold have done this with respect to their notion of support. Lindberg and Scheingold's notion of the 'utilitarian' basis of support and Easton's notion of 'specific' support are nearly identical. Both are thought of as more rational than affective judgements, based on concrete interests and cost–benefit considerations. Moreover, both of them are thought of as sensitive to short-term variations. However, whereas Lindberg and Scheingold's more generalized concept of support is defined as being only 'affective', Easton's concept of support is defined as a value-based and/or affective belief in the legitimacy of an object. Whereas Lindberg and Scheingold's category of affective support does not deal with the stability of support, 'diffuse' support as specified by Easton should not fluctuate greatly over time, at least not with regard to the objects 'political community' or 'regime'. Easton's classification has a clear relevance for the analysis of democratic systems, because diffuse support serves as a barrier against the overflow to the higher levels of the political system of short-term dissatisfaction with outputs from the system. Because of these theoretical implications, and the broader scope of Easton's notion of diffuse support compared with Lindberg and Scheingold's notion of affective support, we shall use Easton's distinction. We therefore distinguish between specific and diffuse evaluations, relating both to all components of the object in question.

The other end of the spectrum of orientations we cover is represented by the mode 'behavioural intentions'. This mode includes all actions which might be taken with different degrees of subjective probability in regard to a particular object. Examples of this mode are the intention to vote, to join a party, to contact a political authority, to sign a petition, to demonstrate, and so on.

Our final conceptualization of orientations towards internationalized governance is shown in Figure 3.5. The available data do not allow us to examine every aspect identified in this schema, but it provides a framework within which to locate the topics and issues considered in this volume.

		MODE			
		Psychological involvement	Evaluations		Behavioural intentions
OBJECT			Specific	Diffuse	
Object as a whole					
COMPONENTS	ELEMENTS				
Political collectivity	Territorial				
	Personal				
Political order	Values/ norms				
	Power structure				
Political authorities					
Policies	Plans/ outcome/ outputs				
	Functional scope				

FIGURE 3.5. *Orientations towards internationalized governance*

PART II

Support for European Integration

4

Trends and Contrasts

OSKAR NIEDERMAYER

Before we can embark on an analysis of the factors which affect support for integration, we must have an overview of the main trends in such support. This is the primary purpose of this chapter. We also examine some of the macro-level hypotheses which have been put forward to explain variations in public opinion between countries. The chapter concludes with a discussion of the impact of one particularly salient event—the signing of the Maastricht Treaty. First, however, we must look at how citizens' attitudes and orientations towards the European Community have been measured in the Eurobarometer surveys, our main data source.

Measuring Support for the EC

Since 1970, four questions dealing with attitudes towards the EC have appeared more or less regularly in Eurobarometer surveys:

(1) 'In general, are you for or against efforts being made to unify Western Europe? If for, are you very much for this, or only to some extent? If against, are you only to some extent against or very much against?' (European Community Study 1970; Eurobarometer, Nos. 0 (autumn 1973), 3 (spring 1975), 4 (autumn 1975), 10 (autumn, 1978), and subsequent surveys). We refer to this question as the 'unification' indicator.

(2) 'Generally speaking, do you think that (your country's) membership in the Common Market is a good thing, a bad thing, or neither good nor bad?' (Eurobarometer, No. 0 (autumn 1973) and

subsequent surveys). This question is referred to as the 'membership' indicator.

(3) 'If you were told tomorrow that the European Community (the Common Market) had been scrapped, would you be very sorry about it, indifferent or relieved?' (European Community Study, 1971; Eurobarometer, Nos. 0 (autumn 1973), 4 (autumn 1975), 8 (autumn 1977), 15 (spring 1981), and subsequent surveys). This is the 'dissolution' indicator.

(4) 'Taking everything into consideration, would you say that (your country) has on balance benefited or not from being a member of the European Community (Common Market)?' (Eurobarometer, Nos. 19 (spring 1983), 21 (spring 1984), and subsequent surveys). This question is referred to as the 'benefit' indicator.

Classifying these indicators according to the typology of orientations developed in Chapter 3 gives rise to some problems. The first indicator does not explicitly refer to the European Community as a specific form of internationalized governance but to 'efforts being made to unify Western Europe'. Inglehart (1977*a*: 168) argues that this question, which has been asked in various surveys since 1952, has a 'floating referent'; that is, the concrete historical situation and the stage reached by European integration are different at any given time. The object of the 'membership' and 'benefit' questions is the respondent's own country rather than the European Community. However, since an important aspect of the evaluation of the EC necessarily relates to the individual's country, we shall use these questions, in line with normal practice in the literature on European public opinion, as indicators of the respondent's orientations towards the EC.

All four questions are aimed at eliciting evaluations. Which type of evaluation, however, is a matter for debate. Whereas the 'unification' question is unanimously classified as operationalizing a diffuse, affective evaluation (Lindberg and Scheingold 1970; Handley 1981*a*; Hewstone 1986; Inglehart, Rabier, and Reif 1987; Niedermayer 1991; Westle and Niedermayer 1991), the membership indicator has been handled in different ways by different scholars. It is viewed by Inglehart, Rabier, and Reif (1987: 140) as an indicator of a specific or instrumental evaluation: 'a calculated appraisal of the immediate costs and benefits of membership in the Community' (see also Inglehart and Rabier 1978). Handley (1981: 348 f.), however, states that 'much of the response is probably the result of a large amount of diffuse affective orientations without any clear idea as to why membership is good or bad'. This view is supported, among others, by Hewstone (1986), Niedermayer (1991), and Niedermayer and Westle (1991). If one accepts Handley's argument, the question asking respondents for their reaction were the EC to be scrapped has also to be classified as operationalizing a diffuse evaluation. The last question, however, refers explicitly to cost–benefit calculations and can therefore be classified as indicating a specific evaluation. Moreover, since in all four questions the evaluation criterion is the respondent's own criterion, we can speak of support instead of evaluation (see Chapter 3).

In order to examine the development of these four indicators and to analyse relationships over time, we need to make them as comparable as possible. In doing this, two problems have to be solved. First, the four questions operationalize the choices which face respondents quite differently. The first difference relates to the number and gradations of the response categories. The 'unification' question uses four categories, two positive ('for very much', 'for to some extent') and two negative ('against to some extent', 'against very much'). The 'membership' question uses an overall positive ('good thing') and an overall negative ('bad thing') category, whereas the 'dissolution' question counterposes a very positive ('very sorry') category to a somewhat negative one ('relieved'). Finally the 'benefit' question simply gives the options 'benefited' and 'not benefited'. The second difference lies in the way in which a neutral or middle position is handled by each question. The response categories of the 'membership' and the 'dissolution' questions explicitly include a category expressing neutrality ('neither good nor bad'; 'indifferent'). This is not the case at any stage with the 'benefit' question. The 'unification' question contained such a response category only for the first four points in time, when the respondents were offered the category 'indifferent'.

To enhance the comparability of the four indicators, we have grouped the various response categories into a positive, an indifferent, and a negative category. Respondents who spontaneously answer 'don't know' or do not answer the question at all are allocated to the neutral category; if the question does not provide a neutral category, then such responses are used as a substitute for a neutral category. The details are summarized in Figure 4.1.

Obviously, the different approaches to the explicit provision of a middle or neutral category in these questions creates a problem. If the response categories include a neutral category, it is a simple matter for respondents to express a neutral attitude or a non-attitude. However,

	Unification	Membership	Dissolution	Benefit
Positive	Very much for	–	Very sorry	–
	For to some extent	Good thing	–	Benefited
Indifferent	(Indifferent)	Neither/nor	Indifferent	–
	d.k./n.a.	d.k./n.a.	d.k./n.a.	d.k./n.a.
Negative	Against to some extent	Bad thing	Relieved	Not benefited
	Very much against	–	–	–

FIGURE 4.1. *Grouping of response categories in the four basic indicators of attitudes towards European integration*

Note: 'd.k./n.a.' = 'don't know/not available'.

if respondents can only choose between a positive or negative answer, it is more difficult for them to express neutrality; the only options are to respond by answering 'I don't know' or not to answer the question at all. Therefore, if an indifference category is not offered to respondents, a higher proportion of positive or negative answers is to be expected. In sum, we have to be very careful about comparing the answers to questions which vary in the way they treat neutral responses.

One way to deal with the problem is to subtract the proportion of negative answers from the proportion of positive answers. If we assume that those who would actually choose a neutral response but are forced (because they wish to answer the question) to give a positive or negative response are randomly distributed between the positive and negative answer categories, then the removal of the middle category affects the proportion of positive and negative answers but not the difference between them. Even if the assumption about the distribution of this group of respondents is not absolutely rigorous, the comparability of the answers to questions with and without a neutral category is improved.

Based on these considerations, we constructed four indices of net evaluation (or net support).[1] Each index is computed by subtracting the proportion of negative answers from the proportion of positive answers. Each index therefore shows the extent to which the positive or negative evaluation of European integration predominates on the dimension in question. The indices range from +1 to −1. A value of +1 means that all respondents evaluate the EC positively; a value of 0 indicates an equal share of positive and negative orientations among respondents;[2] and a value of −1 indicates an entirely negative evaluation.

In contrast to analyses which focus only on positive responses (Inglehart 1977*a*; Inglehart and Rabier 1978; Handley 1981*a*), these indices allow a more meaningful comparative analysis of the four indicators and a more accurate interpretation of their development over time. A description of the development of the indicators referring only to the percentage of positive evaluations creates the impression that an increase in EC support occurs every time this percentage increases. An increase of positive evaluations can be accompanied, however, by a simultaneous and even stronger increase in negative evaluations, if there is a mobilization process which moves neutral or indifferent citizens more towards opposition than towards support. Positive evaluations may increase in this situation, but such a development has to be seen as an overall decline in support which is captured by the net support indices used here.

Europeanization or Nationalization of Public Opinion?

As a summary measure of trends, we shall speak of a 'Europeanization' of public opinion if the index values are increasing over time, and of a 'nationalization' of public opinion if the values are declining. These terms are, of course, a form of shorthand; we note, in particular, that 'nationalization' does not imply a growth of nationalism or nationalist sentiment in the ideological sense. A Europeanization or nationalization of public opinion can be the result of various combinations of the components of the indices. Normally, Europeanization is characterized by an increase in positive evaluations of the EC. This can result from a decline in the proportion of those who are indifferent, or a decline in the proportion who evaluate the EC negatively, or both. In the first case, Europeanization is based on a mobilization process; in the second case, it is based on a decline in opposition. However, Europeanization can also take place if positive EC evaluations are constant over time and negative evaluations decline to the advantage of the neutral or indifferent category; this may be so even if positive evaluations decline and the negative evaluations decline even more. In both instances there is a demobilization process leading to a greater proportion of people who do not have a clear orientation towards the EC. Similarly, a nationalization of opinion is normally characterized by a decline in positive evaluations of the EC along with either an increase in indifference or an increase in opposition, or both. In other words, the nationalization of opinion can be the result of either a process of demobilization or the strengthening of opposition.

The relevance of these distinctions between different forms of Europeanization and nationalization of public opinion becomes obvious if one considers their different political implications. A tendency towards the nationalization of opinion in the EC member states, for instance, is less threatening for the continued development of the EC if it is based on a process of demobilization and not a strengthening of opposition. For example, if some of the citizens with positive orientations turn to neutrality or indifference rather than to negative orientations, any efforts by the political élites to reverse the nationalization process should have a better chance of success.

In Figure 4.2 we show developments on the four indicators for the EC as a whole, based on the weighted average of all EC member states.[3] On average, the index values of all four indicators are clearly positive over the whole twenty-year period. This means that positive evaluations of the EC have predominated during the last two decades. Secondly, the distributions suggest that the four indicators are hierarchically ordered. Support for the EC is lowest if respondents are asked to give a specific or instrumental evaluation of the EC; that is, an answer based on a rational cost–benefit calculation. Support is highest if a diffuse, affective evaluation of European unification is being elicited.

As the 'unification' question was asked in several surveys by the US

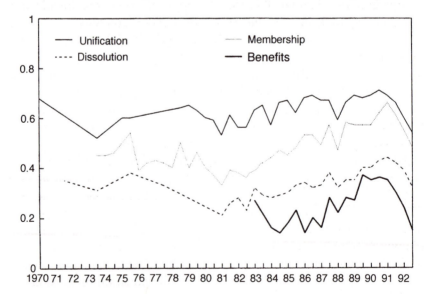

FIGURE 4.2. *Net diffuse support for the European Community, 1970–92*
Sources: European Community Study (1970, 1971); Eurobarometer, Nos. 0–38.

Information Agency between 1952 and 1967, we can trace this particular indicator even further back in time. Figure 4.3 shows that in the 1950s net support for the idea of European unification in the four big countries (Germany, Britain, France, and Italy) followed more or less the same pattern. However, at the beginning of the 1960s, net popular evaluation of this process in Britain, which did not join the EC at its foundation in 1957, dropped well below the level of support in the other three countries. By the mid-1960s support had recovered somewhat but still remained below the level in the three large member states.

Diffuse Support for the EC

If we look at the development of the three indicators used to measure diffuse support for the EC ('unification', 'membership', and 'dissolution'), it becomes clear that there was a tendency towards the nationalization of public opinion at the end of the 1970s.[4] This was followed by a tendency towards Europeanization in the 1980s, and then another reversal or nationalization process in 1991–2. The latter development will be considered at the end of this chapter. However, as we shall see, this overall picture is based on rather different country-specific developments.

Opinion in the six original member states is summarized in Figure 4.4. According to the unification indicator, attitudes in these countries are very similar, with index values ranging from 0.6 to 0.8. The variation is somewhat greater in the case of the membership question, with France and Germany in particular showing a somewhat lower level of support. The general level of support is lowest and the differences between the countries are largest on the 'dissolution' indicator.

Figure 4.5 shows, however, that there is a clear gap between these levels of diffuse EC support in the six original member states and the levels in those states which joined the EC at the first enlargement in 1973. This is most pronounced in the evaluation of EC membership and EC dissolution. In the 1970s and early 1980s, the Danes and the British were divided or even largely negative on these measures. It took until the mid-1980s for positive EC orientations to become clearly predominant. Even now, however, the level of EC support in Denmark and Britain has not reached the average support level in the six original member states. By contrast, the index values have been considerably higher from the beginning in Ireland—largely because the proportion of

Support for European Integration

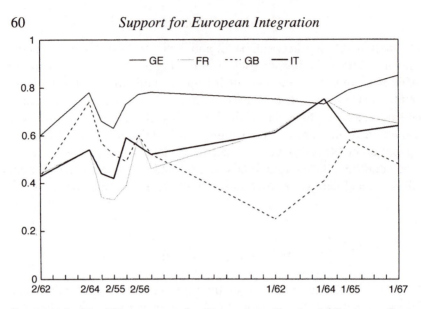

FIGURE 4.3. *Net diffuse support for European unification in Germany, France, Italy and Britain, 1952–67*

Notes: The data for 1952, 1954, 1955, and 1956 relate to the second half of the respective year; the data for 1962, 1964, 1965, and 1967 relate to the first half of the respective year.

Sources: USIA data; Merritt and Puchala (1968).

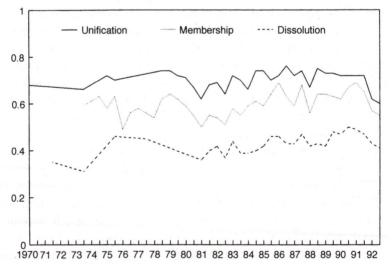

FIGURE 4.4. *Net diffuse support for the EC among the six original member states, 1970–92*

Sources: European Community Study (1970, 1971); Eurobarometer, Nos. 0–38.

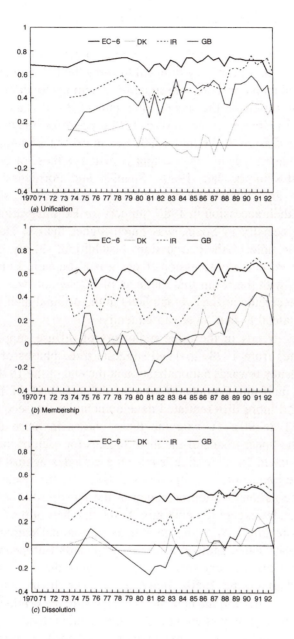

FIGURE 4.5. *Net diffuse support for the EC in Denmark, Ireland, and Britain, 1970–92*

Sources: European Community Study (1970, 1971); Eurobarometer, Nos. 0–38.

explicit EC opponents was much lower in Ireland than in the two other countries.

While the Danes and the British are still—almost two decades after EC accession—less positively oriented towards the EC than the peoples of the original member states, the situation is completely different in the states joining the EC at the second enlargement in 1981 and 1986 (see Figure 4.6). In Greece, the level of diffuse support for integration from the date of accession to the mid-1980s was more or less comparable to the Irish values and, as in Ireland, approximated to those of the original member states in the late 1980s. Spanish and Portuguese data on 'unification' and 'membership' collected since 1980–1 show that, long before their accession in 1986, support for EC integration in these countries, especially in Spain, was much higher than in Denmark or Britain at the time of their accession. In addition, shortly before the Spanish and Portuguese accessions there was a dramatic Europeanization process, with the result that the level of EC support was as high at the time of accession as the average level in the original member states. Support remained at that level subsequently.

Comparing trends in the three indicators of diffuse support in the member states from 1978[5] to 1990 suggests three phases of development: a tendency towards nationalization at the end of the 1970s (1978–80); almost uniform Europeanization in the first half of the 1980s (1981–5); and more differentiated developments in the second half of the 1980s (1986–90). To examine these phases in more detail, we calculated the linear trends of the three indices for each of the member states—calculated by regressing levels on each index against time. The slopes of the trend lines are reported in Table 4.1. It is clear from the table that the nationalization tendency in the late 1970s characterized all member states except Luxembourg. In the first half of the 1980s, this process was reversed. With the notable exception of Denmark, almost all EC member states showed a tendency towards Europeanization—albeit in some cases a very small one—on each of the three indices. In the second half of the 1980s, however, a clear distinction emerges between the original and the new member states. In the original member states Europeanization was either replaced by a minor tendency towards nationalization or at least a considerably weakened Europeanization process. But all six new member states, on all three indicators, showed a considerable tendency towards Europeanization. The Europeanization of public opinion in the second half of the 1980s, shown by the overall

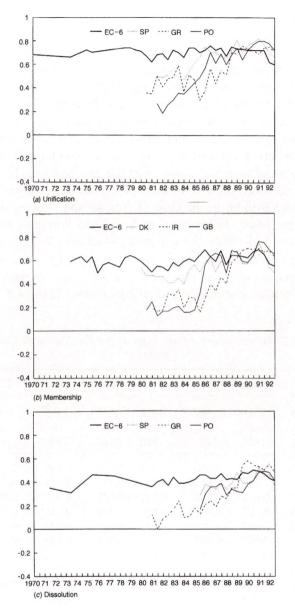

FIGURE 4.6. *Net diffuse support for the EC in Greece, Spain, and Portugal,*
1970–92

Sources: European Community Study (1970, 1971); Eurobarometer, Nos. 0–38.

European average, is therefore almost entirely due to a Europeanization of public opinion in the new member states.

Altogether, one gets the impression that, with respect to support for integration, those states with decades of EC experience reached an upper limit in the level of public support in the mid-1980s which can, if at all, only be increased slightly in the long run. The states which joined the EC in 1973 and Greece, which joined in 1981, started from a considerably lower level of support for the EC, and for a long time the level of support developed more or less in parallel with that of the original states, although in some cases the gap widened. By the end of the 1980s, however, there were signs of a possible closing of the gap in Denmark and Britain; in the case of Ireland and Greece, the gap had already been closed. In the cases of Spain and Portugal, which joined the EC in the mid-1980s, the gap was closed even before accession.

We noted earlier that changes in net support for integration might follow from quite different processes of mobilization or demobilization, from the decline or strengthening of opposition. Table 4.2 shows that

TABLE 4.1. *Trends in net diffuse support for the European Community, 1978–90*

	Unification			Membership			Dissolution	
	1978 to 1980	1981 to 1985	1986 to 1990	1978 to 1980	1981 to 1985	1986 to 1990	1981 to 1985	1986 to 1990
BE	−0.020	0.022	0.008	−0.013	0.019	0.005	0.009	−0.003
DK	−0.023	−0.022	0.040	−0.005	0.003	0.013	−0.006	0.003
FR	−0.028	0.012	−0.010	−0.017	0.023	−0.007	0.019	−0.004
GB	−0.008	0.028	0.005	−0.055	0.036	0.031	0.020	0.020
GE	−0.020	0.003	−0.003	0.001	0.007	0.009	0.005	−0.002
GR	—	−0.002	0.039	–	0.004	0.050	0.009	0.050
IR	−0.041	0.009	0.030	−0.037	0.007	0.032	0.004	0.029
IT	−0.013	0.009	0.003	0.009	0.008	0.001	−0.002	0.020
LU	0.033	−0.005	−0.019	0.031	0.009	−0.012	0.004	−0.012
NL	−0.014	0.007	−0.002	−0.014	0.009	0.001	0.005	−0.001
PO	—	—	0.014	—	—	0.002	—	0.004
SP	—	—	0.008	—	—	0.005	—	0.006
EC	−0.015	0.011	0.003	−0.011	0.015	0.010	0.009	0.010

Note: Entries are the slopes of the linear trend line in each period.

Sources: Eurobarometer, Nos. 10–34.

TABLE 4.2. *Europeanization of public opinion in the new member states*

		Unification		Membership		Dissolution	
		Neutral	Negative	Neutral	Negative	Neutral	Negative
Denmark	1986–90	−0.010	−0.015	−0.009	−0.002	—	—
Britain	1981–90	−0.002	−0.013	−0.001	−0.014	0.008	−0.013
Ireland	1986–90	−0.012	−0.009	−0.012	−0.010	−0.017	−0.006
Portugal	1984–86	−0.064	−0.001	−0.071	−0.017	—	—
Spain	1984–86	−0.035	−0.009	−0.020	−0.007	—	—
Greece	1986–90	−0.010	−0.013	−0.026	−0.012	−0.028	−0.008

Notes: Entries are the slopes of the linear trend line in each period. For Britain, the unification indicator relates to the period 1981–85.

Sources: Eurobarometer, Nos. 15–34.

the Europeanization of public opinion[6] in the new EC member states, which led to a narrowing or even closing of the gap in EC support, was based on quite different processes in different states. In Denmark, Ireland, and Greece, Europeanization was based both on a mobilization process which reduced indifference and on a reduction of opposition. In Britain, however, the Europeanization of public opinion in the 1980s was almost exclusively based on declining opposition. A completely different development occurred in Spain and Portugal. The considerable Europeanization of opinion in these two states from 1984 to 1986 was mainly based on a mobilization process; that is, a fall in the proportion of those who are indifferent at a time when the proportion opposed to the EC was already lower than the EC average.

Differences between Countries

The clear gap between the level of diffuse support for the EC in the six original member states and in those states joining in 1973 has prompted the hypothesis of a societal learning effect arising from, among other things, exposure to the institutions of internationalized governance. In other words, it has been assumed that the difference between old and new members 'seems to reflect the presence or absence of a reservoir of diffuse support built up over a long period of time' (Inglehart and Rabier 1978: 71; see also Inglehart 1970*b*). This hypothesis, however, was severely challenged by the southern enlargement of the EC because, as shown above, diffuse support for the EC among the Spanish and the Portuguese increased dramatically before the accession of their countries. By the time they entered the EC, levels of diffuse support in Spain and Portugal had reached the level found in the original member states. In this respect, then, there was no gap between the old and the new members.

Enthusiasm for the EC in Spain and Portugal suggests a range of political, cultural, and historical characteristics as explanations of cross-national differences in EC orientations. In addition to economic considerations,[7] EC membership was widely seen in these countries, as well as in Greece, as an essential contribution to the democratization, stabilization, and legitimation of the new political systems after the regime transitions of the mid-1970s. EC membership came to symbolize the inclusion of these countries in the community of western democracies. Similar sentiments probably also have some part in explaining the Euro-enthusiasm in Germany during the very early years of the Community. That is, the widespread support for internationalized governance in Germany in the first decades after the Second World War can be seen as a flight from the country's historical inheritance, especially from the period of National Socialism with its perversion of national governance. On the theme of escape from the national situation, we might note that in Italy the EC is often regarded as a cure for the chronic difficulties of government (see Chapter 8).

Apart from these countries, however, it may be that the political and cultural heritage of nation states impedes rather than promotes the development of favourable orientations towards the European Community. This would help to account for attitudes in the United Kingdon with its former status as a world power and its ties with the Commonwealth. As Hoffmann noted, an important influence maintaining the obstinacy of the nation state is the enjoyment, for a long time, of an autonomous status on the world scene (see Chapter 2). External ties of another sort, especially with the other Nordic countries, may help to account for attitudes in Denmark (see Chapter 14). In addition, both Denmark and Britain have traditionally set great store by the protection of their national sovereignty; in the case of Denmark, this is reinforced by the fear of becoming dominated by the big member countries in a supranational, centralized, and bureaucratized EC. But size can work quite differently, with an even smaller country such as Ireland viewing the EC more positively—as an enhancement rather than as a loss of sovereignty.

Specific Support for the EC

Turning to examine specific or instrumental support for the EC, operationalized by the 'benefits' indicator, the trend lines shown in Figure 4.7 reveal that the variation between the original member states is much greater than in the case of the three previous indicators. This is primarily due to the considerably less positive view of the French and the Germans on this dimension. In contrast to the original member states, in which the specific evaluation of the EC was more or less the same at the beginning of the 1990s as it had been in the early 1980s, we find a clear upwards trend in the new member states. But there are differences among these countries: in Ireland, Greece, Denmark, and Portugal evaluations of benefit were positive at the outset and moved upwards thereafter; in Britain and Spain, negative orientations predominated until 1988–9.

If we calculate the linear trends on this indicator, it again becomes clear that the development of this kind of orientation in the individual member states during the second half of the 1980s follows the same pattern as in the case of the more general and diffuse attitudes. Here, too, the general pattern of Europeanization we found is almost exclusively due to a strong Europeanization process in the new member states. By contrast, the index values rose only slightly in the original six member states.[8]

Maastricht and Attitudes to European Integration

Diffuse as well as specific net support for European integration had, by the end of the 1980s, as an EC average, reached the highest level ever measured. This has been attributed largely to the effects of the single European market, 'the galvanizing force which Europe has so sorely lacked over the past twenty years' (Noel 1991: 57). But following the negative result of the first Danish referendum on the Maastricht Treaty in June 1992, there was much discussion in the media about the waning of public support for the Community. Did this major event really cause a general change in attitudes towards European integration in the early 1990s?

Our data show that the referendum result only brought out into the light a development which had already begun in autumn 1991.[9] Since late 1991, there was a distinct nationalization of public opinion, in the

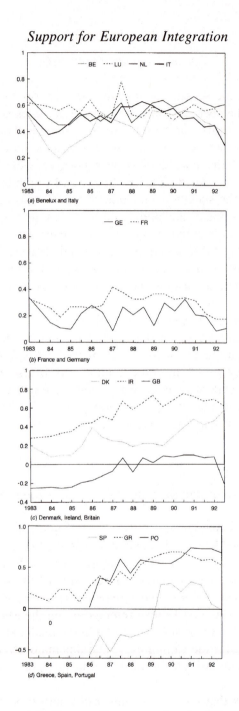

FIGURE 4.7. *Net specific support for the EC, 1983–92*
Sources: Eurobarometer, Nos. 19–38.

sense that both diffuse and specific net support for the EC was in decline. The timing of the onset of this decline means that it could not have been caused by the specific event of the Danish referendum on the Maastricht Treaty but at best by discussions surrounding preparations for the Maastricht Treaty. The impact of these discussions must be seen in the context of two broader developments. First, the Single Market programme had reached a stage at which it had begun to impinge on public consciousness. Secondly, there was the growing uncertainty about the role of the Community in the post-cold war world. In any event, the plausible supposition that attitudes towards the Maastricht Treaty have influenced general orientations towards the EC must not assume that the two are identical. The two sets of orientations have different objects. In the case of the Maastricht Treaty, people were evaluating a proposed future development in European integration, whereas the object of the orientations dealt with in this chapter is the EC as it already existed.

That this is not simply a theoretical distinction is demonstrated by the Danish case. In the first of two referendums, the Danes rejected the Maastricht Treaty by a tiny majority. A few months earlier, in the Eurobarometer survey of spring 1992, the index values for all four indicators of EC support were positive (see Figures 4.5 and 4.7c). After the referendum, in the Eurobarometer survey of autumn 1992, all respondents were asked whether they would vote for or against the Maastricht Treaty in a referendum.[10] Together with the British, the Danes still rejected the Treaty by a tiny majority, but they were the only European people who showed a clear increase in support for the existing Community. In other words, people differentiate between European integration as currently realized, on the one hand and, on the other hand, future plans for further integration.

Comparing the spring 1991 and autumn 1992 values of our four indicators, shown in Table 4.3, reveals the extent to which public opinion underwent nationalization in the early 1990s. The differences in the index values demonstrate that there was a more or less pronounced decline in both diffuse and specific net support for the EC in each of the EC member states except Denmark. The nationalization process was most evident in the big countries, namely in Britain, Spain, Germany, and France.

As emphasized at the outset of this chapter, nationalization tendencies are less threatening for the maintenance of the EC if they are based on a process of demobilization; that is, if there is an increase in the

TABLE 4.3. *Nationalization of attitudes towards integration, spring 1991–autumn 1992*

	Unification				Membership				Dissolution				Benefit			
	VDI	p	n	neg	VDI	p	n	neg	VDI	p	n	neg	VDI	p	n	neg
BE	-0.15	-	0	+	-0.15	-	+	+	-0.06	-	-	+	-0.16	-	+	+
GB	-0.31	-	+	+	-0.26	-	+	+	-0.18	-	-	+	-0.31	-	+	+
DK	-0.13	-	-	+	0.10	+	-	-	0.06	+	-	0	0.09	+	+	-
FR	-0.15	-	-	+	-0.17	-	+	+	-0.09	-	-	+	-0.14	-	+	+
GE	-0.18	+	0	+	-0.15	-	+	+	-0.18	-	+	+	-0.17	-	0	+
GR	0.02	+	-	+	-0.07	-	+	+	-0.05	-	0	0	-0.11	-	+	+
IR	-0.07	-	0	+	-0.11	-	+	+	-0.04	-	+	+	-0.10	-	+	+
IT	-0.10	-	0	+	-0.12	-	+	+	-0.04	-	0	+	-0.20	-	0	+
LU	0.11	+	-	-	-0.06	-	+	+	-0.04	-	-	+	-0.12	-	0	+
NL	-0.03	-	-	+	-0.05	-	+	+	0.00	+	-	+	-0.06	-	+	+
PO	-0.08	-	0	+	-0.11	-	+	+	-0.07	-	+	+	-0.06	-	+	+
SP	-0.16	-	0	+	-0.26	-	+	+	-0.15	-	+	+	-0.34	-	-	+
EC	-0.15	-	0	+	-0.18	-	+	+	-0.12	-	-	+	-0.20	-	+	+

Notes: The entries in the Value Difference Index (VDI) column show the change in each of the four indices of net evaluation of European integration between 1991 and 1992. Entries in the other three columns indicate whether positive (p), neutral (n) or negative (neg) responses have increased (+), declined (−), or remained the same (0).

Sources: Eurobarometer, Nos. 35–38.

proportion who are indifferent to European integration rather than an increase in the proportion who are opposed. Comparision of the responses in spring 1991 and autumn 1992 shows that, although there is an increase in indifference, the nationalization process is to a considerable extent based on strengthening opposition to the EC.

A more detailed examination of attitudes towards the Maastricht Treaty throws some light on possible determinants of this process of nationalization. In the 1991–2 Eurobarometer surveys respondents were asked about their evaluations of three specific aspects of the Maastricht Treaty: a common defence policy, a common foreign policy, and European monetary union.[11] Figure 4.8 shows clearly that net support for a common defence policy increased and net support for a common foreign policy remained more or less stable between spring 1991 and autumn 1992. However, support for monetary union with a single currency replacing national currencies by 1999 declined considerably.

This finding suggests that the monetary implications of the Maastricht Treaty, which had broad and mostly negative media coverage, had an impact on the attitudes of European citizens towards the existing EC. It is certainly the case that the debate about replacing national currencies with a common currency has made purely economic cost–benefit

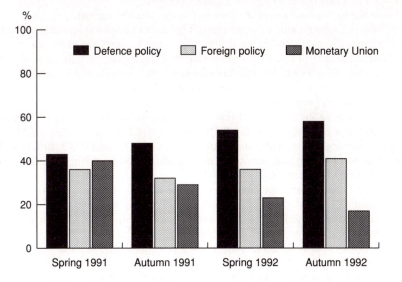

FIGURE 4.8. *Net support for three aspects of the Maastricht Treaty, 1991–2*
Note: Entries are the average level of support across the EC as a whole.
Sources: Eurobarometer, Nos. 35–8.

calculations particularly topical. The debate may also, because of the symbolic aspect of national currencies, have increased fears about a loss of national identities. We return to the question of the relationship between national and European identity in a later chapter. The next task, however, is to examine whether economic calculations do in fact play any role in enhancing or undermining support for European integration.

NOTES

1. In addition to improving the comparability of the four indicators, this procedure ensures better comparability of the 'unification' indicator over time because it reduces the effect of a change in the response format.
2. For completeness, we should note that the indices can take the value 0 also in the hypothetical case where not a single respondent has any orientation towards the EC.
3. The weighting is based on the size of the adult population in each country. The gaps in the data for the unification and dissolution indicator in the 1970s are filled in by interpolation. The new member states are added starting with their official accession date: Denmark, Ireland, and Britain 1973; Greece 1981; Portugal and Spain 1986.
4. On the 'crisis of the 1970s' see Handley (1981a).
5. For the earlier time period the data base is too small to compute a trend.
6. Table 4.2 includes only those periods of time with a substantial upward trend in the indicators in question (see Table 4.1). The values for the slope of the linear trend line between 1984 and 1986 in Spain and Portugal are: Spain, unification = 0.052, membership = 0.035; Portugal, unification = 0.067, membership = 0.105.
7. For a discussion of hypotheses about economic factors underlying attitudes towards European integration, see Ch. 5.
8. The slopes of the linear trend lines for this period are Belgium 0.021, Denmark 0.008, France 0.008, Germany 0.010, Greece 0.052, Ireland 0.033, Italy 0.007, Luxembourg -0.005, Netherlands 0.013, Portugal 0.047, Spain 0.095, Britain 0.031.
9. In some of the original member states a gradual erosion of support started even earlier; see also Reif (1993).
10. In the Danish, Irish, and French surveys the question referred to 'another referendum'.
11. The question wording is: 'Irrespective of other details of the Maastricht Treaty, what is your opinion on each of the following proposals? (1) The EC member states should work towards a common defence policy; (2) The member states of the European Community should have one common foreign policy towards countries outside the European Community; (3) There should be a European monetary union with one single currency replacing by 1999 the (national currency) and all other national currencies of the member states of the European Community.'

5

Economic Calculus or Familiarity Breeds Content?

AGUSTI BOSCH AND KENNETH NEWTON

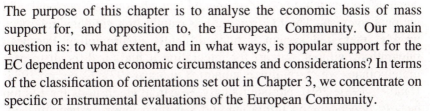

The purpose of this chapter is to analyse the economic basis of mass support for, and opposition to, the European Community. Our main question is: to what extent, and in what ways, is popular support for the EC dependent upon economic circumstances and considerations? In terms of the classification of orientations set out in Chapter 3, we concentrate on specific or instrumental evaluations of the European Community.

Behind this research question lies the matter of the legitimacy of the EC among its citizens. Inglehart argues that 'favourable economic payoffs are conducive to—perhaps even essential to—the processes of national and supranational integration' (Inglehart and Rabier 1978: 69). In much the same way integration theory suggests that economic rewards for the general population are of some significance in the drive towards integration. Nye (1971: 83–4), for example, points out that it is important that economic benefits are perceived to flow from integration.

Some empirically oriented researchers into public opinion have argued that a widespread recognition of rewards is a necessary pre-condition of stronger and more enduring ties of loyalty (Shepherd 1975: ch. 6; Hewstone 1986: 43). In the case of the EC it seems obvious that of the many kinds of reward, economic benefits are likely to be the most important. As Dalton and Eichenberg suggest, 'at the base of any utilitarian model of public support for the European community must be considerations about its economic performance' (1991: 3; see also Reif and Inglehart 1991: 7). To what extent, then, does economic performance underpin utilitarian support for the EC, and is there any evidence to suggest that this sort of support preceded stronger ties of loyalty and legitimacy?

It is equally obvious that economic benefits alone are not enough to establish the legitimacy of the EC. The stability of any political institution is uncertain if it depends wholly, or even largely, on a good economic climate. It is entirely appropriate that economic considerations and performance should enter into the calculus of consent but, like nation states, the Community cannot depend only on utilitarian support of an economic kind. It must build its future prospects to some extent on values which can both transcend and outlast calculations of economic gain and loss. It must have roots which are deep enough and strong enough to weather even severe economic drought.

Some research studies have concluded that the EC lacks democratic legitimacy, that its foundations of 'permissive consensus' are not deeply rooted (Lindberg and Scheingold 1970; Stavridis 1992), and that it depends too much upon instrumental calculations of personal and national interests. The EC, it is said, is caught in a vicious circle: as a weakly integrated system it finds difficulty in promoting European integration; without support for integration it finds it difficult to promote policies which reinforce support (Caporaso 1973; Caporaso 1974; Handley 1981: 360). Not suprisingly, research which finds the EC too heavily dependent on utilitarian and specific support, especially economic support, often finds that adverse economic circumstances tend to undermine its popularity (Caporaso 1974; Handley 1981*a*; Lindberg and Scheingold 1970; Shepherd, 1975; Jowell and Hoinville 1977).

Others have argued that the EC has built up support of a more enduring and diffuse or affective kind. They see signs of a growing European identity and trust, and of beliefs in the goals and ideals of European integration, especially among the younger generation (Hewstone 1986; Inglehart 1977*b*; Inglehart 1990; Inglehart and Rabier 1978; Merritt 1968). Questions about the nature and strength of EC support remain, however. In Easton's terminology, does the EC attract the diffuse and enduring support of its citizens, or is it dependent on specific support of a more short-run kind? (Easton 1965: 249).

The legitimacy of the EC is the first concern of this chapter. The second is a more theoretical interest in the extent to which economic circumstances and factors mould, even determine, our political world view. In the context of the EC, this question turns on whether citizens evaluate the EC in terms of their material interests or in terms of their ideal interests. Economic interests are among the most important material matters; ideal interests include such things as world peace, European co-operation, social justice, and environmental protection. Studies of politics at the national level suggest that economic conditions and perceptions have a strong impact on support for governments and on electoral behaviour. At the same time, these economic influences are not necessarily of a selfish or 'pocket-book' nature, but are often socially aware or 'sociotropic' (Tufte 1978: 65; Lewis-Beck 1986*a*; Lewin 1991; Rattinger 1991*b*: 50). Is the same true of support for the EC? The fact that this study is both cross-national, examining data for between nine and twelve countries, and across-time, with data for some seventeen years, adds to its interest as a test case for the 'economic voting' hypothesis at the level of internationalized governance.

There is no hard and fast distinction to be drawn between economic and non-economic, or between the material and the ideal. Nor is there a simple dichotomy between 'narrow materialism' and 'high-minded idealism'. More to the point, mass opinion about anything as large and complex as the European Community is highly likely to be based upon a mixture of different factors and dispositions, ranging from naked economic self-interest, through sociotropic calculations of an economic nature, to considerations of an idealistic kind. Moreover, the mix of different reasons for supporting or opposing the EC may well change over time in different countries according to different social, political, and economic circumstances.

Analytic Method

Economic conditions and circumstances may affect support for the European Community in three ways. First, they may be related to differences between countries at any given time. For example, it may be that the wealthier nations are inclined to show the highest levels of support because their citizens believe that the EC has helped to create the conditions of their economic success. The first stage of the analysis, therefore, compares levels of support in different nations at the same point in time—a cross-sectional analysis.

Secondly, changing economic circumstances may affect levels of mass support for the EC in the same nation over a period of time. For example, support may grow in those countries whose economies are growing, or whose inflation or unemployment rates are low or falling. According to Dalton and Eichenberg (1991: 13), for example, 'the improvement in national economies during the 1980s yielded a substantial measure of support for the Community'. The second part of our analysis examines how changing economic circumstances in the same country influence support for the EC over a period of time—a time-series analysis.

The first two approaches deal with aggregate data at the national level. The third type of analysis deals with individual citizens. We use the Eurobarometer surveys to analyse EC support among individuals with different economic characteristics. For example, it may be that the employed are more favourably disposed towards the EC than the unemployed, or that wealthier individuals are more favourably disposed than poorer people. In the third section of the chapter, therefore, we examine individual-level data. In this sense, this complements the national, aggregate-level analysis of the first two sections.

And a last preliminary point. Our concentration on economic variables does not imply that these are the only relevant variables, or that we have exhausted the topic of EC support if we deal with them systematically. It simply reflects a division of labour within this volume. Other questions about support for the EC are discussed in other chapters.

The EC as an Economic Organization

First, we need to show that citizens of the EC member countries do, indeed, see it as an economic organization. If they believe it has little or nothing to do with economics, then to investigate the economic basis of support would be pointless. Does the public think of the EC as having an important economic role? Fortunately, it is relatively simple to answer this question, and the answer is fairly clear.

The most direct attempt to answer the question is found in Eurobarometer, No. 27 (1987), which asked, 'What things in your opinion bring the countries of the European Community together most?' Most people (41 per cent) answered in terms of 'the economy' or 'world peace', or both. These two responses tied for first place, some 13 percentage points ahead of the third option. In other words, respondents mixed material and idealistic reasons in equal parts. More circumstantial evidence is available in other Eurobarometer surveys. They show that most people in the EC believe that it does have a significant economic role and that it should play an even larger role. For example, surveys in 1989 (No. 32) and 1990 (No. 33) reveal that a majority (51 and 57 per cent respectively) of people in the EC thought that currency decisions should be taken by the EC; a smaller percentage (40 and 35 per cent) thought these should be national decisions. Similarly, more believed that VAT rates should be decided jointly within the European Community (48 per cent in 1990, 51 per cent in 1989) than believed they should be decided nationally (39 and 36 per cent).

It is not necessary to labour the point. The Eurobarometer surveys show over and over again that the publics of the European member countries see the EC both as an important economic organization, and as an equally important political and diplomatic organization concerned with such things as peace, co-operation, European integration, environmental protection, social justice and development, and equality.[1] Whereas Dalton and Eichenberg (1991: 3, 14) argue that 'For the European Community economic policy is the *raison d'être* . . . the EC is above all an economic institution', the evidence presented indicates that, while the public sees the EC as an important economic institution, it is also seen as having a range of important non-economic goals of a more ideal nature (cf. Inglehart and Rabier 1978: 97).

There are national differences in this respect, some being more utilitarian or economic than others. We can gauge this from answers to an open-ended question asked in 1987: 'When you hear about the European Community what does that bring to your mind?' When the responses are coded into economic and political responses, it appears that some nations, notably Greece, Ireland, Portugal, Spain, and Britain have a preponderance of people who see the EC primarily in economic terms. In some other countries, people are more inclined to see it as a political organization—Italy, Belgium, Luxembourg, and the Netherlands. This is evident in Figure 5.1. We will return to this continuum of economic–political perceptions later. Meanwhile we can safely conclude that it is sensible to ask questions about the economic basis of support for the EC, while recognizing that citizens across Europe see it as having both political and economic functions.

Indicators of Support

Responses to the four standard questions used to measure support for the EC and European integration are used in this chapter and are referred to in shorthand as 'unification', 'membership', 'benefit', and

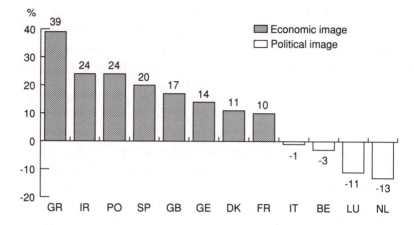

FIGURE 5.1. *Economical–political images of the EC, 1987*

Note: The figures are the percentages of respondents in each country presenting a primarily economic image of the EC minus the percentages presenting a primarily political image.

Source: Eurobarometer, No. 27.

'dissolution' (see Chapter 4). Of the four, the 'unification' question is the most general, and the one which comes closest to asking about diffuse attitudes. Towards the other end of the continuum, the 'benefits' question comes closest to asking about specific support. Although the question is carefully worded and avoids mentioning any particular type of benefit, it seems likely that some respondents will have economic benefits in mind when they respond to it. On the diffuse–specific continuum, the membership question fits somewhere in the middle. The fourth question dealing with 'dissolution' can be set aside for the moment. It is hypothetical and, not suprisingly, a relatively large proportion (about 50 per cent or more) give an 'indifferent'—don't know—response, or no reply.

The discussion in Chapter 4, and the figures and tables which go with it, outline how the main indicators of support for the EC have developed since 1970. That chapter also shows that the trends in individual countries conform to the same general pattern. The 'unification' question clearly produces the highest level of support. Well over 70 per cent of EC citizens regularly endorse this aim, sometimes over 80 per cent. On average, about 10–15 per cent fewer support their country's membership of the EC. Even so, support for membership has claimed a clear majority across Western Europe over the long run. A lower percentage, but still a majority, claim benefits from their country's membership of the EC. Since the question was first asked regularly in 1983 about 50–55 per cent have claimed that they have benefited. The conclusion seems to be that, across the Community as a whole, diffuse support is more widespread than specific support.

Differences between Countries

Support for the EC in any given year varies quite substantially from one country to another, and these differences have persisted over a relatively long period of time. It is tempting, at first, to attribute the differences between countries simply to when they joined the EC. As we can see in Table 5.1, the proportion of positive responses to three of the support indicators is consistently higher among the original six member states than among later members.

However, a closer look at the data shows that the matter is not so simple. For example, Italy has generally shown higher levels of support than Germany, while Denmark and Britain have usually shown support

TABLE 5.1. *Indicators of support by length of EC membership, 1970–89*

	1970	1975	1980	1985	1989
Unification					
EC-6	74	74	76	81	82
EC-10	—	69	72	77	78
EC-12	—	—	—	74	78
Membership					
EC-6	—	67	64	69	69
EC-10	—	59	53	60	65
EC-12	—	—	—	60	63
			1983	1986	1989
Benefit					
EC-10			52	55	59
EC-12			—	46	59

Notes: The entries are the percentages 'very much' or 'to some extent' supporting unification; the percentages who regard membership as 'as good thing'; and the percentages claiming to 'have benefited' from membership.

Source: Commission of the European Communities (1989: 41–78).

levels which are lower than Ireland. Spain and Portugal show higher levels of support than some of the older member states. In other words, there are still differences between nations which joined at the same time, and a certain amount of overlap between some nations which joined at different times. To what extent do these national variations relate, among other things, to the economic circumstances of different countries?

The simplest proposition, and the one which comes closest to a calculation of naked economic self-interest, is that levels of support will be higher in countries which receive more from EC funds than they pay into them. According to Ardy (1988: 425), 'the EC has a budget which derives revenue and distributes benefits in a manner entirely unrelated to levels of national wealth'. This may encourage those who benefit and those who pay to make economic calculations the basis of their support or opposition. Moreover, the publicity surrounding the Common Agricultural Policy, by far the largest part of the EC budget, may also encourage such economic calculations. For example, support for the EC in Britain was relatively low during the period in which Mrs Thatcher was arguing about the British payment, which she claimed, with a great deal of national publicity, was far too high. Support rose substantially after a lower contribution was negotiated. Just before the new financial settlement, as few as 25 per cent of the British claimed that EC membership was 'a good thing'; a year later the figure rose to 37 per cent. Evidently, this highly publicized incident seemed to disturb the long-term upward trend of support in Britain only briefly.

Unfortunately, it is impossible to get satisfactory figures for net country receipts from the EC over a period of years. This is because the annual contributions of member states to Community revenues are published, but the totals of their annual receipts are not (Office for Official Publications of the European Communities 1991). However, precise figures for the average of 1982, 1983, and 1984 have been painstakingly calculated and published (Ardy 1988). Although this provides us with only nine cases (Belgium and Luxembourg are grouped together), we can examine them to see if any pattern emerges.

At this stage of the analysis, support for the EC is measured in terms of responses to the 'membership' question which has the longest run in the Eurobarometer series. Table 5.2 shows the level of support for membership of the EC in 1984 by country, and the average net per capita balance between payments into EC funds and receipts from EC funds over the 1982–4 period. The table displays no obvious pattern. For example, Denmark, which was a substantial net beneficiary of EC finances, shows the lowest level of support (31 per cent) compared with Germany (53 per cent), a substantial net contributor. The Irish combined by far the largest per capita net receipts with a lower than average level of support (43 per cent). In the five countries which were net contributors to EC funds (Belgium, Luxembourg, Germany, France, and Britain) the average level of support was 54 per cent; among the five net receivers of EC funds (the Netherlands, Italy, Ireland, Greece, and Denmark) support averaged 52 per cent. The level of support among the two largest net gainers (Ireland and Greece) averaged 40.5 per cent. For the two largest contributors (Belgium/Luxembourg and Germany) the figure was 61 per cent.

The figures clearly support Dalton and Eichenberg's (1991: 15) conclusion that 'EC budget distributions have no impact on citizen support for European institutions'. In fact, Table 5.2 deepens the mystery. Why was the level of support relatively low among the Irish when the EC contributes so heavily to their national economy? The same might be asked of the Greeks and the Danes, although they benefit less heavily. On the other side of the coin, why should two-

TABLE 5.2. *Net payments/receipts and support for the EC*

	Percentage reporting membership a 'good thing' 1984	Percentage claiming to have benefited 1984	Net per capita payments from EC funds 1982–84
Netherlands	80	64	+17.11
Italy	70	63	+17.28
Belgium/Luxembourg	69	53	−47.07
France	62	47	−9.98
Germany	53	46	−45.02
Ireland	43	61	+205.61
Greece	38	51	+80.00
Britain	32	32	−19.61
Denmark	31	44	+57.83
EC-10	55	52	

Note: Net per capita payments from EC are calculated as receipts minus payments in ECU, averaged over 1982, 1983, and 1984.

Sources: Ardy (1988); Commission of the European Communities (1989: 57–72).

thirds of the French support the EC when, on average, France is a net contributor to EC funds? We return to these questions shortly.

Meanwhile, we can try another tack. Perhaps national variations in EC support can be explained in terms of more general macro-economic considerations, such as national wealth or economic growth. After all the EC budget is an arcane matter, but issues such as inflation, unemployment, and economic growth have an immediate impact on everyday life. One hypothesis is that the wealthier countries with stronger economies will be able to compete more effectively in a larger and more open market and will therefore show higher levels of support for the EC. Germany would be an obvious case in point. Equally, it may be that poorer countries think that they will gain most, in the long run, from the modernizing effects of the EC, and accordingly will show high levels of support. Spain, Greece, and Portugal might be examples. Perhaps both propositions are true, in which case plotting gross domestic product (GDP) per capita against EC support would produce a U-curve.

Table 5.3 presents figures for GDP per capita and support for the EC in 1975, 1980, and 1985. Once again, the small number of cases makes it impossible to draw any hard and fast conclusions. Nevertheless, there is little evidence here to suggest an association between national income and EC support. On the contrary, the figures suggest no kind of linear relationship, either positive or negative, or any kind of U, S, or J-curve. Luxembourg, Germany, and Denmark are the three most affluent countries, but they showed relatively high, intermediate, and low levels of support respectively. Conversely, Italy, Ireland, and Greece have relatively low GDP per capita, but Italy showed much higher support levels than Ireland and Greece. There seems, then, to be a random relationship between GDP per capita and EC support.

Perhaps the relationship is dynamic, related to economic growth: people in countries which are doing well, expanding their economies and growing richer will feel well disposed towards the EC, perhaps attributing some of their success to their membership? Or perhaps it is the other way round; rich countries may feel that they could do even better outside the EC, whereas the poorer ones feel they need to be inside the market in order to expand economically? Once again, there is nothing in the figures to support either hypothesis (see Table 5.4). For example, Germany sustained a rather higher growth rate than Italy over the 1968–85 period, but Italian support for the EC was regularly higher over the same period. In the 1979–85 period, Luxembourg's economy

TABLE 5.3. *GDP per capita and support for the EC, 1975–85*

	Percentage saying membership a 'good thing' 1975	GDP per capita ($'000)		Percentage saying membership a 'good thing' 1980	GDP per capita ($'000)		Percentage saying membership a 'good thing' 1985	Percentage claiming to have benefited 1985	GDP per capita ($'000)
IT	71	6.8	LU	84	12.5	LU	84	73	14.3
LU	65	11.3	NL	75	12.0	NL	77	63	12.3
NL	64	10.9	IT	74	8.1	IT	72	65	8.7
FR	64	10.7	GE	65	13.2	FR	68	50	13.0
BE	57	10.4	BE	54	12.0	BE	64	52	12.4
GE	56	11.2	IR	52	5.7	GE	54	45	14.2
IR	50	4.9	FR	51	12.3	IR	53	62	6.0
GB	47	8.8	GR	42	4.2	GR	45	49	4.3
DK	36	11.6	DK	33	12.9	DK	35	44	14.6
			GB	21	9.5	GB	32	31	10.3

Note: GDP per capita is real GDP per capita in constant prices expressed in thousands of dollars at 1980 exchange rate.

Source: Commission of the European Communities, (1989: 57–72).

grew only marginally faster than Denmark's, but whereas opinion in Luxembourg was strongly supportive, in Denmark it was not. Luxembourg's population was generally favourable whether its economic growth was relatively good (1968–73 and 1979–85) or relatively poor (1973–9). Likewise, Ireland's relatively good growth rate of 3 per cent in 1973–9 was associated with relatively low support for the EC. In short, there is no systematic difference between fast and slow growth countries so far as support of the EC is concerned.

We will go no further in showing that there is no clear relationship between macroeconomic indicators and levels of support for EC membership. It is enough to say that we tried to find patterns for unemployment, for exports and imports both within the EC and outside, for trade dependence, and for the growth of exports and imports and trade dependence. Tables were scrutinized, figures rearranged in different ways, totals and subtotals for different groups of nations aggregated and reaggregated, and scattergrams drawn up. But the data were as randomly arranged as those in the tables presented.

The search for economic determinants should not end here, however. So far we have considered the 'membership' indicator of support, but we might expect economic calculations to be reflected most clearly in response to the 'benefits' question. Although the question does not specifically mention economic benefits, it does ask respondents to think in terms of benefits, and economic benefits may come easily to mind. Perhaps this will be reflected in answers to the benefits question?

At first sight, the figures presented in Table 5.5 suggest that they do. In 1984, the proportion claiming to have benefited from membership was higher, on average, among the five countries which were beneficiaries of EC funding (53 per cent) than the four which made net payments into EC funds (45.5 per cent). The pattern is clearest at the extremes. Belgium/Luxembourg and Germany were the two largest net contributors; 49.5 per cent of their population claimed to have benefited. Ireland and Greece were the two largest beneficiaries, and 56 per cent of their populations claimed benefits.

On closer examination, however, budgetary considerations are evidently muted by other considerations. People in the five net beneficiary countries were barely more likely to claim to have benefited (53 per cent) than the EC average (52 per cent). Both Greece and Denmark were substantial net recipients of funds, but fewer of their citizens claimed to have benefited than the EC average. In fact, fewer of the Danes claimed to have benefited than the Germans, the French, or the

TABLE 5.4. *Economic growth and support for the EC, 1973–85*

	Percentage saying membership a 'good thing' 1973	Growth of real GDP per capita 1968–73		Percentage saying membership a 'good thing' 1979	Growth of real GDP per capita 1973–9		Percentage saying membership a 'good thing' 1985	Percentage claiming to have benefited 1985	Growth of real GDP per capita 1979–85
IT	69	3.9	NL	84	1.9	LU	84	73	2.1
LU	67	5.0	LU	83	0.9	NL	77	63	0.2
NL	63	3.7	IT	78	2.1	IT	72	65	1.2
GE	63	4.0	GE	66	2.5	FR	68	50	0.6
FR	61	5.0	BE	65	2.0	BE	64	52	1.2
BE	57	5.3	SP	58	1.4	SP	62	—	0.7
IR	56	3.7	FR	56	2.6	GE	54	45	1.4
DK	42	3.3	IR	54	3.0	IR	53	62	1.1
GB	31	2.9	DK	37	1.6	GR	45	49	0.4
			GB	33	1.5	GB	32	31	1.1
			PO	24	1.5	DK	29	44	1.9
						PO	28	—	1.1

Source: Commission of the European Communities (1989: 57–72).

TABLE 5.5. *Benefits of EC membership by length of membership and net payments or receipts*

	Net receipts (+) or payments (−) 1982–4 (ECU)	Percentage claiming to have benefited 1984
EARLY MEMBERS		
Net recipients		
Italy	+17.28	63
Netherlands	+17.11	64
Net payers		
France	−9.98	47
Germany	−45.02	46
Belgium/Luxembourg	−47.07	53
LATER MEMBERS		
Net recipients		
Ireland	+205.61	61
Greece	+80.00	51
Denmark	+57.83	44
Net payers		
Britain	−19.61	32

Source: compiled from Table 5.2.

Belgians—countries which were net contributors. In financial terms, the Netherlands and Italy were relatively worse off than Ireland, Greece, and Denmark, but the Dutch and the Italians claimed greater benefit. Interpreting the figures is also complicated by the fact that in the case of Belgium and Luxembourg, the benefits flowing from the location of EC institutions must be added to the direct transfer of budget payments.

A third look at Table 5.5 suggests that budgetary matters are mixed up with the length of membership in the EC. Of the original six, the net recipients (the Netherlands and Italy) perceive greater benefit than the net payers (Belgium/Luxembourg, France, and Germany). And among the later members, the net recipients (Ireland, Greece, and Denmark) perceive greater benefit than the net payers (Britain). The pattern is clearest at the extremes: those who joined early and are net receivers of funds are most likely to perceive benefits (Italy and the Netherlands) compared with those who joined late and are net payers (Britain). In the middle groups, however, the pattern is jumbled. It seems that even when they are asked to consider the benefits of EC membership, many people do not have in mind the hard facts of the distribution of the EC budget.

Attempts to match other economic variables to responses to the 'benefits' question were largely unsuccessful. As before, we do not present the many tables showing random associations, but they can be summarized. Answers to the 'benefit' question do not seem to be consistently or strongly related to any of the macroeconomic variables which have been matched with the membership question: GNP per capita, growth of GNP, exports and imports within and outside the EC, and trade dependency. For the most part, the association was usually non-existent. At best, the associations were weak and marked by many exceptions.

The economic variables used so far are objective measures. Modern voting studies, however, suggest that subjective measures of voter perceptions are better indicators of support for parties and governments, especially measures of consumer confidence and well-being— the 'feel-good factor' (Harrop and Miller 1987: 217–20). Is the same true of support for the EC? Perhaps the best starting point is Figure 5.1 which shows countries on the 'economic–political' continuum. In the light of what was said earlier about the newer and older members of the EC, the figures clearly show that the most recent members of the EC tend to have a relatively strong economic image of the EC—Greece, Ireland, Portugal, Spain, and Britain. Conversely, the older members tend to have a stronger political image, especially Italy, Belgium, Luxembourg, and the Netherlands. Moreover, as shown in Table 5.6, there is a rough fit between economic images and lower levels of support, and political images and higher levels of support. In the four countries where the economic image of the EC was most widespread, the average level of support in 1987 was 64 per cent; in the four countries where the political image predominated, there was an average support level of 80 per cent. Unfortunately, Britain and Denmark decisively spoil this neat pattern.

These two major exceptions apart, however, this evidence suggests that the more the population of a country regards the EC as an economic organization, the less supportive of the EC that population is likely to be. But this generalization has to be tentative at this stage. First, it is based on individual-level data aggregated at the national level, and therefore must be treated cautiously. Secondly, it tells us nothing about the direction of causality. Do people in countries which have a political image of the EC support it because of its political benefits; or do people

TABLE 5.6. *Economic images and support for the EC, 1987*

	Percentage with an 'economic image' of the EC	Percentage believing membership a 'good thing'
GR	39	58
IR	24	64
PO	24	68
SP	20	64
GB	17	46
GE	14	62
DK	11	39
FR	10	74
IT	−1	79
BE	−3	70
LU	−11	87
NL	−13	83

Source: Commission of the European Communities (1987: 1–7).

in countries which generally support the EC focus on its political aspects; or is there a third, common factor, which underlies both support and political images? We leave these questions to the last section of the chapter which deals with the individual-level analysis.

Clearly, then, from this first part of the analysis, we cannot conclude that macro-economic conditions do not affect levels of support for the EC. First, there are far too few countries to draw any firm conclusions. Secondly, we have found some evidence, albeit weak and secondary, of an association between the 'benefits' question and net payments into or receipts from the EC budget. Thirdly, we have found some evidence of an association between political images of the EC and levels of support. However, with these two exceptions, the analysis so far has come up with rather little to suggest that macro-economic variables are associated with popular support for, or opposition to, the EC. To this extent the results reinforce the conclusion that economic determinants of support are 'weak and casual' (Treiber-Reif and Schmitt 1990: 45).

There are, perhaps, some simple reasons for this conclusion. It is unlikely that many people in Europe know even the broad features of such things as EC payments and receipts, or the degree of trade dependency upon the EC. On the occasions when such matters become headline news, they may have some affect on EC support but it seems to be fairly short lived. Moreover, the economic trends and circumstances which citizens are aware of, such as unemployment, inflation, or GNP growth, are not seen as related to, or caused by, the EC. In Lewis-Beck's term (1986b: 108) there is little or no 'attribution of responsi-bility' to the EC for economic conditions. A general mood of consumer confidence may rub off on to general feelings about governance at the international level, but the association is likely to be distant and contingent. It may also be that a substantial proportion of EC citizens weigh the ideal of European unification and co-operation more heavily than more instrumental considerations of an economic kind. The circumstantial evidence is that they do.

Changes within Countries over Time

Support for the EC has increased gently and unevenly but consistently over the long run (see Table 5.1). Furthermore, the overall trend is fairly similar in most member states, although the rise from comparatively low levels has been rather more steep in recent years in Spain, Greece, and Portugal. Most countries, however, impose their own short-term bumps and slumps in support from year to year, and most recently problems with the increased pace and scope of integration have been associated with a slump in support. To what extent is the overall upward trend or the year-on-year variation in particular countries the conse-quence of economic circumstances and change?

Inglehart and Rabier (1978: 74) conclude from a time-series analysis of the nine member states in the 1973–7 period that 'public evaluations of membership in the Community seem linked with economic growth or decline'. Handley (1981a: 360) agrees, stating that 'inflation, un-employment and stagnation [in the mid-1970s] were undoubtedly influencing public attitudes and government policy stands toward Europe, its institutions, and peoples'. Dalton and Eichenberg (1991: 13) find that 'the improvement in national economies during the 1980s yielded a substantial measure of support for the Community'.

In this section we examine changes in support over time, using the 'membership' question as the main indicator. This is the longest running question in the Eurobarometer survey and provides a time-series from 1973 to 1990. We also use the 'unification' question because it provides a time series from 1978 to 1990. The macro-economic variables related to these two questions are those used in the previous section, namely unemployment, inflation, GDP, trade relations (both exports and imports within and outside the EC as a percentage of GDP), and trade dependence.

In addition, we used a set of non-economic control variables to test the relative strength of the economic factors. These were drawn from the Eurobarometer surveys in the form of questions tapping 'satisfaction or dissatisfaction with life on the whole', 'happiness or unhappiness with all things taken together', 'satisfaction or dissatisfaction with the way democracy works in your country', and whether respondents thought next year would be 'better, worse, or the same, as this year'. Responses to these questions were aggregated for each country, and for each year of the time series. In addition, because the most cursory inspection of the graphs and previous research (Treiber-Reif and Schmitt 1990: 56-7) shows that support is strongly related to the length of membership of the EC and the simple passage of time, these two variables were also entered into the time-series regressions.

As the time series for Spain, Greece, and Portugal is too short for reliable analysis, only the data for nine member states were analysed. Each indicator of support was analysed in two ways. The first related absolute levels of support to absolute levels in the independent variables. The second related year-on-year changes in both the dependent and independent variables as a way of maximizing the variance from one year to the next. Each analysis was run twice, first for concurrent years, and, secondly, lagging the support measure by twelve months.[2]

The result of these analyses was eight regression equations for each of the nine countries. Rather than presenting such a large array of statistics, most of them inconclusive or insignificant, or both, we summarize the results. First, most of the variables are insignificant; and even when statistically significant they are substantively small, explaining some 5 per cent or less of the variance. Secondly, the pattern of significant variables varies from one country to the next and from one dependent variable to the next. Sometimes the same variable has a positive effect in one country, a negative effect in another. Thirdly, economic variables do not generally appear in the equations. So far as economic change has an impact at all, it seems to be a short-term effect which is smoothed over by the long-term trend. Simple correlations suggest a moderately strong relationship between levels of economic confidence and EC support, but the regressions show that this is more likely to be attributable to a more general 'feel good' factor which includes economic, political, and personal satisfaction with life and with future prospects.

Even so, fourthly, at first sight there seems to be a close correlation between attitudes towards the EC and various indicators of trade within the Community. Countries with a high proportion of exports and imports within the EC show higher levels of support. On closer inspection, however, this turns out to be a spurious relationship. If we control for inflation, the correlation is reduced to insignificance. Moreover, support for the EC continues to rise even in the countries, such as Britain, with an increasingly adverse balance of trade within the EC. Moreover, fifthly, social and political rather than economic attitudes seem to be more influential, especially happiness, satisfaction with democracy, and optimism about the next year. However, they are often not significant at all, and when significant, their effect is generally fairly weak. Yet support for EC membership seems to be rather more closely related to these attitude variables than support for European unification, which, if anything, seems to be slightly less sensitive to changes in popular mood.

One variable, however, stands out as important—the passage of time. Support for EC membership and for European unification simply grows slowly in the long term. Each year seems to add, on average, about a fifth to a quarter of 1 per cent to approval of European unification and EC membership. The rate of growth does not seem to vary much according to the year of joining the EC. However, the inclusion of Greece, Spain, and Portugal might change this conclusion. Their support increased dramatically just before membership and continued to rise relatively steeply thereafter.

A seventeen-year time series is not a particularly reliable basis for statistical generalization. It is more satisfactory than a cross-sectional analysis of six, ten, or twelve countries, but the results are still tentative. Nevertheless, the results of the cross-sectional and time series analysis we carried out are consistent. And both are consistent with the conclusions of the ZEUS study which pooled data for different countries and different years to produce a larger number of observations. The study concluded that socio-economic variables generally have a weak and variable impact on the four Eurobarometer indicators of support, while length of membership has a strong and consistent impact: 'The longer a country belongs to the Community, the more its people appreciate it.' (Treiber-Reif and Schmitt 1990: 59)

It is possible that individuals with different economic characteristics may vary in their support for the EC even though countries with different economic characteristics do not. For example, relatively wealthy individuals within countries may support the EC, even though the level of support in a wealthy country is relatively low. The difference between aggregate figures and individual-level data is, of course, the basis of the psychological and ecological fallacies, and we must be careful not to fall for either. In this section we concentrate on individual-level explanations. A plausible example might be that wealthier people may approve of the EC because they believe that it promotes the business which is the basis of their affluence. This proposition may also be reversed: perhaps the poorer sections of a population support the EC on the grounds that it will help to improve their economic circumstances, whereas the rich tend to be opposed to it because of its attempts to redistribute resources.

We are on stronger statistical ground in dealing with the individual-level explanations because we have a much larger number of cases. Even so, the common core questions asked in each Eurobarometer survey in each country and in each year do not include the full range of data required for our analysis. Therefore, we must rely on questions which have been asked at irregular intervals since 1973. Since there are still gaps in the data it is necessary to analyse slightly different sets of variables, and slightly different sets of years for different countries. Nevertheless, it is possible to use the Eurobarometer surveys to achieve a reasonable degree of comparability across different countries and over time.[3]

The individual economic data are of two types. The first deal with the objective economic characteristics of respondents: social class, family income, and whether or not they are employed.[4] In addition, it is possible to identify farmers and fishermen. They are of particular interest because they are strongly and directly affected by EC spending and policy. The second type deals with subjective economic expectations and attitudes, which include whether respondents expect more or fewer strikes in the next year (a measure of economic optimism); whether governments should play a greater role in reducing income inequality; whether government should intervene more in economic affairs; and whether governments should expand public ownership.[5]

Thus, altogether, the Eurobarometer surveys have data about four objective and four subjective economic variables.

These variables are contrasted with a set of seven non-economic control variables which are included in many, but not all, Eurobarometer surveys. The three objective indicators are age, gender, and the age at which the respondent left school.[6] The four subjective indicators are overall life satisfaction, satisfaction with democracy, optimism or pessimism about next year, and left–right party support.[7] A final variable, grouping people according to their materialism and postmaterialism scores (Inglehart 1977*b*: 1990), straddles the distinction between the economic and the non-economic.[8]

Support for EC Membership

As before, the first indicator of support for the EC we examine is the 'membership' question. And as before, the analysis is on a country-by-country basis. Pooling the survey data for the whole of the EC is possible, but the persistent differences between countries means that this is likely to confuse rather than clarify. Instead, as a first step, we examined the simple correlations between economic and non-economic variables and support for the EC in each member state. The results of this initial analysis can be summarized in a few sentences.

The table contains 486 cells related to the eight economic variables. Of these, 195 (40 per cent) contain significant correlations. The table contains 669 cells relating to non-economic variables, and of these 375 (56 per cent) are significant. The figures which are statistically significant show rather low levels of significance and are not of great substantive significance.[9] This is generally true of non-economic and economic variables alike. The same economic variable was significant in some countries but not in others; for example, class was significant in Denmark, Britain, Ireland, and France but not in Italy, Belgium, the Netherlands, and Luxembourg. The direction of the association sometimes varies from year to year, and country to country. Some of the non-economic control variables, however, are more consistently related to support for the EC, most notably satisfaction with life, education, and party support in left–right terms.[10]

However, these observations are based on simple correlations. Could it be that the real effects of economic circumstances are revealed only after making allowances for social and political variables? To address this question, we used multivariate regression analysis; the results are presented in Table 5.7. The table does not show regression coefficients for the non-economic control variables because those are discussed in greater detail in other chapters in this volume. But bear in mind that the table reports results from a multiple regression model which includes the non-economic control variables of life satisfaction, happiness, satisfaction with democracy, expectations for next year, age, education, left–right party, and gender.

The regression results do not reveal powerful or widespread economic effects. On the contrary, the economic variables do not contribute much to the regression equations. Those which are statistically significant generally make a scattered, weak, and fairly random appearance in different countries and in different years. The only economic variable to make much of a showing is the occupational category 'farmers and fishermen'. Nor are the effects of the non-economic variables particularly strong, but a few of them, including education, gender, and life satisfaction, are persistently more significant than any of the economic measures. In particular, the general measure of optimism about next year emerges as significant in most countries in at least some years. The left–right political variable is important in Denmark, Britain, and France, and sometimes in other countries. Life satisfaction and optimism about next year also made modest contributions, as they did to the time-series analysis reported earlier.

The time-series analysis suggested that simply the passage of time is associated with growing support for unification and for the EC. This may be explained in two ways, or in a combination of the two. First, support may grow as the population as a whole becomes accustomed to EC membership, or, secondly, support may grow as the older population is replaced by younger people who are more favourable (see Chapter 6). In the latter case, we would expect age to be associated with attitudes towards Europe. However, age is not generally significant. It would seem, therefore, that support is growing in the population as a whole, and not especially in the younger age groups.

Overall the results of the regression equations are not particularly encouraging in the sense that, taken together, economic and non-economic variables do not explain a substantial proportion of the variance—generally less than 30 per cent and often less than 10–15 per cent. Non-economic variables are generally more significant than economic variables, but neither are powerful.

TABLE 5.7. *Economic and non-economic variables and support for membership of the EC*

	Equality	Public ownership	Government management	Class	Employment	Farmers/ fishermen	Income	Post-materialism
France								
1973	—	—	—					
1976	—	—	—	0.16**	—			
1979								—
1981								
1984		—						
1986	—	—	—			0.14*		
1990	—	—	—					
Belgium								
1973	—	—	—					
1976	—	—	—		—		0.13*	
1979					−0.23*	−0.20*		—
1981	−0.17*							
1984		—						
1986	—	—	—					
1990	—	—	—			−0.15*	−0.23**	
Netherlands								
1973	—	—	—			−0.34**		
1976	—	—	—		—			—
1979			0.17*					
1981								
1984		—						
1986	—	—	—					
1990	—	—	—					
Germany								
1973	—	—	—					0.11*
1976	—	—	—			—		
1979		−0.13*			—			—
1981	0.15*							
1984	−0.14*	—	0.15**	0.25**			−0.15*	
1986	—	—	—			−0.13*		
1990	—	—	—			−0.12*		
Italy								
1973	—	—	—					
1976	—	—	—		—			
1979		−0.23**						—
1981								
1984		—						
1986	—	—	—		0.19*			−0.16*
1990	—	—	—					
Luxembourg								
1973	—	—	—					
1976	—	—	—		—			
1979					0.40**			—
1981					—			
1986	—	—	—					

TABLE 5.7. *Cont.*

	Equality	Public ownership	Government management	Class	Employment	Farmers/ fishermen	Income	Post-materialism
Denmark								
1973	—	—	—	0.12*		0.20**		
1976	—	—	—		—	0.13*	0.13*	
1979		−0.16**						
1986	—	—	—					
1990	—	—	—					
Ireland								
1973	—	—	—			0.11*		
1976	—	—	—	0.23**	—	0.29**		
1979								—
1981					−0.25**			
1986	—	—	—					
Britain								
1973	—	—	—					
1976	—	—	—		—			
1979	−0.12*							—
1981						—		
1984			—			—		
1986	—	—	—	0.18**	0.16*			
Greece								
1981		−0.16*						
1986	—	—	—					
1990	—	—	—					
Spain								
1986	—	—	—					
1990	—	—	—					
Portugal								
1986	—	—	—	0.21*	−0.22**			−0.18**
1990	—	—	—	0.26*				

* *p* <0.05 **p <0.01

Notes: Entries are data coefficients. Only significant coefficients are shown. Some variables are not available in all years. Dashes have been entered in cells for which there are no data. As there are no significant correlations for 'strikes', the indicator for economic optimism is excluded from the table. No results are shown for the eight non-economic control variables included in the regression analysis.

Sources: Eurobarometer, Nos. 0, 8, 12, 16, 22, 26, and 34.

Support for European Unification

The same set of regressions as those reported in Table 5.7 were run using support for European unification as the dependent variable. The 'unification' question was not asked regularly in the Eurobarometer survey until the autumn of 1978, so we do not have the same number of years for analysis. Nevertheless, it is possible to run separate regressions for each member state in 1979, 1984, and 1990.

The results are even worse, if anything, than those already presented in Table 5.7, so once again they can be summarized in a few sentences. Of the 142 cells for the economic variables, 11 beta coefficients (8 per cent) were statistically significant. Of the 138 cells for non-economic variables, 17 (12 per cent) were statistically significant. This means that neither economic nor non-economic variables are closely associated with support for European unification, although the non-economic variables show marginally less weak correlations. No single variable stands out as worthy of note even in this array of poor results. The result is a thin and patchy distribution of weak coefficients which have different effects in different countries and in different years. In sum, we have what might be called a Jackson Pollock—no discernible pattern.

Farmers

We complete our analysis with two cases which put the economic hypothesis to the acid test. The first involves farmers. The Common Agricultural Policy (CAP) is the largest item in the EC budget. Irrespective of payments to, and receipts from, EC funds in any country, farmers in all countries benefit directly from EC payments and subsidies from the CAP. Some benefit very substantially. If any social or occupational group has an incentive to support the EC on grounds of personal financial interest, it is the farmers in member states. At the same time, it is not difficult to imagine why some farmers might be strongly opposed to the EC. Perhaps farmers associate the EC with the painful restructuring of the agricultural sector over the past two or three decades. It may be that farmers will support the EC because it provides them with a high proportion of their income. It is also possible that they will oppose it strongly in spite of CAP payments and subsidies and, more recently, because of CAP reform and cut-backs. Either way it is to be expected that farmers will have stronger feelings about the EC one way or the other than their compatriots.

Do farmers support or oppose EC membership more often than other employed citizens in their own country? Several difficulties arise in pursuing this question. First, in most Eurobarometer surveys, farmers and fishermen constitute a single occupational category. However, they were coded separately in Eurobarometer, No. 33 (spring 1990), and examination of the frequencies in these data shows that fishermen either do not appear in the samples or are negligible in proportion to the number of farmers. Accordingly, in the analysis which follows the category 'farmers and fishermen' is treated as if it refers only to farmers. Secondly, the samples of farmers in individual Eurobarometer surveys are quite small. We dealt with this problem in two ways: by combining the data from both Eurobarometers in any one year; and by expanding the category to include the dependent spouses of farmers who, we reasoned, are likely to share any economic logic which might be at work. Thirdly, even with these measures, we had to omit the case of Britain, where the number of farmers even in the combined samples is usually in single figures, and we combined the samples from the Benelux countries in order to produce a reasonable number of farmers. Table 5.8 summarizes the differences between farmers and their dependents and other sectors of the employed population.

At first sight, it appears that being a farmer makes only a marginal difference and, even then, only in the first half of the twenty-year period under consideration. If we take the Community as a whole (the bottom

TABLE 5.8. *Balance of support for EC membership among farmers and dependent spouses compared with other employed people, 1973–92/3*

	1973	1976	1979	1981	1984	1986	1990	1992/3	Average N (farmers)
Benelux	9.5*	2.8	1.3	6.3	9.4	11.0	−8.9	−0.4	86
Denmark	41.0*	38.4*	38.7*	30.8*	21.6*	31.6*	17.3*	21.2*	79
France	3.5	−13.8*	−6.4	−19.1*	−10.6*	−15.5*	−25.5*	−2.2	107
Germany	6.8*	−24.4*	5.6	−41.3*	−15.3	−15.5	−30.8*	−36.7*	58
Ireland	4.9	25.9*	14.8*	20.9*	18.4*	5.8	−0.1	−2.0	288
Italy	1.1	−13.1*	−3.3	0.2	−16.3*	−8.5	−12.7	−19.1*	67
Greece	—	—	—	5.7	12.7*	2.7	−0.1	4.6	264
Spain	—	—	—	—	—	−6.5	−6.9	−15.0*	50
Portugal	—	—	—	—	—	−3.6	−7.8	−13.5*	112
EC	10.3*	5.7*	9.0*	5.2*	2.6	−0.3	−0.3	−2.2	952

* $p < 0.05$

Notes: Entries are percentage-point differences derived by subtracting the proportion supporting EC membership among non-farmers from the proportion among farmers and their dependent spouses.

Sources: Eurobarometer cumulative data; Eurobarometer, Nos. 38 and 39.

row of Table 8.5), farmers were marginally more supportive of EC membership than those in the non-agricultural sector for the first four time points but they were no different in the subsequent four. However, this overall picture masks contrasts among the member states. Half the cells in the table (30 out of 59) show statistically significant differences and, within this set, half (14 out of 30) show farmers to be more positive while the other half show them to be more negative.

The main basis of the contrast is the diffference between France, Germany, and Italy on the one hand, where farmers tend to take a more negative view than other people in employment, and Denmark and Ireland on the other hand where they tend to be more positive. Moreover, this contrast varies over time. For example, French farmers usually show lower support for the EC throughout the 1973–93 period by comparison with other employed people in France. The same is true for Italy, although the differences are less often statistically significant. Strong support for the EC among farmers seems to have waned substantially in Denmark and Ireland in the late 1980s, but as often as not Benelux farmers are no different from their compatriots in employment. In other words, the picture is a mixture of significant and insignificant, positive and negative, results. Looking at them as a clear and strong test of the economic interpretation of support for integration, they constitute, at best, no more than a partial exception to the finding that support for the EC is not generally rooted in economic calculations.

Spain and Portugal

The second acid test of the economic hypothesis centres on Spain and Portugal. We showed earlier (see Figure 5.1) that citizens in some member states see the EC primarily as an economic organization. This was particularly the case in the newer member states, notably Greece, Spain, and Portugal. Moreover, generally, although not invariably, levels of support are lower in countries which have a primarily economic image of the EC. We suggested that there are different interpretations of this three-cornered relationship.

We now investigate this set of associations in greater depth, focusing on Spain and Portugal because they are among the most 'economic' nations. Moreover, the Eurobarometer surveys asked some interesting questions in these two countries just before they joined the EC. First, in the autumn 1985 survey, respondents were asked what future economic benefits were expected of the EC. Generally, those who expected economic benefits also supported membership (gamma = 0.70 and 0.87 respectively). The survey also asked about the political benefits for democracy, and about benefits for the roles of Spain and Portugal in the world. Not surprisingly, responses to the three questions about economic, political, and diplomatic benefits are closely associated (gamma = 0.80, 0.73, 0.91 for Spain; 0.87, 0.84, and 0.87 for Portugal). Moreover, there is also a close association between expectations for all three benefits and support for EC membership (gamma = 0.70, 0.54, and 0.61 for Spain; and 0.87, 0.78, and 0.83 for Portugal). In short, those who expected their country to benefit economically also expected it to benefit politically and diplomatically, and these people, in turn, supported EC membership. In other words, economic expectations appear to play an important role in stimulating EC support, but not necessarily a more important role than political and social factors. Moreover, we cannot even assume causal primacy for the economic variable. On the contrary, the survey results seem to suggest a generally favourable disposition towards the EC, from which flow a set of economic, political, and diplomatic expectations, and support for membership. This serves to qualify our earlier conclusion.[11]

We might offer some tentative suggestions as to why economic variables have rather little impact on the attitudes of the general population towards either European unification or EC membership. First, the EC is fairly remote from the everyday experience of ordinary citizens. As a result, the sorts of economic circumstances and attitudes which typically have an impact on national voting and political attitudes may have a looser association with attitudes towards the Community. Citizens are more likely to praise or blame their national government than the EC for economic gains or losses.

Secondly, the strong support for European unification as a general goal suggests that individuals see the EC more in terms of ideal rather than material interests. Of course, it might be argued that the very remoteness of the EC is precisely why the harsh facts of economic reality do not intrude much upon popular support. Hence, even the unemployed, the poor, and the working class do not evaluate the EC in a significantly different way from the employed, the rich, and the upper class.

Following this line of argument, it might be suggested that people do not so much support the EC for diffuse or ideal reasons, but rather fail to make the connection between the EC and their own life experiences. The physical and political distance from Brussels, the democratic deficit, and the fact that national governments may intervene between the citizen and economic circumstances all help to protect the EC from economic accountability and judgement. Hence, circumstances may conspire to protect the average European's idealistic view of European unification and the EC. Is this a case where distance makes the heart grow fonder?

Conclusion

In some respects the results of this study are frustrating and inconclusive. So far as economic variables do appear to be associated with support or opposition to the EC and European unification, they seem to have different effects in different countries and in different years. This makes it difficult to draw out any general conclusions. But in other respects, the results suggest some clear generalizations and conclusions.

First, we have rather little evidence that the EC or European unification are evaluated in primarily economic terms. Of course, the fact that we have been unable to find the evidence even after exhaustive analysis does not prove that it does not exist. At the same time, the results of this study are consistent with the systematic and wide-ranging study produced by ZEUS (Treiber-Reif and Schmitt 1990), which shows a weak, variable, and patchy association between a wide range of economic variables and the four indicators of support. Those who find evidence of an economic impact (cf. Inglehart and Rabier 1978; Handley 1981*a*; Dalton and Eichenberg 1991) seem either to be generalizing about rather short-term effects, which, although significant at the time, tend to be smoothed out by long-term trends, or to be using a narrower range of control variables than the range employed in the present study.

Secondly, support seems to be associated more strongly with social and attitudinal variables of a non-economic kind. In the individual-level regression analysis it emerged that optimism about the coming year, left–right orientation, education, and satisfaction with life in general are more closely associated with support than income, class, or unemployment. In this sense the results of the individual-level analysis, based on a large number of observations, are generally consistent with the conclusions of national-level analysis, which is necessarily limited to a small number of countries or a fairly short time-series. There is no reason to expect the results of the different levels of analysis to be the same. Nevetherthelss, the fact that they support each other lends strength to the conclusion that support for the EC is not generally or powerfully determined by economic considerations.

Thirdly, the figures suggest that diffuse and somewhat idealistic reasons for supporting unification and EC membership tend to out-weigh more specific reasons. Not only is there rather little evidence of economic calculation as the basis of support, but there is clear evidence that the general goal of unification is supported more strongly than EC membership. Membership, in turn, has more supporters than those who see benefits in EC membership. The conclusion seems to be that support for membership, and even more for unification, is at a high level, even among some of those who see few benefits.

Fourthly, a solid foundation of inertia, custom, and national tradition seem to maintain support and make it grow. This is apparently true in two rather different ways: the countries which joined the EC first still maintain the highest levels of support; support tends to increase slowly and unsteadily over the long term. In spite of short-term disturbances, some of them associated with economic circumstances, the long-term trend is for support to increase, suggesting that the people of the EC like it more as they grow accustomed to it. There is no evidence that support grows because an older and less favourable age group is replaced by a younger and better disposed one. It seems that the population as a whole is growing slowly but steadily more supportive. Familiarity breeds content.

We conclude with some further observations. We found little evi-dence that specific calculations of an economic nature have gradually been replaced by, or converted into, stronger and deeper ties of loyalty, as some theorists of integration and institution building have suggested (Shepherd 1975; Hewstone 1986: 43). Rather, the EC seems to have accumulated both material and ideal support over the years, at least since the Eurobarometer surveys started. Finally, so far as the study suggests a role for economics at all, it indicates sociotropic rather than pocket-book calculations. Variables such as household income and employment/unemployment are weakly related to EC support, whereas variables such as anticipated national benefits of an economic, political, and diplomatic kind are more strongly associated.

However, behind the conclusions of this study there lurks a general problem which we cannot tackle here, and which is scarcely touched upon by the Eurobarometer surveys. It concerns the possibility that support for the EC, although widespread, is rather flimsy and without great conviction. The EC is not a particularly salient issue for most people most of the time, and therefore favourable attitudes might easily be eroded or even reversed. The not infrequently high level of 'Don't know' or non-committal responses to the four questions tapping support for European unification and the EC suggest that this may be the case. The evidence we present here suggests, however, rather slow, long-term changes in support, punctuated by more extreme but generally short-lived fluctuations. This long-term stability combined with glacial changes suggests that EC support has fairly substantial foundations.

The EC has recently suffered set-backs following the Maastricht Treaty and turbulences within the European Monetary System. However, if we can generalize from the past—a beguiling but dangerous activity—the effects on popular support for the EC, although considerable in the short run, are likely to wear off. The trends for support are likely to pick up and continue much as they were for most of the last twenty years.

NOTES

1. See e.g. Eurobarometer, No. 31 (1989): 20–1; No. 24 (1985): 79–80. Individual-level preferences in allocating these issues to the European or national level are examined in Ch.12.
2. Inglehart and Rabier (1978: 72) suggested that 12 months would be the optimum time period for detecting lagged effects.
3. Full information about the data and the variables for the individual-level analysis in this chapter is presented in the codebook of the Cumulative Eurobarometer, 1973–91, created by Dr Richard Topf, Department of Politics and Government, London Guildhall University for the Beliefs in Government project of the ESF. The codebook is available from the Zentral Archiv, University of Cologne.
4. The social class variable is based on five occupational groupings: professionals, business owners, executives and managers, white collar workers, and manual workers. Family income is computed in quartiles. The employed are coded 1, the unemployed 0.
5. The questions wordings are: 'Looking ahead to next year, 19__, do you think that strikes and industrial disputes [in this country] will increase, decrease, remain the same?' 'Do you agree or disagree that greater effort should be made to reduce inequality of income?' 'Do you agree or disagree that public ownership of private industry should be expanded?' 'Do you agree or disagree that government should play a greater or smaller role (intervene less) in the management of the economy?' Except for the first question, there are five response options from 'agree strongly' to 'disagree strongly'.

6. Age is coded in years. Education is coded 1–9 according to the year the respondent left school between 'up to 14' and '22 or over'. Men are coded 1, women 2.

7. The question wordings are: 'On the whole, are you very satisfied, fairly satisfied, not very satisfied or not at all satisfied with the life you lead?' Coded 1–4 respectively; 'Taking all things together, how would you say things are these days—would you say you are very happy, fairly happy, or not too happy these days?' Coded 1–3; 'On the whole are you very satisfied, fairly satisfied, not very satisfied or not at all satisfied with the way democracy works in your country?' Coded 4–1. 'So far as you are concerned, do you think 19__ (next year) will be better or worse than 19__ (this year)?' Coded 3–1. The Cumulative Eurobarometer file codes party preference according to whether the respondent supports a party of the right, centre, or the left, coded 1–3 respectively.

8. The standard Inglehart variable is used, coding postmaterialists 3, materialists 1, and mixed 2.

9. The sample size of a thousand in most countries (except Luxembourg) means that quite small correlations can be statistically significant. Few rise much above 0.20, and most are generally lower.

10. On the importance of left–right party support and party cues, see Hewstone (1991: 99), and Worre (1988).

11. For a more detailed discussion of the Spanish and Portugese cases see Bosch (1992, 1993).

6

Development of Support: Diffusion or Demographic Replacement?

BERNHARD WESSELS

As the Danish and the French referendums have amply demonstrated, the role of public opinion in the process of European integration is becoming increasingly more important. But public opinion is not homogeneous; indeed, considerable variation in mass attitudes towards European integration is found between member countries. Moreover, there are also remarkable differences within countries, both over time and between groups or sectors in society. Examining these variations should provide insight into the dynamics of public support for the EC and might even throw some light on future developments. This chapter examines factors which may give rise to differences in people's awareness of, and support for, the EC—such as demographic and social factors, general political orientations, political involvement, and party affiliation. We start from the assumption that whatever the causal processes or mechanisms, they operate in more or less the same way in each EC country. We then also take into account cross-national differences in attitudes and in the array of factors which influence such attitudes.

The General Hypothesis

Research over the last thirty years on the determinants of attitudes towards European integration has been voluminous. Micro-analytic studies have looked into short-term factors, such as particular events (Inglehart, Rabier, and Reif 1987: 136ff.) as well as into long-term social factors, such as gender (Rabier 1965; Cayroll 1983), stratification, and education (Handley 1981a; Inglehart 1970; Inglehart and Rabier 1978; Cayroll 1983; Inglehart, Rabier, and Reif 1987: 143ff.), and age or generation (Handley 1981a; Inglehart 1967, 1970a). There has also been some research into dynamic aspects, such as cognitive mobilization, political involvement, and value change (Inglehart 1971a, 1977b, 1990: 393ff.; Janssen 1991). What all these studies have in common is that they emphasize the persistence of differences between social and demographic groups within countries in their awareness of the EC and their attitudes towards this form of internationalized governance.

The most prominent approaches seeking to explain increasing support for the EC are based on either the hypothesis of intergenerational value change, or the hypothesis of cognitive mobilization, or a mix of the two. As early as 1967, Inglehart formulated the hypothesis of persisting age group differences in support for European integration, with the implication that, in the long run, these will lead to an increase in support through generational replacement. In short, differences between age groups persist but through replacement the overall distribution of support will increase over time.

Much the same kind of argument applies in the case of cognitive mobilization. According to Inglehart (1970a: 47) cognitive mobilization:

increases the individual's capacity to receive and interpret messages relating to a remote political community. As such, cognitive mobilization is a necessary but not sufficient condition for the development of support for a European community . . . If we regard formal education as an indicator of cognitive mobilization, for example, we would expect the more educated groups to be more aware of European level politics.

Higher overall levels of support are only possible through generational replacement of less-educated groups by groups with higher education.

In contrast to these approaches, the general hypothesis advanced in this chapter is that processes of intra-societal diffusion—not cohort replacement—are responsible for developing awareness of, and support for, the EC. The first implication of this idea is that awareness of the EC and access to this still remote institution have a tendency to become less dependent than they were on political skills, knowledge, involvement, and the like. In other words, differences in orientations between particular segments of society tend to decrease over time. The second implication is that attitudes towards the EC, whether favourable or not, become more consensual among mass publics within and across countries.

Plausible as the hypothesis of diffusion may be, the literature offers only a few relevant clues to the problem of intra-societal diffusion of political innovations. One reason is that diffusion theory and research concentrate mainly on technological innovations. Secondly, even when cultural innovation is the focus, as in sociology, anthropology, and ethnology, inter-societal diffusion is the main concern (Heine-Geldern 1968). But our concern is intra-societal diffusion. Thirdly, this chapter deals with a political innovation, but diffusion theory is not well developed in political sociology or political science. However, 'obstacles to the spread of diffusion theory among political scientists do not exist in the essential nature of political phenomena' (Walker 1973: 1186). Political innovations can be treated like any other innovation, and the EC is probably the most distinguished political innovation of the post-war period in Western Europe.

Diffusion, in the EC context, means the spread of awareness of this special kind of institutional innovation as well as support for it within the twelve nation states over a certain time span (see Reimann 1973: 167; Katz, Levin, and Hamilton 1963: 240). In empirical terms, diffusion can be measured by the extent of awareness and, later on, of adoption. Few people adopt an innovation on the basis of awareness alone (Hägerstrand 1968: 180), since adoption happens by stages, beginning with awareness, continuing through interest, evaluation, trial, and finally acceptance (Lionberger 1960; Rogers 1962). Diffusion includes an individual learning process which spreads intra-societally from one cultural subsystem to another, through socialization from one generation to the next, or vertically from one social stratum to the next, whether higher or lower (Reimann 1973: 167).

Diffusion processes often follow an S-curve: 'a slow take-off stage of varying length, an intermediate stage of more rapid development, and a final stage of declining growth, which seems to approach a ceiling asymptotically' (Hägerstrand 1968: 174). Rogers (1962: 162) distinguishes between 'adopters' according to their location on the S-curve, identifying them as innovators, early adopters, early majority, late majority, and laggards. Rural sociology shows that these groups are characterized by their specific social situation. Innovators normally enjoy high socio-economic status, are involved in community affairs and in informal and formal communication networks, whereas the late majority have low socio-economic status and education, low involvement, and limited communication networks (Reimann 1973: 171). Larsen (1962) proposes that, in general, categories of adopters form a continuum from the highest to the lowest in terms of socio-economic status, specialization, contacts, and information (cited in Reimann 1973: 172).

Such results from diffusion research point to factors similar to those which feature in theories of demographic change and replacement. However, the consequences of an explanation based on diffusion differ quite markedly from those following from theories of demographic changes. In particular, the diffusion concept assumes that differences in awareness and adoption or acceptance of an innovation, an idea, or a culture will, in the end, diminish in an ongoing and successful process of dissemination. Obviously, this expectation differs fundamentally from the ones created by hypotheses of value change and cognitive mobilization.

In empirical terms, this line of reasoning leads to two expectations. First, there should be a noticeable increase in awareness of, and in supportive attitudes towards, the EC over time. Secondly, this overall increase is not primarily caused by intergenerational replacement—related to value change or the educational revolution—but by an assimilation of opinion across all groups of society. This general hypothesis does not, of course, assume that group differences do not count. Quite the contrary: specific social characteristics lead, as diffusion research shows, to different patterns of resistance to changes over time. The point is that change occurs without generational replacement.

Whether diffusion or inter-generational replacement is responsible for the growth of favourable attitudes towards the EC is crucial for the integration process. These implications are discussed in the concluding section of this chapter. But first we explore the factors responsible for creating awareness of the EC. Then we go on to explore how social and demographic characteristics as well as general political orientations are related to attitudes towards the EC, and whether persisting group differences or diffusion characterize these relationships over time. Finally, the impact of directly political factors—such as party orientation—on attitudes towards the EC are examined.

Awareness of the EC

One of the necessary conditions of support for the EC is that awareness of it as a political object is strong enough to develop an attitude towards it (Inglehart 1970a: 47; Janssen 1991: 447). However, the conditions under which awareness of a remote object like the EC develops depend very much on the individual position of a person within the social structure of their society, on individual interests as expressed in general political orientations, and on an individual's involvement in political life. Diffusion research suggests that diffusion is much more likely to occur from a higher social stratum—defined by occupation or education—to a lower one than vice versa (Bonfadelli 1987: 316; Reimann 1973: 169). More specifically, the degree to which an occupation is specialized has an impact on the likelihood of adopting an innovation (Rogers and Shoemaker 1971: 187) and is often related to education and, in any case, to skills. Education and the educational process create an enduring receptiveness to knowledge (Genova and Greenberg 1979: 80; Hyman, Wright, and Reed 1975) and the ability 'to receive and interpret messages relating to a remote political community' (Inglehart 1970a: 47).

At first sight, gender also seems to be related to receptiveness. Bivariate analyses show that women tend to be less interested and less involved in politics than men. For many people, even in advanced societies, gender still defines a life space which is connected to specific social roles, such as the division of labour between men and women, and with lower education and less attractive jobs for women. Against this background, Inglehart (1970a: 53) as well as McKenna and Niedermayer (1990: 4ff.) argue that apparent gender differences are due to their interaction with other socio-structural variables.

Age, like gender, represents a specific position in life space. Its impact can be construed in terms of life-cycle or generational effects. However, whereas the concept of generations plays no part in diffusion research,[1] it is prominent in research on EC orientations, especially comparisons between pre-war and post-war cohorts. As we noted earlier, Inglehart (1967: 94 ff.) advanced a model of generational replacement to predict steadily increasing support for the European movement. But later research shows no consistent pattern of intergenerational differences. The results even suggest that, at some points in time, pre-war generations are more supportive than younger generations (Janssen 1991: 460; Handley 1981a: 346). Research on the receptiveness of age groups is similarly inconclusive. For example, as measured by exposure to European election campaigns, older people follow campaigns on TV more often and more regularly than younger people (Cayroll 1983: 174). All in all, then, no clear results can be found in previous research regarding the influence of age, and research on the EC orientations of different generations also does not reveal consistent results. So, instead, we explore the more plausible hypothesis that, since younger people are more receptive, the EC as a political object is more accessible to them than it is to older people. However, this hypothesis relates only to awareness. Different hypotheses need to be formulated for attitudes towards the EC.

Diffusion research also suggests that the size of the community in which an individual lives is likely to be another important factor influencing awareness of the EC. Fischer (1978: 152) argues that the variety of population types in cities, their concentration as 'critical masses', and their intermingling, foster the diffusion of innovations because personal contact and network density increase with the size of a community. These factors also increase the probability of sub-cultures emerging which are receptive to innovations. Several studies have found faster diffusion in urban areas (Reimann 1973: 172; Katz, Levin, and Hamilton 1963: 248). Thus our hypothesis here is that people living in urban areas are more aware of the EC and are better placed to develop attitudes towards it.

Finally, a word about how we measure the availability of the EC as a political object; that is, psychological involvement, according to the schema developed in Chapter 3. One possibility might be to use direct measures of knowledge or perception. Another possibility is to tackle the question indirectly by asking whether people have developed an orientation towards the EC. For practical reasons, we chose the second method. As diffusion occurs as a continuous flow over time, we need data covering a considerable time span. Moreover, the multivariate approach we use requires a sufficient number of cases. Hence, we use data from the questions about EC support which have been asked most often in the Eurobarometer series of surveys.

We use two of the indicators discussed in Chapter 4. The 'member-ship' indicator is based on a question asking respondents whether their country's membership of the EC is a good or a bad thing. The second question is whether or not further efforts for unification should be made. This is the 'unification' indicator. Awareness of the EC, or what we can think of as the availability or accessibility of the EC (Aldrich, Sullivan, and Borgida 1989: 125), is measured by the proportion of respondents able to express an attitude towards the EC, regardless of what kind of attitude that is. The proportion of respondents in the EC-12 countries unable to answer the questions are shown in Table 6.1.

Large segments of the population in all EC countries have developed an attitude towards the EC. In the surveys for the 1973–91 period, the proportion of respondents unable to answer the questions is quite low, ranging, on average, from 14 per cent in Portugal to 4 per cent in Luxembourg on the membership question, and from 24 per cent in Ireland to 9 per cent in Luxembourg on the unification question (see Table 6.1).[2] However, the differences here suggest that the evaluation of EC membership comes to people much more readily than the evaluation of unification efforts.[3]

To explore differences in the ability of respondents to articulate an attitude towards the EC, we performed a contrast group analysis using multiple analysis of variance. This allows one to compare bivariate differences and, in addition, to check whether the bivariate effect holds up after controlling for the effects of other variables. At this stage, our purpose is to investigate the effect on non-attitudes of different locations in the social structure within countries. Our results are presented in Table 6.2.

First, we look at the effect of gender. On the question of EC membership, the difference between men and women ranges from 9 percentage points in Greece and Spain to 2 percentage points in Luxembourg. On the question of European unification, the difference ranges from 17 percentage points in Greece to 6 percentage points in Luxembourg. These differences are statistically significant for all countries except

TABLE 6.1. *Percentage of respondents without an orientation towards membership and unification, 1973–91*

	EC Membership	N	European Unification	N
BE	11.1	37,199	20.5	33,115
DK	8.1	36,485	16.1	32,618
FR	6.1	38,782	13.0	34,064
GB	5.8	38,311	16.4	34,063
GE	8.4	38,282	12.4	34,275
GR	10.5	24,226	17.9	24,226
IR	6.2	36,322	23.8	32,337
IT	6.7	39,545	11.9	35,138
LU	4.0	11,372	9.4	10,102
NL	5.5	37,337	10.3	33,190
PO	14.4	13,998	23.6	13,998
SP	12.9	14,053	18.6	14,053

Source: Eurobarometer cumulative data.

TABLE 6.2. *Non-attitudes towards membership and unification: mean percentage-point differences between contrast groups*

	Bivariate contrasts			Multivariate controlled contrasts		
	Mean percentage-point difference	Percentage-point range across countries	Inverse relation to modal result in:	Mean percentage-point difference	Percentage-point range across countries	Inverse relation to modal result in:
NON-ATTITUDES TO MEMBERSHIP						
Social structure						
Women–men	5.6	2 to 9		3.7	2 to 6	
Manual workers–professionals	4.8	2 to 8		0.5	0 to 2	
Small–large communities	2.2	–3 to 10	GB, IR	1.2	–2 to 5	GB, IR
Primary–tertiary education	7.0	3 to 10		2.3	1 to 5	
Born before WWII–1960 and after	5.5	–1 to 17	GB	2.3	–1 to 10	DE, GB, IR
Political orientations						
Left–right self-placement	–1.2	–10 to 1	DE, GB	0.4	–3 to 3	SP
Materialists–postmaterialists	6.0	2 to 14		1.5	0 to 5	
Religious Catholics–secularized[a]	1.2	–1 to 6	LU, NE	–1.5	–3 to 0	
Religious Catholics–Catholics[a]	–1.6	–4 to 0		–1.9	–4 to 0	
Religious Protestants–secularized[a]	0.8	–1 to 1	GB	0.5	–1 to 0	
Religious Protestants–Protestants[b]	–2.3	–3 to –1		–1.8	–2 to –1	
Religious Catholics–religious Protestants[c]	–0.3	–2 to 2	GB	–0.3	–1 to 1	GB
Political involvement						
Discussion: never–frequent	10.6	6 to 16		5.4	4 to 10	
Persuasion: never–often	5.0	1 to 8		1.4	0 to 2	

NON-ATTITUDES TO UNIFICATION

	Bivariate effect	Range	Contrast groups flagged	Multivariate controlled contrast	Range	Contrast groups flagged
Social structure						
Women–men	10.3	6 to 17		6.8	4 to 10	FR, GB, IT
Manual workers–professionals	10.3	7 to 16		1.8	−1 to 5	GB, IR
Small–large communities	2.3	−10 to 15	BE, GB, IR	0.8	−9 to 8	
Primary–tertiary education	14.3	8 to 21		5.8	2 to 9	
Born before WWII–1960 and after	8.3	0 to 21		2.5	−1 to 8	GE
Political orientations						
Left–right self-placement	−1.5	−10 to 6	DE, GB	1.0	−3 to 6	DE, PO, SP
Materialists–postmaterialists	11.4	6 to 19		3.7	2 to 8	
Religious Catholics–secularized[a]	3.3	−1 to 8	BE	−1.7	−5 to 0	
Religious Catholics–Catholics[a]	−3.2	−7 to 1		−3.2	−6 to −1	
Religious Protestants–secularized[b]	0.0	−2 to 2		−1.5	−3 to 1	NE
Religious Protestants–Protestants[b]	−5.0	−8 to −2		−2.8	−5 to 0	
Religious Catholics–religious Protestants[c]	1.0	−1 to 3	NE	0.0	−1 to 1	NE
Political involvement						
Discussion: never–frequent	19.9	12 to 28		10.7	8 to 15	
Persuasion: never–often	9.2	4 to 14		3.2	2 to 5	

Notes: The multivariate controlled contrasts are the bivariate effects after controlling for the effects of all other variables in the table. Denmark is not included in the contrast groups flagged[a]. Contrast groups flagged[b] include only Denmark, Britain, Germany, and the Netherlands. Contrast groups flagged[c] include only Britain, Germany, and the Netherlands. *N* are given in Table 6.1.

Source: Eurobarometer cumulative data.

Germany and Luxembourg. Generally speaking, the gender differences are largest in more traditional societies such as Greece, Portugal, and Spain, but also in Italy. None the less, generally, the phenomenon of women being less likely to develop an attitude towards the EC persists. But do these bivariate differences hold up when we control for their interaction with other variables? We imposed controls for the impact of several kinds of independent variables: the socio-structural variables age, education, occupation, and community size; left–right self-place-ment, the materialism–postmaterialism index, and religious orientations as indicators of general political orientations; political discussion and attempts at political persuasion as indicators of political involvement. However, although the range of the bivariate gender differences declines when these controls are applied, the differences still persist. And they remain highest in the southern and more traditional societies.

In analysing the impact of occupation, manual workers and profes-sionals and managers are the two contrast groups. These groups provide the largest range with respect to specialization, a factor known to be a key variable affecting receptiveness to the diffusion of innovations. Of course, these two locations in the social structure are related to quite different individual interests: dependent employment, low status, and low income on the one hand, and more or less independent employ-ment, high status, and high income on the other. Accordingly, diffusion effects may be difficult to disentangle from class effects. In any event, this becomes a moot point because, while the bivariate analysis revealed quite strong differences between the two groups, these effects did not hold up in the multivariate analysis. This aspect of the diffusion hypothesis fails.

In the analysis of community size, the results are even weaker and more inconsistent. Differences between respondents living in the largest and smallest communities in their country are generally very small. In Belgium, Britain, and Ireland, the results even run counter to expecta-tions. This failure to corroborate previous findings from diffusion research with respect to occupation and community size might be related to the fact that political innovations are quite distinct from technical innovations. Political innovations can be much more easily communicated via the mass media, and their adoption is less dependent on direct experience. In other words, political innovations are more readily accessible to people, and probably easier to adopt compared to technical innovations, without direct experience, because they address people in their role as citizens.

The weak impact of occupational position and community size on EC awareness suggests that the development of attitudes towards the EC may be more strongly influenced by cognitive resources which foster receptiveness and the ability to interpret and store messages relating to a remote political object. The empirical results strongly support this view. For both the membership and unification questions, the difference between respondents with a primary and tertiary level of education is high in all countries in the bivariate comparison. In fact, these contrast group differences are the highest of all differences between social groups and range up to 21 percentage points. However, the effect of education becomes rather weaker when controlled by the social structural variables, general political orientations, and political involvement. Even so, the remaining differences amount to a noteworthy maximum of 9 percentage points on the unification indicator. Education, then, seems to be one of the central factors influencing the accessibility of this issue. Certainly, it is the most important of the socio-structrual variables examined in Table 6.2.

Differences between the age cohorts born before the Second World War and after 1960, however, are neither strong nor show a consistent pattern. The results for Greece, Portugal, and Spain show a certain consistency which, presumably, reflects the experience of dictatorship until the mid-1970s. In general, however, neither the hypothesis of higher receptiveness among the young nor the expectation of generation-specific socialization effects finds support in the data.

General Political Orientations and Accessibility

Diffusion theory suggests that a traditional rather than a modern value climate may lead to closed- rather than open-minded attitudes towards innovation (Rogers and Shoemaker 1971: 31). It has also been argued that innovations have to be compatible with an existing cultural or value system if they are to be adopted (Katz, Levin, and Hamilton 1963: 249; Rogers and Shoemaker 1971: 145). But what kinds of political orientations might be the most important in influencing individuals in their selection of political objects and their openness to European political issues? The left–right dimension is, undoubtedly, the most general instrument for selecting what is relevant in politics. Fuchs and Klingemann (1989: 206) argue that the left–right dimension has structural properties which permit symbolic generalization, limitation, and binary schematization. In this sense, an individual's political position is connected, for example, to perceptions of which issues and problems are important and which are not. Here, of course, the question is whether being to the left or to the right makes for greater receptiveness concerning EC matters.

Inglehart (1977b: 57–60) has proposed that there exists a strong affinity between postmaterialist and cosmopolitan orientations, the latter implying receptiveness to issues ranging beyond small circles like family, friends, and the nation state. Thus a remote political object such as the EC becomes more familiar to postmaterialists than to others. In contrast to the 'modern' value orientations encapsulated in the notion of left and right and postmaterialism, traditional orientations, such as those related to religion are rarely used in the analysis of attitudes towards the EC. One general hypothesis might be that religious people—of whatever denomination—are more traditional in orientation and are therefore more resistant to change (cf. Rogers and Shoemaker 1971: 31–2). A second hypothesis can be formulated which relates to denomination. According to Max Weber, Protestantism is more rational and more modern than Catholicism (Weber 1972: 329, 339) and has contributed enormously to social, cultural, and economic modernization (Troeltsch 1928: 46–85). In a continuum of positions from traditional (Catholic), through intermediate (Protestant), to modern (secular), receptiveness to innovation should increase. Yet we have also to bear in mind that the idea of a universal church is a Catholic concept, whereas the process of nation-building led to the Protestant Reformation and to the forming of national churches—which suggests that Catholicism might be more strongly related to internationalization than Protestantism.

Turning first to the evidence relating to political orientations (left–right and postmaterialism), we can see from Table 6.2 that it is only the latter which shows strong and consistent effects cross-nationally on awareness of the EC. Bivariate comparison of materialist–postmaterialist contrast groups produces quite impressive differences, reaching up to 14 percentage points on the question of EC membership and up to 19 percentage points on the unification question. Although these differences decline substantially once social structural variables and political involvement variables are included in the analysis, differences between materialists and postmaterialists in awareness of the EC continue to exist even controlling for such factors. As to the impact of religious orientations,[4] the only persisting pattern is that nominal Protestants and

Catholics are less likely to articulate an attitude towards the EC than their religious counterparts. This difference, which is small in the bivariate comparison, is not affected by controlling for other individual characteristics.

Political Involvement and Accessibility

Diffusion research has shown that involvement in a community or in organizational activities (Reimann 1973: 172) creates a certain readiness to be receptive to innovations and diffusion processes. Similarly, broader social contacts and embeddedness in reference groups are related to greater openness to new political issues (Bonfadelli 1987: 310). In the political arena, people involved in political discussions have a higher chance of learning about remote political objects.

We have two measures of political involvement: participation in political discussion and the frequency of trying to persuade friends to one's own political opinions. Of these indicators, participation in discussion clearly shows a higher impact on adoptiveness. Especially for the unification question, the differences between those who never discuss politics and those who frequently discuss politics far exceed the differences between the other contrast groups. Looking again at Table 6.2, we find that, in the bivariate comparisons, only education shows effects on awareness of the EC as strong as political involvement. In the multivariate comparisons, the effects of involvement in political discussion weaken a little but still persist at quite a high level. This is not equally true for the indicator 'trying to persuade friends'. In regard to all of this, of course, it has to be kept in mind that political involvement is closely related to education, the most important factor facilitating EC awareness and the accessibility of attitudes.

Most explanations of the evolution of EC awareness and support are based on hypotheses related to demographic and social changes. But we have argued that increasing awareness of the EC is not predominantly generated by demographic replacement, but by diffusion processes. This hypothesis can be tested by drawing a time-ordered comparison (Rogers and Shoemaker 1971: 77–8; Rogers and Eveland 1978: 283). Diffusion processes, similar to other processes, flow as a temporal stream. Although the Eurobarometer surveys would, in principal, allow continuous monitoring, we compare the two time periods 1973–82 and 1983–91. This comparison can only be drawn for those countries which

entered the EC long before 1983: the 'original' EC-6 which entered in
1958 (Belgium, France, Germany, Italy, Luxembourg, and the Netherlands) and the three countries (Britain, Denmark, and Ireland) which
joined in 1973. The comparisons are reported in Table 6.3.

In eight of the nine countries, the ability of citizens to articulate an
attitude towards the EC proved to be higher in the 1983–91 period.
Ireland, which showed a reverse development, was the exception. The
increase was highest in Belgium, with a 7 percentage point decline of
non-attitudes towards EC membership between the two periods and a 15
percentage point decline in non-attitudes towards unification. The
decline of non-attitudes was lowest in Britain and Luxembourg. However, note that in these two countries the proportion of respondents
having an attitude towards EC membership is at the top of the league
(94 per cent in Britain, 95 per cent in Luxembourg for 1973–82). Here
the ceiling of attention had already been reached in the earlier period.

However, the decisive question with respect to the generational

TABLE 6.3. *Change in proportion and determination of non-attitudes towards
membership and unification 1973–82 compared with 1983–91*

	Non-attitude towards EC membership				Non-attitude towards EC unification			
	Percentage non-attitude 1973–82	Percentage-point change	Determination		Percentage non-attitude 1973–82	Percentage-point change	Determination	
			R^2*100 1973–82	R^2*100 change			R^2*100 1973–82	R^2*100 change
Belgium	14.7	−6.9	18.2	−11.3	29.4	−15.3	23.0	−14.0
Denmark	9.2	−2.2	7.1	−1.7	20.8	−8.0	12.7	−1.4
France	7.4	−2.7	7.4	−2.8	17.1	−7.3	12.4	−4.5
Britain	6.2	−0.8	4.3	−0.1	19.9	−6.1	11.4	−0.8
Germany	9.4	−2.0	11.3	−2.1	15.5	−5.4	16.0	−5.8
Ireland	5.5	1.2	4.7	0.3	25.7	−3.2	12.2	1.3
Italy	7.7	−1.9	8.8	−1.9	15.0	−5.5	11.8	−2.3
Luxembourg	4.7	−1.4	6.9	−1.8	9.7	−0.5	9.1	−1.8
Netherlands	6.8	−2.4	11.2	−5.8	12.6	−3.9	14.6	−7.3
Mean	8.0	−2.1	8.9	−3.0	18.4	−6.1	13.7	−4.6

Notes: Determination is the proportion of explained variance from a multivariate analysis including
social structure political orientations, and political involvement as independent variables. The
percentage-point change is for 1983–91 compared with 1973–82. For details of the variables, see
Table 6.2. For the 1973–82 data, approximate N for membership support are more than 17,000 per
country except Luxembourg (5,379); for unification support, more than 13,000 per country except
Luxembourg (4,107). For the 1983–91 data, approximate N are more than 19,000 for both
questions except Luxembourg (more than 5,000).

Source: Eurobarometer cumulative data.

replacement and diffusion hypotheses is whether group differences provide as strong an explanation of awareness of the EC in the second period (1983–91) as in the first period (1973–82). This can be measured by the change in the explained variance between the two periods, with non-awareness as the dependent variable and social-structural characteristics, general political orientations, and political involvement as independent variables. The results, shown in Table 6.3 reinforce the finding about the decline of non-attitudes: in eight of the nine countries, the explained variance drops quite dramatically. Again, Ireland is the exception. On average, the fall is 3 percentage points for EC membership and almost 5 percentage points for European unification. Given that the average explained variance for the nine countries was 8.9 per cent for the membership question and 13.7 per cent for the unification question for the 1973–82 period, this amounts to a reduction of more than 30 per cent in the explanatory strength of the independent variables taken together. Changes in explained variance, however, differ from country to country. The decline is strongest in Belgium and the Netherlands, moderate in Denmark, France, Germany, Italy, and Luxembourg, and fairly minor in Britain. Summing up, we can say that the result is more consistent with the diffusion hypothesis than with the cohort-replacement hypothesis.

Some of the independent variables reveal different developments in each country. In Denmark, for example, the impact of education increases somewhat, whereas the effects of gender, community size, and occupation decline. In Belgium the effect of religious orientations increases slightly, while the impact of the left–right dimension and postmaterialism declines markedly. There are many different patterns of this kind. However, these findings do not contradict the diffusion hypothesis. Rather, they suggest that the diffusion process is not uniform. Taken as a whole, the impact of social structure, general political orientations, and political involvement declines between the first and the second period. More particularly, the effects of the two indicators of political involvement (discussion, persuasion)—which are closely related to cognitive mobilization and therefore central to the replacement hypothesis—decline uniformly in eight of the nine countries. In sum: differences in the ability of people of varying levels of political involvement to develop an attitude towards the EC are disappearing—except in Ireland. All of this points to the conclusion that diffusion processes are much more important for the development of orientations towards the EC than cohort replacement.

Three Models of Awareness and Support

Most approaches seeking to explain positive orientations towards the EC are based on a simple assumption: if people are able to cope at all with a complex and remote object like the EC, after a while it will also become better known to them and they will support it. According to Janssen (1991: 447), 'A higher level of skills is supposed to influence attitudes because it makes European integration and the EC less threatening and more familiar; that is, it brings into being a sort of "positive" awareness.'

Heuristically, we can think of this 'positive awareness' in terms of three models of the linkage between people's knowledge of foreign affairs and their opinions on foreign policy (Gamson and Modigliani, 1966). In the 'enlightenment model', knowledge is seen as an indicator of sophistication; the more enlightened someone is, the more positive is their orientation towards internationalization. In the 'mainstream model', greater mainstream attachment results from enhanced knowledge and involvement; participative citizens are seen as both more aware of official government policy and more susceptible to government influence. Thirdly, in the 'cognitive consistency model', endorsement of a specific policy position stems from the application of general attitudes and orientations to a specific situation. Thus, foreign policy attitudes are developed which are consistent with the general political orientations of an individual.[5]

The advantage of these models, compared to other approaches, is that they focus on why awareness tends to lead to support. However, our purpose here is not to test these models against each other, but, rather, to use them as complementary concepts to explain support for the EC. In the following sections, we apply each model in turn.

The 'Enlightenment' Model

This model is closely related to an explanatory approach relying on social structural factors. Gamson and Modigliani argue that the knowledgeable segment of the citizenry has a sophisticated understanding of the complexity of foreign affairs. The greater people's understanding, the more likely it is that they see the solutions to international problems to lie in friendly instead of hostile relations, in alliances instead of demarcations, and in peacefulness instead of belligerence. Although

Gamson and Modigliani deal with foreign relations, it is not difficult to transpose their general argument to European integration: sophisticated, 'enlightened' people are more likely to develop a positive attitude towards the EC. Obviously, in our data, education is the main indicator of 'enlightenment'. However, because of the interconnections between variables, we examine, at the same time, the impact of occupation, gender, density of social communication (indicated by community size), and differences between political generations. Our findings are presented in Table 6.4.

The empirical findings indeed support the 'enlightenment' model. In all countries the groups with higher educational status show higher levels of support for the EC. On average, there is a 17 percentage point difference across countries between educational groups with respect to EC membership and 16 percentage point difference with respect to EC unification. Differences between occupational groups are of the same order (20 and 18 percentage points). When controls are entered for other relevant variables, the differences between these groups remain sizeable: between the educational groups across countries there is a difference of about 10 percentage points for both EC membership and EC unification; between occupational groups the differences are about 10 and 8 percentage points respectively.

Differences between men and women are generally smaller, with men being more supportive on both membership and unification. The bivariate differences across countries, on average, amount to 8 and 11 percentage points on the two indicators. But differences of 5 and 8 percentage points, respectively, persist even after controlling for other social-structural factors, general political orientations, and political involvement. In Germany and Luxembourg, however, the differences between the sexes disappear on the membership question. The results for the community size variable are inconsistent and often insignificant. Thus the argument that larger communities provide more dense political communication structures and therefore create differences in political knowledge and enlightenment does not hold up.

The findings for generational differences are similarly inconclusive. The bivariate comparisons of the cohorts born before the Second World War and after 1960 generally show differences in support for EC membership in the expected direction, except in Denmark and Greece. However, the differences disappear in most countries when other social and political characteristics are taken into account. Our results are even more inconclusive on support for unification. In Belgium, Britain,

TABLE 6.4. *Support for membership and unification: mean percentage-point differences between contrast groups*

Orientation/contrast groups	Bivariate contrasts			Multivariate controlled contrasts		
	Mean percentage-point difference	Percentage-point range across countries	Inverse relation to modal result in:	Mean percentage-point difference	Percentage-point range across countries	Inverse relation to modal result in:
SUPPORT FOR MEMBERSHIP						
Social structure						
Men–women	8.0	2 to 13		4.9	0 to 9	
Professionals–manual workers	20.1	11 to 31		10.2	5 to 18	
Large–small communities	1.1	–7 to 7	GB, IR, IT	–0.4	–7 to 4	DE, FR, GE, GR, NE
Tertiary–primary education	17.2	7 to 29		9.9	2 to 19	DE, FR, GR
Born 1960 and after–before WWII	6.2	–6 to 16	DE, GR	1.3	–6 to 7	
Political orientations						
Right–left self-placement	15.7	0 to 51		16.1	4 to 49	
Postmaterialists–materialists	11.8	8 to 18		4.8	1 to 9	
Religious Catholics–secularized[a]	4.7	–1 to 10	SP	8.2	6 to 12	
Religious Catholics–Catholics[a]	7.2	–1 to 23	PO	5.5	–1 to 18	PO
Religious Protestants–secularized[b]	5.0	0 to 14		5.0	1 to 8	
Religious Protestants–Protestants[b]	8.3	4 to 12		5.0	1 to 9	
Religious Catholics–religious Protestants[c]	2.3	–1 to 6	GE	3.0	1 to 5	
Political involvement						
Discussion: frequent–never	16.1	7 to 29		8.3	3 to 9	
Persuasion: often–never	8.8	3 to 16		3.7	1 to 6	

SUPPORT FOR UNIFICATION

Social structure						
Men–women	11.2	6 to 15		8.2	2 to 12	
Professionals–manual workers	17.8	11 to 24		7.6	5 to 12	GB, IT
Large–small communities	3.1	−5 to 15	GB, IT	1.3	−4 to 9	
Tertiary–primary education	16.2	8 to 22		9.7	6 to 15	
Born 1960 and after–before WWII	−0.7	−14 to 14	BE, GB, IR, IT, PO, SP	−4.8	−13 to 7	GB, PO
Political orientations						
Right–left self-placement	4.9	−13 to 34	GE, NE, SP	7.3	−9 to 37	SP
Postmaterialists–materialists	10.6	−4 to 18	DE, GR	4.9	−3 to 10	DE, GR
Religious Catholics–secularized[c]	−1.9	−10 to 3	GB, LU, NE	2.9	−3 to 7	IR
Religious Catholics–Catholics[c]	1.5	−5 to 9	LU, SP	0.8	−4 to 7	GB, GE, LU, NE, SP
Religious Protestants–secularized[b]	−3.0	−9 to 3	DE	−2.5	−0 to 1	DE
Religious Protestants–Protestants[b]	2.0	−3 to 6	NE	−0.3	−5 to 4	
Religious Catholics–religious Protestants[c]	4.7	1 to 10		5.3	2 to 10	DE, GB
Political involvement						
Discussion: frequent–never	22.7	11 to 34		14.5	7 to 24	
Persuasion: often–never	8.7	2 to 13		4.1	0 to 6	

Notes: Membership support is based on proportion who say membership is a 'good thing'; unification support on proportion who are 'completely for'. The multivariate controlled contrasts are the bivariate effects after controlling for the effect of all other variables in the table. Denmark is not included in the contrast groups flagged[a]. Contrast groups flagged[b] include only Denmark, Britain, Germany, and the Netherlands. Contrast groups flagged[c] are for Britain, Germany, and the Netherlands. *N* are given in Table 6.1.

Source: Eurobarometer cumulative data.

Ireland, Portugal, and Spain (see Table 6.4), the bivariate analysis reveals more support in the younger cohort. But this pattern does not persist after controlling for other characteristics. Rather, in some countries the older cohort is clearly more in favour of EC unification (Denmark, France, Germany, Greece, Luxembourg, the Netherlands), while in two countries (Britain and Portugal) the younger cohort is more in favour. In sum, those characteristics which are most closely related to political and social stratification—education and occupation—show the strongest impact on support for the EC. This result is consistent with the 'enlightenment' model.

The Cognitive Consistency Model

According to this model, a specific policy position or attitude stems from the application of more general principles to a given problem or situation. Thus, differences between people's attitudes are expected as a consequence of differences in general political orientations. We investigate the effects of three such orientations: left–right self-placement, postmaterialism, and traditionalism (denominational affiliation and religiosity).

The problem with the cognitive consistency model, however, is how to derive specific hypotheses. One might argue that left-wing positions are connected to the general idea of an internationalized communist or socialist society. Thus, those on the left should favour European integration. However, the European idea has been developed in the context of integration into the western alliance and a commitment to free market principles. Accordingly, socialist internationalism seems incompatible with what the EC is about. On these grounds, the hypothesis put forward here is that a left-wing orientation should lead to a non-supportive or even an antagonistic orientation towards the EC, whereas a conservative or right-wing position should square well with the idea of European integration in economic, political, and defence terms.

In the case of postmaterialism, Inglehart has argued that the shift to postmaterialist values is linked to the development of a cosmopolitan sense of identity, whereas materialist orientations are more concerned with the nation state and parochial orientations (Inglehart 1977*b*: 320ff.; Inglehart 1990: 412). Thus, support for the EC should go along with postmaterialist rather than materialist orientations. As for traditional or religious orientations, we shall follow the arguments put forward earlier. First, for the secular and, therefore, 'modern' individual, the consistent position is a positive orientation towards European integration (Rogers and Shoemaker 1971: 31–2). Secondly, although Protestantism is institutionally regarded as more rational and more modern than Catholicism (Weber 1972: 329, 339; Troeltsch 1928: 46–85), the idea of internationalization is close to Roman Catholic ideas of universalism—in contrast to the more national orientation of Protestantism. Thus, support for the EC is more consistent with a Catholic than a Protestant affiliation.

Our results shown in Table 6.4 tend to corroborate our hypotheses about left–right location and postmaterialism. Support for EC membership, on average, is 16 percentage points higher for those on the right than for those on the left, even when controlled by social-structural factors, other general political orientations, and political involvement. But the variation between countries is striking. In Denmark and Greece the differences amount to 49 percentage points, indicating very strong polarization along left–right lines on the question of EC membership. Differences between the left and the right are also quite high in Portugal and Spain. In the other countries, the differences, although smaller, are still quite sizeable. But the picture is much more mixed on support for European unification. In most countries differences exist in the direction one would have expected, but they are very small in Belgium, France, Germany, Ireland, Italy, and the Netherlands. Denmark and Greece again show high polarization. In Spain, interestingly, the left is significantly more in favour of efforts to unify Western Europe than the right, while at the same time, as we have seen, they are less inclined to regard Spanish membership as a good thing.

As to the influence of postmaterialism, the bivariate comparisons show that support for EC membership among postmaterialists is, on average, some 12 percentage points higher than for materialists. Moreover, there are no large variations between countries. But in contrast to left–right self-placement, postmaterialism loses most of its impact when controlled by social structural factors, other general political orientations, and political involvement. With these controls, the average difference between postmaterialists and materialists drops to just under 5 percentage points. The picture is again more mixed on support for unification, largely because in Denmark and Greece a reverse, though not statistically significant, effect can be observed. In summary, the hypothesis that support for the EC is more consistent with postmaterialist orientations is generally upheld, but the effects are not very strong and, to a large degree, they are dependent on interactions with other factors.

Concerning religious traditionalism, the hypothesis that secular orientations are more consistent with the 'modern' idea of internationalization must be rejected. Although the picture is mixed, especially when support for EC membership and EC unification are compared, it is obvious from Table 6.4 that the hypothesis does not match reality. Religious Catholics especially, but also religious Protestants, are much more supportive of EC membership than secular individuals, and they are also more supportive than those who are only loosely affiliated with the Catholic or Protestant church. However, our results, although rather weak, are consistent with the hypothesis that Catholicism is more compatible with internationalization. In Britain and Germany, differences between religious Catholics and Protestants in support for the EC are very small, but they are quite large in the Netherlands, rising as high as 10 percentage points. These differences persist even after controlling for all the other independent variables. Compared to the effects of postmaterialism, denomination and religiosity have a certain 'stand-alone' status and might well be regarded as neglected factors in the study of citizen's orientations towards European integration.

Summarizing the results for the 'consistency model' and comparing them to those for the 'enlightenment model', it is clear that individuals develop attitudes towards European integration in line with their general orientations. Yet, with a few exceptions, general political orientations show less impact than social structural variables, especially education and occupation. This suggests that 'enlightenment' is more important in support for European integration than the distribution of value preferences in society.

The 'Mainstream' Model

This model, with its emphasis on 'not so much better understanding of the world as greater participation in it and attachment to the mainstream' (Gamson and Modigliani 1966: 188), serves as a frame of reference for considering the relationship between political involvement and support for the EC. The more involved people are in politics, the more aware they are of government policy and the discourse of political élites. Furthermore, they are more exposed to the mass media and other institutions which explain policy and its rationale (Modigliani 1972: 965).[6] Both mass media coverage and political élite discourse since the early 1970s has been largely favourable to European integration; that is, the mainstream or predominant policy has not changed. According to the 'mainstream model', then, our hypothesis is that the more people are involved in politics the more they favour EC integration.

The empirical results shown in Table 6.4 support this hypothesis. Especially remarkable are the differences between those involved in political discussion and those not involved—averaging 16 percentage points on support for EC membership and 23 percentage points on support for unification. The differences are rather less—about 9 percentage points on both questions—between those who often try to persuade others to share their views and those saying they never do so. Controlling for social structural factors and general political orientations reduces the percentage point differences in support levels by about 50 per cent compared to the bivariate results. Nevertheless, political involvement remains a relatively strong determinant of supportive orientations towards the EC. Especially in Belgium, Germany, Luxembourg, and the Netherlands, involvement in political discussion, together with education, is one of the strongest predictors of EC orientations.

Diffusion or Demographic Change?

Our analysis of the effects of social characteristics, political orientations, and political involvement on attitudes towards the EC has, so far, been largely static. This might create the impression of stable and persisting group differences. However, the key question is: do group differences persist over time? Or, to spell out the question, is support for European integration dependent on demographic replacement in general and intergenerational change in particular, or does growing support result from a diffusion process by which group differences disappear and support for the EC becomes an increasingly consensual feature of European societies?

Again, and for the same reasons as earlier, the longitudinal analysis is limited to the two time periods 1973–82 and 1983–91. To show that diffusion is at work, it has to be shown, first, that support for the EC is higher in the second period; and, secondly, that group differences have less impact on orientations towards the EC in the later period compared with the earlier period. Again, we include only those nine countries which entered the EC long before 1983. Our results are shown in Table 6.5.

The answer to the first question—whether support, on average, is higher in 1983–91 than in 1973–82—is two-fold. With respect to EC membership, support is higher in all countries in the later period. The differences between the two periods are highest in Britain (11 percentage points) and lowest in Germany (2 points), with an average increase of support across countries of almost 7 percentage points. Support for unification, however, does not increase in all countries. In Germany, Luxembourg, and the Netherlands support is lower in 1983–91 than in the previous period. The fall is not dramatic, averaging about 4 percentage points. Moreover, the increase of support in the other countries is not as strong as in the case of support for membership, averaging only 4.5 percentage points.

TABLE 6.5. *Change in proportion and determination of support for membership and unification 1973–82 compared with 1983–91*

	Support for EC membership				Support for EC unification			
	Percentage support 1973–82	Percentage-point change	Determination		Percentage support 1973–82	Percentage-point change	Determination	
			R^2*100 1973–82	R^2*100 change			R^2*100 1973–82	R^2*100 change
Belgium	58.0	+8.7	14.2	−6.2	23.0	+3.2	10.4	−1.8
Denmark	34.9	+6.5	12.7	+3.4	14.0	+1.6	6.0	+1.1
France	57.9	+8.2	8.0	−0.5	24.3	+6.4	9.2	−0.5
Britain	33.0	+10.5	10.9	−2.6	19.4	+4.9	8.1	−1.1
Germany	58.2	+1.6	8.1	−2.2	36.5	−1.9	9.6	−3.6
Ireland	53.2	+8.2	9.4	−1.0	20.3	+5.7	6.4	−0.2
Italy	70.5	+4.8	6.4	−1.1	36.2	+2.1	7.9	−1.2
Luxembourg	74.6	+3.9	5.3	−0.7	43.2	−5.9	6.1	+1.4
Netherlands	74.4	+6.6	8.7	−3.2	31.8	−3.6	6.1	−0.7
Mean	57.2	+6.6	9.3	−1.6	27.6	+1.4	7.8	−0.7

Notes: Membership support is based on the proportion who say membership is a 'good thing'; unification support on the proportion who are 'completely for'. Determination is the proportion of explained variance from a multivariate analysis including social structure, political orientations, and political involvement as independent variables. The percentage-point change is for 1983–91 compared with 1973–82. For the 1973–82 data, approximate N for membership support are more than 17,000 per country except Luxembourg (5,379); for unification support, more than 13,000 per country except Luxembourg (4,107). For the 1983–91 data, approximate N are more than 19,000 for both questions except Luxembourg (more than 5,000). For details of the variables, see Table 6.2; for N, see Table 6.1.

Source: Eurobarometer cumulative data.

This result qualifies rather than invalidates the general hypothesis of the diffusion of support. It underlines that the two indicators of support measure different things: the membership indicator evaluates the status quo whereas the unification indicator is more prospective. Declining support for further unification in Germany, the Netherlands, and Luxembourg suggests that the present stage of EC integration is sufficient for a majority of the population. It does not imply that support, as such, has declined. Rather, increasing support for EC membership in these three countries reveals a growing consensus regarding the status quo on European integration.

These results, however, are compatible with both the diffusion hypothesis and the hypothesis of demographic replacement. The ultimate test for the diffusion hypothesis is whether group differences persist from one time period to another. As before, this can be measured by the increase or reduction of explained variance in EC orientations produced by the entire set of independent variables. In eight of the nine countries the proportion of explained variance is smaller in the second period. The exception is Denmark, where the explained variance increases by 3.4 percentage points. Given the relatively low level of explained variance for the 1973–82 period (12.7 per cent), this increase is not negligible. But the same argument applies to the opposite findings. Although the reduction in explained variance in the remaining eight countries is quite small (averaging 2.2 percentage points), it amounts to a considerable portion of the total explained variance. The reduction is largest in Belgium (from 14.2 per cent explained variance for 1973–83 down to 8 per cent) and smallest in France (from 8 to 7.5 per cent). The explained variance in support for unification between the two periods also declines overall, although here Denmark is joined by Luxembourg as countries where the explanatory power of the independent variables has increased.

In general, then, in most countries, diffusion processes have taken place. Group differences are not as significant in the period 1983–91 as in the 1970s and the early 1980s. A more detailed review of the impact of the independent variables on attitudes towards integration in Denmark and Luxembourg show that the increase in explained variance is caused solely by general political orientations. Thus, the results for Denmark and Luxembourg support the diffusion hypothesis with respect to the social stratification variables. But the EC issue has apparently been politicized in these two countries, leading to a polarization of people of different general political orientations in the second period—in Denmark on the left–right dimension, in Luxembourg on the religious–secular dimension. This finding brings us to our final question: what is the impact on attitudes towards the EC of the agents most likely to be responsible for politicizing issues—the political parties?

Party Affiliation and Support for the EC

Political parties represent more or less coherent programmatic profiles which provide the citizenry and, in particular, party followers with specific policy positions as well as general yardsticks with which to evaluate policies and political developments. They put forward blueprints incorporating a more or less coherent view of a complex world (Klingemann 1990). The analysis in this section starts from the assumption that, as parties offer individuals a means of political orientation, as well as a means of political participation and representation, individuals affiliated with a particular party tend to adopt the political stand-point of that party.

Rather than analysing EC policy positions party-by-party, we define a number of 'party families' and identify the European policy of each family. Klingemann's (1990) classification of parties is based on both institutional characteristics, such as being a member of the same supranational party organization, and programmatic profiles. Thus, the parties of the EC countries are grouped together as the green, communist, socialist, liberal, religious, conservative, and nationalist party families. We review the policy position in each party family and examine how this is reflected among party supporters.

The green parties in the European Community do not share a common position on European integration. It is not a prominent issue for the green parties in Belgium, so party adherents can be regarded as neither supporters nor opponents of the EC. In Denmark, De Groene is opposed to the EC and European integration; Les Verts in France support a Europe of the regions. Die Grünen in Germany similarly opposes the EC in its present form, calling for a confederal Europe of the regions. The Green Party in Britain has urged British withdrawal from the EC. The Federazioni Liste Verdi in Italy—a heterogeneous alliance focusing narrowly on ecology—supports EC environmental directives. Similarly, although critical in other policy areas (Jacobs 1989), the Greens in Luxembourg support the EC where it benefits the environment. As we can see from Table 6.6, the heterogeneity of the green parties' position on EC integration is fully reflected in the orientations of their followers. In France, Britain, and Italy, adherents of the green party are more supportive of the EC than the population at large. In Denmark, green voters are clearly opposed to the EC membership as well as EC unification. In Britain, Germany, and Luxembourg, the position of the green parties differs from the orientations of their voters, indicating that factors other than party affiliation shape the EC orientations of green party supporters.

Although there are substantial differences in European policy among the communist parties in EC countries, we expect communist party supporters to coalesce around the pole opposing the EC. Communist parties have generally been suspicious of the EC, seeing European integration as a manifestation of capitalist forces and part of the Atlantic bloc.[7] Hence, overall, the traditional communist parties have been strongly opposed to the EC, especially in Denmark, France, Germany, Greece, Luxembourg, and Portugal (Timmermann 1976: 91–114, 123–8). The expectation that communist party followers are generally opposed to European integration is borne out by our findings. Across all countries, support for EC membership among communist party supporters was 18 percentage points lower than the average; support for European unification was a little lower. However, there were large differences between communist supporters in different countries. They were least supportive in Denmark, Greece and the Netherlands, with support figures about 30 percentage points lower than the average on EC membership. But, as anticipated, Spanish communists did not deviate from the average level of support among the Spanish people. However, contrary to expectation, Italian communists were less supportive than the average Italian citizen.

The socialist family consists of parties with quite different standpoints on European integration: 'The disparate response of European socialist parties to issues of integration has been paralleled by a confused debate over the relationship between socialism and supranationalism' (Featherstone 1988: 339). An emphasis on national sovereignty and objections to supranationalism have been articulated at various times by the Danish Social Democratic Party, the British and Irish Labour parties, and by PASOK in Greece (Featherstone 1988: *passim*). By contrast, the EC is a symbol of freedom and democracy for the socialist parties of Portugal and Spain. This range of policy positions is well reflected in the attitudes of socialist party voters (see Table 6.6). In Denmark, Britain, Greece, and Ireland they are much less supportive

TABLE 6.6. *Support for membership and unification by party family:*
percentage-point differences in mean support

	BE	DE	FR	GB	GE	GR	IR	IT	LU	NE	PO	SP
SUPPORT FOR MEMBERSHIP												
Mean support (%)	62.5	38.3	62.0	38.3	59.1	53.2	57.5	73.0	76.7	77.9	63.6	64.8
(a) Bivariate effects												
Greens	+8	−23	+5	+14	+2	—	—	+12	−5	—	—	—
Communists	−7	−32	−20	—	−19	−33	−13	−8	−19	−20	−20	+1
Socialists	−2	−7	+3	−9	+2	−8	−12	+4	−2	0	+9	+9
Liberals	+10	+24	+9	+3	+8	—	—	+8	+5	+6	—	—
Religious	+7	+4	+10	—	0	+29	—	+4	+4	−2	—	+7
Conservatives	—	+25	+4	+11	—	—	—	—	—	—	—	−4
Nationalists	—	—	−3	—	−21	—	+3	−1	—	−19	—	—
(b) Controlled effects												
Greens	−2	−21	+1	+5	−4	—	—	+8	−9	—	—	—
Communists	−9	−27	−17	—	−22	−22	−14	−7	−19	−27	−17	−6
Socialists	0	−5	+2	−8	+2	−8	−11	+3	−2	0	+5	+8
Liberals	+5	+21	+10	+1	+5	—	—	+3	+3	+4	—	—
Religious	+5	+3	+8	—	0	+21	—	+3	+4	+2	—	+3
Conservatives	—	+17	+4	+9	—	—	—	—	—	—	—	−4
Nationalists	—	—	−3	—	−23	—	+3	−2	—	−19	—	—
SUPPORT FOR UNIFICATION												
Mean support (%)	24.9	14.9	27.8	22.2	35.4	38.0	23.6	37.4	39.8	29.7	45.8	37.7
(a) Bivariate effects												
Greens	+7	−9	−1	+6	+3	—	—	+9	−13	—	—	—
Communists	−2	−10	−11	—	−8	−20	+1	−5	−7	−8	−6	+6
Socialists	−1	−2	+3	−2	0	−5	−1	+6	0	+1	+6	+5
Liberals	+7	+7	+8	+3	+9	—	—	+11	+7	+8	—	—
Religious	+2	−6	+8	—	0	+23	—	+2	+4	−3	—	+3
Conservatives	—	+10	+2	+4	—	—	—	—	—	—	—	−1
Nationalists	—	—	0	—	−15	—	0	0	—	−5	—	—
(b) Controlled effects												
Greens	−1	−8	−3	+3	−4	—	—	+4	−12	—	—	—
Communists	−7	−9	−11	—	−15	−17	−2	−6	−10	−9	−6	−3
Socialists	0	−1	+1	−2	0	−6	−1	+5	0	+1	+4	+5
Liberals	+3	+5	+10	+1	+7	—	—	+7	+5	+7	—	—
Religious	+2	−6	+8	—	+1	+18	—	+3	+3	−2	—	0
Conservatives	+7	+3	+3	—	—	—	—	—	—	—	—	−1
Nationalists	—	—	+1	—	−17	—	0	−1	—	−4	—	—

Notes: Membership support is based on the proportion who say membership is 'a good thing'; unification support on the proportion who are 'completely for'. Party effects are controlled for level of education; left–right self-placement; materialism–postmaterialism; religion; involvement in political discussion. Empty cells indicate either no party or only minor party of this party family. For details of *N*, see Table 6.1.

Source: calculated from Eurobarometer cumulative data.

than the population at large, while in Portugal and Spain they are much more supportive than the population at large. In France, Germany, and Italy, socialist voters are a little more supportive than the average; support for integration is about average among Belgian socialists; socialists in Luxembourg are a little less supportive than the population at large.

As we move towards the centre of the party systems, however, support for the EC tends to increase and to become more uniform. The liberal, religious, and conservative parties share a positive attitude to European integration; to a certain extent it is their brain-child. Liberal parties have supported European integration from the beginning (Ficker *et al.* 1976: 19), and their supporters concur with this view. In all countries where liberal parties can be regarded as politically relevant, support for integration among liberal party voters far exceeds the average level of support (see Table 6.6). The same is true for religious parties, although their adherents—except in Greece—are not as supportive as liberal voters. The conservatives in Denmark, France, and Britain are also more supportive than average; indeed, only in Spain are conservative voters less supportive of the EC than the population at large. Given the extent to which the European issue has wracked the Conservative Party in Britain for more than a decade, the more positive orientation of conservative voters in Britain is particularly interesting. As we move to the right of the party systems, however, support for the EC declines (see Table 6.6). Supporters of the nationalist parties in France, Germany, Italy, and the Netherlands are less positive about integration than, on average, is the population as a whole.

These findings demonstrate that the views of parties and their followers on European integration are quite closely matched. But in which countries are attitudes towards the EC most politicized and polarized, and in which are they more consensual? We can answer this question by examining the differences in levels of support among party followers in each country. These data are shown in Table 6.7. The differences are largest in Denmark and Greece, where the EC has been a more politicized issue than in any other countries. In contrast, in Belgium, Ireland, and Spain, there are relatively narrow differences between the views of followers of different parties. In the remaining countries, the differences between followers of different parties are somewhere between these two extremes. Interestingly, polarization shows no systematic relationship with the level of support for the EC or how long a country has been a member of the EC.

In general, then, when it comes to the EC, party followers tend to reflect the stance of their party. Looking at the matter the other way around, the policy positions of the parties shape the attitudes of their partisans towards European integration. This general conclusion holds up when the relationship is examined after controlling for education, left–right self-placement, postmaterialism, and political involvement. It seems, then, that the diffusion of political orientations and the politicization of orientations are two distinct mechanisms generating support for EC integration. Moreover, as the impact of social and political stratification on EC orientations declines, political actors and mediating institutions such as political parties assume an important role in the development of support for European integration. We analyse this role in more detail in Chapter 7.

TABLE 6.7. *Politicization of the EC issue by party politics*

	Support for					
	EC membership			EC unification		
	Minimum	Maximum	Range	Minimum	Maximum	Range
Belgium	−7	+10	17	−2	+7	9
Denmark	−32	+25	57	−10	+10	20
France	−20	+10	30	−11	+8	19
Britain	−9	+14	23	−2	+6	8
Germany	−21	+8	29	−15	+9	24
Greece	−33	+29	62	−20	+23	43
Ireland	−13	+3	16	−1	+1	2
Italy	−8	+12	20	−5	+11	16
Luxembourg	−19	+4	23	−13	+7	20
Netherlands	−29	+6	25	−8	+8	16
Portugal	−20	+9	29	−6	+6	12
Spain	−4	+9	13	−1	+6	7

Notes: Membership support is based on the proportion who say membership is 'a good thing'; unification support on the proportion who are 'completely for'. The minimum is lowest level of support among party followers compared with average level of support. The maximum is the highest level of support among party followers compared with average level of support. For details of *N*, see Table 6.1.

Source: Eurobarometer cumulative data.

Conclusions

The research literature on EC orientations has tended to assume, implicitly or explicitly, that an individual's location in the social and political hierarchy has a persistent influence on individual awareness of, and support for, the EC. The higher the location, the higher the support for the EC. If these differences persist, then an increase in EC awareness and support can be achieved only by a process of replacement.

In this chapter we have put forward an alternative hypothesis: that European integration is a political innovation which follows the logic of diffusion. Accordingly, differences in attitudes between socio-economic and other status groups towards the EC tend to decline. The findings presented here provide strong evidence that the generation of awareness and support for the EC is a diffusion process. The impact of stratifying characteristics—education and occupation in the social realm, degree of political involvement in the political realm—on attitudes towards the EC has declined in almost all EC countries. The Community has become more familiar to all social groups in society and has obtained support across all social segments. When diffusion is the mechanism for generating support, the political consequences for EC integration are very different from what they would be if rising levels of support depended on cohort replacement.

While differences in EC orientations between various strata decline, the same is not uniformly true for groups defined by left–right and materialist–postmaterialist orientations, and party affiliation. Even more important than the persistence of such differences is that these factors have an impact independent of socio-economic status and political involvement. In particular, parties play an important role in the way their followers view European integration. Indeed, where EC membership is politicized by the political parties as in Denmark and Greece, it polarizes society. In sum, while structural factors have become less important to the formation of attitudes towards the EC, political factors not only show persistence, but have even increased their impact.

One might argue that the expansion of EC competences as well the intensification of EC activities tend to accelerate diffusion processes, while, at the same time, creating scope for politicization. The decline in support for the EC since 1991 is in line with the general argument of this chapter. The interaction between the process of diffusion, the increase in EC competences and penetration represented by the

Maastricht Treaty, and the growing politicization of support for the EC helps to explain recent developments in European public opinion.

NOTES

1. Rather, the general hypothesis is simply that younger people are more receptive than older ones (Reimann 1973: 169). In empirical terms, however, this hypothesis does not always hold up. After a review of 228 studies, Rogers and Shoemaker (1971: 185) concluded that there is no consistent evidence of a positive relationship between youth and innovativeness.
2. Note that there are quite marked differences between countries which seem to be related to the length of time the country has been a member state of the EC. The southern countries which entered the EC in 1981 (Greece) and 1986 (Spain and Portugal) show a relatively high proportion of respondents who are unable to answer the question.
3. However, we should note that the membership question specifically includes an 'indifferent' response option whereas the unification question allowed for an indifferent or neutral response only in the first four surveys in which the question was used. The absence of a middle or indifferent category may have the effect of increasing the proportion of 'don't knows' or non-response, or both. For a discussion of these measures, and variations in response categories, see Ch. 4.
4. Traditionalism is measured by combining denominational affiliation and degree of religiosity. In Eurobarometer, Nos. 1–23, religiosity is measured by the question: 'Do you personally feel, irrespective of how often you go to church, that your religion is of great importance, some importance, or only of little importance in your life?' People who regard religion as of great importance are classified as religious. The question in Eurobarometer, Nos. 24–34, is: 'How important is God in your life?' The original 10-point scale is recoded: 1–2 = little importance, 3–8 = some importance; 9–10 = great importance.
5. Research shows that the mainstream model performs somewhat better than the other two; see Sigelman and Conover (1981: 489).
6. There are parallels here with Inglehart's views on the effects of cognitive mobilization: 'Over the last two decades, the topic of European integration has received predominantly favorable coverage in the mass media . . . National opinion leaders, moreover, have been relatively strong supporters of European integration. Hence, we expect that the more educated groups . . . have a favourable orientation' (Inglehart 1970: 48). This point is discussed at greater length in Ch. 7.
7. There are exceptions, however. For example, the Italian Communist Togliatti pressed the concept of European decentralization and regionalization on the Moscow world conference of communist parties in 1969; and the Italian and Spanish communists were able to persuade the other communist parties to adopt a European declaration in Brussels in 1974.

7

Support for Integration: Élite or Mass-Driven?

BERNHARD WESSELS

The relationship between élite and mass orientations towards the European Community is often regarded as the crucial element in the process of European integration. Two opposing arguments have been distinguished in the so-called 'pull' and 'push' models: in the one, élites pull publics; in the other, publics push élites. Neo-functionalist theory stresses that European integration was pulled by political élites. In similiar, although negative, vein Feld and Wildgen (1976) concluded that the 'politics of rejection' among élites is mirrored in mass orientations. Quite the opposite perspective is suggested by the 'push' model, which emphasizes the importance of modernization, value change, and cognitive mobilization (Inglehart 1967, 1970).

The role of public opinion and political culture in the integration process was discussed in Chapter 2. Attention was drawn to the 'transactionalist' approach and to the role attributed to cultural factors and to a variety of attitudes and perceptions among 'the politically relevant strata'. It was also noted that Deutsch laid particular emphasis on connections and communications across strata. Building on these ideas, Deutsch subsequently developed a more differentiated—'cascade'—model of élite–mass linkage than is suggested by either the 'pull' or 'push' analogies.

Deutsch's cascade model of communication and action comprises five different levels, in which the political stratification system consists of a series of interconnected opinion pools. At the top there are the socio-economic élites (2–3 per cent of the population), followed by the political élites. Just below, there are the opinions represented by the mass media. Between the mass media and the ordinary citizens is situated the 'net of opinion leaders' (5–10 per cent of the population). At the bottom level of the cascade are the 'politically relevant strata of society'; that is, the politically effective part of the population (60–90 per cent of the adult population). The communication flow is more intense and more open within each level compared to communication between levels (Deutsch 1968: 147–59). Reviewing these ideas, Putnam argues that 'even in countries where levels of political sophistication are quite high, the "bubble-up" theory is less accurate than the one which Deutsch has termed the "cascade" model' (Putnam 1976: 138).

Not surprisingly, the cascade model finds echoes in discussion of the role of public opinion and the nature of opinion formation in the domain of foreign policy. A well-known example is the four-step model developed more than three decades ago by Rosenau (1961: 7–8):

News and interpretations of an event are first carried by, say, a newspaper; this then is read and adapted by opinion-makers, who assert (step 2) their opinions in speeches on the subject that are reported (step 3) by the press and thereupon picked up by 'opinion leaders' in the general public who in turn pass on (step 4) the opinions through word-of-mouth.

Obviously, in such a model élite opinion guides mass opinion: élite views influence the attentive groups of the mass public and from there opinion trickles further down. Although Rosenau's model is often cited, research based on it is rare.[1] But one piece of research which can be found (Peterson 1972) strongly supports the model. Peterson asked whether, for the period 1955–64, evaluation of the Soviet Union by the American public and by decision-makers had been congruent. Her findings were that the relationship holds, even after controlling for political events and conflicts. Moreover, time-lag correlations suggest that the direction of influence was from élite orientations to mass opinion (Peterson 1972: 265–8).

Opinion leaders play a similar role for Lazarsfeld, Berelson, and Gaudet (1944). In their classic study *The People's Choice* they came up with the notion of a two-step opinion flow whereby opinion flows from the mass media to the public via opinion leaders. However, there is an important difference between the two-step model and the Deutsch approach. Research on the two-step model questioned its general appropriateness because it neglects the fact that most interpersonal communication occurs among people who are equally attentive to politics. This point is also stressed by Robinson (Robinson 1976; see also Merten

1988). However, this criticism cannot be levied against the Deutsch cascade model, given the way he emphasizes that the communication flow is more intense and more open within levels of attentiveness than between different levels of attentiveness.

We noted above that Inglehart seems to suggest that, by means of intergenerational value change and increasing political mobilization, the process of European integration has become 'mass pushed'. Although, in principle, it is possible to put Inglehart and Rosenau or Deutsch into opposing camps, such a confrontation would over-emphasize the differences between the two positions. Moreover, Inglehart's model is not that simple. First, an output from the political system has to be perceived and evaluated by the mass public. Only after that can the feedback from the public to the élites have an important impact on the political system. The younger the generation and, by implication, the more politically mobilized, the greater the impact (Inglehart 1967: 95). Furthermore, cognitive mobilization itself is an expression of political stratification. High cognitive mobilization allows for high accessibility to issues, even if they are remote from day-to-day life. Therefore, the more educated groups in society may be the agents who trigger off the diffusion of opinions and orientations in remote issue areas. Inglehart's argument (1970a: 48) is summed up thus:

The more educated groups have a greater facility to receive and absorb messages relating to a remote political community. If the content of the messages concerning Europe were predominantly negative, we would then expect the more educated groups to be more strongly opposed to integration then the less educated. . . . Over the last two decades, the topic of European integration has received predominantly favourable coverage in the mass media and schools of Western Europe. National opinion leaders, moreover, have been relatively strong supporters of European integration. Hence, we expect that the more educated groups among the public would not only be more likely to have an opinion concerning European integration; they would also be more likely to have a favourable orientation towards it.

To explore these issues, we adopt a three-pronged strategy. First, using some 'historical' data from mass and élite surveys, orientations towards a political federation of Western Europe are examined. Secondly, the population of the Eurobarometer surveys is divided into opinion leaders and ordinary citizens in order to seek out evidence of a cascade model of opinion flow. Thirdly, as the core of the analysis, we test a process model of opinion formation, which relates the opinions of party supporters to official party stances in pre-election, election, and post-election periods.

Citizens, Opinion Leaders, and Élites

Although data sources on élite orientations are rare, some comparisons with mass orientations are possible. We have to keep in mind, however, that research in the early élite studies focused more on international security alliances rather than European questions. Moreover, the élite groups as well as the question wordings in the various studies differ.

In their early work on the development of the cultural, political, and defence relations between Western Europe and the United States, Lerner and Gordon carried out the European Élite Panel Survey (TEEPS) in 1955, 1956, 1959, 1961, and 1969 (Lerner and Gordon 1969). Although this study is important for understanding 'Euroatlantica' relations, it hardly touches on European integration. Rather, it emphasizes European defence, relations between nations and peoples, and the importance of several international organizations. Nevertheless, in France and Germany in 1956 and 1959, and in Britain in 1959, élites were asked to what extent they would approve of a reduction in national sovereignty in favour of a common policy for Europe. Their responses show that during the second half of the 1950s, the willingness of élites to support European integration 'beyond alliance to confederation' (defined as common policy by majority rule) or to a 'supranational institution' (defined as a single common decision-making body) increased (Lerner and Gordon 1969: 198). As illustrated in Table 7.1, agreement was greatest in Germany in both years, followed by France. Compared to France and Germany, British élites in 1959 were at the 'bottom of the league'. The orientations of the public towards a political federation of Western Europe show the same rank order and the same positive development in this period, although they lag behind in time (Merritt and Puchala 1968: 104).

A second élite–mass comparison, for the mid-1970s, is also shown in the table, using élite data from a study by Free (1976: 22) and mass data from Eurobarometer, Nos. 4 (1975) and 5 (1976). Again, on the question of a political federation in Western Europe, support was lowest among élites and the public in Britain, highest in Germany, and the French were in a middle position. Because the wording of the questions at the élite level in 1959 and 1974 differs substantially, a strict assessment of differences in support between élites and mass publics is not possible. The final comparison, which is only possible for West Germany, shows more consistency than inconsistency regarding the development of élite and mass opinion about a European political federation.

In any case, it is clear that support for a European political federation emerged much earlier, and was more widespread, among élite groups than among mass publics. During the mid-1950s, the development of support at the mass level is similar to that at the élite level. Moreover, as is evident in Table 7.1, the rank orders of élites and publics in country comparisons are always the same. The overall correlation of élite and mass opinion is quite high (0.68) and statistically significant. In brief, there is a systematic and strong relationship between élite and mass opinion. But the causal nature of this relationship—whether it is due to 'push' or 'pull' processes—cannot be identified, given the limitations of these data.

TABLE 7.1. Élite and mass attitudes towards joining a political federation in Western Europe, 1956–76

	1956	1957	1959	1962	1974	1975	1976
Germany							
Élites	57		74		71	79	
Publics		46		53		67	64
France							
Élites	53		68		59		
Publics		35		40		66	
Britain							
Élites			48		32		
Publics				20		34	

Notes: The correlation between élites and public (Pearson's *r*) is 0.68 (p< 0.02). Élite entries for 1956 and 1959 are percentages of promoters of a confederation or supranationality; for 1974, percentages in favour of 'joining a political federation . . . in which final authority would lie with the central government rather than member countries'; and for 1975, percentages favouring federation or one common state. Entries for publics 1957 and 1962 are percentages in favour of '[name of country] joining a political federation of western Europe in which the final authority would lie with a central government rather than with the member countries'; for 1975 and 1976, percentages who 'totally approve' and 'approve on the whole' of a plan for European political union.

Sources: Lerner and Gordon (1969: 198); Free (1976: 22); Reif (1978: 66); Merritt and Puchala (1968: 104); Eurobarometer, Nos. 4 and 5.

Opinion Leaders and Public Opinion

Before embarking on a detailed examination of the relationship between attitudes among opinion leaders and public opinion more generally, it may be useful to summarize the expectations deriving from the Deutsch cascade model, taking into account Robinson's (1976) findings. First, opinion leaders (in Robinson's language, opinion givers) pay more attention to the mass media and all forms of political information than others. Secondly, opinion leaders communicate more frequently with each other than with the attentive non-leaders (opinion receivers). Thirdly, because opinion leaders are more exposed to politics and because they have their own communication 'culture', they react faster and in ways different from non-leaders. Fourthly, opinion formation among opinion receivers or attentive non-opinion leaders is influenced more strongly by interpersonal communication with opinion leaders than by the mass media. Finally, a cascade model of opinion formation probably works among people who discuss politics, but a large proportion of the public are not involved in discussing politics and are much more open to direct influence from the mass media. Among these people, the cascade model does not work. There might still be a correspondence of opinion and opinion change between opinion leaders and non-discussants, but this is not an effect of a communication cascade but due to the fact that they are both exposed to the same mass media.

In examining the appropriateness of this model, we use the index Inglehart constructed for analysing the Eurobarometer data. The index is derived from combining responses to two questions: 'When you get together with friends, would you say you discuss political matters frequently, occasionally or never?' and 'When you, yourself, hold a strong opinion, do you ever find yourself persuading your friends, relatives or fellow workers? If so, does this happen often, from time to time, or rarely?'[2] This operationalization of opinion leadership comes close to the two questions used by Lazarsfeld, Berelson, and Gaudet (1944): 'Have you tried to convince anyone of your political ideas recently?' and 'Has anyone asked your advice on a political question recently?' However, both Eurobarometer questions emphasize the active role of the respondent, whereas the questions in *The People's Choice* tried to strike a balance between the active and passive role of respondents in the persuasion process. Nevertheless, Inglehart's index can be accepted as a valid indicator of opinion leadership. In Table 7.2

TABLE 7.2. *Opinion leadership and support for the European Community,*
1973–91

	Opinion leadership index				
	Low	Medium–Low	Medium–High	High	All respondents
(a) Support for EC membership					
Belgium	47.1	64.4	74.8	79.3	62.5
Denmark	29.0	38.6	41.8	42.1	38.3
Britain	26.6	37.1	45.2	49.4	38.3
France	48.5	61.3	68.6	69.4	61.2
Greece	44.4	53.8	56.9	54.4	53.4
Ireland	47.7	57.7	64.4	67.0	57.5
Italy	62.1	72.9	79.4	77.9	73.0
Luxembourg	66.4	76.0	78.5	84.0	76.7
Portugal	54.6	64.5	74.3	71.5	63.6
Spain	54.8	66.5	74.4	76.0	65.3
Netherlands	59.0	75.2	82.9	83.9	77.7
West Germany	39.1	57.3	65.7	73.2	58.8
East Germany	39.8	35.5	40.6	43.4	40.2
(b) Support for European unification					
Belgium	14.2	23.5	32.8	51.0	24.9
Denmark	11.0	13.6	15.7	21.8	14.9
Britain	13.3	20.3	26.6	36.7	22.3
France	17.2	25.6	32.3	43.8	27.6
Greece	25.3	34.0	41.4	44.3	38.1
Ireland	15.6	21.6	29.2	39.3	23.7
Italy	24.3	34.1	44.4	55.1	37.4
Luxembourg	30.3	35.9	40.7	54.4	39.8
Portugal	35.5	47.7	55.4	62.8	45.8
Spain	27.6	37.6	47.6	60.6	38.3
Netherlands	20.6	27.1	31.0	41.4	30.1
West Germany	19.2	31.3	39.7	57.1	35.2
East Germany	28.3	29.7	35.5	47.7	37.5

Notes: Except for East Germany, entries are 1973–91 averages; entries for East Germany are 1990–1 averages. For construction of opinion leadership index, see ICPSR (1980). The membership question is: 'Generally speaking, do you think that [country] membership of the European community (Common Market) is . . . good thing, a bad thing, or neither?' Entries are based on percentages saying membership is a good thing. The unification question is: 'In general, are you for or against further efforts being made to unify western Europe? Are you completely for, to some extent against, completely against?' Entries are based on percentages responding 'completely for European unification'.

Source: Eurobarometer cumulative data.

TABLE 7.3. *Difference in EC support between opinion leaders and non-leaders, 1973–91*

	Percentage-point difference between opinion leaders and non-leaders				
	1973–91	1973–9	1980–4	1985–9	1990–1
(a) Support for EC membership					
Belgium	31.0	39.5	34.5	21.7	22.7
Denmark	11.6	16.4	8.2	9.4	13.0
Britain	21.2	24.8	14.9	21.1	29.7
France	21.1	18.0	22.6	22.6	21.6
Greece	5.7	—	1.3	8.5	8.8
Ireland	19.2	18.8	25.9	14.9	14.4
Italy	15.6	17.0	12.9	16.2	18.1
Luxembourg	17.8	23.5	17.2	13.4	14.9
Portugal	17.8	—	—	18.3	16.1
Spain	20.8	—	—	23.5	11.8
Netherlands	22.4	29.5	20.2	18.0	20.0
Germany	33.3	39.9	30.9	29.3	32.1
Mean difference	19.5	24.2	19.9	17.4	19.0
(b) Support for European unification					
Belgium	36.4	41.2	34.3	35.2	36.9
Denmark	9.8	13.5	7.9	8.3	13.3
Britain	23.0	24.0	19.7	24.3	26.8
France	26.4	27.9	24.3	27.8	24.6
Greece	16.8	—	15.3	17.2	19.6
Ireland	23.8	24.8	25.9	20.3	27.7
Italy	30.4	34.8	28.8	30.1	26.7
Luxembourg	25.2	30.1	26.3	23.0	18.0
Portugal	27.6	—	—	27.5	28.2
Spain	32.6	—	—	33.4	29.9
Netherlands	21.2	32.9	16.1	19.7	16.8
Germany	36.7	48.2	33.2	32.6	36.8
Mean difference	24.8	29.1	22.4	24.0	24.1

Note: Calculations are based on percentage-point differences between the proportion of supporters at the highest level of opinion leadership minus the proportion at the lowest level of opinion leadership.

Sources: Eurobarometer cumulative data.

we present the results from applying this index to Eurobarometer data on attitudes towards EC membership and European unification over the 1973–91 period.

Clearly our expectation that the social strata close to élite positions are more favourable towards European integration than the public at large is confirmed. It is worth noting, however, that the difference between opinion leaders and the rest of the public is larger on support for European unification than support for EC membership. This may be because evaluation of EC membership is concerned with the status quo, whereas the unification question—asking about future engagement and the willingness to use the political and economic resources of one's own country to deepen integration—demands a more active degree of support from respondents.[3]

Using the average distributions of these attitudes over a period of almost twenty years neglects the possibility that there may have been a fundamental change in the mechanisms of opinion formation, as well as in the importance of European issues, during that time. If that were the case, the relationship between political stratification and levels of support for the EC might decline over time, due to the growing importance of mass communication and the greater relevance of European matters in people's day-to-day life. However, looking at differences in the extent of support among opinion leaders and non-opinion leaders at different time periods between 1973 and 1991, shown in Table 7.3, we detect no major changes. For the whole period, the mean difference between opinion leaders and non-opinion leaders is about 20 percentage points on support for membership and about 25 points on support for European unification—although a small decline in differences is evident from comparing periods before and after 1980.

As we can see from the table, the differences in the degree of support are quite similar for the periods of 1980–4, 1985–9, and 1990–1. Only for the period 1973–9 are the differences slightly larger than in the periods which follow. Whether the greater difference between opinion leaders and non-leaders before 1980 signals a fundamental change in opinion formation is doubtful, because it is not a consistent pattern in all the countries. It is true only for Belgium, the Netherlands, Germany, and Luxembourg. The explanation here may have something to do with either, or both, the central role of the Benelux countries and Germany in European integration or the very high levels of communication density found in each country (Gabriel 1992: 283, 428, 529).

Whether these findings reflect a cascade model of opinion flow is difficult to address empirically. One piece of evidence is that the political stratum closest to the political élites shows the highest degree of positive evaluation of the EC. Again, the level of positive evaluation falls monotonically with each step down the political stratification ladder. Moreover, these patterns have been consistent over the last two decades.

Looking at the dynamics of the development of European orientations at different levels of opinion leadership provides stronger evidence that a cascade model may be at work. Following Robinson's (1976) findings, we would expect greater congruence in the development of European attitudes between levels of opinion leadership which are closer to each other. This accords with Deutsch's proposition that the communication flow and, therefore, processes of opinion formation, are more open within equal levels of attentiveness. A corollary is that the pattern of development among those who do not take part in political discussion at all should show the weakest congruence with opinion leaders, because opinion formation in their case is not influenced by opinion leaders but primarily by the mass media. Taking the support level among opinion leaders as our reference point, we would expect, according to the cascade model, that the dynamics of EC support are most similar between opinion leaders and the stratum next to them, getting weaker and weaker as we follow the cascade down. This can be tested by examining the correlations of support levels among the reference group (opinion leaders) with the other groups over time. Our findings are presented in Table 7.4.

These findings sustain our argument, although the results are rather clearer on support for European unification than on support for EC membership. In both cases, the correlations between opinion leaders and the other three groups drop linearly. In other words, the correlation between the proportion of supporters at different levels of opinion leadership across more than thirty time points provides a good deal of evidence for the cascade model, particularly as this pattern holds across all EC countries. The results for Denmark and Greece, however, are not as convincing as in the other countries.

A Political Process Model

So far, our analysis has shown only that political élites and opinion leaders may influence orientations towards the EC among ordinary citizens. But this kind of analysis cannot uncover the interactive and dynamic nature of the processes of opinion flow and opinion formation. Consequently, we need to think in terms of a political process model

TABLE 7.4. *Development of support for the EC by levels of opinion leadership, 1973–91*

	Time-series correlation of support level among opinion leaders and lower levels of opinion leadership			
	Medium–high	Medium–low	Low	Time points correlated
(a) Support for EC membership				
Belgium	0.71	0.52	0.24	35
Denmark	0.75	0.66	0.69	35
Britain	0.87	0.82	0.82	35
France	0.82	0.81	0.77	35
Greece	0.87	0.91	0.87	23
Ireland	0.96	0.89	0.75	35
Italy	0.58	0.47	0.53	35
Luxembourg	0.63	0.47	0.46	35
Portugal	0.93	0.76	0.78	13
Spain	0.85	0.76	0.49	13
Netherlands	0.81	0.54	0.24	35
Germany	0.59	0.34	0.30	35
Mean correlation	0.79	0.66	0.56	
(b) Support for European unification				
Belgium	0.63	0.53	0.30	31
Denmark	0.52	0.45	0.53	31
Britain	0.74	0.66	0.50	31
France	0.78	0.70	0.63	31
Greece	0.78	0.77	0.69	23
Ireland	0.86	0.83	0.60	31
Italy	0.62	0.54	0.21	31
Luxembourg	0.69	0.60	0.37	31
Portugal	0.71	0.63	0.74	13
Spain	0.64	0.74	0.02	13
Netherlands	0.38	0.20	0.09	31
Germany	0.48	0.31	0.28	31
Mean correlation	0.66	0.58	0.39	

Note: Entries are Pearson's correlations based on the percentages of respondents in each group supporting the EC correlated over time.

Sources: Eurobarometer cumulative data.

which allows us to separate input from output effects. Ideally, such a model would be traced through time in order to look for feedback processes, especially the reactions of the mass public to political outputs or outcomes which then influence the orientations and behaviour of the political élites. Easton in particular emphasizes the importance of this aspect of the political process (1975*b*: 28):

The significance of outputs is not only that they help to influence events in the broader society of which the system is a part; in doing so, they help to determine each succeeding round of inputs that finds its way into the political system.

In system theory this feedback loop is significant for the capacity of a system to cope with stress. Note, too, that in distinguishing input from output, one must distinguish between demands and support on the input side, and policies or policy intentions and policy positions on the output side. In adopting the political process model, we focus on two research questions. Does the public's evaluation of the EC have any influence on the policy intentions or policies of political élites? And, vice versa, do the policy intentions or policies of political élites affect the public's evaluation of the EC?

In the analysis which follows, we focus only on the most important channel of political representation—the linkage between political parties and party supporters. We compare the level of support for the EC among party supporters with party support for the EC as expressed in election manifestos. The use of documents rather than surveys as the data base for élite opinion is not unusual (cf. Peterson 1972). Nevertheless, this design raises two important questions. Are we still dealing with the problem of élite–mass linkages or with a different topic? Why should election manifestos influence party supporters or, more generally, public opinion?

The crucial point concerning the first question is how party platforms are created. Generally, modern political parties appoint a commission or working group which submits a programme proposal; members of the working group are, normally, from the upper echelons of the party hierarchy, not rank-and-file members (Greven 1977; Volkens 1989). In this sense, party platforms articulate the policy options and intentions of party leaders—that is, of the political élites. As Niedermayer (1989: 226–32) shows for the German Social Democrats, the involvement of rank-and-file members in this process is quite low, but the involvement of party office holders is quite high. In a nutshell, party platforms are predominantly an expression of the political positions of party élites.

As to the second question, election manifestos, although not read by a large proportion of the electorate, have high visibility via the mass media. The policy positions of parties are prominently presented via the mass media during election campaigns. Policy options are discussed and presented by journalists and politicians, both of whom rely heavily on the collectively accepted policy profile, the election platform. For party supporters the argument is even more straightforward. They are interested in a specific party and its programme is of at least some importance to them in terms of integration, identity, and 'we-feeling'. The probability that party supporters at least glance through 'their' party platform is therefore somewhat higher than for the average elector.

In summary, the political process model runs as follows: party supporters and especially party members may influence party platforms before election campaigns through intra-party channels. But since the genesis of party platforms is dominated by party élites, the influence of party supporters is relatively minor. However, the high visibility of party positions in election campaigns may lead to a reorientation of the views of party supporters. But once again, although the influence of party platforms on the opinion of party supporters might be stronger than vice versa, parties cannot entirely determine opinion among their supporters. None the less, in most of the countries under observation, there are two situations in which policy positions and, therefore, the content of party platforms are highly visible; during the election campaign, and during a post-election period with the government declaration on its future policies and the challenge to it by the opposition forces. This gives us three time points when different effects from party platforms can be expected. Our arguments are summarized in Figure 7.1.

Operationalization and Data

In all countries except Italy, party supporters are identified by responses to the question: 'If there were a General Election tomorrow, which party would you support?' For Italy the question is 'Do you feel closer to any one of the parties on the following list than to all the others? [If yes:] Which one?'

The indicators of the orientations of party supporters towards the EC are, as before, evaluation of the membership of one's own country in the EC, and evaluation of the efforts designed to lead to European unification. Party positions towards the European Community are measured by two categories used by the Party Manifesto Research Group in the content analysis of party manifestos.[4] The two categories are 'EC positive' and 'EC negative'. The 'EC positive' code records favourable

Period	Pre-election period	Election campaign	Post-election period
Activity	Create an election programme	Mobilization; winning elections	Government declaration; critique of government declaration
Issue accessibility	Low to moderate (intra-party it might be high)	High	High
Expected relation	Party followers' opinions influencing party platform	Party platform influencing party followers and public opinion	Party platform influencing party followers and public opinion
Strength of influence	Low to moderate	High	Moderate to high

FIGURE 7.1. *Expected effects during time periods in the political process model*

mentions of the European Community in general, the desirability of expanding the European Community and/or increasing its competence, and the desirability of the country in question joining (or remaining) a member of the EC. The 'EC negative' code refers to hostile mentions of the European Community, the undesirability of expanding the European Community and/or its competence, and negative positions about joining the EC or remaining a member (Volkens and Klingemann 1991: 96).

From the two questions in the Eurobarometer surveys and the two categories in the party manifesto analyses, we created an aggregate data set consisting of three variables. Two are based on the Eurobarometer survey data: the percentage of party supporters saying that the EC membership of one's own country is a good thing; the percentage of party supporters saying that they are very much in favour of European unification.[5] The third variable is the percentage of mentions in party manifestos which are 'EC positive' among all EC-related mentions in a party manifesto. This measure seems to be fairly comparable to the variables based on the survey data.[6]

According to the political process model of opinion flow discussed in the previous section, the orientations of party supporters are of special interest at three time points in particular: around nine months before elections; around three months before elections; and around three months after elections. These three time-points cover the relevant periods as presented in Figure 7.1. Nine months before elections, the election campaign normally has not yet started, but parties are about to prepare their manifesto. Three months before elections the 'hot phase' of the election campaign has started, in which the mobilization of the voters and winning the election have highest priority, and inter-party competititon is highly visible. About three months after elections, the new government is inaugurated, and, in most countries, the parties (in parliament) again present their policy intentions to the public—in the government declaration by parties in government and in criticism of the government's programme by the opposition parties.

On the question of support for EC membership, the data set consists of a maximum of 215 comparisons between the opinion of party supporters and the position of a party. For nine countries (Denmark, Belgium, the Netherlands, Luxembourg, France, Italy, Germany, Britain, and Ireland) altogether fifty-seven party pairs are compared. The average number of time-points is about 3.61 and covers the period 1973–91. However, the question about support for European unification was not asked over the entire time span, and time lags reduce the number of cases. Hence, the data set for the unification question allows for a maximum of 172 comparisons. Finally, note that the definition of the three time periods is approximate. It is subject to country variations, particularly in the case of elections which are precipitated by political crises or tactical decisions by a head of government. Consequently, our test of the model tends to the conservative side, and likely, if anything, to underestimate the strength of the hypothesized relationships.

Parties and Party Supporters

Research on various aspects of the Community has shown time and again that 'nation', whatever the term represents, is the best 'explanatory' variable in cross-national analysis, including the study of élite attitudes towards the EC (see Feld and Wildgen 1976: 145–57). This finding is reinforced by our analysis; and it is true for both élite orientations and mass orientations. The commitment of élites to political integration shows a pattern very similar to the orientations of the citizenry in the EC countries. But, as we would expect, there are differences between the countries: the lowest levels of support are evident amongst legislators and civil servants in Denmark, Britain, and Ireland; the highest levels of commitment are evident in the Benelux and Italy; France and Germany are in a middle position.

Is this also true for the position of the parties as represented in election manifestos? The result is shown in Figure 7.2, which presents the average proportion of pro-EC references out of the total number of EC references in the party manifestos of each country. The Dutch, German, Belgian, and Italian parties show, on average, the highest proportion of positive positions towards the EC. Conversely, the Danish parties show the most negative positions towards the EC. The parties in Luxembourg tend to be in favour of the EC, but not as strongly as the Dutch, Belgian, and German parties. The parties in France, Britain, and Ireland, on average, fall between the negative extreme represented by the Danish parties and the parties which are most supportive of the EC.

Although the picture fits very much what is known from research on the relationship between elite and public orientations, such country comparisons conceal important differences between parties. Following Klingemann (1990), we can group parties into four 'party families': left parties (communists, socialists, new left); liberal parties; conservative, and Christian or religious parties; and nationalist parties (including

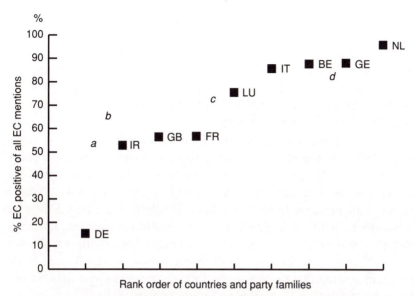

FIGURE 7.2. *Positive references to the EC in party manifestos by country and party family*

Note: *a* = nationalist/regional parties; *b* = left/green parties; *c* = liberal parties; *d* = Christian/conservative parties

Source: Comparative Manifestos Project.

regional and single-issue parties). Employing this classification reveals large differences between parties of the same family in different nations. The range within the left parties across countries is 83 percentage points, being lowest for the Danish left parties (12 per cent positive mentions of the EC) and highest for the Belgian left (95 per cent positive mentions). For the liberal parties, the range across countries is 90 percentage points; for the conservative or Christian parties 62 points. Irrespective of party family, Danish parties are at the bottom and Belgian parties at the top of the league. Within the nationalist parties category, the range is 77 percentage points across countries.

As to the proportion of positive mentions of the EC by parties of different families in a particular country, the range is less, on average, but still remarkable. The range is greatest in Britain (from 14 to 100 per cent), least in the Netherlands (5 percentage points). The next narrowest range is found in the Belgian party system (16 points), then Germany (22 points), Denmark, Ireland, and France (all a little above 30 points), and Italy and Luxembourg with a range of about 45 percentage points.

That the range is less between different parties in the same country compared to the range between parties of the same family across countries indicates that national peculiarities influence party positions more than ideological similarities. None the less, the differences between parties within most countries remain quite large. Our next question, then, is how this political differentiation relates to orientations among the public in each country.

Quite close linkages exist in all countries between the positions adopted in party manifestos and the positions of party supporters, shown in Figure 7.3. The greatest similarities between the average position of parties and the average position of party supporters can be found in France, Luxembourg, Ireland, and Italy. Similarities are only a little less in the other countries. In this respect one should not over-emphasize the numerical differences, but look at the structure, because the results stem from different data sources and different indicators. Looked at in this way, it is striking that quite a strong linkage or similarity exists between the average position of parties and party supporters.

The same is true if one looks at political rather than national differences, as shown in Figure 7.4. The relationship between the

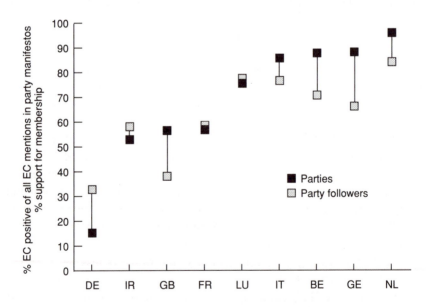

FIGURE 7.3. *Positive orientations towards the EC: comparison of parties and party supporters, by country, 1973–91*

Sources: Comparative Manifestos Project; Eurobarometer cumulative data.

positions of the parties and party supporters in particular party families again show quite strong linkage. Although there are slight differences in the strength of linkage between the parties and party supporters of the left, liberal, conservative or Christian, and nationalist parties, a transmission process—in whichever direction—is evidently at work.

Testing the Political Process Model

In the model under discussion, support for the European Community is seen as a result of a process of interaction and exchange between party supporters and political parties. National political systems mediate between the transnational system and national publics. The EC is still not a fully-fledged political system. Support and success depend to a considerable extent on actions taken at the national level. This means, as discussed in Chapter 2, that the political process at the national level is still crucial to the legitimacy of the European Community and the support it enjoys.

To test the model, we examine the interaction between the orientations

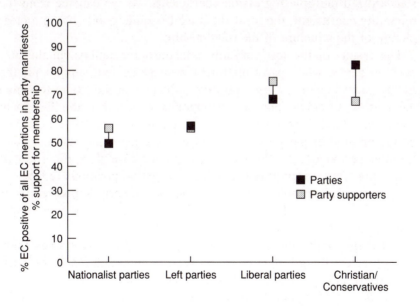

FIGURE 7.4. *Positive orientations towards the EC: comparison of party families and party supporters, 1973–91*

Sources: Comparative Manifestos Project; Eurobarometer cumulative data.

of parties and their supporters at three time points. First, the influence of the orientations of party supporters on party platforms nine months before elections; secondly, the influence of party manifestos on the opinion of party supporters three months before the elections; and, thirdly, the influence of party manifestos on the opinion of party supporters three months after elections. As noted in Figure 7.1, we expect the opinion of party supporters to have a low to moderate effect on party platforms, and we expect party platforms to have a strong effect on the orientations of supporters during election campaigns, and a moderate to strong effect after elections. In testing such a model, however, we have to control for the impact of nation, otherwise the effect of belonging to a particular nation could predominate, leading to an over-estimation of causal relationships. For the purpose of controlling differences between countries, we transformed all the variables within countries so that country differences disappear.[7]

The model was tested using a technique known as LVPLS (Lohmoeller 1984). This path model for latent variables combines confirmatory factor analysis and multiple regression analysis. The path diagram is shown in Figure 7.5. The path coefficients can be interpreted as standardized multiple regression coefficients. As we can see from the reliability coefficient, the fit of the model is quite good, giving a clear picture of the structure of the relationships.

The results of the test conform with our expectations. In the pre-election period when party platforms were generated, support for the EC by party supporters has a positive influence on the extent to which the parties articulate positive standpoints concerning the EC (path coefficient 0.29). Party platforms, in turn, have a remarkable influence on the opinion of party supporters in the election campaign and post-election period (0.32). Positive positions increase the proportion of party supporters supporting the EC, and negative positions reduce the proportion. But without testing the opinion of party supporters over time, this tells only half the story. Therefore the same model was calculated with paths between opinion variables.

Not surprisingly, the paths between public opinion variables show much greater strength than those between opinion and manifesto variables (0.67 and 0.53 respectively). This means that the best explanation for the degree of support by party supporters at any point in time is the degree of support they have shown previously. There is a basic level of support which does not change much. But, in so far as there is change in the support level between time points, one of the factors explaining

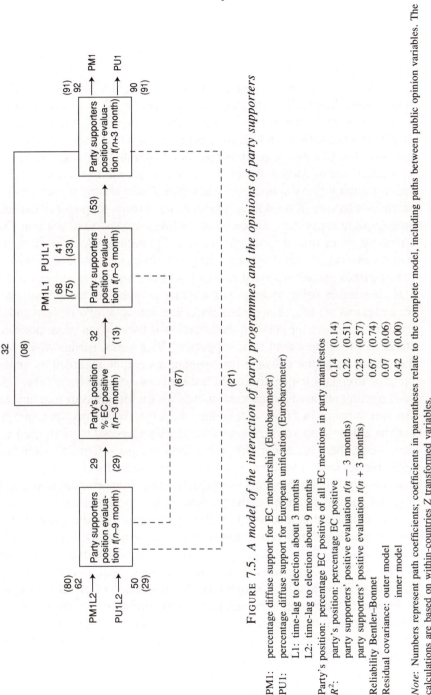

FIGURE 7.5. *A model of the interaction of party programmes and the opinions of party supporters*

PM1: percentage diffuse support for EC membership (Eurobarometer)
PU1: percentage diffuse support for European unification (Eurobarometer)
      L1: time-lag to election about 3 months
      L2: time-lag to election about 9 months
Party's position: percentage EC positive of all EC mentions in party manifestos

R^2:		
party's position: percentage EC positive	0.14	(0.14)
party supporters' positive evaluation $t(n-3$ months)	0.22	(0.51)
party supporters' positive evaluation $t(n+3$ months)	0.23	(0.57)
Reliability Bentler–Bonnet	0.67	(0.74)
Residual covariance: outer model	0.07	(0.06)
inner model	0.42	(0.00)

Note: Numbers represent path coefficients; coefficients in parentheses relate to the complete model, including paths between public opinion variables. The calculations are based on within-countries Z transformed variables.

such change is the position of the respective parties on EC issues. Party platforms still have an impact on party supporters, even when their opinion at the preceding time point has been considered in the model (path coefficent 0.13).

Taking into account the continuity of opinion over time, two conclusions can be drawn. First, the position of parties on EC matters presented to voters and party supporters during election campaigns and the process of government formation influence support—whether positive or negative—for the EC among party supporters. Secondly, because the mobilization efforts of parties do not lead to linear growth in the level of EC support among party supporters, party manifestos should be seen as an essential element in up-dating and thus stabilizing support for the EC among party supporters. Indeed, our findings suggest that, without the mobilization efforts of political parties, EC issues, which tend to be remote anyway, might disappear altogether from the public's agenda.

But parties are not always successful. At any given time, parties can be characterized as being under pressure either to mobilize stronger support for or against the EC, or not being under pressure at all. Parties are under pressure to engage in positive mobilization if they take a more positive stand on EC matters than their supporters. Vice versa, parties which are less in favour of the EC than their supporters can be regarded as under pressure to engage in negative mobilization. As we can see from Table 7.5, in 41 per cent of the cases analysed, parties were under pressure to mobilize stronger support; in 51 per cent of the cases, they were under pressure to convince their supporters to be less favourably disposed towards the EC. But, again, there are some differences between party families. Left and green parties tend to be more in favour of integration than their supporters and therefore under pressure to mobilize more support; nationalist and regional parties tend to be under pressure of the opposite kind.

Are parties more successful in closing the gap with their supporters during election campaigns? When party supporters evaluate the EC more positively than their party, the proportion of positive evaluations should decline during the election period; when parties regard the EC more positively than their supporters, the proportion of positive evaluations among their supporters should increase during the election period. The evidence, presented in Table 7.6, suggests that parties are successful in about two-thirds of the cases. Those parties under pressure to mobilize against the EC are a little more successful than parties which have to mobilize support for the EC. In regard to attitudes towards EC membership and attitudes towards European unification, parties are able

TABLE 7.5. *Parties under pressure to mobilize for or against the EC, 1973–91*

	All parties	Party families			
		Left/greens	Liberals	Christian/ conservatives	Nationalist/ regional
(a) Pressure to mobilize support for the EC	41	59	43	50	39
(b) Pressure to mobilize against the EC	51	32	48	43	52
No pressure/congruence	8	9	9	7	9
N	216	96	42	44	33

Notes: Row (a) shows that party manifestos favour the EC more than party followers (about 9 months before elections). Row (b) show that party manifestos favour the EC less than party followers (about 9 months before elections).

Sources: Comparative Manifestos Project; Eurobarometer cumulative data.

TABLE 7.6. *Success of parties under pressure to mobilize for or against the EC, 1973–91*

Change in support level among party followers 3–9 months before elections	Pressure to mobilize:	
	Against the EC	For the EC
(a) Diffuse support for EC membership		
Declining support level	68	37
Increasing support level	32	63
N	87	105
(b) Diffuse support for European unification		
Declining support level	78	42
Increasing support level	22	58
N	62	87

Note: Entries are percentages of all cases in which support level changed.

Source: Eurobarometer cumulative data.

to reduce the support level of their supporters in 68 and 78 per cent of cases respectively. Increasing the support level seems to be a more difficult task. Here, parties are successful only in 63 and 58 per cent of the cases respectively.

The extent to which parties can influence party supporters during the election campaign and during the post-election period of parliamentary debate about the government's programme can be shown by the average change in the support level of party supporters between nine months and three months before elections and between three months before and three months after elections. All in all, as shown in Figure 7.6, in both situations—being under pressure to mobilize positively or negatively—parties, on average, are able to influence party supporters in such a way that supporters come closer to the party's position. The impact of election campaigns is, as expected, of greater significance for opinion formation. The change between nine months and three months before elections is obviously larger on average than between pre- and post-election periods.

There are also some very successful parties which are not only able to influence their supporters strongly during the election campaign but also during the subsequent period of parliamentary debate. This is true for 26 per cent of the cases where parties are under pressure to mobilize for or against support for the EC. With respect to successful parties, it is true for 40 per cent of the cases. These parties are even able to influence their supporters, positively or negatively, to such an extent that supporters change their positions from being considerably above average in their level of support—or opposition—to being clearly below average.

We conclude from these findings that the influence of political parties on the way their supporters evaluate the EC is quite substantial.

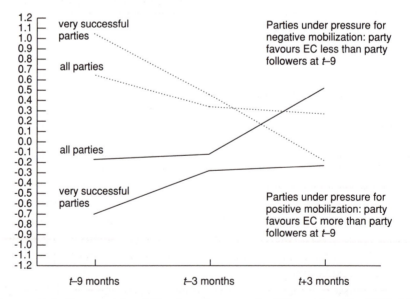

FIGURE 7.6. *Patterns of mobilization of support for EC membership, 1973–91*
Source: Eurobarometer cumulative data.

Moreover, if parties were not to mobilize for or against the EC, support for, and opposition to, the EC by the mass publics would not reveal such relatively stable and structured patterns as they do. In other words, party action at the national level contributes to European integration by regularly returning to the issue and so directing public attention to it.

Conclusion

The general question addressed in this chapter is whether or not support for the EC among the mass public is generated by élite action. More precisely, we asked whether opinion flow and opinion formation concerning the EC functions according to the cascade model proposed by Karl Deutsch. Our empirical findings provide evidence for a cascade model by showing that the development of support is more congruent between opinion leaders and the highly attentive publics than between opinion leaders and the less attentive strata of society. In the second stage of the analysis, employing a dynamic model, we showed that generating support for the EC follows the logic of the normal political process, with stages of articulation, aggregation, and output.

The position of parties, as expressed in election manifestos, has served as a measure of élite orientations which has been compared to the opinion of party supporters. Although the orientations of party supporters have, as expected, only a minor influence on party platforms, they do have an influence. But the content of party platforms is substantially reflected in the attitudes of party supporters in both the election and post-election periods, when party policy intentions have a high degree of visibility.

We have shown that in about two-thirds of the cases there is a discrepancy between the EC orientations of party supporters and the position of parties regarding the EC. However, we have also seen that parties are able to mobilize their supporters, bringing them closer to the party, whether for or against the EC. Although parties are quite successful in the mobilization of opinion, it is difficult to detect trends in the orientations of party supporters. This sheds some light on the process of opinion formation. If, on the one hand, parties are successful in mobilizing their supporters, while, on the other hand, that does not lead to identifiable trends over time, the inference must be that parties recurrently update support. If there was no mobilization effort, one major precondition of European integration—a more or less stable basic level of support for the EC—might be weakened or even vanish.

Successful mobilization by parties to change the orientations of their supporters must, then, be seen as a contributory factor to the process of European integration. It revives otherwise remote EC issues in the public mind and, by doing so, contributes to stabilizing mass orientations towards European integration. Putting it another way, the inference is that a system of internationalized governance such as the EC could not expect support if there were no political élites, political parties, and attentive publics who care about it. That does not turn the European integration process into a process independent of mass opinion. Quite the contrary: because support and legitimacy are necessary, élites and political actors have to work to secure them.

NOTES

1. According to Bardes and Oldendick (1990: 243), there has been virtually no research based on Rosenau's model, or, if there has, it has focused on only one level of analysis.
2. Inglehart has referred to this index variously as an 'index of cognitive mobilization' and as an 'opinion leadership index'. We prefer the latter designation, but the measure shows a strong relationship to processes of cognitive mobilization.
3. See Ch. 4 for a discussion of the development of these two indicators of diffuse support.
4. The content of party manifestos is generally coded into fifty-six different common categories described by the researchers as follows: 'Each of the 56 categories sums up specific themes or policy positions in a way that changes over time can be measured across parties and countries. The coding unit of the analysis is the "quasi-sentence". A quasi-sentence comprises an argument. An argument is the verbal expression and evaluation of a political idea or issue . . . Because of the different length of election programmes, the number of quasi-sentences in each category is standardized taking the total number of quasi-sentences in the respective election programmes as a base . . . These variables represent percentages' (Volkens and Klingemann 1991: 4–5).
5. The calculations are base on weighted data.
6. I am grateful to Philip Everts for his advice on using this measure instead of a measure based only on a positive emphasis on the EC.
7. This has been checked in different ways, for example by regression analysis using country dummies.

8

Europeans and the Nation State

GUIDO MARTINOTTI AND SONIA STEFANIZZI

One view of the construction of the European Union sees it as just another step in an almost ineluctable process of progressive evolution from the simple to the more complex—from the individual, to the commune, to the nation state, to ever more inclusive supranational units, up to world government. The end of the cold war Manicheism, the increasingly proactive role of the United Nations and other supranational organizations, and above all the institutional web of the European Community, combine with the daily experience of a world reachable at the touch of a button to make this evolutionary view appear not wholly imaginary. Perhaps unconsciously rooted in the Spencerian tradition, this conception of the process involves the application to history of the principle *natura non facit saltus*. Even so, while we now more than suspect that nature does in fact jump, seamless and evolutionary visions of history have to bite on the hard surface of facts. First, there are the examples of the disintegration of neighbouring political systems, and the painful realization of the seeming impossibility of preventing such dire consequences with concerted action. Then there are the very concrete anxieties over the short-term impact of German unification on local economies and life destinies which prompted the post-Maastricht reactions in several European countries. And yet these dramatic developments linger somehow on the horizon of events, and are seen, by governments and the general public alike, as annoying disturbances rather than signs of reverse trends.

Europe, moreover, is not only a new object being smelted now, to be completed sometime in the near future when its rather uncertain features will emerge from the furnace of the work of this generation:

it is also a reality which comes from the past, inscribed in our collective memory. For the many millions of Europeans with some more or less direct experience of the Second World War and the world it buried, the process of European integration is an established historical fact. Moreover, the 'construction of Europe', in the very literal and non-rhetorical sense of the phrase, is not just a product of the recent past. As Namer emphasizes: 'In a way it is a conscious memory of Europe constructed in reaction to the '39–'45 war, which is seen as an absurd reiteration of conflicts between European nations, and particularly France and Germany. But the *memory of recent projects refers to the faraway ones: from Henry IV and Sully to Kant via Leibniz*' (Namer 1993: 25).[1] In sum, the construction of Europe is part of the definition of the conceptual map of the world, much as the construction of walls and temples defined the *polis* in the past.

Various aspects of how this new *polis* is perceived are dealt with in this volume. Here we are interested in the relationship between the integration of the individual in the national system and their attachment to the new polity under construction. Is integration in the national political system a precondition for becoming a good citizen of Europe? Are nation states going to melt away into the larger European whole, or does the creation of a more inclusive unit require some kind of *saltus* and the painful, conflict-ridden overhaul of current national beliefs and institutions? Or are the paradoxes of mass politics so pervasive that the prevailing mood is indifference and apathy for both national polities and the European polity?

Our research question can be summed up by saying that we are interested in the relationship between legitimacy at the national level and legitimacy at the supranational level. Hoffmann (1966), in particular, points to the tensions in the relationship between the legitimacy of the nation state and supranational political integration. He argues that national consciousness must not be too strong; nor must it be too weak. A negative, non-purposive national consciousness inhibits integration, but, at the same time, the very strength and comprehensiveness of the nation state in the sense of its broad functional scope, authority, and popular basis may also be an obstacle to integration. In terms of our interests, Hoffmann's proposition that 'integrating units must themselves be integrated political communities' is particularly relevant.[2] Hoffmann also suggests that the legitimacy of several European states is relatively recent and that many states which have endured through nationalist struggles (either for unification or secession) do not want to abandon what has been gained. But recent developments may require qualification of this view. In some of the weaker and younger national states, such as Italy, national solidarity is now questioned both through the traditional reluctance of richer regions to share their wealth with poorer ones, and by a new rationalization of this concept emboldened by the existence of a European Community in which the richer regions seek to integrate. Such an orientation might be behind localist and regionalist movements manifesting themselves sometimes under the label of 'federalism'. This is clearly the case of movements such as the Lega Nord, which indicate that localism and parochialism rather than nationalism might be the counterpart of European integration.

The Data

In pursuing these lines of inquiry, we are very conscious of the gap between what we would like to know and be able to measure and the available evidence and indicators. What we have done is to select two variables as the main focus of the analysis, each measuring a central aspect of the dimensions we are interested in: the orientations of citizens towards their national political system, and their orientations towards the European Community. For the first dimension—orientations towards the nation state—we selected from the Eurobarometer surveys the question concerning satisfaction with the working of democracy in the respondent's country: 'On the whole, are you very satisfied, fairly satisfied, not very satisfied or not at all satisfied with the way democracy works [in your country]?' For the second dimension— orientations towards the EC—we focused on the membership question: 'Generally speaking, do you think that [country's] membership in the Common Market is a good thing, a bad thing or neither good nor bad?' The relationships between the two indicators highlight the link between the political life of the member states and the process of European integration.

Many factors may condition European developments; the data we are dealing with show only an aspect of the relationship between the national political culture and the creation of supranational institutions. It is an important aspect, however, because the sources of legitimacy for the Community's institutional system are rooted at the national level. This does not necessarily mean—as in the case of Italy— that there is a positive relation between the legitimacy of national political institutions and the process of international integration. The national and international integration of citizens need not be a linear process; it can be discontinuous and conflictual. For citizens, the European Community may represent a symbolic threat or, alternatively, a chance to make up for the bad governance of the national state.

One hypothesis is that the citizens of the most solid and centralized countries of Western Europe—France and Britain—may regard European unity as creating a new European state. This would imply transferring sovereignty and identity from one level to another, a transfer which would offend against long-established national traditions. Those who belong to a weaker or less institutionalized state are probably less worried about integration because (as in the case of Italy) their idea of national sovereignty is less fixed and because they accept that their government is divided according to institutions and political groups with different degrees of power and authority (Wallace 1990*b*).

In the next two sections, we examine trends in orientations towards the European Community and towards the national state. These trends are dealt with singly in greater detail in other chapters in this volume (see Chapters 4 and 6) and in one of the companion volumes (see Volume i, Chapter 11). Here, we look in particular at national differences because our research question implies that differences between national political systems are central to our inquiry.

Trends in Orientations Towards the National System

In Table 8.1 we show the percentage of those who declare themselves either 'highly satisfied' or 'somewhat satisfied' with the way democracy works in their own country. The data are presented at five-year intervals—1975, 1980, 1985, 1990—and in the spring of 1993, with countries ranked in ascending order for the average of the results for 1975–90. Greece is shown only from 1980, Portugal and Spain only from 1985. The German entry for 1993 refers to post-unification Germany.

Starting from a low level which presumably reflected the economic and political crises of the mid-1970s, the average satisfaction level across all member states, taken together, rose steadily until 1990 (from 46 to 62 per cent) but by spring 1993 it had fallen back sharply (to 51 per cent). Given our primary interest in the relationship between orientations towards the national political system on the one hand and the European political system on the other, cross-national variations in assessments of democratic performance are particularly important. In spring 1993 these variations ranged from the low levels of satisfaction in Greece, and in particular Italy, to remarkably high levels in Denmark and Luxembourg. In between but towards the low side are France, Germany, and Spain, while Portugal, West Germany, Ireland, and the Netherlands are towards the higher end of the middle range. Britain and Belgium, with 49 per cent satisfied with democracy, are plumb in the middle.

Of course, these comments on country differences derive from a single snapshot, perhaps reflecting quite particular situations in individual countries. So we extend the analysis by combining the cross-national and cross-temporal perspectives. Examining the development of satisfaction with democracy over time enables us to distinguish two groups of countries. In the first group, shown in Figure 8.1, there is an overall increase in satisfaction. This group includes Denmark, Ireland, Luxembourg, the Netherlands, Portugal, and Britain. There are, of course, differences within the group. Ireland starts from a relatively

TABLE 8.1. *Satisfaction with democracy in EC countries, 1975–93*

	1975	1980	1985	1990	Average 1975–90	Spring 1993
Italy	14.8	21.3	27.3	25.9	23.7	13.0
France	38.1	39.5	45.9	52.2	49.5	41.0
Belgium	56.4	40.1	58.5	63.8	55.8	49.0
Greece	—	54.1	59.5	39.9	56.6	28.0
Ireland	42.0	51.2	50.3	67.6	57.5	62.0
Britain	32.4	55.2	54.7	52.5	57.6	49.0
Spain	—	—	57.6	58.7	57.9	41.0
Portugal	—	—	39.4	73.6	62.6	54.0
Netherlands	54.1	52.8	60.5	73.2	64.2	68.0
Denmark	49.3	63.3	73.8	72.7	68.0	81.0
Luxembourg	60.4	77.6	73.8	78.8	72.5	82.0
West Germany	63.8	77.6	72.1	82.3	76.1	(55.0)
Germany	—	—	—	—	—	45.5
Average	45.7	53.3	56.1	61.8	56.5	51.1
EC-9 average	45.7	53.2	57.4	63.2	58.3	55.5

Notes: Entries are percentages. Countries are listed in ascending order according to the average level of satisfaction with democracy 1975–90. The average sample size is over 1,000 except in Luxembourg (488).

Sources: Eurobarometer, Nos. 3, 14, 24, 35, and 39.

low position in 1975. The Netherlands, starting from a somewhat higher level, show a more decisive upwards movement; the movement in Denmark runs in parallel. The level of satisfaction in Portugal moved sharply upwards between 1985 and 1990, but had fallen back again by 1993. Even so, the average level of satisfaction with democracy in Portugal was higher in 1993 than in 1985.

In each of the other five countries, the gains made during the 1980s were more or less retained in the face of increasing dissatisfaction with democracy among other member states of the Community after 1990. One factor common to five of the six countries is their relatively small size. The exception is Britain where the rise in satisfaction was concentrated in the period 1975–80, taking off from a very low base which presumably reflected the political crisis in Britain prior to the 1974 election. By contrast, the second group of countries is characterized by an overall decline, or, at best, stability in satisfaction with democracy over the period as a whole (see Figure 8.2). Moreover, except in Greece, this decline is concentrated between 1990 and 1993.

In all of these instances we can hypothesize that the observed patterns reflect changes in the internal political dynamics of the countries

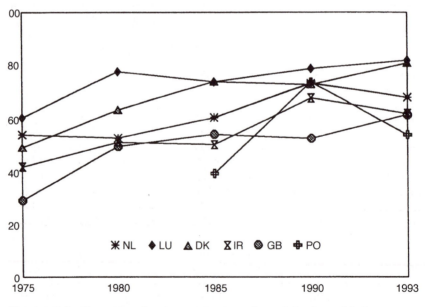

FIGURE 8.1. *Countries showing an increase in satisfaction with democracy, 1975–93*

Sources: Eurobarometer, Nos. 3, 14, 24, 35, and 39.

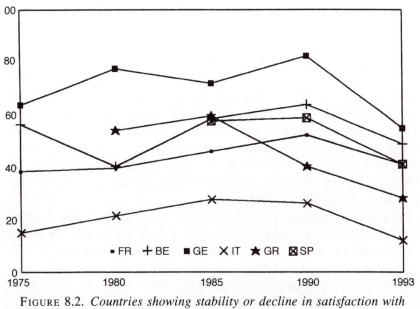

FIGURE 8.2. *Countries showing stability or decline in satisfaction with democracy, 1975–93*

Sources: See Figure 8.1.

concerned. In Germany since 1989, the issue of re-unification gave rise to heated public debate (Janning 1991; Massari 1991; Ferrera 1991). In cases like this, dissatisfaction with specific policy options, especially related to such a fundamental and encompassing decision as unification, may carry over to the level of the political system. In addition, incidents involving racial or ethnic tension may have given rise to concerns about the 'working of democracy' in Germany. Indeed, we have seen those concerns expressed in mass pro-democracy and anti-racist demonstrations. In Portugal and Spain, the democratic system had to be restored before these countries could secure entry to the European Community. In this sense, the transition to democracy was more a precondition than a consequence of European integration. However, although these data do not allow us to assess how much the democratic requirements of the European Community have influenced the establishment and maintenance of democracy in Spain and Portugal, it is reasonable to think that pressures in this sense were indeed at work. It remains to be seen whether the recent figures are a temporary blip or reflect the experience of coming to grips with the mundane realities and imperfections of democracy.

In France, until 1980, the crisis of the centrist government and the close race with the socialists kept the public's satisfaction with the functioning of the national system low. After the turn to the left, prepared by the victory of the left-wing coalitions in the local elections of 1978, the initial enthusiasm for Mitterrand and the Union de la Gauche, followed by the responsiveness of the system shown in the policy U-turn of 1983, seem to have raised the overall level of satisfaction with democracy. Again we observe that the success of a specific political orientation overflows on to the political system. The problem is that such gains are vulnerable to changing political fortunes and Mitterrand's fortunes may well be reflected in the decline in satisfaction with democracy in 1993.

Similarly in Britain, the observed trend can be explained with the unfolding of Mrs Thatcher's policies and their aftermath. The period begins with the rescue of Britain from being 'the sick man of Europe' but, thereafter, the Conservative government found itself in considerable difficulty on both the internal and external fronts. In particular, it was caught severely off-balance by the deeply modified European scenario (Wallace 1991) and, in the end, the Thatcherite position on the British political scene as well as Britain's position on the European scene were substantially weakened.

Greece shows a very specific trend. Looking at 1980 and 1985, satisfaction with the democratic system was fairly high and growing. But in 1990, no doubt as a consequence of the internal political crisis of PASOK and the Papandreou government, satisfaction with the democratic system among people in Greece drops sharply. During 1990, Greece had two general elections, neither of which changed the *malgoverno* of the country which started in 1988. For the first six months of 1989, Papandreou's government survived in spite of many difficulties; after the election of June it was replaced by a conservative–communist coalition. But not even the new coalition proved able to take the urgently needed steps in economic policy. As a consequence the Greek economy was not able to develop and to keep pace with the other EC countries (McDonald 1989). The challenge for Greek democracy is whether the return of a Papendreou-led government with a self-proclaimed new orientation will restore confidence at this basic level.

Italy is the most peculiar case. On the one hand, it is consistently at the bottom of the ranking. On the other hand, in the early part of our period, the proportion satisfied with democracy almost doubled, going from a scant 15 per cent in 1975 to 27 per cent in 1985. One can say that, having such a low starting point, Italy could not but go up. But what goes up can come down, and in the Italian case did so between 1990 and 1993, as Italians reacted to the unfolding *tangentopoli* crisis. In this instance, something akin to a 'crisis of democracy' would seem to have brought the system to the point of fundamental political change and institutional reform.

Over and above all these country-specific developments, however, there was a continuing common development in the governance of these countries during the period: the evolution of the European Community. Accordingly, we now turn directly to the analysis of trends in attitudes to Community membership.

Trends in Orientations towards the Community

Like satisfaction with democracy, average support for EC membership declined between 1990 and 1993. Unlike satisfaction with democracy, however, this was not the first dip in support—a falling-off had also

TABLE 8.2. *Evaluation of EC membership, 1975–90*

	1975	1980	1985	1990	Average 1975–90	Spring 1993
Britain	54.7	25.2	38.7	56.2	40.2	48.0
Denmark	42.6	35.1	36.0	54.9	40.8	61.0
Greece	—	43.9	47.3	80.2	58.5	68.0
Ireland	61.0	52.8	56.9	79.3	60.7	75.0
West Germany	63.0	70.9	62.2	69.1	63.8	59.0
France	69.8	56.3	70.0	67.8	65.6	56.0
Belgium	70.1	66.6	67.6	75.9	70.1	64.0
Portugal	—	—	60.5	73.4	73.6	64.0
Spain	—	—	67.3	71.9	73.7	56.0
Italy	77.1	78.1	78.9	81.7	78.0	71.0
Luxembourg	76.4	80.7	84.6	77.5	79.7	76.0
Netherlands	77.7	80.4	84.5	85.9	82.5	83.0
Germany	—	—	—	—	—	58.5
Average	65.8	59.0	62.9	72.8	63.2	65.0
EC-9 average	65.8	60.7	64.4	72.0	64.6	65.8

Notes: Entries are percentages. Countries are listed in ascending order according to the average level of support for EC membership 1975–90.

Sources: See Table 8.1.

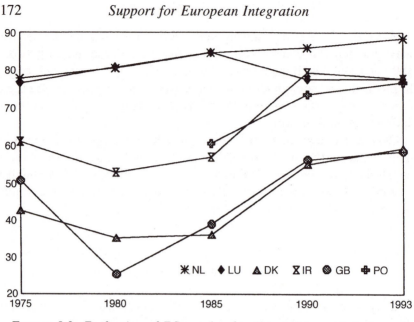

FIGURE 8.3. *Evaluation of EC membership in countries with increased satisfaction with democracy, 1975–93*

Sources: See Figure 8.1.

occurred between 1975 and 1980 (see Table 8.2). Given our research question, and the fact that orientations towards EC membership are examined extensively elsewhere in this volume, we are interested mainly in the interaction between support for EC membership and satisfaction with democracy.

As a first step in exploring the relationship between the two variables, we display the trends in support for membership for the two groups of countries as defined by the pattern of satisfaction with democracy. In the countries with increased levels of satisfaction (see Figure 8.1), the picture is mixed. The Netherlands and Luxembourg show high levels of support for the EC, but Denmark and Britain show low levels. Ireland, which is in the same group, moves from a moderate to a high level of support, whereas the support level in Portugal increases at first but then falls back a bit (see Figure 8.3). With the exception of Luxembourg, however, a common feature of these countries is a net increase in support for EC membership over the period considered; in Luxembourg, support for membership was at the same level at the end of the period as at the beginning.

In contrast, in the countries with stable or declining satisfaction with democracy, there is a net decline in support for membership over the whole period. Greece is an exception to that general pattern, but support for EC membership in Greece had started (in 1980) from a relatively low base (see Figure 8.4).

More striking is the concomitant decline in both indicators which occurs between 1990 and 1993 in the second group of countries. Some countries, however, show startlingly inverse patterns in the distribution of the two orientations. Italy is bottom of the table in approving the functioning of the democratic system but is among those at the top in support for membership of the EC. Denmark shows quite a high degree of satisfaction with democracy and low—but growing—support for EC membership. Greece moves from moderate satisfaction with democracy and overall disapproval of the EC to a pattern of decided dissatisfaction with the working of national democracy combined with growing support for EC membership—although the latter trend is partially reversed between 1990 and 1993.

In order to explore this matter further, in Figure 8.5 we set out a general mapping of the relations between support for the EC and trust in the national democratic political system. As the former is normally

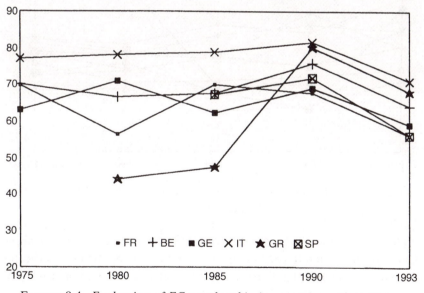

FIGURE 8.4. *Evaluation of EC membership in countries with stable or declining satisfaction with democracy, 1975–93*

Sources: See Figure 8.1.

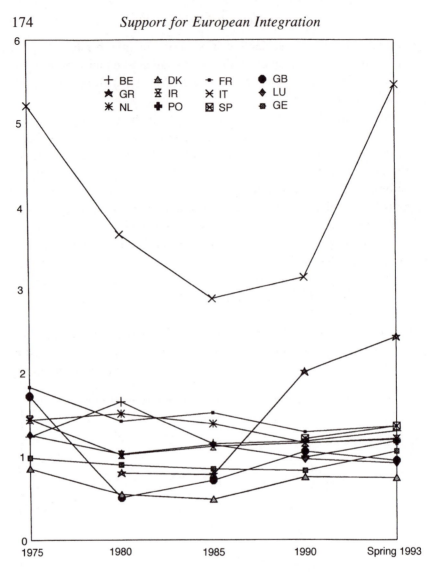

FIGURE 8.5. *Ratio of evaluation of EC membership to satisfaction with democracy, 1975–93*

higher we created a ratio of positive European orientation over positive national orientation in each country.[3] A high score on the ratio indicates that support for EC membership outstrips satisfaction with the functioning of democracy in the national political system.

The ratio measure brings out quite clearly the anomaly of Italy. Indeed, the most striking feature of Figure 8.5 lies in two aspects of the Italian case: its exceptional nature, and the dramatic change in the Italian ratio over time. It was extremely high in the mid-1970s, indicating a huge predominance of satisfaction with the European Community over satisfaction with Italian democracy. Over the next decade, the discrepancy declined substantially, although the decline still left Italy looking remarkably different from its fellow member states. Then, between 1990 and 1993, the ratio shot up again as Italians reacted to the developing crisis in their political system. The combination of strong—almost fideistic—support for Europe with low regard for the national political system is such a particular aspect of *il caso italiano* that one cannot pass over the suspicion that this dyscrasia has something to do with the emerging brew of separatist and federalist humours. Intimations of crisis are also evident in the upward movement of the Greek ratio which, although well short of the Italian position, distinguished Greece from the majority of the member states in 1990 and 1993.

Turning to the other member states, it is evident that the exceptional nature of the Italian case has the effect of compressing the display of the range of differences in their ratios. The display rather suggests that they are all in the same boat, whereas, in fact, the ratios range from around one and lower in West Germany and Denmark to close to two in France (1975). Morover, the relationship between the two orientations cannot be fully explored by means of a solely quantitative ratio. The ratio has the advantage of dramatizing the singularity of the Italian case but runs the risk of overdramatizing it and of exaggerating the extent of change which occurred in Italian orientations during this period. In addition, from a strictly statistical point of view, the ratio may even be inappropriate because, as already emphasized, the two measures are not exactly comparable. Thus, in order to explore further the relationship between Community and national orientations, a better strategy may be to concentrate on the categorical level of analysis.

A Typology of Orientations

By cross-tabulating the two measures—satisfaction with national democracy and evaluation of EC membership—we can create a useful typology of national and supranational orientation. The fourfold typology is displayed in Figure 8.6. In attaching labels to each type, we borrow from a distinction suggested by Umberto Eco. Analysing the

		ORIENTATIONS TOWARDS THE NATIONAL POLITICAL SYSTEM	
		Positive	Negative
ORIENTATIONS TOWARDS THE EC	Positive	Integrated	Innovators/escapists
	Negative	Nation statist	Alienated

FIGURE 8.6. *A typology of orientations towards the national political system and the European Community*

theories of mass culture in the early 1960s, Eco (1964) speaks about the 'integrated' and the 'apocalyptics'. These are polar types, the 'integrated' showing full acceptance and positive evaluations regarding the growing mass culture while the 'apocalyptics' express a deep alienation, equating mass culture with the apocalypse of culture. We draw an analogy from the attitude towards mass culture to political culture in general, although for the negative orientation we change the term 'apocalyptic' to 'alienated' as more appropriate for the kind of operational definition implicit in the data. Thus we define as 'integrated' those respondents who have a positive orientation both towards the EC and their own political system. At the opposite pole we find the 'alienated': citizens of Community countries who feel alienated both in regard to their own political system and the projected European system. The alienated are mainly retreatists and marginal, but they might host a strong potential for protest.

The intermediate types are located on the reverse diagonal. Those in the positive/negative cell (positive towards the national system but sceptical about the European system) put their faith primarily in the nation state. Without necessarily being nationalists, they are those in whom, in Hoffmann's (1966) terminology, national consciousness is too strong relative to supranational consciousness or commitment. They are a source of the obstinacy of the nation state, hence the label 'nation statists'. It is likely that the numbers in this cell will swell as the difficulties of European integration become increasingly apparent.

The 'innovators' or 'escapists' in the negative/positive cell include those who, on the contrary, are sceptical about their own system but have positive expectations *vis-à-vis* the European Community. We interpret these respondents as innovators or escapists in the sense that they hope either that European integration will provide leverage for innovation or reform in their own national system or they regard it as an escape hatch through which the deficiencies of the national system can be circumvented. In terms of their potential contribution to integration, these people might be thought of, again in Hoffmann's terms, as those in whom national consciousness is weak or in whom 'an intense and positive general will or enlightened national patriotism' is absent. The innovator-escapist orientation may not make as strong a contribution to stable political integration as might at first sight appear.

In Figure 8.7 we show the development of the four types at five-yearly intervals between 1975 and 1993 The salient European-level trends are, first, a substantial increase in the proportion of the integrated, an increase which largely took place between 1985 and 1990. These are now clearly the preponderant group. At the same time, secondly, the innovators/escapists constitute a group of significant size. They declined somewhat in numbers between 1975 and 1993, but they remain the second largest group, clearly outnumbering the nation statists and the alienated. Thirdly, the period of maximum strength of the nation-statist orientation would appear to have been

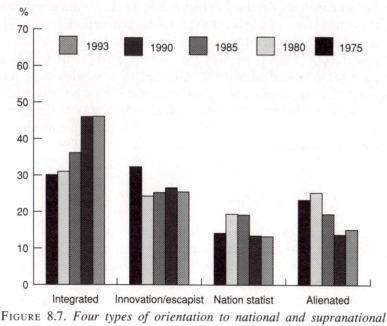

FIGURE 8.7. *Four types of orientation to national and supranational governance in the EC, 1975–93*

Sources: See Figure 8.1.

around 1980–5, but even then they were a minority. Finally, the last two decades have seen a substantial decline in alienation—as we use the term here to signify those who are negative about both national politics and European integration. In 1980, the alienated substantially outnumbered the nation statists, were as large a group as the innovator-escapists, and were not much smaller than the integrated. In 1990 and 1993, they were much more clearly in the minority, although still large enough to make an impact.

Of course, beneath this Community-wide surface there are conflicting currents and undercurrents. None the less, certain common features are detectable and, based on these, we can arrange the twelve member states in four sets: the predominantly integrated; the integrated plus innovator/escapist; the integrated plus nation statist; and the predominantly innovator/escapist. We look at these sets in turn, identifying the characteristic profile of orientations in each of the member states.

The Predominantly Integrated

This set of countries, depicted in Figure 8.8, has an absolute majority in the integrated category and lacks a substantial concentration in any other group. In particular, the levels of nation statist and alienated orientations are low. Luxembourg is perhaps the clearest example of the pattern, which it has exhibited since 1980. Although of somewhat more recent origin (1985), the pattern is also well established in the Netherlands, and was consolidated in the last two time points (1990 and 1993). Ireland and Portugal are the most recent arrivals in this set, both having undergone a substantial change in orientation between 1985 and 1990.

The Integrated plus Innovator/Escapist

Characterized by the absence of an integrated majority, by relatively high levels of innovators/escapists and by particularly low levels of nation statists, the integrated plus innovator/escapist set of countries consists of France, Belgium, and Spain (see Figure 8.9). France is the most clear-cut case. There, the integrated and the innovator/escapist jostle for position and there is a very substantial alienated segment. Belgium has a larger group of integrated citizens; indeed in 1990 it might have been placed in the predominantly integrated set, alongside

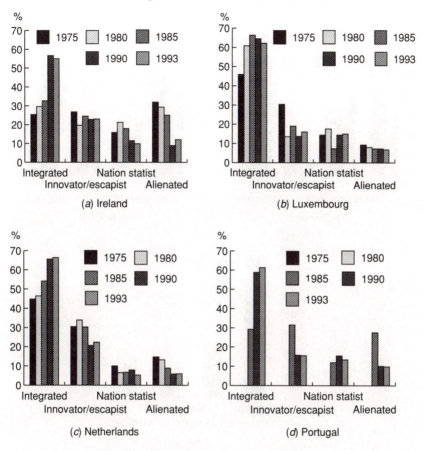

FIGURE 8.8. *The predominantly integrated: Ireland, Luxembourg, the Netherlands, and Portugal, 1975–93*

Sources: See Figure 8.1.

its Benelux neighbours. However, the pre- and post-1990 data fail to show an integrated majority and, on average, Belgium has a higher level of alienation than is found in the predominantly integrated set of countries. The third member of this group, Spain, exhibits a pattern quite close to that in Belgium, including the fact—common to all three countries in the set—that the alienated outnumber the nation statists. Unlike its neighbour, Portugal, which would have belonged to this set in 1985, Spain shows quite a stable pattern over time.

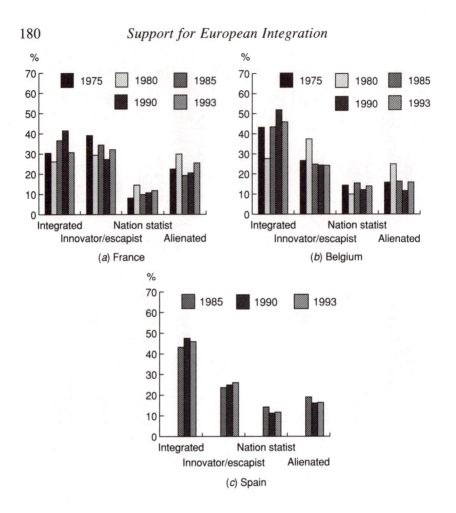

FIGURE 8.9. *The integrated plus innovator/escapist: Belgium, France, and Spain, 1975–93*

Sources: See Figure 8.1.

The Integrated plus Nation Statist

As indicated by the label, the integrated plus nation statist set has a substantial proportion of integrated citizens but a proportion which, with two exceptions, falls short of a majority (see Figure 8.10). The exceptions are West Germany in 1980 and 1990, and Denmark in 1992. The second characteristic of this set of countries is that they have a significant nation-statist segment which outnumbers either the innovators or the alienated. Although West Germany had integrated majorities in 1980 and 1990, it is perhaps the clearest example of the pattern. It has been joined by Denmark since 1985 and, less decisively, by Britain in 1993. If we take account of the sample from the former East Germany to give a picture of orientations in the unified Germany after 1993, we find that the proportion of nation statists drops slightly and that there is a corresponding increase in the proportion of innovators/escapists. However, the change is not sufficient to warrant moving Germany to a different group.

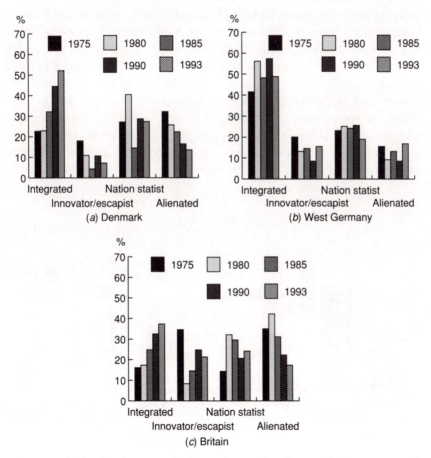

FIGURE 8.10. *The integrated plus nation statist: Denmark, Germany, and Britain, 1975–93*

Sources: See Figure 8.1.

The Predominantly Innovator/Escapist

It was apparent from our earlier discussion that Italy is virtually in a class of its own, in terms of the combined orientations of its citizens towards national and internationalized governance. The uniqueness of Italy is confirmed by the clear and stable majority of citizens who are innovators/escapists. The remainder are either integrated or alienated, and there is a virtual absence of nation statists. Despite the intensifying political crisis in Italy, the distribution of Italian citizens among the four types shows relatively little change between 1975 and 1993.[4]

We have placed Greece in this set as well. It lacks the innovator/escapist majority found in Italy, but, unlike any other country in the Community, innovators/escapists have constituted a clear plurality since 1990. Moreover, like Italy, Greece is marked by the virtual absence of nation statists. Although in this analysis we have avoided going below the level of the nation state, we should note the case of the former East Germany, for which we have only one data point. In 1993 (data not shown here), it belonged to the predominantly innovator-escapist set of countries, having a slightly larger proportion of integrated citizens than Greece but, like Greece, having an innovator/escapist plurality and a very low proportion of nation statists.

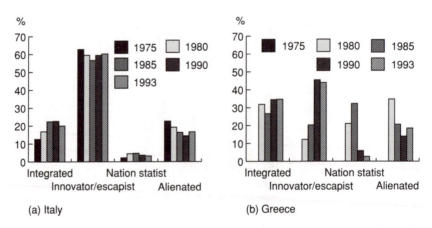

FIGURE 8.11. *The predominantly innovator/escapist: Italy, 1975–93, and Greece, 1990, 1993*

Sources: See Figure 8.1.

Social and Political Correlates of Orientations

The balance between the integrated, the innovators/escapists, the nation statists, and the alienated in any particular country is a function of both historical and contemporary political circumstances. In order to understand the origin and logic of these orientations and their consequences for the Community's dynamics, we would need to delve into the politics of each member state to examine not just the historical background but also the domestic politics and policies, the nature of electoral competition, the ideology and the role of political actors and national interest groups. We cannot perform such an analysis here, but we can broach the question of the sources of the four orientations by analysing to what extent and in which ways certain basic social and political variables are related to these orientations, both across the Community as a whole and within each member country.

The independent variables in this analysis are occupational class, education, age, left-right orientation, frequency of political discussion, and level of awareness of the European Community.[5] The dependent variable is the four types of orientation described in Figure 8.3. As this is a categorical variable, discriminant analysis is an appropriate statistical technique. Our objective is not to provide a comprehensive explanation of why individuals belong to one type rather than another but to see if the variables in question are significantly related to the four types of orientation.

In the discriminant analysis for the European Community as a whole, the independent variables show statistically significant associations with the four types of orientation but the associations are quite weak and the level of discrimination is low. The canonical correlations for the two functions extracted are 0.22 and 0.15. From all that we said earlier about the different patterns in the member states, this is not surprising. One would expect that, given the historical and political context of each state, the incidence of the four types would vary significantly by country and that there would be different configurations of social and political variables associated with each type in the different countries. That this is indeed the case is confirmed by entering into the model dummy variables representing each member state. The canonical correlation coefficient for the first function then increases to 0.36 and for the second function to 0.28. The new first function is defined mainly by the dummy variables representing Italy, Denmark, and Greece.

In light of these results, the most appropriate strategy is to pursue the analysis at the level of the member states. After a preliminary analysis, a single function was extracted for each member state incorporating the variables with significant effects for that country. The functions are reported in Table 8.3.

There are three main items of information in the table. The first is the set of discriminant function coefficients. These can be interpreted in a manner analogous to beta weights in multiple regression analysis, or alternatively, they are similar to the loadings which emerge from factor analysis. The second item of information is the average score on the function of each of the groups defined by the typology. These scores indicate how the groups are arrayed on the dimension, or discriminant function, and which groups are furthest apart and which are closest together. The group scores which are furthest apart are set in bold type. Finally, the first column in the table provides a means of assessing the importance of each of the functions. This is the canonical correlation which is a measure of the ability of the functions to discriminate among the groups.

On the basis of the contrasts in the group scores shown in Table 8.3, the countries can be arranged in two sets. Set A consists of countries where the functions discriminate between the integrated on the one hand and the alienated on the other; in Luxembourg, however, the distinction is between innovators/escapists and the alienated. In set B the functions discriminate between the integrated and the nation statists. In this instance, Britain is a partial exception as the distinction is between innovators/escapists and nation statists.

The contrast between the integrated and the alienated can be seen most clearly in Greece and Denmark. In Greece, being right-wing and having a high level of awareness of the Community are associated with an integrated orientation. In the Danish case, these same two variables play a similar role, with left–right orientation again the dominant variable. However, being middle class and being young are also significantly associated with an integrated orientation in Denmark. At a somewhat lower level of association, the more aware, right-wing, and integrated syndrome appears also in Ireland and Portugal. France shows the same contrast between the integrated and the alienated, with innovators/escapists and nation statists in between. In this case, however, the relevant independent variables are EC awareness and education, with left–right orientation apparently playing no role.

In the second set of countries, the main distinction generated by the combination of independent variables is between the integrated at one

TABLE 8.3. *Discriminant analysis of orientations towards national and internationalized governance, 1992*

	Canonical correlation	Standardized discriminant function coefficients		Average scores			
				Integrated	Innovator/escapist	Nation statist	Alienated
Pattern A							
Greece	0.43	Left–right	0.98	**0.56**	−0.19	−0.21	**−0.75**
		EC awareness	0.31				
Denmark	0.42	Occupational class	0.29	**0.39**	0.13	−0.47	**−0.72**
		Left–right	0.82				
		Age	−0.35				
		EC awareness	0.34				
Ireland	0.25	Occupational class	0.53	**0.16**	0.04	−0.48	**−0.55**
		Left–right	0.24				
		EC awareness	0.67				
France	0.24	Education	0.64	**0.26**	0.10	−0.19	**−0.37**
		EC awareness	0.72				
Portugal	0.24	Education	0.05	**0.16**	−0.01	−0.36	**−0.53**
		Left–right	0.51				
		EC awareness	0.87				
Luxembourg	0.24	Political discussion	0.67	0.06	**0.30**	−0.38	**−0.59**
		Age	0.47				
		EC awareness	0.30				
Pattern B							
West Germany	0.34	Occupational class	0.24	**0.28**	0.14	**−0.64**	−0.24
		Left–right	−0.40				
		EC awareness	0.83				

TABLE 8.3. *Cont.*

	Canonical correlation	Standardized discriminant function coefficients		Average scores			
				Integrated	Innovator/ escapist	Nation statist	Alienated
Britain	0.34	Left–right	0.89	0.01	**-0.60**	**0.46**	0.09
		Political discussion	-0.33				
		EC awareness	-0.36				
Netherlands	0.25	Education	0.21	**0.13**	-0.03	**-0.82**	-0.61
		Age	-0.67				
		EC awareness	0.73				
Spain	0.24	Left–right	0.30	**-0.16**	-0.12	**0.50**	0.34
		Age	0.82				
		EC awareness	-0.44				

Notes: In each case, following preliminary analysis, a single discriminant function was derived. All functions shown are significant at $p \leq .001$ (calculated using Wilk's Lambda). Belgium and Italy were omitted because preliminary analysis showed that the variables had minimal discriminatory power.

Source: Eurobarometer, No. 38.

end and the nation statists at the other. West Germany is the clearest example. In this case, high levels of awareness of the EC, left-wing self-placement, and middle-class occupation are associated with an inte-grated orientation; being less aware, right-wing, and working class are associated with a nation-statist orientation. A somewhat similar combi-nation of independent variables is found in Spain, where nation statists are more likely to be older, to be less aware of the EC, and right-wing. Right-wing orientation and low levels of awareness are also associated with a nation statist position in Britain. Here, however, low levels of political discussion also play a role. Finally, in the Netherlands, the integrated are more aware of the Community, younger, and better educated than nation statists.

The qualification we made earlier bears repetition: in no sense do our findings provide an explanation for the allocation of individuals to the four types of orientation. The association between the dependent variable and the independent variables is not strong enough to warrant such an interpretation. However, the associations are statistically sig-nificant in all cases and moderately strong in a few. With these qualifications in mind, we can summarize the results of our analysis.

Awareness of the Community has a significant effect in all countries. In particular, level of awareness distinguishes between the integrated and the alienated in Ireland, France, and Portugal, and between the integrated and the nation statists in Germany and the Netherlands. The second distinguishing factor is left–right orientation. This plays some role in a majority of the member states and is the dominant factor in Denmark, Greece, and Britain. It plays a moderately strong role in Portugal and Germany. Even so, the effect of left–right orientation varies according to country. Thus, in Denmark, Greece, and Portugal, being right-wing is associated with being integrated rather than alie-nated. In Britain and, to a lessser extent, in Germany, a right-wing position is associated with being a nation statist as opposed to being either an innovator/escapist (the British case) or integrated (the German case).

Conclusion

Our analysis is exploratory. This is so, in particular, because of the limitations which the data impose on operationalizing our key concepts—orientation to the national and supranational systems.

However, even this preliminary exploration confirms that the line of inquiry is interesting and fruitful. It also indicates that the questions raised at the outset are not susceptible to simple answers. There is not a straightforward relationship between satisfaction with democracy at the national level and support for EC membership, nor between dissatisfaction with national democracy and support for membership. On the contrary: the relationship between national and supranational orientations is complex, as evidenced in the systematic variations in the relationships examined here—both between countries and between sets of countries.

Some purchase on this complexity can be obtained from our typology of orientations—the integrated, the innovator/escapist, the nation statist, and the alienated. There has been considerable change in the balance of these orientations in Europe over the last twenty years or so. The proportion of the integrated has increased substantially, mainly at the expense of the nation statists and the alienated. The proportion of innovators/escapists has fallen compared to 1975, when they were actually marginally ahead of the integrated. It should be noted, however, that, having fallen sharply in 1980, since then the proportion of innovators has increased at each time point examined. Nation statists are also more rare than in the early 1980s and the proportion of alienated citizens has declined substantially.

What is most striking, however, is the diversity of orientations revealed by applying this typology at the national level. Placing most weight on the distribution of opinion in 1990 and 1992, we have suggested that the member states can be arranged in four groups: (1) the predominantly integrated (the Netherlands, Luxembourg, Ireland, and Portugal); (2) the integrated plus innovator/escapist (France, Belgium, and Spain); (3) the integrated plus nation statist (Denmark, West Germany, post-unification Germany, and Britain); and (4) the predominantly innovator/escapist (Italy and, with a less clear predominance, Greece). We can also divide the member states on the basis of the social and political variables associated with the types of orientation. In the first pattern, being right-wing and well informed is associated with being integrated, while being left-wing and having a high level of awareness is associated with being alienated. This pattern applies particularly in Greece and Denmark but also in Ireland and Portugal. In the second pattern, being politically right-wing and having low levels of EC awareness are associated with being nation statist rather than integrated (West Germany and Spain) or innovator/escapist (Britain).

However, these associations, while significant, are not particularly strong. Thus, we have to presume that historical and contextual variables have the most effect in shaping the various combinations of attitudes towards governance at the national and international levels. From this perspective, the legitimacy of internationalized governance depends as much on what happens within nation states as on what happens between them.

NOTES

1. The original is in Italian: 'In un certo modo, si tratta comunque di una memoria intenzionale dell'Europa che vuole essere una risposta alla guerra del '39–45, intesa come l'assurda reiterazione delle guerre tra nazioni europee e in particolare tra Francia e Germania. Ma la memoria dei progetti recenti rimanda a quella di progetti lontani nel tempo: da Enrico IV e del suo ministro Sully fino a Kant, passando da Leibniz.'
2. See Ch. 2, where Hoffmann's theory of the obstinacy of the nation state is examined in some detail.
3. The ratio is calculated by dividing the level of positive evaluation of EC membership (see Table 8.2) by the level of satisfaction with democracy (see Table 8.1). Thus, for example, for Italy in 1975, the ratio is 77.1/14.8 = 5.2. Except for Italy, the values of the ratio range from a low of 0.4 (Britain 1980) and a high of 1.8 (Britain 1975). In Italy, the ratio ranges between 2.9 (1985) and 5.5 (1993).
4. This confirms that the wide fluctuations in the ratio of support for EC membership to satisfaction with democracy in the Italian case (see Fig. 8.5) tends to exaggerate the degree of change in orientation among Italians.
5. The index (level of awareness of the EC) was compiled using variables based on the following questions: (i) Have you recently heard or read anything about the EC or not? (ii) All things considered, how well informed do you feel you are about the EC? (iii) Have you recently seen or heard in the papers, on the radio, or on TV, anything about the European Commission? (iv) Have you recently seen or heard in the papers, on the radio or on TV, anything about the European Parliament? (v) Have you recently heard anything about the Summit of the Heads of State and Government of the EC in Maastricht, or about the signing of the Treaty of Maastricht on European Union?

PART III

Levels of Legitimacy

9

Is There a European Identity?

SOPHIE DUCHESNE AND ANDRÈ-PAUL FROGNIER

The dream of the Community's founding fathers was, ultimately, to see the emergence of a European identity. That does not mean that European identity should replace national identities but that it should become strong enough, and be perceived as 'inclusive' enough by European citizens, for Europe to develop as a genuine political entity. How has this dream fared among the citizens of the Community? This is the main question we address in this chapter.

'Identity' is a very general term. We do not intend to examine all the dimensions or components of what might constitute a European identity. Instead, we focus on whether or not European citizens consider themselves members of a political community. In this sense, we are interested in people's sense of political identity—a notion which is close to the concept of citizenship. Specifically, we focus on the relationship between the different levels of 'belonging', from the local to the European, and even the world level, and on the feeling of being a 'European citizen' or 'a European'.

A key question is to determine at what point the link between the individual and the European Community can be considered to amount to an 'identity'. As the institutions of the EC have largely been created independently of the expressed will of national populations, we might anticipate that people's attitudes are basically instrumental. The people of the Community could very well have formed a favourable opinion of the EC as an effective decision-making system—in the economic field

We thank Anne-Marie Aish for her methodological support and Benoit Rihoux for computations and translation.

or in specific policy areas such as the environment or international relations—without developing any genuinely 'identitive' link to it as a political community. According to this hypothesis, the fact that they are European citizens would not intrude on people's self-definition.

One difficulty here is that, although the question about identity in the Eurobarometer surveys seems to elicit responses in terms of a feeling of belonging, this might be merely an indicator of instrumental evaluations rather than affective orientations. Our first task, then, is to investigate the extent to which responses to this question differ from responses to the four 'support questions' used in Chapter 4 ('unification', 'membership', 'dissolution', and 'benefit'). For sure, simply on account of the 'spill-over' process of European integration, we do not expect these questions to produce entirely independent responses. None the less, we have to check whether or not there exists a dimension which we can interpret as a European 'identity'.

We also need to investigate the relationships between this putative 'new' identity and national identities. It is likely that this new 'European identity' does not emerge *ex nihilo* but, rather, is built on the basis of existing identities—particularly, of course, national identities. This will lead us to explore the alleged 'antagonism' between national and European identity. Indeed, both Hoffmann (1966) and Inglehart (1970*a*) have hypothesized that national identity is the springboard, not the gravedigger, of European identity, with national identity providing a model of what it is to belong to a remote political community.

This hypothesis highlights two important elements in the development of political identity: education and 'cognitive mobilization' (Inglehart 1970*a*, 1977*b*, 1990). Hence, we extend our analysis to take in a number of socio-demographic variables which can be supposed to interact with education and cognitive mobilization: age, income, gender, and size of locality. We also consider the influence of several political variables, particularly party identification, left–right orientation, postmaterialist values, and satisfaction with democracy. Only then do we attempt to assess the relationship between the evaluative and identitive dimensions which are at issue when one considers people's feeling of belonging to the EC. This will bring us back to the relationship between national and European identity.

European Identity, 1975–1979

One of the questions in the Eurobarometer surveys seems particularly appropriate for measuring European identity. It was asked in 1975, 1978, and 1979, and was explicitly formulated in terms of belonging: 'To which one of the following geographical units would you say you belong to first of all: the locality or town where you live; the region or county where you live; [name of the country] as a whole; Europe; the world as a whole?' Respondents were asked to state a first and second preference. The average percentages of the first and second choice over the three time points are displayed in Figure 9.1. [1]

The pattern of responses is pretty much alike across the countries. In the aggregate, 'Europe' and 'the world' were consistently marginal, whereas in all cases 'country' and 'town' were either the first or second preference among some two-thirds, even three-quarters, of respondents. But 'town' shows much higher percentages as first choice than 'country', except in France and Britain (and Denmark in 1979). For example, in 1978, 60 per cent of Irish respondents mentioned their town as a first choice, while 25 per cent mentioned their country; the gap was even greater in Belgium and Germany.

Although 'country' and 'town' share the first place in all cases, followed by the region in third place, there are some differences. In Belgium, Germany, and Denmark, the town is by far the dominant choice; in 1979, for example, 'town' was either first or second choice among three-quarters of respondents. The other alternatives always followed in the order: the country, the region, Europe, and the world. In contrast, in France, the Netherlands, Italy, and particularly in Britain, 'country' dominates, gathering some 60–75 per cent of respondents' first and second choices. Generally, the region and the town share second place, while Europe and the world share fourth place. Ireland is the only country in which the structure of responses varies from one year to the other, with the country and the town alternatively obtaining the highest score.

In most instances, 'Europe' is in fourth position. Between 1 and 9 per cent of the whole sample selected Europe as their first choice; between 6 and 26 per cent selected Europe as either first or second choice. Again, in most instances, there is little point in searching for trends because the percentages are too low and the observed variations seldom significant. But it is worth noting that in the Netherlands and Ireland there was a perceptible growth in the 'Europe' choice (particularly as a

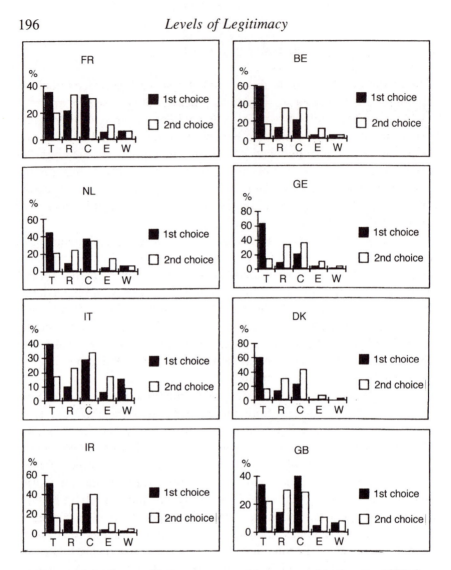

FIGURE 9.1. *Sense of belonging to various geographical units, 1975–9*

Notes: Entries are the average percentages for 1975, 1978, and 1979; T = town; R = region; C = country; E = Europe; W = world

Sources: Eurobarometer, Nos. 6, 10*a*, and 12.

second choice) whereas in Germany and Denmark there was a perceptible decline.

With such uniformly low percentages, this question about 'belonging' provides an inadequate basis for classifying the 'Europeanness' of the member countries. However, two countries can be singled out as extreme cases: Italy, where some 20–25 per cent of respondents chose Europe as the unit to which they belong (either as first or second choice); and Denmark, where the proportion feeling they belonged to Europe reached 6 per cent in 1979 (and less than 1 per cent as first choice). Finally, we might note that 'Europe' and 'the world' obtain similar scores in France, Italy, and Britain, whereas in Belgium, the Netherlands, Germany, Denmark, and Ireland, the proportion selecting 'Europe' is often about twice as high as 'the world'.

European Identity, 1982–1991

To examine developments since 1979, we rely on a question in which respondents were asked to state if it occurs to them 'often', 'sometimes', or 'never' that they are not only citizens of their country but also citizens of Europe. The question wording varies from one survey to another, and from one country to another; in particular, the term 'citizen' appears in some formulations of the question but not others.[2] Even so, we consider the wordings sufficiently similar to allow comparisons.

The average results for this indicator over eight time points between 1982 and 1992 are displayed in Figure 9.2. In Figure 9.3 we display a 'net' measure of identity through time, calculated by subtracting the proportion of 'never' responses from the proportion of 'often' and 'sometimes' responses. However, this measure does not yield an unequivocal classification of the 'Europeanness' of each country since the identity variable is not dichotomous. Our estimates depend on whether one considers 'sometimes' to be nearer to 'often' or 'never'. We opted for the first alternative, especially as it is better suited for making comparisons with the indicators of support for integration— even though it risks overestimating European identity.

The most 'European' countries are assuredly France, Italy, Greece, Spain, and Portugal. It is in these countries—except Portugal—that we usually observe the highest percentage of 'often' answers as well as the lowest percentage of 'never' answers. Germany and Portugal show fairly similar means but opposite trends. Portugal is a stable case, and rather inclined to Europeanism. Germany, however, one of the most favourably disposed countries in 1982, shows such a steadily downward trend during this period that, by the early 1990s, German levels of

'Europeanness' were among the lowest in the Community. The least 'European' countries are Britain and Ireland, although there is an upwards trend in both. Belgium and Denmark show more middle-of-the-road positions, and the Netherlands tends to come closer to Britain and Ireland.

Figure 9.4 displays responses to the European identity question alongside responses to the indicators of support for European integration discussed in Chapter 4: attitudes towards unification, EC membership, possible dissolution of the EC, and benefits associated with participation in the EC.[3] Thus, we can compare evaluations of the EC and people's sense of European identity.

Clearly, the level of European identity is consistently lower than the level of positive attitudes towards the EC. This might perhaps be explained by the differential rhythms of political integration, with instrumental acceptance being relatively rapid whereas affective involvement is more internalized and thereby slower.[4] However, although the level of the identity variable is clearly lower than the levels of the other variables, the shape of the curve is quite similar for the beginning

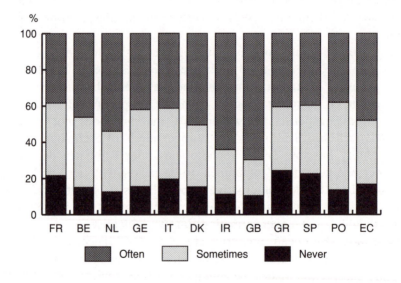

FIGURE 9.2. *Average sense of European identity, 1982–92*

Notes: Entries are average proportions in each category of response over eight time points. For question wording see n. 2 in text. Weighted data.

Sources: Eurobarometer, Nos. 17, 19, 24, 26, 30, 31, 33, 35, and 37.

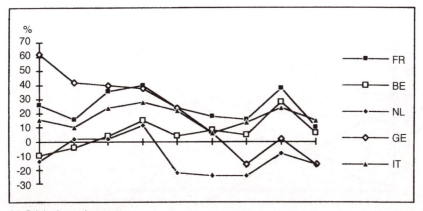

(a) Original member states

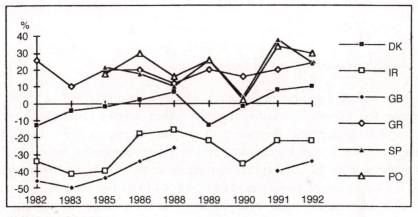

(b) New member states

FIGURE 9.3. *Net sense of European identity in original and new member states, 1982–92*

Notes: Entries are the proportion of 'Often' and 'Sometimes' responses minus the proportion of 'Never' responses.

Sources: See Figure 9.2.

and the end of the period.[5] More precisely, three distinct periods are evident from Figure 9.4.

The first period is 1982–6 during which, despite a decline in 1983, there is a general increase in consciousness of European identity, Germany being the notable exception (see Figure 9.3). Except for evaluations of benefits from EC membership, the EC support variables also increase in strength in this period. The second period is 1986–90

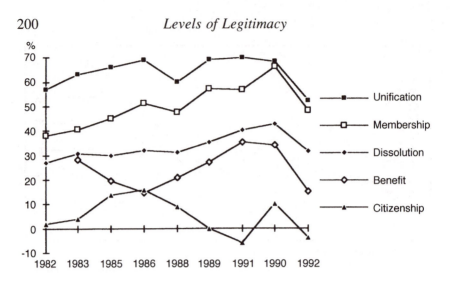

FIGURE 9.4. *Net support for the EC and sense of European identity,*
1982–92

Sources: Eurobarometer, Nos. 17, 19, 24, 26, 30, 31, 33, 35, and 37.

when we find a decline in European identity, mainly in 1989 or 1990, while the support variables remain rather stable (unification) or increased in strength—despite a short-term reverse in 1988. Clearly there is some loss of the sense of European identity among the original members of the EC, and sometimes the decline is abrupt. For example, in the Netherlands 'never' increases from 44 to 62 per cent; in France, 'never' increases from 30 to 42 per cent. But in Germany, the decline is continuous, the 'never European' group increasing from 31 to 58 per cent! The more recent members of the EC again show more differentiated development. European identity progressed in Denmark, Britain, and Ireland in 1989 but fell back in 1990. The position in Greece is largely stationary, whereas there are ups and downs in Spain and Portugal but with a noticeable decline in European identity in 1990.

The third period is 1990–2 when there was a general increase in European identity in 1991 followed by a sudden fall. The support variables show a rather similar trend for 'dissolution' and 'membership' in 1991, then the fall is general. A glance back at Figure 9.3 shows that this picture is clearest among the original members of the EC, with more recent members again showing more differentiated development. Among these more recent member states, a negative trend is evident only in Spain and Portugal, but from a high starting point, whereas in

Denmark, Britain, and Ireland, European identity progresses, but from a relatively low starting point.

These results clearly run counter to the hypothesis that the sense of European identity depends on the length of EC membership. First, the turning points of 1986–8 and 1991–2 question the idea of a steady increase in this form of belonging; attitudes in the EC founding member states do not seem any more stable than attitudes among more recent member states. Secondly, differences in the levels of the responses do not justify contrasting older and newer member states: early members, especially Germany and the Netherlands, suffer the larger decline during the period; the sense of identity is higher in Greece and Spain than in Britain and Ireland.

We might try to explain the 1986 peak in the sense of European identity, followed by an abrupt decline in 1988, as a consequence of the extension of the EC to Spain and Portugal in 1985, reflecting fear of increased competition in fields such as agrarian policy. However, Greece, the main potential victim of this new competition, is one of the few countries in which European identity does not decline. Alternatively, the downturn might reflect concern amongst northern countries about a southern over-extension of the EC. In that case, we would have to explain the increased sense of European identity in Denmark in 1990.

Another explanation for peaks in the sense of European identity might be the 'notoriety' effect. The 1986 peak perhaps reflected heightened attention to the EC following the 1985 Single European Act while the 1991 peak reflected the 'notoriety' of the EC in the run up to the Maastricht Treaty. If so, the effect is short lived, for the sense of European identity had dropped again by 1988 and by 1992. Moreover, the support variables behaved differently in the wake of these peaks, showing either stability or modest decline after 1986 but a very similar sharp decline after 1991. Probably more to the point is that the Maastricht Treaty represents a much bigger jump towards European identity, a jump into the unknown before the feeling of belonging has had time to stabilize. Indeed, we might surmise that it is not overall evaluations of the Community which have a negative impact on the sense of European identity and citizenship, but, rather, that the approaching reality of European citizenship has a negative impact on evaluations.

National and European Identity

Earlier we noted the view that the completion of European integration would require the creation of a 'supranational' identity, which, some have argued, would be at the expense of national identities. To test this claim, we should see, first, if the two identities are related. We can use the question about 'national pride' in the Eurobarometer data as an indicator of national identity: 'Would you say you are very proud, quite proud, not very proud, not at all proud, to be [nationality]?' In several surveys, this question has been asked at the same time as the question about European identity. In Table 9.1, we report the correlations between national pride and European identity in member states at five time points.

Even a quick look at the correlation coefficients reveals that there is no direct relationship between declaring pride in one's nationality and considering oneself to have a European identity. The coefficients are low and they fluctuate from one year to the other, whereas we would have expected them to be relatively stable. Even worse, in several instances the direction of the relationship switches from one year to another. In other words, the hypothesis of an 'antagonism' between national pride and European identity does not stand up against the data. In so far as they are related, it seems—at least in France, Belgium, Italy,

TABLE 9.1. *Relationship between national pride and sense of European identity, 1982–8*

	1982	1983	1985	1986	1988
France	0.15	0.08	0.07	0.07	−0.03
Belgium	0.10	0.04	0.01	−0.06	−0.02
Netherlands	−0.01	−0.03	−0.10	−0.07	−0.06
Germany	0.18	−0.04	0.11	−0.03	−0.04
Italy	0.07	0.09	0.02	−0.01	0.00
Denmark	−0.00	0.04	0.05	0.05	0.03
Ireland	0.01	−0.02	−0.03	0.00	−0.03
Britain	−0.02	−0.06	−0.03	−0.09	−0.09
Greece	−0.03	−0.02	−0.08	−0.07	−0.11
Spain	—	—	−0.01	0.12	−0.06
Portugal	—	—	0.11	0.00	0.02

Note: Entries are correlation coefficients (Pearson's *r*).

Sources: Eurobarometer, Nos. 17, 19, 24, 26, and 30.

Denmark, and Greece—that this relationship is quite the opposite of what might be expected: national pride tends to foster the development of European identity.

The weakness and instability of the coefficients are not sufficient evidence of the independence of the two variables, however. There are two other possibilities: that there is a linear relationship but it is disrupted by a third variable; that there is a relationship but it is non-linear, and thus cannot be detected by correlation analysis. To examine the first possibility, we assumed that age, education level, or political orientation might be intervening variables. For example, perhaps national pride and European identity are positively correlated among respondents on the political left but negatively correlated among respondents on the right. However, all our attempts to uncover a significant intervening variable came to nothing.[6]

The second possibility, that the relationship is non-linear, stems from evidence that a subjective sense of national belonging is the outcome of two distinct processes.[7] The first is a genuine identification process, since calling oneself 'French' (Belgian, German, . . .) is an assertion about being part of a community. It is about inheriting nationality, about acknowledging duties towards one's country based on fidelity and gratitude to those who made the country what it is—rather than *a priori* sympathy or solidarity with fellow nationals. The ties uniting people with their country are very emotional and give rise to love as well as anger. In that sense, to say that one is 'very proud' or 'not proud' to be French (Italian, or Spanish, . . .) are opposite poles of the same process of belonging.[8] According to the other process, more appropriately referred to as 'attachment' rather than belonging, individuals consider their birth and life in a particular country as fortuitous. They may call themselves French (Danish, English, . . .),[9] but their attachment to the national community is based on recognizing that living in this particular country produces a certain community of interests, habits, and feelings. Duties are balanced against benefits. Although people probably say that life is rather better in their own country than abroad, the affective dimension of their 'national consciousness' remains limited. We expect such people to say that they are 'rather' or 'not very proud' to be French (Dutch, Portuguese, . . .) as their orientation towards national identity, positive or negative, is weak.

In our view, these two modes of belonging constitute a fundamental characteristic of the individual which goes far beyond the question of national identity. Some people feel the need to define themselves in relation to the different circles in which they move, whereas others do not, despite objectively 'belonging' in such circles. The internationalization of the feeling of belonging is an extension of the same process at the national level. People who fully identify with their country will tend to identify with Europe as well, provided 'Europe' is visible enough— hence the importance of the cognitive variable. Similarly, those who are merely attached to their country will also be only attached to Europe. The outcome of both these processes of identification and attachment can be positive or negative, but the key distinction is the different intensities of feeling to which they give rise. Thus, we consider being 'very proud' or 'not proud at all' of one's nationality as indicators of national identification (positive or negative), and 'rather proud' or 'not very proud' as indicators of national attachment. Similarly, at the European level, we treat 'often' or 'never' feeling oneself European as measuring European identification, and 'sometimes' as measuring European attachment. If our hypothesis about the internationalization of identification and attachment is valid, cross-tabulation of the two variables should reveal a structure to these attitudes, as depicted in Table 9.2.

We should find over-representation in the (+) cells, indicating that the same identification process is operating at both the national and the European level. That is, according to our hypothesis, people who identify positively with their nation—by saying they are 'very proud' of being French, Belgian, and so on—also identify positively or negatively with Europe. On the other hand, people who just feel attached to their nation, and are 'rather proud' or 'not very proud' of their nationality are more likely to think only sometimes of themselves as European. Our findings from cross-tabulating the two variables at four time points are shown in Table 9.3.

TABLE 9.2. *Expected structure of attitudes towards European identity and national pride*

National pride	European citizenship		
	Often	Sometimes	Never
Very proud	+	−	+
Rather proud	−	+	−
Not very proud	−	+	−
Not proud at all	+	−	+

TABLE 9.3. *Cross-tabulation between national pride and European identity, 1983–8*

National pride	European identity		
	Often	Sometimes	Never
1983			
Very proud	+14	−14	+5
Rather proud	−9	16	−4
Not very proud	+1	9	−6
Not proud at all	+36	−18	0
1985			
Very proud	+12	−11	+3
Rather proud	−14	14	−3
Not very proud	+5	0	−1
Not proud at all	+29	−8	−4
1986			
Very proud	+9	−10	+5
Rather proud	−17	+13	−3
Not very proud	+7	+6	−8
Not proud at all	+56	−32	+2
1988			
Very proud	+2	−9	+6
Rather proud	−8	+9	−4
Not very proud	+6	+2	−4
Not proud at all	+46	−12	−5

Notes: Entries indicate over-representation in comparison with expectations of independence, calculated according to the margins of the table. To obtain the over-representations, the proportional differences between observed and expected frequencies were computed.

Sources: Eurobarometer, Nos. 19, 24, 26, and 30.

A close look at the table reveals a picture which broadly conforms with what we expected. However, the over-representations in the table are generally weak (the chi-square is seldom significant), and the structure varies from one country to another. Even so, we should note the high over-representation in the bottom left cells, in which being 'not proud at all of one's nationality' goes along with 'often feels a European citizen'. This is probably a compensation process: people who need to define themselves as belonging to something but who, for some reason, lack national identity may find in the European community a valid object of identification.

Do we have to conclude, then, that European identity grows

independently of national pride? This would tend to confirm Hoffmann's claim (1966) that for people who have achieved statehood, 'national consciousness' is neutral. National identity does not imply hostility towards other nations or towards internationalization processes, for 'it is perfectly conceivable that a nation convinces itself that its 'cohesion and distinctiveness' will be best preserved in a larger entity' (Hoffman 1966: 867). This possibility calls for further exploration of the notion 'national pride'.

To assess more precisely what 'national pride' really measures, we recall Michelat and Thomas's (1966) study of the dimensions of nationalism.[10] One dimension is national pride, centred on the feeling of being better characterized by one's nationality than by one's adherence to other communities. In the typology of various kinds of nationalism, this 'belonging to the nation' is characteristic of left-wing nationalism, which they label 'affective nationalism'. This is described as a 'nationalism of belonging, which accepts the determinism of the national fact', but is free of 'the feeling . . . of this nation's superiority over others' and ideological or dogmatic content (Michelat and Thomas 1966: 119). National pride would thus be the expression of a neutral feeling, in Hoffman's meaning of the term, since it refers to belonging to the nation without implying superiority or hostility towards other nations. It is thus not surprising that 'national pride' varies independently of 'belonging to Europe', provided the latter is not understood in terms of exclusivity or opposition. [11]

Other data tend to confirm this interpretation. In 1987 and 1988, the Eurobarometer asked a question designed to measure to what extent European unification is perceived as hostile or favourable to national identities and national interests. Respondents were asked to indicate, on a seven-point scale, how they stand as between two propositions: (1) 'If one day the countries of Europe were really united, this would mark the end of our national, historic, cultural identities and our national economic interests would be sacrified'; (2) 'The only way of protecting our national, historic, cultural identities and our national economic interests against a challenge put up by the Great World Powers is for the countries of Europe to become truly united.' Responses to this question (data not shown here) proved totally independent of national pride.[12] This confirms that 'pride' measures a dimension of national identity which is not centred on the fear of losing national identity. Thus 'national pride' is not opposed to the process of internationalization, nor, moreover, is it a determinant of attitudes towards the EC.

Belonging and Attachment

We can tackle the question of identity from another direction. Even if one or more dimension(s) of nationalism are, indeed, indifferent to the internationalization of governance, it seems improbable that a feeling of belonging to an international community would arise without any reference to the pre-existing systems of belonging, especially belonging to the national community. To see how these different levels of belonging fit together, we return to the question asked in 1976, 1978, and 1979: 'to which one of the following geographical units . . . do you feel that you belong, in the first place? And in the second place?'

Unfortunately, this question does not express different intensities as between one level and another. However, since all the levels are on an equal footing, we shall assume that the sense of belonging is the same for each level. To analyse the structure of the relationships between the various levels of belonging, we have calculated the under- and over-representation of the second choices compared with the first choices. This is shown in Table 9.4.[13] In particular, those whose first choice is their town are expected to choose their region or their country as second choice more often than they would if the first and second choices were independent.

The table represents a synthesis of the structures which are observed in all eight countries [14] and at each of the three time points. The positive and negative signs indicate that the combination of first and second

TABLE 9.4. *Over- and under-representation of second choice of belonging according to first choice*

First choice	Second choice				
	Town	Region	Country	Europe	World
Town	*	+	+	−	−
Region	+	*	0	(−)	(−)
Country	+	−	*	0	+
Europe	0	−	(+)	*	(+)
World	0	(−)	0	+	*

Notes: Plus signs indicate over-representation; minus signs indicate under-representation. Brackets around a sign indicate that one or two countries are exceptions to the pattern of over- or under-representation. Zeros indicate no dominant pattern. The diagonal cells, which are by definition empty, are indicated by asterisks.

choices is over- or under-represented in all the countries; the signs in brackets indicate that there is a tendency towards over- or under-representation but that one or two countries, at most, are exceptions to the pattern. The zeros indicate that there is no dominant pattern—both over- and under-representation of that combination is found.

The feelings of belonging are clearly structured around the local and international poles, with 'country' appearing as an intermediate level. Those whose first choice is their town or their region or district tend to choose either the other local level or their country as a second choice. Europe and the world are under-represented in these second choices. By contrast, those whose first choice is 'Europe' tend to favour the world as a second choice, and vice versa. Those whose first choice is their country tend to select either their town or Europe, or even the world (in Britain, Belgium, France, Ireland, and the Netherlands) as their second choice. But in all these cases, 'region' or 'district' is under-represented as a second choice.

In other words, identification with one's country, Europe, and the world do not stand in opposition at all. This confirms the impression one gains from observing the evolution of the choices from one year to the other: whenever choices favouring 'Europe' and 'the world' increase, they seem to do so to the disadvantage of 'town' and 'region', but seldom to the detriment of 'country'. These tendencies can be found in all countries except Britain and the Netherlands, where, moreover, the variables measuring 'national pride' and 'European identity' tended to be negatively correlated.

According to these results, it seems that the development of a European identity—at least in the later 1970s—is accompanied by the weakening of local attachments, not the weakening of national identities. These results also question notions of 'Europe of the Regions': the priority of belonging to a region appears to be at odds with a feeling of belonging to Europe. When the local level is over-represented among those whose first choice is Europe or the world, it is the town—not the region—which is selected.

These findings support the view that it is the nation which enables the individual to learn abstract solidarity stripped of personal life experiences, the very type of solidarity which is needed at the European level. In this respect, our findings concur with Inglehart's (1977*b*: 337) description of the relationship between support for the European and the national levels: 'The two levels tend to function as one cosmopolitan communications network rather than as separate competing networks.' Inglehart then goes on to attribute this linkage to cognitive mobilization, which 'increases the individual's capacity to receive and interpret messages relating to a remote political community. As such, the process is a necessary but not sufficient condition for the development of support for a European Community; one must be aware of it before one can develop a sense of commitment.' Accordingly, we now turn to analyse the effects of the main social and political variables which might be influential at the individual level, especially education and cognitive mobilization.

Socio-Demographic Correlates of European Identity

The main socio-demographic variables available in all the Eurobarometer surveys for this period are education level (measured by school-leaving age), income (in quartiles), gender, size of locality (rural municipalities, small and middle-size towns, and large towns), and age (divided into four groups). The correlation coefficients between the independent variables and the feeling of European identity in the member states over time are presented in Table 9.5. Except for age, the relationships follow much the same pattern, although the strength of the relationships vary.

Educational level shows the strongest relationship to a feeling of European identity. In all instances, a larger proportion of the highly educated respondents state that they 'often' consider themselves European, and a smaller proportion of them give the 'never' answer. Exactly the opposite obtains among respondents who left school at fifteen or younger. The correlations between education and the feeling of European identity are sometimes quite high; for example, 0.30 and 0.32 respectively in Greece and Portugal in 1986. Indeed, in Portugal (1986), a mere 10 per cent of the less educated responded 'often' compared with 36 per cent of those who, at twenty, were still studying; conversely, 43 per cent of the former give the 'never' answer, compared with 14 per cent of the latter. Similarly, differences in pro-EC feelings according to education level are commonly in the 20–40 per cent range in Spain, Greece, and Britain. But the influence of education is somewhat weaker in other countries. In Denmark, for example, in 1983, educational level produces variations in the 6–10 per cent range.

Income is the second most influential variable, although its effect is

TABLE 9.5. *Relationship between socio-demographic variables and sense of European identity, 1983–91*

	Age	Age left school	Gender	Size of locality	Income
France					
1983	−0.14				
1985		−0.15		−0.12	−0.11
1986					−0.14
1988		−0.19	0.11		−0.15
1991		−0.16	0.11		−0.17
Belgium					
1983		−0.20			
1985		−0.18			
1986		−0.21		−0.14	−0.18
1988	0.10	−0.16			−0.15
1991		−0.26			−0.21
Netherlands					
1983		−0.16		−0.12	
1985		−0.15	0.11		−0.12
1986		−0.22			
1988		−0.14			−0.12
1991		−0.12			
Germany					
1983		−0.11			
1985					
1986		−0.21		−0.10	
1988	0.14	−0.16	0.11		
1991	0.15	−0.24			−0.09

	Age	Age left school	Gender	Size of locality	Income
Ireland					
1983		−0.14			−0.13
1985		−0.19		−0.14	−0.14
1986		−0.14		−0.13	−0.15
1988		−0.18	0.12		−0.15
1991		−0.22			−0.31
Britain					
1983		−0.13			
1985		−0.15	0.10		
1986		−0.13			
1988		−0.15	0.14		
1991		−0.22	0.11		−0.20
Greece					
1983	0.11	−0.19	0.23		−0.20
1985	0.21	−0.26			−0.21
1986	0.22	−0.28	0.15	−0.11	−0.21
1988	0.16	−0.30	0.12	−0.15	−0.28
1991	0.15	−0.29	0.13		−0.21
Spain					
1985	0.13	−0.25	0.13		−0.19
1986		−0.21		−0.15	−0.23
1988	0.12	−0.22	0.17		−0.20
1991	0.14	−0.21	0.14		−0.21

Italy					
1983	−0.24	−0.14		0.13	−0.30
1985	−0.24			0.11	−0.25
1986	−0.22	−0.10		0.18	−0.20
1988	−0.19	−0.12		0.12	−0.21
1991	−0.22	−0.12		0.13	
Portugal					
1985	−0.25	−0.14	0.19	0.14	−0.13
1986	−0.32		0.20		−0.15
1988	−0.19	−0.10			−0.16
1991	−0.15	−0.12	0.18	0.15	−0.13
Denmark					
1983		−0.12			−0.07
1985		0.12			
1986		0.11			−0.05
1988	−0.17	0.12			−0.05
1991	−0.14	0.11			−0.05
EC					
1983	−0.16		0.05	0.07	−0.09
1985	−0.16		0.03	0.08	−0.10
1986	−0.17		0.06	0.09	−0.10
1988	−0.16		0.07	0.12	−0.13
1991	−0.20	−0.13		0.11	−0.15

Notes: Entries are correlation coefficients (Pearson's *r*). Only coefficients significant at $p < 0.001$ are shown. The 'age left school' education variable was coded as those who left school at 15 years or younger, those who have completed their studies between 16 and 19 years, and those who continued to 20 years or older. The EC results are based on weighted data.

Sources: Eurobarometer, Nos. 19, 24, 26, 30, and 35.

less predictable than education. For instance, none of the correlation coefficients for Germany, Denmark, and Britain is significant except in 1991. Moreover, in some cases, such as Germany in 1983, the proportion of respondents in the lowest income quartile who 'often' feel they are European citizens is higher than among the highest income quartile. Some statistically significant but none the less weak relationships can be detected in France, Belgium, the Netherlands, Italy, and Ireland. But interestingly, with coefficients often exceeding 0.20, income displays a stronger impact on feelings of European citizenship in the southern countries than in the other member states. Indeed, the impact of income is greater than the impact of educational level in Portugal.

Gender is also a differentiating factor in that, generally, men more often consider themselves to be European than women. Even so, the coefficients are weak,[15] except in the Mediterranean countries. In the tables, we find differences of up to 20 per cent between male and female respondents: in the 1986 data, for example, 40 per cent of Italian men 'never' considered themselves to be European compared to 60 per cent of Italian women. Differences between the attitudes of men and women are becoming narrower in contemporary European societies, and feelings about European identity are no exception. However, this has to be seen in the light of greater educational opportunities for women. Some discrepancies remain but notably less so among the highly educated.

Where people live exerts little influence on feelings of 'Europeanness'. But one difference is observed throughout the Community: people living in urban areas are more likely 'often' to feel themselves to be European than people living in rural areas. This relationship is only significant in Ireland, Greece, and, especially, in Portugal. In 1985, among urban Portuguese respondents, 15 per cent 'always' considered themselves to be European and 35 per cent 'never' thought of themselves as European; the corresponding figures among rural respondents were 7 per cent and 47 per cent. All things considered, however, the impact of locality is decidedly modest.

Finally, age is not perceptibly related to feelings about European identity except in Greece, Spain, and Portugal. Not only are the correlations seldom significant, but we also find contradictory trends. In the three most recent member states, it is younger respondents who are more likely 'often' to feel European, whereas in the other member states the feeling of belonging to Europe is stronger amongst older respondents. In Britain, the two variables are entirely independent of each other in each instance. But in the newer member states differences between young and old in the degree of subjective 'Europeanness' rise to as high as 30 per cent.

In assessing these findings, we can separate the countries into two groups. On the one hand, we have countries such as Greece, Portugal, Spain, and, to a lesser extent, Ireland and Italy, where socio-demographic factors clearly influence attitudes towards European identity. On the other hand, in countries such as Denmark, Britain, and even Germany and France, the feeling of belonging to the EC seems to be quite independent of these factors. In the first group of countries, the correlations between education and income are particularly strong (above 0.40): the stronger the influence of education, the greater the influence of income. This suggests that the level of economic development in a country influences, in a specific way, the development of individual feelings of belonging to Europe. In those countries where economic development is more recent and less advanced, the feeling of belonging to Europe is much more dependent on socio-demographic factors than in more economically advanced countries. To put it simply: if we classify EC member states according to the relative impact of socio-demographic factors on the feeling of belonging to Europe, the ordering corresponds closely to a classification of the countries on the basis of gross national product per capita.

Political Correlates of European Identity

In his work on political integration, Inglehart associates both the national and supranational level of belonging not only with a process of cognitive mobilization but also with 'postmaterialist' value change. Cognitive mobilization is a concept derived from Deutsch's notion of 'social mobilization', defined as 'the . . . distribution of the political skills necessary to cope with an extensive political community' (Deutsch 1961: 47). The shift to postmaterialism amounts to stressing the quality of life rather than material considerations such as security and economic well-being.

Inglehart's arguments have been challenged from several directions. In particular, Janssen (1991) shows that if both cognitive mobilization and postmaterialism are linked with a cosmopolitan sense of belonging to Europe, then cognitive mobilization renders spurious the link between postmaterialism and the sense of Europeanness. The rationale behind the argument is that today's Europe is more oriented towards economic development and trade than towards values. In short: it is difficult to associate postmaterialism with the question of potato prices!

To test these claims we examined the effects of five political variables on European identity: two variables measuring 'political mobilization' (cognitive mobilization and party identification) and three variables measuring 'political values' (postmaterialism; left–right self-placement; and satisfaction with democracy). Table 9.6 shows the correlations between these five variables and European identity for the time points when all the relevant variables are available for analysis.[16]

We consider cognitive mobilization first, operationalized as an 'opinion leadership' index based on the frequency of political discussion and trying to persuade others to one's own opinion (see also Chapter 6). [17] It is evident from the table that cognitive mobilization is significantly correlated with European identity. The coefficients are significant in every country and in every year, and they have the highest values of all the coefficients in the table. The lower values in Britain and Denmark are the only notable differences between countries. For the EC as a whole, we see a drop in the correlations in 1986 and some recovery in 1988, followed by a decline again in 1991. This general pattern across the Community as a whole is principally reflected in France, Belgium, Italy, the Netherlands, and Portugal.

These results accord with Inglehart's findings about the importance of cognitive mobilization. However, the relationship between cognitive mobilization and identity is more complex than appears at first sight. In particular, we find that variations in the strength of the correlations go in the opposite direction to changes in the proportion of people who feel they are European—which increased in 1986, declined in 1988, and increased again in 1991! This is accounted for, in part, by growing polarization. The contingency tables for the two variables (not shown here) reveal that, between 1986 and 1988, among those of high or fairly high cognitive mobilization, there was an increase across the Community as a whole in both the proportion of people who 'often' feel European and people who 'never' feel European. In 1991, when European identity increases but the correlations with cognitive mobilization are lower, there was an increase in the proportion who 'never' feel European among the cognitively more highly mobilized.[18]

Party identification has a more variable and generally weaker influence than cognitive mobilization. Across the Community as a whole,

TABLE 9.6. *Relationship between five political variables and sense of European identity, 1983–91*

	Cognitive mobilization	Party identification	Left–right	Materialist–postmaterialist	Satisfaction with democracy
France					
1983	0.21	0.19			
1985	0.24	0.17		−0.11	0.14
1986	0.12	0.13		−0.16	
1988	0.23	0.17		−0.20	
1991	0.17			−0.10	0.17
Belgium					
1983	0.29	0.12		−0.16	
1985	0.33			−0.18	
1986	0.25	0.14		−0.19	
1988	0.23	0.21		−0.16	n.a.
1991	0.25	0.16		−0.15	
Netherlands					
1983	0.26	0.12		−0.13	
1985	0.22	0.16	0.11	−0.17	
1986	0.19		0.10	−0.12	
1988	0.18			−0.10	n.a.
1991	0.24				
Germany					
1983	0.17	0.12	0.13	−0.23	
1985	0.28	0.15			0.10
1986	0.30	0.13		−0.14	
1988	0.25	0.15		−0.17	n.a.
1991	0.26				0.13
Italy					
1983	0.28	0.11		−0.17	
1985	0.31	0.15		−0.17	
1986	0.25	0.11		−0.18	
1988	0.27			−0.16	n.a.
1991	0.31				
Denmark					
1983	0.17		−0.15		
1985	0.12		−0.13		0.11
1986	0.13		−0.19		
1988	0.17	0.21	−0.13		n.a.
1991	0.13		−0.14		0.10
Ireland					
1983	0.21	0.13		−0.13	
1985	0.20				
1986	0.19		0.12	−0.11	
1988	0.26				n.a.
1991	0.19				

TABLE 9.6. *Cont.*

	Cognitive mobilization	Party identification	Left–right	Materialist–postmaterialist	Satisfaction with democracy
Britain					
1983	0.17				
1985	0.11	0.11			
1986	0.15	0.12			
1988	0.27	0.15		−0.11	n.a.
1991	0.25	0.08			
Greece					
1983	0.18				
1985	0.22			−0.12	
1986	0.24			−0.17	
1988	0.24	0.15		−0.13	n.a.
1991	0.20		−0.20		0.21
Spain					
1985	0.23	0.17		−0.21	
1986	0.26	0.14	0.15	−0.14	0.18
1988	0.30	0.16	0.11	−0.14	n.a.
1991	0.23				
Portugal					
1985	0.29	0.16		−0.14	
1986	0.23	0.11			
1988	0.27	0.21		−0.11	n.a.
1991	0.33				
EC					
1983	0.23	0.12	0.07	−0.12	
1985	0.23	0.14	0.09	−0.11	0.06
1986	0.21	0.14	0.03	−0.13	0.05
1988	0.24	0.15	0.09	−0.13	n.a.
1991	0.21	0.06	0.05	−0.14	

Notes: Entries are correlation coefficients (Pearson's r). Only coefficients significant at $p < 0.001$ are shown; n.a. = not available (in 1988 the formulation of the question is different, so comparison could be misleading). The EC results are based on weighted data. For question wordings, see n. 16, in text.

and in several countries, from 1983 to 1988 the correlations come second in importance among the variables shown in Table 9.6. Then, suddenly, in 1991 the coefficients drop. Only in Belgium and Britain does the correlation between party identification and European citizenship remain significant in 1991. This finding suggests that we might be witnessing a general weakening of party mobilization as a factor in building a sense of European identity.

Turning to the indicators for political values, the correlations between left–right self-placement and a sense of European identity are generally positive. However, they are seldom significant—except in Denmark where people on the right consistently feel more European. Even so, it is interesting to note the contrast between the steadily growing sense of European identity among the right in France and Belgium but among the left in Spain, and the constant, and sharp, opposition towards Europe among the right in Spain and Portugal.

In most countries, the correlations between European identity and postmaterialist values are significant. The exceptions are Denmark and Britain, and, to a lesser extent, Ireland and Portugal. These results, too, are in the line with Inglehart's findings about the relevance of postmaterialism for political integration. We noted earlier, however, that Inglehart combined postmaterialism and cognitive mobilization to explain support for political integration whereas Janssen argued that cognitive mobilization renders spurious the link between postmaterialism and Europeanism. We report below on our tests of these relationships.

Finally, the correlations between European identity and satisfaction with democracy are intermittent, appearing in some years and not in others. An examination of country-by-country cross-tabulations of the two variables suggests that part of the explanation for these low correlations is the existence of a degree of curvilinearity in the relationship, with those who often see themselves as European being found disproportionately among the most satisfied and the most dissatisfied with democracy in their own country. On the whole, then, identification with Europe does not appear to be a 'democratic resort' for those who are dissatisfied with democracy in their own country—which is consistent with the findings reported in the previous chapter.

The analysis reported in this section suggests that cognitive mobilization, party identification, and postmaterialist orientations are directly relevant to the development of a European identity. But, so far, we have looked only at the bivariate relationships between these variables and the sense of being a European citizen. How do these variables interact with one another to foster European identity?

Pathways to European Identity

Along with the significance of cognitive mobilization, Inglehart (1970*a*) also showed that in the absence of the cognitive mobilization variable, level of education became the most important determinant of

Europeanism. But when cognitive mobilization was introduced, the impact of education vanished. Inglehart also demonstrated that among pro-Europeanists, high cognitive mobilization notably reduces the effect of education but does not abolish it (1970*a*: 54).

In Table 9.7 we report our findings on the interaction between cognitive mobilization and education and its impact on people's sense of European identity. The more recent picture is clearly different from the picture reported by Inglehart: high cognitive mobilization does not eliminate the link between education and Europeanism. Indeed, in 1983, 1986, and 1991 the two variables seem to be quite independent of each other.[19] Education appears to have become an important factor in its own right and cannot be replaced by cognitive mobilization. In 1991, in particular, the increase in European identity is more evident among the highly educated than among those who are high in cognitive mobilization.

What of the interaction between cognitive mobilization and party identification? In other words, has cognitive mobilization taken over from party identification in shaping people's sense of European identity? Our findings here, reported in Table 9.8, are qualified. The correlations between European identity and party identification are positive and not insubstantial, but when we control for cognitive mobilization, the coefficients fall to about half the size up until 1988, and then, in 1991, vanish. Evidently, cognitive mobilization is the major factor and its influence has increased with time.

Finally, we return to the question of whether or not cognitive mobilization renders spurious the relationship between postmaterialist orientations and European identity. Our findings, reported in the third and fourth columns of Table 9.8, reveal intermediate results. The partial correlations between postmaterialism and European identity, after controlling for cognitive mobilization, are about 50–70 per cent of the zero-order correlations between postmaterialism and European citizenship. In other words, cognitive mobilization only partially eliminates the effect of postmaterialist values. This persistence of postmaterialist values is rather close to Janssen's results for the intermediate category of European identity. People's sense of European identity is perhaps less 'idealist' than a generally positive attitude towards integration, but it is more value-laden than simply support for a specific policy.

We conclude, then, that while cognitive mobilization and postmaterialist values are highly relevant for European identity, their influence on a sense of 'Europeanness' is not straightforward. Moreover, recall

TABLE 9.7. *Sense of European identity by education and high cognitive mobilization, 1983–91*

Age when left school	'Often' feeling European					High cognitive mobilization and 'often' feeling European				
	1983	1985	1986	1988	1991	1983	1985	1986	1988	1991
Under 15	12	16	15	12	16	28	31	30	30	28
N	4,431	5,443	5,241	4,683	4,263	310	392	429	344	403
16–19	17	19	19	15	20	33	36	37	33	33
N	2,999	3,635	3,696	4,382	3,519	350	368	431	486	421
20 and over	27	32	35	26	32	40	39	48	39	46
N	1,127	1,473	1,419	2,314	2,406	233	273	289	467	436
Difference	15	16	20	14	16	12	8	18	9	18

Note: Entries are percentages in each cell.

Sources: See Table 9.5.

TABLE 9.8. *Correlations between European identity, materialism–postmaterialism, party identification, and cognitive mobilization*

	European citizenship by party identification	European citizenship by party identification controlling for cognitive mobilization	European citizenship by materialism–postmaterialism	European citizenship by materialism–postmaterialism controlling for cognitive mobilization
1983	0.12	0.06	−0.12	−0.06
1985	0.14	0.08	−0.11	−0.07
1986	0.13	0.08	−0.13	−0.08
1988	0.15	0.09	−0.13	−0.08
1991	0.06		−0.14	−0.10

Notes: Entries are correlation coefficients (Pearson's *r*). Data pooled and weighted.

Sources: See Table 9.5.

the division among highly mobilized people between those who 'often' feel European and those who 'never' feel European. Hence, we suggest that, during 1983–8, there were two distinct paths leading to a European identity: one path ran cognitive mobilization —> party identification —> European identity; the other path ran cognitive mobilization —> post-materialist values —> European identity. The distinctiveness of these two paths is borne out by the low correlations between party identi-fication and postmaterialist values.[20] Moreover, such weak relation-ships are congruent with postmaterialist theory which claims that postmaterialists are more detached from party identification and its associations with 'old' politics (cf. Dalton 1988: 177–205; Inglehart 1990: 363ff.). Thus, we might describe one path as relating to 'old politics' and one to 'new politics'. In 1991, only the latter path is significant. Finally, we can confirm the importance of education and cognitive mobilization—although it is also clear that we should not confuse them. Moreover, what also emerges is the importance of postmaterialist values, and that their relevance seems to grow with time.

Too Soon to Speak of a European Identity?

We noted earlier (see Figure 9.4) that a sense of European identity is far weaker than four other measures of attitudes to European integration. However, the evolution of a sense of identity shows similarities with these other variables. We interpret this as a transitional or formative phase of political identity resulting from the spill-over effects of European integration. Moreover, this sense of identity is not linked, negatively or positively, with national pride. Rather, it seems to challenge only local feelings of belonging. According to our analysis, the main feature of this sense of identity is its link with education, cognitive mobilization, and postmaterialism—which reflect basic capa-cities for coping with an extended community. If this sense of identity is to become autonomous, it will have to be less linked with instrumental evaluations and more affective in nature. The only known model of such a form of political identity is the nation state. Indeed, we already see an affective element in the desire for integration associated with postmaterialist orientations, but that is probably inadequate compared with the classical idea of 'love of the motherland' associated with the nation state. But will an affective European identity develop?

Moreover, will it develop in a conflictual way, in opposition to the nation state, or in a co-operative way, integrating a European identity along with national identity?

To explore these questions, we carried out a factor analysis using seven variables: national pride, the four support indicators, sense of European identity, and whether or not national and European identities are contradictory. Pooling the data and analysing all the countries together, produces only two factors, shown in Table 9.9. All the support questions and both 'identity' questions load on the first factor; national pride and, less strongly, 'being a European' load on the second factor. Similar results are obtained for each country, except for the Netherlands and Ireland.[21] In the Netherlands, the two identity questions load on a third factor; in Ireland, the two identity indicators load on the second factor along with the item 'for or against European unification' but national pride does not load on either factor.

Thus, the identity variable shows the strongest links with the four evaluative, or support, variables—confirming our earlier findings. Yet the loading of European identity on the national pride factor as well appears to question our earlier conclusion that national pride and citizenship are not correlated (see Table 9.1). Does this mean that a specific European identity is in the process of formation in opposition to, or in contrast to, national pride?

Two simple models of such a new identity can be formulated. In the first, identity is a characteristic acquired through formative socialization,

TABLE 9.9. *Factor analysis of attitudes towards identity and European integration*

Variables	Factor I	Factor II
1. National pride	0.088	0.931
2. Unification of Western Europe	0.774	−0.020
3. Membership of country in EC	0.832	0.076
4. Country has benefited from EC membership	0.694	0.107
5. Sorry if Common Market scrapped	0.817	0.105
6. European identity	0.487	−0.347
7. European unity and rational identity contradictory?	−0.632	0.132
Proportion of variance explained	44%	15%

Note: Entries are factor loadings from orthogonal rotation.
Source: Eurobarometer, No. 30.

with the implication that the geopolitical frame of reference already exists. According to this model, we would expect to find the new 'European identity' only among younger people, as a generational phenomenon, and only in the older member states (thus not in Greece, Spain, and Portugal). A second model proposes that before a European identity can be a reality for younger generations, it has to be 'constituted' by a symbolic transformation, producing a new complex of affective attitudes. This process is more likely among those with high 'cultural capital'—that is, among the most highly educated.[22] If a European identity is in the process of developing according to either of these two models, a factor analysis based on pooling the data for 'first', 'second wave', and 'recent' member states, and differentiating between age groups and education levels, should produce different results. Our analyses produced no such differences. On the contrary, we found the same two factors for each group of countries, with the same variables loading on the same factor in each group.

As an economic, political, and administrative construction, Europe evidently elicits evaluative attitudes, but not a real community of belonging of the kind experienced in nation states. If the European Union is able, in the future, to generate a new system of belonging, it is difficult to imagine, from what we know, what it will be like. We could imagine a new form of citizenship based on a commitment *à la carte*. This might be linked with the apparently contradictory characteristics of postmaterialism: a desire for belonging and, at the same time, a higher level of individualism which is translated, in the political sphere, into more direct participation in resolving issues (and is thus based on instrumental evaluations) than on an all-encompassing political loyalty. As far as people's attitudes are concerned, such a stance would generate affective orientations based more on sympathy than on love, for sympathy implies a certain distancing which allows individuals to elaborate a self-definition independently of the group to which, nevertheless, they feel attached.

Such observations are speculative. Meanwhile our empirical analysis makes clear that, whatever the tendencies and processes involved, it is too soon to speak of the internationalization of identities. For the present, a European identity is a vanguard phenomenon.

NOTES

1. Luxembourg and Northern Ireland are excluded due to small sample size.
2. In Britain, for example, the wordings were as follows. 1982: 'Do you ever think of yourself as a citizen of Europe?' (often, sometimes, never, don't know/no reply); 1983, 1985, and 1986: 'Do you ever think of yourself not only as a British citizen but also as a citizen of Europe?' (often, sometimes, never, don't know); 1988, 1989, and 1990: 'Does the thought ever occur to you that you are not only British but also European? Does this happen often, sometimes, never, don't know?' 1991: 'Do you ever think of yourself as not only British, but also European? Does this happen often, sometimes, never, don't know?' In most of the other countries, the changes of wording were along the same lines but the introduction to the question varied. In the French wording (used also in French-speaking Belgium), 'un citoyen' was reintroduced in 1989 and 1990: 'Vous arrive-t-il de penser que vous êtes non seulement un citoyen de la France (ou de la Belgique) mais aussi un citoyen de l'Europe? Cela vous arrive-t-il souvent, parfois, jamais, ne sait pas?' In Portugal, 'cidadao' was used until 1991. The term 'citoyen', 'Bürger', 'citizen', 'cittadino', 'ciudadano' or the like might be expected to lead to quite strong national differences in the understanding of the question. In some countries, the word 'citizen' is frequently used in public discourse, incorporating notions of political and social equality, and is clearly affectively loaded. In other countries, the word is primarily an administrative term, and is rarely used to stimulate emotional reactions. The designers of the Eurobarometer questions are, of course, aware of these complexities—hence the frequent changes to the question, and the dropping of 'citizen' from the question since 1988 (except in 1989 and 1990 in France and Belgium). Fortunately, the effect of including/excluding the word 'citizen' has been tested. In 1992, a split-half sample was taken, using both formulations of the question. The results show that the different wordings make little or no difference to the pattern of responses. Hence, we can use the variable to analyse sense of European identity without taking into account changes in wording. We thank Juergen Hofrichter (ZEUS, University of Mannheim), who retrieved the question formulation in every language and for every year.
3. For the evaluative variables, we subtracted the positive reponses from the negative responses, without taking into account the neutral answers, or don't know/no answer.
4. These findings are in line with the results obtained by Lindberg and Scheingold (1970), who found that 'utilitarian' commitments were, on average, more frequent than 'affective' commitments. They used evaluations of policies as indicators of utilitarian commitments and 'approve or disapprove of the Common Market idea'. For affectivity, they used questions similar to those of the evaluative type; for example, 'for or against making efforts towards uniting Western Europe'. Questions more directly linked to the issue of citizenship were not used (1970: 55–60).
5. Indeed, the five measures are intercorrelated. But the evaluative variables are more correlated with each other than with identity. These results are almost the same in each Eurobarometer.
6. Several four-dimensional cross-tabulations were constructed, examining European

identity by national pride and the following variables: age, level of education, sex, urban–rural residence, income level, regret if the EC was to disappear, frequency of political discussion, and the postmaterialism index.

7. The following hypotheses are based on the qualitative interviews conducted by Sophie Duchesne as part of her doctoral research about feelings of citizenship in France. Part of the analysis seeks to understand what 'to feel French' means. See Duchesne, 'Citoyenneté à la Française', doctoral thesis, Institute d'Etudes Politiques de Paris, 1994.

8. Indeed, rejection and hatred go along with the same need to define oneself as a 'member of', or 'part of a whole', when this need is not satisfied. It is not inconsequential to be positively or negatively identified with one's country, but what matters here is that it is a full identification process, a real sense of belonging.

9. Especially if respondents are being asked this question! During the interviews, respondents often turned the question round to ask themselves when they actually feel French.

10. Michelat and Thomas (1966) stress the limits of their survey. It was based on a small sample (223) of students during the Algerian war, which was an untypical period marked by 'maximum politicization in the student milieu'.

11. Remember that, after 1987, the Eurobarometer question implies the complementarity of the feelings of belonging: 'Have you ever considered yourself not only a German/Belgian/ Danish/ . . . citizen, but also as a citizen of Europe?'

12. Only in Britain is the coefficient significant (although weakly). The question on the complementarity of national and European identities has been asked three times, but only one of these surveys also includes the question on national pride. However, a significant coefficient of about 0.1 is unlikely to be stable over time.

13. Since it is not possible to give the same answer for the first and second choice, the diagonal cells are empty. We have thus had to adjust the expected frequencies per line which means that the table can only be read horizontally.

14. Luxembourg is not included due to the small sample size. As the data are for the late 1970s, Greece, Spain, and Portugal are not included.

15. We computed such correlations in order to give a common measure for all the independent variables. However, Pearson's r is not, strictly, an appropriate measure of dependence for dichotomous variables.

16. The cognitive mobilization index is based on two questions: 'When you yourself hold a strong opinion, do you ever find yourself persuading your friends, relatives or fellow workers to share your views? If so, does this happen frequently, occasionally or never?' and 'When you get together with your friends, would you say you discuss political matters frequently, occasionally or never?' The left–right self-placement scale (1–10) is based on the question: 'In political matters, people talk of the "left" and the "right". How would you place your views on this scale?' Materialism–postmaterialism is based on Inglehart's standard four-item battery (1990: 132). The party identification question is: 'Do you consider yourself to be close to any particular party? If so, do you feel yourself to be very close to this party, fairly close, or merely a sympathizer?' Satisfaction with democracy is based on the question: 'On the whole, are you very satisfied, fairly satisfied, not very satisfied, or not all satisfied with the way democracy works in [country]?'

17. Operational definitions of cognitive moblization which include education make it impossible to analyse the specific effects of education. Introducing the level of information might have been useful, as information is relevant to both cognitive mobilization and opinion leadership. Unfortunately, the relevant questions are not available in the Eurobarometer surveys which include the citizenship variable. These problems are reflected in Eurobarometer publications where the index we use is sometimes labelled 'cognitive mobilization' and sometimes (more recently) 'opinion leadership'. Also, see Inglehart (1977*b*: 339–40; 1990: 359).

18. Among people who are high and fairly high in cognitive mobilization, the proportion who 'often' feel European increases from 56 per cent in 1986 to 62 per cent in 1988; the proportion who 'never' feel European increases from 32 per cent in 1986 to 35 per cent in 1988, and to 41 per cent in 1991.

19. One could argue that this difference is due to operationalizing cognitive mobilization as opinion leadership. But opinion leadership could be supposed to be linked with educational level, and probably more strongly than in Inglehart's (1970*a*) operationalization of cognitive mobilization based simply on general information.

20. The correlations are: -0.07 in 1983, -0.06 in 1985 and 1986, -0.07 in 1988. But the correlation is not significant (at the 0.001 level) in 1991.

21. Germany and Denmark are also exceptions, as only one factor emerged. However, this factor regroups all the Europe-related questions, whereas the contribution of the variable 'national pride' is almost nil.

22. See Percheron (1991), who analyses attitudes towards Europe in terms of reaction to innovation.

10

Trust and Sense of Community

OSKAR NIEDERMAYER

Discussion of European integration usually means talking about institutional integration. Theoretical approaches to this subject, however, stress that institutional integration has to be accompanied by other forms of integration. According to the classification schema outlined in Chapter 3, these other forms can be defined in terms of orientations towards the personal element of the political collectivity. Nye (1971) argues that integration must be disaggregated into economic, social, and political dimensions, and further sub-divides the political dimension into institutional, policy, security-community, and attitudinal integration. The latter can also be referred to as 'identitive appeal'. Wallace (1990a) considers expectations, common identity, and a sense of community as essential elements of political integration. Both themes derive in part from the work of Karl Deutsch (see Chapter 2). The transactionalism approach of Deutsch and his colleagues describes integration as 'the attainment, within a territory, of a "sense of community" and of institutions and practices strong enough and widespread enough to assure, for a "long" time, dependable expectations of "peaceful change" among its population' (Deutsch *et al.* 1957: 5). The sense of community is further specified as 'a matter of mutual sympathy and loyalties; of "we-feeling", trust, and mutual consideration; of partial identification in terms of self-images and interests; of mutually successful predictions of behaviour, and of cooperative action in accordance with it' (Deutsch *et al.* 1957: 36).

To establish empirically whether such a sense of community exists between the peoples of the European Community, we have to analyse the orientations of citizens towards both aspects of the personal element of the political collectivity; that is, we have to include not only 'others' but also 'the self' as the object of orientations. Chapter 9 dealt with the self as object, that is with the question of European identity. In this chapter, we concentrate on orientations towards the other peoples in the EC.

Our analysis of mutual orientations focuses on mutual trust, which is one of Deutsch's main concepts in defining 'sense of community'. We distinguish between three dimensions of trust: level, salience, and uniformity or diversity. Although all three dimensions are relevant for a comprehensive analysis of mutual trust, the most important is the level of trust. A sense of community can only exist if the people of the EC evaluate each other positively; that is if they trust each other. An increase in the level of mutual trust over time would indicate a growing sense of community.

Deutsch's 'sense of community' clearly refers to the mass population and not just to the élite level. This means that the growth in trust in the peoples of the other member states must not be restricted to the élites or small parts of the population. In other words, for the majority of EC citizens, the peoples of other member states have to be salient enough to develop an orientation towards them. Therefore, for a sense of community to exist within the EC, both a relatively high level of mutual trust must exist and it must be based on relatively high mutual salience.

In addition to the level and the salience dimensions, the uniformity or diversity of the evaluation is an important aspect of the analysis of trust. This dimension is particularly relevant in the socio-psychological literature about images and stereotypes. The term 'image', defined as 'the organized representation of an object in an individual's cognitive system' (Kelman 1965: 24) has been used by various authors to describe the views of other peoples and nations,[1] and the term 'stereotype, as commonly employed, refers to oversimplified, overgeneralized images' (Scott 1965: 94). Bearing in mind the operationalization of stereotype used in Taft (1959), and thereafter by many others, we can treat a high degree of uniformity in responses to a question dealing with the image of another people as indicating a stereotyped image. Extreme stereotyped mutual images of the peoples of the other EC member states— even positive ones—are, at least in the long run, unlikely to provide a solid basis for a sense of community. Rather, a sense of community is more firmly based on differentiated mutual images.

We approach the empirical analysis of mutual trust from the perspective of both those being evaluated and those doing the evaluating.

Hence, first, we present an aggregate-level analysis of the average level of trust in the people of other member states among people in all the member countries of the Community, the salience of these other people, and the uniformity or diversity with which they are evaluated. This part of the analysis focuses on whether we can speak of a sense of community within the EC and whether this sense is increasing over time. Then, secondly, we present an individual-level analysis examining the average level of trust which individuals in a particular country have in the peoples of the other member states taken as a whole, the salience of these other peoples, and the uniformity or diversity of these evaluations. This part focuses on the factors which influence individual levels of trust in the other peoples of the European Community. Here, we try to identify groups which are in the vanguard in establishing or fostering a sense of community within the Community.

Data Base and Operationalizations

The Eurobarometer surveys provide our data base. A question dealing with this topic was asked as early as 1970, in the first European Community Study. The question has been replicated in five subsequent Eurobarometer surveys: autumn 1976, autumn 1980, spring 1982, spring 1986, and in spring 1990. The question wording in the English-speaking countries from 1970 to 1986 was as follows:

Now, we would like to ask about how much you would trust people from different countries. For each country please say whether, in your opinion, they are in general very trustworthy, fairly trustworthy, not particularly trustworthy, or not at all trustworthy.

In 1990, a slightly different wording was used:

Now, we would like to ask you a question about how much trust you have in people from various countries. For each, please tell me whether you have a lot of trust in them, some trust, not very much trust, or no trust at all.

There have been no corresponding changes in the question wording in France, Luxembourg, the Netherlands, and the Flemish questionnaire in Belgium. In Germany, the slight changes in the wording do not include altering the keyword 'trust'. In the other countries, changes in the wording occur as part of the change in the keyword in the British questionnaire from 'trustworthy' to 'trust'. It could be argued that the new version in 1990 aims at trust in other peoples on a more personal level than the previous version. However, we believe that the two versions of the question can be interpreted as equivalent because both aim at responses suggesting the respondent's 'underlying emotional predispositions' (Merritt 1968: 112) about other peoples—that is, in our classification of modes of orientation, their diffuse evaluations. Moreover, the results of our analysis do not indicate a general and systematic effect from the changed wording.[2]

The lists of peoples to be evaluated were not the same in each of the five surveys. In 1970, the peoples of four big European countries (Britain, France, Italy, Germany) were evaluated along with the Swiss and three major non-European nationalities, the Americans, Russians, and Chinese. Since 1976, all peoples of the EC member countries are included in the list. In 1980, the list included the Spanish, the Portuguese, and the Japanese in addition to the other non-EC peoples included since 1970. In 1986, the Turks were added to the list, and peoples from Eastern Europe were added in 1990. In spring 1982, the question was asked only for some non-EC peoples. In addition, the first survey in spring 1970 was carried out in only five of the six EC member countries; in Belgium, France, Germany, Italy, and the Netherlands, but not in Luxembourg. Our analysis, therefore, concentrates on the surveys conducted in 1976, 1980, 1986, and 1990, when representative samples in all EC member countries were asked to report their feelings of trust in the peoples of all the other Community countries.

The trust question has four response categories, coded from 0 ('not at all trustworthy') to 3 ('very trustworthy'). In the empirical analysis, we use the question in two ways. For the aggregate analysis, focusing on those being evaluated, the Community-wide level of trust in a specific people is operationalized by the weighted mean of the responses of all other Europeans to the people in question. Thus, the indicator ranges from 0 to 3 with a mid-point of 1.5; values above 1.5 indicate that the average evaluation of a particular people by all other EC peoples is positive. In the individual-level analysis, focusing on those doing the evaluating, the level of trust is operationalized as the mean of individual responses to all the trust items concerning the peoples of other Community countries. This indicator, too, ranges from 0 to 3 with a mid-point of 1.5; again, values above 1.5 indicate that an individual, on average, evaluates other EC peoples positively.

If an individual does not respond to the trust question, this may be due to lack of knowledge about, or interest in, the peoples concerned.

Or it may be because the respondent considers the question inadequate, and therefore refuses to answer it. In the first instance, the extent of non-response can be seen as an indicator of the salience of these other peoples for the respondent. To find out which of the two interpretations is true, we have to examine the reasons for non-response. This is possible for the spring 1990 survey, where both the 'don't know' and 'refused' codes for non-responses are available for seven of the twelve countries; in the earlier surveys, only one missing data code was used.

A country-by-country examination of the data reveals that, overwhelmingly, non-responses are instances of 'don't know'. Usually less than 2 per cent of the sample refuse to answer the question. Based on these findings, the proportion of valid responses is used to indicate the salience dimension at both levels of analysis. In the aggregate-level analysis, the Community-wide salience of a particular people is operationalized as the weighted percentage of all other Europeans giving a valid response on the trust question. This indicator therefore ranges from 0 to 100. In the individual-level analysis, the salience of other EC peoples is operationalized by the number of peoples for which the respondent gives a valid response. Thus, in the case of the 1990 data, this indicator ranges from 0 to 11, since there were twelve EC member countries at the time—requiring respondents to evaluate the people of eleven other countries.

The third dimension, uniformity and diversity, is operationalized by the standard deviations of the indicators used to measure the level of trust. In the aggregate-level analysis, this is the average deviation from the mean of all responses given by all other Europeans. In the individual-level analysis, this is the average deviation from the mean of an individual's responses to all the trust items concerning other EC peoples. Since the maximum value of the standard deviation in our case is 1.5, the indicators used to operationalize the uniformity–diversity dimension range from 0 to 1.5.

Whom do the Europeans Trust?

Here we concentrate on the Community-wide level, examining levels of trust in the people of other EC states expressed by all other Europeans. We start by presenting the results from the most recent survey in spring 1990. Then, we move to a longitudinal perspective to show the development of trust between peoples of the member states from 1976 to

1990. The four time points used in this analysis cover a period in which the EC was joined by Greece (1981), and by Spain and Portugal (1986). To avoid changes in the basis of calculation, the comparative presentation of the Community-wide results for the whole time period only refers to the Community of nine as it existed before the southern enlargement.

We do not deal with the development of mutual trust between the people of each country and every other country. To do this for all possible pairs of countries would involve a vast amount of data and the analysis would go beyond the scope of this chapter. Moreover, we are interested in the development of a sense of community within the EC, not mutual trust between peoples *per se*.[3] Therefore, in this part of the analysis, we do not test the hypotheses to be found in the literature which seek to explain why, at the aggregate level, mutual trust between some pairs of peoples or countries is higher than between other pairs.[4]

Concentrating on the Community-wide evaluation of the people of each member state, Table 10.1 shows that in 1990 there was a positive trust rating of all the nationalities concerned. The Community-wide level of trust in the people of each member state is above the mid-point of the trust scale (1.5), indicating that, on average, the peoples of the Community trust each other, although the values for some of the member states are only marginally above the mid-point.

TABLE 10.1. *Trust in the peoples of the European Community, 1990*

Trust in:	Level (means)	Salience (%)	Diversity (st. dev.)
Belgians	1.91	83	0.78
British	1.57	91	0.91
Danes	1.95	78	0.77
Dutch	1.93	83	0.78
French	1.71	91	0.86
Germans	1.79	88	0.83
Greeks	1.54	81	0.83
Irish	1.64	82	0.85
Italians	1.61	89	0.83
Luxemburgers	1.97	77	0.77
Portuguese	1.57	81	0.83
Spanish	1.72	89	0.81

Note: Entries are EC-12 averages.

Source: Eurobarometer, No. 33.

The most trusted people are those in certain smaller countries: Luxembourg, Denmark, the Netherlands, and Belgium. The next group comprises the West Germans, the French, and the Spanish, followed by the Irish and the Italians. The group least trusted consists of the Portuguese, the British, and the Greeks. In general, therefore, there is some evidence of north–south and centre–periphery contrasts in perceived trustworthiness, though, it should be emphasized, such patterns are not entirely consistent.

The second column in Table 10.1 shows that nine out of ten respondents gave a valid response to the question about trust in the peoples of the big European countries. Clearly, these countries are the most salient. This is not surprising, since these major countries have taken a prominent role in European history and are more often referred to in the mass media. About four out of five respondents expressed an opinion about the people of the other, smaller, EC countries, whilst salience is lowest in regard to the peoples of the two smallest countries: Denmark and Luxembourg. And, lastly, from the third column, we see that the peoples of the small countries are evaluated more uniformly than the peoples of other countries. Diversity is highest in regard to the British and the French.

Turning to developments over time on the first of our three dimensions, level of trust, Table 10.2 shows that the Belgians, the Danes, the Dutch, and the people of Luxembourg were the most trusted throughout the whole period 1976–90. The level of trust in these peoples was high and stable over time, and, moreover, it was always higher than trust in the peoples of the four big countries and trust in the Irish. Within this group of countries, between 1976 and 1986, trust in the West Germans was always highest, followed by the British, the French, the Irish, and the Italians. The Italians were generally the least trusted people throughout the period, although in 1990 they were displaced by the Portuguese. The Irish received a particularly low rating in 1976. Bear in mind that a value below 1.5 indicates that lack of trust in the people in question predominates.

Trust in those who were ranked lowest in 1976 increased between the mid-1970s and the early 1980s—most notably for the British (from 1.57 to 1.72) and the Irish (from 1.33 to 1.6).[5] Between 1980 and 1986, trust in Italians increased substantially (from 1.27 to 1.47). Only in the case of the British is there a noticeable decline in trust between 1980 and 1986 (from 1.72 to 1.64). Trust in the other peoples remained stable. Then, trust in four peoples uniformly increased between 1986 and 1990;

Levels of Legitimacy

TABLE 10.2. *Development of trust among the peoples of the European Community, 1976–90*

	1976	1980	1986	1990
Belgians	1.84	1.90	1.82	1.96
British	1.57	1.72	1.64	1.62
Danes	1.93	2.00	1.98	2.01
Dutch	1.94	1.97	1.94	1.97
French	1.54	1.60	1.63	1.83
Germans	1.68	1.76	1.75	1.84
Greeks	—	1.45	1.50	1.55
Irish	1.33	1.60	1.60	1.67
Italians	1.22	1.27	1.47	1.61
Luxemburgers	1.90	1.97	1.91	2.03
Portuguese	—	1.38	1.50	1.59
Spanish	—	1.42	1.53	1.72

Note: Entries are EC-9 means.

Sources: Eurobarometer, Nos. 6, 14, 25, and 33.

only trust in the British remained fairly stable at a relatively low level. The French gained most (from 1.64 to 1.83) and they were trusted to the same extent as the Germans in 1990. In 1990, too, the Italians attained a positive trust level for the first time since 1970—being trusted to the same degree as the British.

The results for the three southern countries joining the EC in the 1980s reveal a pattern which could be described as a movement from scepticism to trust via neutrality. The Greeks, Spanish, and the Portuguese were steadily considered to be more and more trustworthy by the other nine EC members between 1980 and 1990. The Greeks, shortly before their accession in January 1981, were trusted somewhat more than the Portuguese and Spanish were in autumn 1980. After the accession of these two countries, trust in their peoples increased to about the same level as trust in the Greeks in 1986 and to a higher level than trust in the Greeks in 1990. The outstanding development is the substantial rise of trust in the Spanish between 1986 and 1990 (from 1.53 to 1.72).

To sum up, in spring 1990 the peoples of the various member states received their highest trust rating in the entire period since the mid-1970s, with the single exception of the British. At the end of the period, the British were at much the same point on the trust scale as at the begining, having experienced a decline in trust between 1980 and 1986.

The outstanding positive developments were the increase in trust in the Italians in 1986 and 1990 and the substantial increase in trust in the Spanish and the French between 1986 and 1990.

Our second dimension is the salience of the peoples being evaluated. Table 10.3 reveals that the peoples of the four big EC countries were consistently the most salient between 1976 and 1990. The level of salience of these four countries varies between 83 per cent for the Italians in 1986 to as high as 92 per cent for the French and British in 1990. The salience of all these peoples was highest in spring 1990, and there are no outstanding or systematic developments over the 1976–90 period. Compared to the peoples from the large EC countries, the peoples of the small countries were less often evaluated. In their case, the level of salience ranges between 67 per cent for Luxemburgers in 1976 and 85 per cent for the Belgians in 1990. Salience was always at its lowest for the Luxemburgers and Danes. However, the peoples of the small countries were perceived more prominently in 1990 than in earlier years. All peoples in the small countries undergo a uniform and substantial increase in salience between 1986 and 1990. A similar development is evident for the three southern peoples. Their salience to the other nine EC countries increased substantially between 1986 and 1990 after having remained at almost the same levels in 1986 as in 1980. In 1990, the response rate in the case of the Spanish people was the same as for the other four big European countries. The salience of

TABLE 10.3. *Salience of the peoples of the European Community, 1976–90*

	1976	1980	1986	1990
Belgians	74	79	74	85
British	88	90	88	92
Danes	68	72	69	80
Dutch	75	79	75	84
French	85	89	84	92
Germans	87	89	85	89
Greeks	—	73	72	83
Irish	74	74	73	84
Italians	85	86	83	90
Luxemburgers	67	71	67	80
Portuguese	—	70	71	81
Spanish	—	83	82	89

Note: Entries are EC-9 average percentages of valid responses to the trust question.

Source: See Table 10.2.

the Greeks and the Portuguese in 1990 is similar to that of the other smaller nationalities.

The results for the third dimension of our analysis, shown in Table 10.4, can be readily summarized. The diversity of evaluations is lower for the peoples of the four smaller northern countries (below 0.8) and higher for the peoples of all other countries (above 0.8). Diversity is highest with respect to the evaluation of Germans, the Irish, and the French between 1976 and 1986. There is some tendency to evaluate the Germans and the French rather more uniformly in 1986 and 1990, whereas the British are judged least uniformly in 1990.

Having reported Community-wide developments on the three dimensions, we can move on to consider whether or not a sense of community exists in the EC as a whole. To do this, we need to combine the separate measures into one overall figure. To get an accurate picture, not only those peoples doing the evaluating but also those being evaluated have to be weighted according to their population size as a proportion of the EC's total population. Therefore, the weighted averages of the figures for all the individual EC peoples have been calculated to provide the overall values we need. The results are shown in Table 10.5.

A sense of community exists within the European Community when the level of mutual trust rises above 1.5; at this level positive evaluations begin to predominate. According to this operationalization, a

TABLE 10.4. *Diversity of evaluation of the peoples of the European Community, 1976–90*

	1976	1980	1986	1990
Belgians	0.73	0.75	0.74	0.76
British	0.80	0.82	0.82	0.89
Danes	0.73	0.76	0.73	0.74
Dutch	0.77	0.79	0.75	0.77
French	0.83	0.91	0.85	0.83
Germans	0.90	0.91	0.88	0.82
Greeks	—	0.84	0.85	0.82
Irish	0.90	0.88	0.84	0.84
Italians	0.82	0.86	0.80	0.83
Luxemburgers	0.74	0.75	0.72	0.74
Portuguese	—	0.85	0.87	0.82
Spanish	—	0.83	0.81	0.80

Note: Entries are EC-9 average standard deviation.

Sources: See Table 10.2.

TABLE 10.5. *Sense of community between the peoples of the EC-9 member states, 1976–90*

	1976	1980	1986	1990
Level of trust (means)	1.55	1.63	1.66	1.75
Salience (%)	85	87	84	90
Diversity (st. dev.)	0.83	0.86	0.83	0.83

Sources: See Table 10.2.

sense of community already existed in the mid-1970s and increased during the period up to 1990. As the very high salience figures show, the sense of community is solidly embodied in the mass population and, as indicated by the moderate diversity figures, the mutual images are not highly stereotyped.

Even so, compared to the maximum value of the level of trust scale (3.0), the 1990 overall level of trust (1.75) might be thought to indicate a rather low sense of community within the EC. However, we suggest that a more appropriate point of reference should be not the maximum value of the scale but the level of trust in one's own people. The weighted average of the level of trust in our respondents' 'own people' is 2.39. This figure indicates that respondents evaluate their own people very positively but not extremely positively. Compared to this figure, an overall level of mutual trust of 1.75 indicates at least a modestly developed sense of community within the EC.

Thus, the results of the aggregate-level analysis allow us to state that the institutional integration of the EC is accompanied by a sense of community between the European peoples. From an integrationist point of view, the good news is the increase in this trust over time; the not so good news, that the level of trust is rather modest. In the next section we investigate which groups of European citizens can be seen as the frontrunners in this development.

Who Trusts the Other Europeans?

Our analysis now turns to the individual level. First, we examine the average level of trust in all the other EC peoples among respondents in each member state, the salience of others, and the uniformity or diversity with which respondents evaluate the other peoples.

Secondly, we examine those factors which may lead to higher or lower levels of trust.

As Table 10.6 shows, the Danes, the Dutch, and the Belgians show the highest levels of trust in the peoples of the other member states. The Spanish and the Italians are considerably less positive in their evaluations. In each of the member states, however, positive evaluations predominate: trust predominates over mistrust. With the exception of Portugal, the salience figures demonstrate that only a tiny minority of respondents from all countries, about 5 per cent, are totally parochial—in the sense of not having developed an orientation towards any of the peoples of the other member states.[6] Usually at least half and sometimes more than four-fifths of respondents evaluated all the eleven other EC peoples.

The means of the salience scale in the table reveal a clear pattern: the salience of other EC peoples is higher among citizens of the six original member states of the EC than among citizens of member states which joined the EC in the first and second round of enlargement. As to the diversity of respondents' evaluation of other EC peoples, the citizens of the various Community member states evaluate other EC peoples rather uniformly.[7] This absence of great variation in respondents' evaluation of other EC peoples encourages us to proceed with the last part of the analysis in which we focus on which factors may influence the tendency to trust or distrust the peoples of the other member states.

In the introduction of this volume, we identified a number of variables which are thought generally to influence orientations towards the EC. Some of these variables can be linked theoretically to the question of trust: social structure, psychological involvement in politics, personality characteristics, values and norms, contact and events. Before looking at the data, a word about the relevance of these variables to trust in other peoples.

The pertinent socio-structural variables are age, education, and residential location. With respect to age, we can assume generation effects; that is, we can anticipate that the different political socialization experiences of different age cohorts shape individual evaluations of other peoples. At least, we can expect to find that citizens who grew up in the period of intense nationalism before the Second World War and those who experienced the war years show a generally lower level of trust in other peoples than those who did not go through those experiences. A negative relationship between education and trust is likely because of the more cosmopolitan orientation of the highly educated,

Table 10.6. *Trust in the peoples of all other EC member states, 1990*

	BE	DK	FR	GB	GE	GR	IR	IT	LU	NL	PO	SP
Level of trust (means)	1.9	2.0	1.8	1.8	1.8	1.7	1.8	1.6	1.8	2.0	1.8	1.5
Salience (scale values)												
0	3	5	5	4	5	5	5	4	8	4	16	6
1–5	3	6	7	11	2	21	22	10	3	4	7	11
6–10	23	16	24	28	11	31	26	30	26	27	11	28
11	71	72	64	57	82	43	48	56	63	65	66	55
Means	9.9	9.6	9.4	9.0	10.1	8.0	7.9	9.1	9.2	9.7	8.4	8.7
Diversity (st. dev.)	0.66	0.47	0.54	0.54	0.52	0.63	0.54	0.58	0.53	0.55	0.40	0.56

Source: Eurobarometer, No. 33.

and their greater capacity to absorb and process information about remote entities. In so far as trust in foreigners is an expression of parochialism–cosmopolitanism, we can assume that people living in rural areas evaluate other peoples less positively than those living in urban areas.

As to psychological involvement in politics, awareness and interest in politics should lead to more benign and complex images of the outside world. Thus, high positive values on these variables are taken to indicate fewer difficulties in dealing with a wider world, thereby leading to less ethnocentric views. The personality characteristics of individuals are relevant because we assume that people with low ego-strength who experience feelings of marginality and anxiety tend to project their problems upon the external world. Thus, mistrust of other people—as a scapegoat mechanism—is likely to be relatively high among individuals with such personality characteristics.

Values and norms probably have a generalized influence on trust in other peoples. More specifically, it is possible that some of the norm-providing groups within a society, such as political parties, shape the views of their adherents with respect to other countries and peoples. In addition, certain value priorities may have an effect. In particular, we anticipate that postmaterialist orientations (Inglehart 1977*b*) are positively related to trust in other peoples. Individuals who give priority to the need for belonging, solidarity, and self-realization are likely to be more open to other peoples than those giving priority to subsistence and physical safety—values associated with the nation state and its traditional functions of protecting the ingroup against outgroups. The argument with regard to contacts is that interactions and communication between different peoples lead to learning processes. As Pentland (1973: 263) puts it, 'the more such contacts are seen to have mutually beneficial results, the more that mutual feelings of trust and loyalty are created'.

Broadly, we anticipate that the level of trust in others should be relatively stable over time because the given structure of evaluative orientations serves as a screen for the selective reception of new information. But it might also be the case that dramatic events, especially when mediated by external messages, affect people's orientations. However, as we have no data about the effect of contact and events on levels of trust,[8] we cannot include this last consideration in our analysis.

We use analysis of variance to determine whether there is a relationship between these variables and the average level of trust. The analysis is based on data for spring 1990. In Tables 10.7–10.10, we show the mean values of the level of trust scale for each category of the independent variables. In addition, the eta coefficients are displayed as measures of the strength of the relationship, together with reporting whether or not the relationship is significant ($p < 0.05$).

Looking first at the socio-structural variables, Table 10.7 shows that the age of respondents is significant in only half the countries. In the other half, people who are 65 years or older—thus socialized during the pre-war and war years—do not show a notably lower level of trust in other EC peoples. There is a clear relationship between education and trust. And in almost all countries this is a linear positive relationship. This is consistent with the results of many other studies.[9] The community size, however, is not clearly and consistently related with trust in other peoples in the Community.[10]

To analyse the relationship between psychological involvement in politics and trust in other peoples, we combined two variables into an index: respondent's interest in politics and the opinion leadership status of the respondent.[11] The results, shown in Table 10.8, reveal a significant positive relationship between political involvement and trust in other peoples for citizens in all EC member states except Luxembourg.[12]

Many empirical studies have found strong relationships between the kinds of personal characteristics we discussed above and trust or related concepts.[13] Only one indicator of this aspect is available to us: overall life satisfaction. Of the seven ego-strength scales which McClosky used in his study of the related concept of isolationism, life satisfaction was the only one which did 'not consistently yield correlations that are statistically significant' (McClosky 1967: 73). The same is true for our data. As Table 10.9 shows, a significant correlation between life satisfaction and trust in other peoples exists in only about half of the EC member states.

For the last group of possible determinants, values and norms, we use the materialist–postmaterialist scale developed by Inglehart (1971*b*, 1977*b*) to test the relationship between values and trust. The scale is dichotomized for this analysis. As Table 10.10 shows, there is a positive correlation between trust and this scale in nearly all countries: individuals with postmaterialist value priorities evaluate other EC peoples much more positively than those with materialist or mixed value priorities.

TABLE 10.7. *Socio-structural variables and trust in the peoples of all other EC member states, 1990*

	BE	DK	FR	GB	GE	GR	IR	IT	LU	NL	PO	SP
Age												
Under 64	1.9	2.0	1.8	1.8	1.8	1.8	1.8	1.7	1.8	2.0	1.8	1.5
Over 65	1.8	1.8	1.8	1.6	1.7	1.6	1.6	1.6	1.9	1.8	1.7	1.4
Eta	0.10*	0.13*	0.02	0.11*	0.05	0.09*	0.15*	0.07*	0.06	0.17*	0.03	0.01
Education												
Low	1.8	1.8	1.7	1.6	1.7	1.6	1.6	1.5	1.9	1.9	1.8	1.4
Middle	1.9	1.9	1.8	1.8	1.8	1.8	1.8	1.7	1.7	2.0	1.9	1.5
High	2.0	2.0	2.0	2.1	1.9	2.0	2.0	1.8	1.8	2.0	1.8	1.6
Eta	0.17*	0.15*	0.20*	0.27*	0.12*	0.21*	0.17*	0.21*	0.13	0.14*	0.09	0.12*
Residence												
Rural	1.9	1.9	1.8	1.7	1.9	1.5	1.7	1.6	1.8	2.0	1.8	1.5
Small town	1.9	2.0	1.8	1.7	1.8	1.8	1.8	1.7	1.8	2.0	1.7	1.5
Big town	1.9	2.0	1.8	1.8	1.8	1.9	1.9	1.6	1.6	2.0	1.8	1.4
Eta	0.04	0.04	0.06	0.07	0.09*	0.20*	0.11*	0.02	0.12	0.03	0.07	0.05

* $p < 0.05$

Note: Entries are means of level of trust scale and eta coefficients.

Source: See Table 10.6.

TABLE 10.8. *Involvement in politics and trust in the peoples of all other EC member states, 1990*

Involvement in politics	BE	DK	FR	GB	GE	GR	IR	IT	LU	NL	PO	SP
Low	1.8	1.8	1.7	1.6	1.7	1.4	1.8	1.6	1.7	1.9	1.8	1.4
Middle	1.9	1.9	1.9	1.7	1.8	1.8	1.7	1.7	1.9	2.0	1.9	1.5
High	2.1	2.1	1.9	1.9	1.9	1.9	1.9	1.8	1.8	2.0	1.9	1.6
Eta	0.20*	0.20*	0.18*	0.22*	0.17*	0.24*	0.10*	0.16*	0.10	0.16*	0.10*	0.12*

* $p < 0.05$

Note: Entries are means of trust scale and eta coefficients.

Source: See Table 10.6.

TABLE 10.9. *Overall life satisfaction and trust in the peoples of all other EC member states, 1990*

Life satisfaction	BE	DK	FR	GB	GE	GR	IR	IT	LU	NL	PO	SP
No	1.7	1.8	1.6	1.6	1.6	1.7	1.5	1.6	1.9	2.0	1.7	1.3
Yes	1.9	2.0	1.9	1.8	1.8	1.8	1.8	1.7	1.8	2.0	1.8	1.5
Eta	0.14*	0.05	0.18*	0.13*	0.14*	0.08*	0.16*	0.06	0.03	0.01	0.06	0.1*

* $p < 0.05$

Note: Entries are means of trust scale and eta coefficients.

Source: See Table 10.6.

TABLE 10.10. *Postmaterialism and trust in the peoples of all other EC member states, 1990*

Postmaterialist orientation	BE	DK	FR	GB	GE	GR	IR	IT	LU	NL	PO	SP
No	1.9	1.9	1.8	1.7	1.7	1.8	1.8	1.6	1.8	1.9	1.8	1.4
Yes	2.1	2.1	2.0	2.0	2.0	1.7	1.9	1.7	2.0	2.1	1.8	1.6
Eta	0.15*	0.12*	0.19*	0.18*	0.14*	0.04	0.08*	0.08*	0.19*	0.18*	0.01	0.07*

* $p < 0.05$

Note: Entries are means of trust scale and eta coefficients.

Source: See Table 10.6.

Even so, all the eta coefficients reported here are rather low, indicating that these relationships, while statistically significant, are rather weak. Nevertheless, the association between trust and education, involvement in politics, and postmaterialist value orientations is consistent across all twelve EC countries.

Conclusion

To sum up our analysis of the orientations of Europeans towards each other, our results for feelings of trust indicate that institutional integration within the EC is accompanied by a sense of community between the peoples who make up the Community. Although up to 1990 this sense of community has not been very pronounced, it is solidly embodied in the mass population, was not based on highly stereotyped images, and was increasing over time. Those Europeans with higher education, a high psychological involvement in politics, and postmaterialist value orientations were, in general, the frontrunners in this development. Set against these findings, however, we have to bear in mind that the last time point for which we have data about trust is spring 1990. At that time, there were very high levels of public support for the EC in general, which were considerably reduced in 1991–92 in the wake of discussions about the Maastricht Treaty and other developments in European integration (see Chapter 4). We do not know whether these events negatively influenced the sense of trust and community between the peoples of the Community. However, the results of our analysis of the development of mutual trust since 1976 suggest that feelings of this kind change gradually in the long run and seem to be generally resistant to dramatic short-term fluctuations.

NOTES

1. See, e.g. Oskamp (1977).
2. The possibility that there are some consequences from changes in the wording cannot be totally excluded. But a systematic effect, such as a uniform increase or decline of trust in other peoples, does not emerge in those countries where the key word was altered.
3. The development of mutual trust between the people of pairs of EC states is documented in Hofrichter and Niedermayer (1991).
4. Buchanan and Cantril (1953) classified the relationships between nations which are

relevant for mutual friendliness into five 'contexts': 'the bi-polar world', 'World War II', 'common boundaries', 'common language or culture', and 'neutrality'. Nincic and Russett (1979) distinguished between 'similarity' (in terms of race, language, religion, political system, level of economic activity) and 'interest' (both economic interest, operationalized by direct investments and trade, and security interest, operationalized by military bases and military personnel). Inglehart (1991) grouped the factors influencing international trust into three main categories: primordial ties (race, religion, language, geographic proximity), societal learning (military and economic alliances, exchanges, communication flows) and economic development (see also Inglehart and Rabier 1984).

5. The low level of trust in the Irish in 1976 could be due to interviewees confusing the Republic of Ireland with Northern Ireland. In the 1980 survey, the question specified 'Irish from the Republic of Ireland'. This change of wording was followed by a marked increase in trust in the Irish between 1976 and 1980.

6. One-sixth of Portuguese respondents fell into this category.

7. Bear in mind that the standard deviation ranges from 0 to 1.5. A value of around 0.5 is rather low.

8. For reviews of the effects of contacts on the evaluation of other peoples, see Davidson and Thomson (1980: 40 ff.), Scott (1965: 93 ff.), and Pool (1965). On events as determinants, see Deutsch and Merritt (1965).

9. See, e.g. Davidson and Thomson (1980: 49), Inglehart (1991: 16), and McClosky (1967: 63). Education is operationalized as the age when respondents finished full-time education, and recoded to: low level = up to 15 years; intermediate level = 16–19 years, high level = 20 years and older.

10. Other studies using similar concepts have found such a relationship (see McClosky 1967: 78–9).

11. The opinion leadership variable is based on responses to two questions: 'When you get together with your friends, would you say you discuss political matters frequently, occasionally or never?' 'When you, yourself, hold a strong opinion, do you ever find yourself persuading your friends, relatives or fellow workers to share your views? If so, does this happen often, from time to time or rarely?' The response categories for both questions were combined to form a 4-point index of opinion leadership. The political interest variable has four response options (a great deal, to some extent, not much, not at all). Both variables were dichotomized and combined to form a 3-point index of psychological involvement in politics. The analyses were first conducted separately for both variables and showed positive relationships in almost all countries.

12. In interpreting the figures for Luxembourg, it has to be kept in mind that until 1990 a very small sample of only 300 was taken.

13. See, e.g. Scott (1965: 87 ff.).

11

Policy, Subsidiarity, and Legitimacy

RICHARD SINNOTT

❖

In reviewing the evolution of integration theory in Chapter 2, it was evident that as public opinion and political culture were reinstated in theoretical endeavour, attitudes towards issues became a major focus of attention. Hoffmann put the point succinctly: 'transnational political issues of interest to all political forces and publics across boundary lines are a prerequisite to political integration' (Hoffmann 1966: 893). This raises several questions. What is a transnational or, in our terms, an internationalized issue? Is there any empirical evidence that there are issues which are of interest to all (or any) political forces and publics across boundaries? If there are, what is the salience of such issues and what are the preferences of the public?

The centrality of these questions in a study of orientations towards internationalized governance is underlined by the classification scheme outlined in Chapter 3. The scheme identified policies as one of the four main components of internationalized governance and suggested that plans, outcomes, outputs, and functional scope are elements within this broad policy category. In pursuing at least some of these elements, it will become apparent that policy orientations have an important bearing both on the operation of the principle of subsidiarity and on the legitimacy of internationalized governance.

The Internationalization of Issues

Issues may become internationalized in three ways: attributed internationalization, exogenous internationalization, and endogenous internationalization. From the perspective of public opinion, the most obvious way in which an issue may be internationalized is if competence in problem-solving or policy-making is attributed to an international agency by the public—which here we call *attributed internationalization*. This is a subjective basis for the internationalization of an issue; in this case, internationalization is based on how the public perceives problems and the means of solving them. It is also a normative attribution. What matters is how the public thinks problems ought to be tackled rather than how it perceives the actual competences of various levels of governance, perceptions which may be more or less in accord with reality.

In this regard, note that all issue orientations and policy preferences have either an implicit or explicit attribution dimension. In fact, all policy orientations have a dual object: the preferred solution to a problem, and the agency to which the public looks for a solution. In dealing with attitudes and policy preferences in the context of a unitary state, we do not usually refer to the attribution aspect because competence for most major issues is simply assumed to belong to the national government. It will usually be quite obvious if a particular issue falls within the remit of local government. In established federal systems the attribution of competence is usually implicit but is likely to become explicit in cases of jurisdictional conflict between the various levels of the federal system. Because internationalized governance is a developing process rather than an established system, the dual nature of policy-relevant attitudes and, in particular, the extent to which the public attributes competence to the international level, become important matters, especially in relation to the legitimacy of internationalized governance.

Attributed internationalization of issues is only one source of the agenda of internationalized governance. Indeed, arguably it is the least important source. Of far greater significance, in terms of impelling governments to take concerted action in a form which tends towards the creation of regimes or stronger modes of internationalized governance, is the nature of certain problems. Some problems require the intervention of internationalized governance if they are to be tackled at all. Here, internationalization arises from the nature of the issue and exists whether or not it is perceived by the public. This is because the problem which gives rise to the issue penetrates or transcends borders; it simply cannot be dealt with within the confines of national policy-making. Because the internationalization of the issue arises from the very nature of the problem to be tackled, it is referred to here as *endogenous internationalization.*

Over and above these two modes, an issue may be internationalized by being claimed by some agency of internationalized governance as lying within its competence. Here the international dimension is external to the issue and can be referred to as *exogenous internationalization.* Once agencies of internationalized governance have been established and have set about their work, there is a strong probability that they will seek to expand the range of their activities. This is fundamental to the notion of 'spill-over', which is the key mechanism by which, according to neo-functionalist theory, the integration process develops.

The relationship between endogenous and exogenous internationalization immediately raises the issue of subsidiarity. In general, the debate about subsidiarity centres on a normative question: what should be the allocation of functions between subnational, national, and supranational levels of governance? The principle of subsidiarity is embodied in Article G (para. 5) of the Maastricht Treaty as a modification of Article 3 of the Treaty establishing the European Economic Communities. The relevant passage reads as follows:

In areas which do not fall within its exclusive competence, the Community shall take action, in accordance with the principle of subsidiarity, only if and in so far as the objectives of the proposed action cannot be sufficiently achieved by the Member States and can, therefore, by reason of the scale or effects of the proposed action, be better achieved by the Community.

This provision, and indeed the whole theory of subsidiarity implies, first, that the priority lies with endogenous internationalization in the sense that this is the determining criterion. Secondly, it implies that the categories of exogenous and endogenous internationalization of issues ought to overlap perfectly: that all those issues and only those issues which by their nature require an internationalized response should be claimed by agencies of internationalized governance. From the broader perspective of normative democratic theory, one could add that the category of attributed internationalization should also coincide with these two categories. That is, all issues which are by their nature internationalized, and are, therefore, in this ideal conception, claimed by some internationalized agency, would be perceived by an attentive public to be within the remit of internationalized governance. An attempt to represent this ideal situation diagramatically would involve three equal and concentric circles and only one circle would appear.

A perfect overlap of this kind is highly unlikely. More realistically, we might think of the situation as a set of three circles arranged as an outer, a middle, and an inner circle. The outer circle would represent those issues which are by their very nature internationalized. The next circle would be the subset of these issues to which agencies of internationalized governance lay claim. And the inner circle would represent the subset of these in regard to which the public attributes competence to agencies of internationalized governance. These relationships are depicted in Figure 11.1.

However, even this model is highly fanciful. In reality, the relationship between the three forms of internationalization is likely to be complex, variable, and issue dependent. Instead of being concentric, the circles will overlap and intersect, with different issues falling into the different subsets created by the intersections. Thus, it is useful to approach the problem using set notation and a Venn diagram in order to provide a systematic account of the overlaps and the intersections.

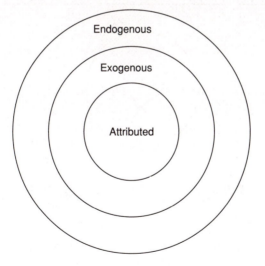

FIGURE 11.1. *Preliminary model of the relationship between categories of internationalization of issues*

We take all issues and designate the three subsets of internationalized issues by the letters A, B, and C. Set A represents issues internationalized by attribution; set B, issues exogenously internationalized; and set C represents issues endogenously internationalized. The universal set, encompasssing all the problems and policy options facing society—including issues at both national and sub-national level—is designated U. We can then categorize the variety of ways in which issues can be internationalized (see Figure 11.2). Thus, the simple case in Figure 11.1 above can be written as: $A \subset B \subset C$. That is, A is a subset of B which, in turn, is a subset of C. Likewise, we could describe the ideal situation according to the theory of subsidiarity in terms of the equality of the three sets of issues: namely $A = B = C$ and $A \cup B \cup C = A \cap B \cap C$.[1]

We have suggested that neither of these accounts of the internationalization of issues is very plausible. Thus, for example, the public may attribute to agencies of internationalized governance issues which do not inherently require internationalized action. They may even attribute competences to such agencies which the agencies do not possess or to which they do not aspire. Moreover, in a process of aggrandisement, agencies may claim competences in relation to issues which do not inherently require an internationalized response. Much

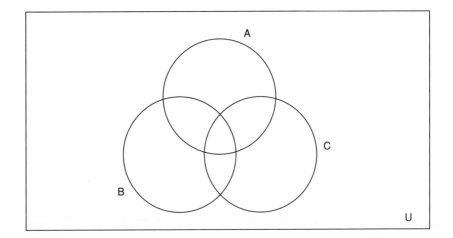

FIGURE 11.2. *Internationalized issues as intersecting subsets of all issues*

A: attributed internationalized issues
B: exogenously internationalized issues
C: endogenously internationalized issues
U: all issues

of the debate about the European Community in the wake of the Danish 'no' vote in May 1992 assumed that just such aggrandisement was a significant source of the difficulties experienced in the ratification process.

Before considering the complexities which arise from the inter-relationships of the three modes of the internationalization of issues, it is important to emphasize that the problem of legitimacy in this area is not limited to attributed internationalization—that is, to instances involving the explicit attribution of competence by the public to an agency of internationalized governance. Suppose, for example, that a given problem is international by its very nature but suppose that the public does not see the problem in these terms; suppose further that there is no regime or institution to deal with the problem. Although this is a situation of purely endogenous internationalization, public opinion may play an important role, either as a source of pressure to get the problem solved or as a constraint on establishing an international regime or institution. It is essential, therefore, to review each of the subsets of internationalized issues, specifying the role of public opinion in each situation. The subsets are highlighted in Figure 11.3. Considering each of them in turn makes it possible to deal in a systematic way with some of the legitimacy issues that arise as nation states and international institutions grapple with a variety of problems.

The World According to Delors (A ∩ B ∩ C). This is set A intersection B intersection C shown in Figure 11.3*a*. This is a world in which the principle of subsidiarity ensures a link between the nature of the issue and the claim to competence by the agency of internationalized governance, and in which a rational and attentive public is fully informed both about the nature of the issues and the policy competences of the various levels of governance. Interestingly, in terms of our focus on internationalized governance in general rather than just the European Community, Delors himself envisaged that the principle of subsidiarity would extend up to the international level, creating 'a real equilibrium between the Community level, the national level and the local level [and], I dare also add, the international level . . . ' (Delors 1991: 11). The immediate questions for empirical investigation, then, are: how extensive is the area included in the overlap defined in Figure 11.3*a* and how salient are the problems in that area?

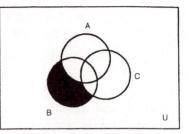

(a) The world according to Delors (A ∩ B ∩ C)

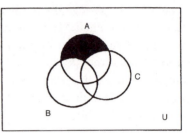

(b) The imperious centre (B~A ∪ C)

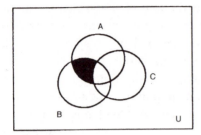

(c) *De facto* legitimacy (A ∩ B~C)

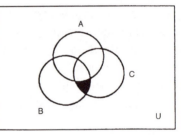

(d) Delegitimizing demand (A~B ∪ C)

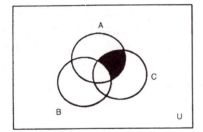

(e) Fertile ground (A ∩ C~B)

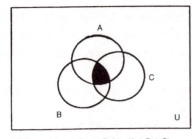

(f) Proceed and persuade (B ∩ C~A)

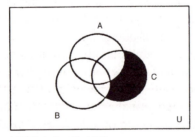

A: attributed internationalized issues
B: exogenously internationalized issues
C: endogenously internationalized issues
U: all issues

(g) Virgin territory (C~A ∪ B)

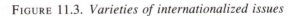

FIGURE 11.3. *Varieties of internationalized issues*

The Imperious Centre (B ~ A ∪ C). Going by the flood of political analysis and sometimes heated debate which followed after the Danish referendum and beyond, the part of set B not included in either A or C (set B negation A union C, shown in Figure 11.3*b*) was a major factor underlying popular misgivings about the Maastricht Treaty. Thus, the task here, having defined the set of issues in which the European Community claims competence or seeks to exercise jurisdiction without an endogenous basis for such claims or efforts, is to identify those issues on which the public is resistant to initiatives by the Community. In other words, to identify issues which have low attributed internationalization.

De Facto *Legitimacy* (A ∩ B ~ C). In the subset of issues in A intersection B negation C, depicted in Figure 11.3*c*, attributions in public opinion confer a certain *de facto* legitimacy on the claimed competences of agencies of internationalized governance. However, because the claims are not underpinned by endogenous internationalization, they are vulnerable to challenge on the basis of the principle of subsidiarity. If successfully challenged, and if public attribution of competence does not rapidly adapt to the new situation, then what had been a source of *de facto* legitimacy for internationalized governance could be transformed into a threat to that legitimacy. It could become a source of delegitimizing demand.

Delegitimizing Demand (A ~ B ∪ C). The sub-set A exclusive of issues in B or C, shown in Figure 11.3*d*, has a particular bearing on legitimacy because it contains explicit demands for internationalized action which are neither rooted in the nature of the issues involved nor in competences claimed by the agency of internationalized governance. It represents, therefore, an excessive demand on the agency to which the agency neither does, nor could, respond. If the issues involved are salient, there is the potential for a rapid loss of legitimacy as the agency of internationalized governance fails to deliver on the expectations which mass publics have of it. As suggested above, a significant roll-back of Community competences could further enlarge the number of issues in this subset as the Community is prevented from acting in areas in which expectations have grown or have been fostered.

Fertile Ground (A ∩ C ~ B). In contrast to the difficulties arising in the previous three subsets, in which an agency of internationalized govern-ance should rein in its ambitions or at least tread warily, the subset here—Figure 11.3*e*—represents issues on which such an agency should forge ahead decisively. These (A intersection C excluding issues in B) are endogenously internationalized issues which are recognized as such by the public. Internationalized action would be legitimate both in principle and in the perceptions of the public. The empirical question, of course, is whether any such issues exist, and how significant and salient are they?

Proceed and Persuade (B ∩ C ~ A). Figure 11.3*f*, by contrast, represents an area already claimed by an agency of internationalized governance. However, while the claim is supported by the principle of subsidiarity, persuasion is required if the public is to accept the claim and not regard internationalized action as 'interference in national affairs'. Here, in particular, national differentiation becomes important and it will be necessary to uncover the extent to which issues in this subset vary from one member state to another.

Virgin Territory (C ~ A ∪ B). Issues in sub-set C exclusive of those in A or B, depicted in Figure 11.3*g*, represent virgin territory in the sense that the agency of internationalized governance has not made any claims in the area, the public does not attribute competence to the agency in respect of it, but the problems are inherently transnational. Here we would expect an expansion of agency competence but antici-pate that, particularly in the current climate in Europe, it might be done only with difficulty in so far as competences not founded either on precedent or on public attribution may well be contested.

A particularly trenchant aphorism in political analysis was Harold Lasswell's statement that politics is about 'who gets what, when, how' (Lasswell 1936). Looked at from the perspective of public opinion, this can be transformed into 'who wants what, when, how'. In the discussion of the various subsets of issues outlined above, the focus has been mainly on 'how'. That is, on the attribution and distribution of competences and, in particular, on the relationship between attributed competence, claimed competence, and any basis such claims might have in a principle of subsidiarity. However, this is only one part of orientations towards internationalized issues. A full treatment of the topic would also consider evaluations of outcomes and outputs, exploring the substantive content of policy preferences and evaluations, and the priority or salience attached to them. In our terms, it is necessary to consider 'what' and 'when' as well as 'how'.

We deal with these aspects, where possible, in the analysis which follows in this chapter. However, we should point out the limits of the possible in this regard. While there are some data on the salience and priority of issues, data on the substantive policy preferences and evaluations of the public *vis-à-vis* internationalized issues are rare. But we have an embarrassment of riches in the area of attribution, at least so far as the quantity of indicators is concerned. The quality and, in particular, the comparability of these indicators is another matter. This brings us to the question of operationalization, which we discuss both in relation to indicators of attributed internationalization and in relation to indicators of exogenous and endogenous internationalization.

Operationalizing Attributed Internationalization

What we are looking for here is an empirical operationalization of a normative outlook. The problem is to identify the evidence by which to measure the extent to which the public looks to one level of governance rather than another as the most appropriate agency to tackle a particular problem or range of problems. There have been three main indicators of the attributed internationalization of issues in this sense in the Euro-barometer surveys. The first poses the alternative 'better dealt with by a European Government' versus 'better dealt with by a (country) government'. This can be labelled 'European government attribution'. This question has been applied to ten issues, ranging from broad policy areas such as economic growth, poverty, and unemployment, to quite specific issues such as scientific research and drug addiction. The ten areas are: pollution of the environment, military defence, scientific research, investment by foreign firms in [country], drug addiction, economic growth, poverty and unemployment, aid to underdeveloped countries, rising prices, major political negotiations with the Americans, the Russians etc.

The 'European government attribution' question was asked in six Eurobarometer surveys between 1973 and 1987. Thus, the indicator has the advantage of covering a substantial time span, although with significant gaps; in particular, there are no data for 1975–82. It is also a stark question in that it poses the radically opposite alternatives of decision by a European government versus decision by the national government. Moreover, when the question was first posed in this form, the notion of a European government was hardly central to the Community agenda.

A more realistic attribution question was introduced in 1974 and used quite often since. However, both the basic question and the issues to which it has been applied have varied. The common elements in the questions are, first, the presentation to the respondent of a list of problems and, secondly, whether, in each instance, the problem would be better dealt with, or decided upon, by the individual member states acting independently or separately, or whether it should be dealt with by action in common. The precise wording of the question varies, as does the list of problems presented. The way in which national versus Community action was described also varies. The latter variations are the most important and they are listed in Figure 11.4.

This series of questions has several advantages over the European government attribution question. In particular, the questions are more in tune with the realities of the attribution of competence in the European Community. However, this means that we must take account not only of the variations in question wording, but also recognize that the object in

---

1. . . . better to deal with it by combined action through the common market or rather by an action of our government independently of other countries (Eurobarometer, Nos. 2 and 3)

2. . . . prefer the decisions on how to deal with this problem were taken by the European community as a whole, or by each country separately. (Eurobarometer, Nos. 6 and 10)

3. . . . better that decisions about it should be taken by each country separately or by the members of the European Community (Common Market) acting together? (Eurobarometer, Nos. 19, 22, and 24)

4. . . . decisions about it should be taken by the countries of the Community acting together or by each one separately? (Eurobarometer, No. 28)

5. . . . decisions about it should be taken by the member countries of the European Community acting together or by each country separately? (Eurobarometer, Nos. 31*a* and 36)

FIGURE 11.4. *Variations in question wording in EC attributions*

the question is a floating referent, depending on how the phrases specifying European Community action were understood at the time.[2] A further advantage of the measure is that it covers quite a wide span of policy issues. Moreover, it provides data over an extended period. Lastly, although the question wording varies, several of the variations are minor, such as the reversal of the order in which the options of Community and national action are listed.[3] This indicator is labelled 'European Community attribution (problems)', or 'problems attribution' for short, and it is the basis for one of our main presentations of evidence on the attributed internationalization of issues.

A major change in the wording of the attribution question was introduced in 1989 and the new form has been used regularly since then. Rather than referring to problems, the new question refers to policies and how they should be determined or decided. The original version of the question, in Eurobarometer, No. 31*a*, reads as follows:

Some people believe that certain areas of policy should be determined by the (national) government, while other areas of policy should be determined in common with the European Community. Which of the following areas of policy do you think should be determined by the (national) government and which should be decided in common with the European Community as a whole?

In the next survey, Eurobarometer, No. 32, this wording was altered slightly and the alteration became the standard version. This question reads:

Some people believe that certain areas of policy should be decided by (national) government, while other areas of policy should be decided jointly within the European Community. Which of the following areas of policy do you think should be decided by the (national) government, and which should be decided jointly within the European Community?

This indicator can be labelled 'European Community attribution (policies)'—or 'policies attribution'. The shift to this policies attribution indicator actually involves three changes. First, the change in question wording noted above; secondly, changes in how the individual issues are described; and, thirdly, a change in the set of issues dealt with. The latter change is the most problematic when it comes to comparability. Even so, in cases where the same broad issue area is covered by a problems indicator in one period and a policies indicator in another, there is at least the possibility of achieving reasonable comparability. But we shall need to examine the degree of comparability in each case.

Given that we have to rely on comparable but non-identical measures, we are fortunate that when the policies attribution question was first introduced, the problems attribution question was also asked. Moreover, two issues were common to the lists of problems and policies: the environment and development aid. This allows us to check the functional equivalence of the two indicators, although there are variations both in the question asked and in the item which describes the issue. For the environment, the item in the problems question was 'the protection of nature and the struggle against pollution', whereas the item in the policies question was 'protection of the environment'. In response to the problems question, 73 per cent felt that decisions should be taken by the member countries of the European Community acting together; in response to the policies question, 71 per cent felt that policy should be decided in common with the European Community as a whole. The match between responses to the two questions dealing with development aid is less close. The items were, 'Help the poor countries of Africa, South America, Asia, etc.' and 'Cooperation with developing countries, Third World'. In response to the first question, 68 per cent favoured decisions being taken together; in response to the second, 75 per cent favoured policies being decided in common with the European Community as a whole. Even so, a 7 percentage point difference is not startling and could be thought not seriously to dent the comparability of the indicators.

However, cross-tabulation of the responses to both versions of each of the questions suggests that, in both issue areas, the data produced by the different questions are not as consistent as they seem at first sight. In fact, as Table 11.1 shows, in both cases, some 20 per cent of respondents gave inconsistent responses; that is, opting for the national response on one question and the Community response on the other. As already emphasized, we do not know whether the inconsistencies arise from the change in the wording of the question or the specification of the issue area. None the less, the indications of some inconsistency between the two kinds of indicators of attributed internationalization suggest that each type of indicator should be dealt with separately. Moreover, if we want to compare the evolution of attributed internationalization over a time period which spans the change in question wording, we should do so with careful attention to the transition from one indicator to the other.

TABLE 11.1. *Consistency of policy and problem attribution on environment and development aid, 1989*

Policy attribution	Problems	
	Decisions should be taken by member countries acting together	Decisions should be taken by each country acting separately
(*a*) Environment		
Should be decided by (national) government	14.2	9.5
Should be decided in common with EC	70.0	6.3
$N = 10,108$		
(*b*) Development aid		
Should be decided by (national) government	10.9	8.8
Should be decided in common with EC	70.0	10.2
$N = 9,693$		

Note: Entries are percentages.

Source: Eurobarometer, No. 31*a*.

A final problem with the operationalization of attributed internationalization is that the earlier conceptual discussion suggests a dichotomy —issues are either internationalized or not—whereas the data reflect a continuum. This arises because the variable is measured as a dichotomy at the individual level but the aggregation of responses reveals that some issues are highly internationalized, in the sense of being attributed to an internationalized agency by a large majority of the public, some are only moderately internationalized, and some are internationalized only to a minor extent. Clearly, the either/or implication of the concept as originally discussed is an over-simplification. Hence, the review of the evidence on attribution has to take into account degrees of attributed internationalization.

Operationalizing Exogenous and Endogenous Internationalization

The problems of operationalizing attributed internationalization pale into insignificance beside those which arise when tackling exogenous and endogenous internationalization. Such operational definitions must be rooted in an understanding of both the actual competences of the agencies of internationalized governance and what those competences ought to be. It is apparent from current political debate in the Community and in the member countries, however, that both of these are what philosophers call 'essentially contested concepts'.

Of the two concepts, it might seem that exogenous internationalization would be easier to operationalize. Certainly, if we confine our attention to the European Community, then the various EC treaties, the procedures actually adopted, and the programmes pursued by the Community should provide a reasonable guide. But the notion of 'claims to competence by the Community', or exogenous internationalization, is complex. In reality, many issues, perhaps even a majority, lie in a middle ground of 'concurrent powers' rather than belonging exclusively to national or Community competence (Wilke and Wallace 1990: 6). Clearly, this plays havoc with any notion of a simple dichotomy between (exogenously) internationalized and noninternationalized issues. However, it can probably be dealt with by, again, allowing for degrees of internationalization and focusing on those cases where the agency of internationalized governance assumes a major role either exclusively or concurrently with the nation states.

A more fundamental difficulty arises from the fact that treaties, as well as being justiciable, are subject to political interpretation and ongoing political conflict. Political conflict is even more prevalent in regard to the *ad hoc* programmes and the procedures of the Community. Depending on the issue in question, action by the Community can imply a relatively high degree of autonomy and initiative, or it can mean a painfully slow pace of movement dictated by the reservations of the most reluctant member state. Finally, there is the complicating factor of the changing competences of the Community, especially the major developments in this regard which are embodied in the provisions of the Single European Act and the Maastricht Treaty. However, all of these are complications and challenges rather than insuperable obstacles to operationalizing our concepts. If we focus on the question of whether or not a particular issue is decided exclusively at national level, reasonably valid operational definitions should be possible.

More problematic still is the third category—endogenous internationalization. Looking at the principle of subsidiarity from a normative and constitutional perspective in the context of the European Community, Wilke and Wallace ask (1990: 6): 'If the concept of subsidiarity has such fuzzy edges and rests on subjective, not objective, analysis, does it make sense to give it a quasi-constitutional character or to entrench it in primary Community law?' Looked at from an empirical perspective, we might ask: does it make sense to attempt to operationalize it? The answer to this question must be that the concept of subsidiarity—or the underlying notions of exogenous and endogenous internationalization—is so central to our research task that we cannot evade the problem, if only to minimize the fuzzy edges.

A major pitfall here is to see virtually all problems as internationalized. This may arise from a perception of the pervasiveness of interdependence or from the implicit assumption that, because national governments are unsuccessful in dealing with a particular problem, both the problem and the policy should be internationalized. To avoid over-extending the concept of endogenous internationalization, we stipulate that either the nature of the problem or the scale of the policy appropriate to dealing with it require a response at the internationalized level. This stipulation mirrors the two approaches to the principle of subsidiarity in the d'Estaing Report prepared for the Institutional Affairs Committee of the European Parliament. The first is based on the criterion of 'effectiveness': 'that the States will transfer to a higher level only those tasks which will be better accomplished at Community level than by the States acting individually'. The second approach is based on a 'transnational criterion', assigning to Community level 'only those tasks the dimension or effects of which extend beyond national frontiers' (Giscard d'Estaing 1990, 6–37).[4] This distinction was originally outlined in Article 12 of the Draft Treaty establishing the European Union (European Parliament 1984).

Even these criteria of policy effectiveness and transnational impact, however, may not point to an objective feature inherent in every issue which makes it an internationalized or non-internationalized issue. One must also take into account that all issues are embedded in a context of prior agreement and prevailing political perspectives and commitments. Thus, a particular issue may be internationalized because it is intimately linked to the achievement of other objectives agreed between a number of nation states. Article 235 of the Treaty of Rome caters for this aspect of the internationalization of issues:

If action by the Community should prove necessary to attain, in the course of the operation of the common market, one of the objectives of the Community and this treaty has not provided the necessary powers, the Council shall, acting unanimously on a proposal from the Commission and after consulting the European Parliament, take the appropriate measures.

We can sum up this discussion by emphasizing that operationalizing our key concepts is problematic in all three cases. But the implications for the legitimacy of internationalized governance of the different combinations of the three types of internationalization of issues set out in Figures 11.3*a*–11.3*g* are sufficiently significant to make the effort worthwhile. In this chapter, we focus on the aspect which is central to the theme of this volume and is most likely to yield immediate dividends: the public opinion or attributed internationalization aspect. In regard to the other two dimensions of internationalization which, we have argued, are essential in interpreting the legitimacy implications stemming from attributed internationalization, we shall proceed on the basis of reasonable assumptions rather than definitive demonstration.

Empirical Evidence

Tables 11.2 and 11.3 show the extent of the attributed internationalization of issues in the European Community over a twenty-year period. Table 11.2 is based on what was described above as 'problems attribution'; with some gaps, the data cover the period 1974–91 at reasonably regular intervals. Table 11.3 is based on 'policies attribution', an indicator which, as we have seen, is available only since 1989.

Before examining the tables, two preliminary comments about Table 11.2 are required. The first relates to the notably low level of attributed internationalization in 1976 and 1978 relative to levels in preceding and succeeding years. This corresponds to—but is considerably greater than—a dip in the membership indicator in approximately the same period (see Chapter 4). However, the wording of the attribution question in 1976 and 1978 was much stronger (in the sense of being more supranational) than the wordings in previous or subsequent surveys. That the stronger version of the question seems to have depressed the level of attribution is of substantive as well as methodological interest. It suggests that the attributed internationalization which the citizens of the Community have in mind is more likely to be intergovernmental rather than supranational (compare version 2 to other versions of the attribution question shown in Figure 11.4). In any event, in order to avoid the methodological artefact reflected in the 1976 and 1978 data, the average levels of internationalization have been calculated for the data since 1983 where these are available.

TABLE 11.2. *Attributed internationalization of problems in the European Community, 1974–91*

	1974	1975	1976	1978	1983	1984	1985	1987	1989	1991	Average
Fight terrorism/crime							73	74		75	74
Development aid	66	63	46	62	69	74	77	72	68	75	72
Fight pollution/protect environment				49	70	71	69	68	73	74	71
Scientific and technical research							70				70
Defend interests (US, USSR, Japan)	74				70	70	68	62	64	68	68
Ensure energy supplies		67								65	67
Fight rising prices	70	66	49	51	65	64	57				62
Reduce differences between different regions	52	50			57	66	63				62
Defend interests (US, USSR)	68	64	53	60	62	61	58	59			59
Defence			44	47	65	61	59	51		57	58
Fight unemployment			38	48				53	54	54	58
Reduce income inequalities			31	41				54	60	57	57
Modernize agriculture	54	51	49	53							53
Control multinationals			33	36							51
Protect consumers			29	33			50				50
Reduce difference between regions in our country								45	48	48	47
Modernize education			24	31							28
More self-government for the regions			15	20							18
Provide housing			15								15
N	9,060	9,610	9,210	8,677	9,790	9,909	11,849	11,583	11,819	13,044	10,455

Notes: Entries are percentages attributing responsibility for the problem to the European level. For items for which data are available since 1983, the average is based on the period 1983–91 (see text). Other averages are based on the available data.

Sources: Eurobarometer, Nos. 2, 3, 6, 10, 19, 22, 24, 28, 31a, and 36.

The second preliminary comment is also methodological. In two instances the descriptions of the problems varied to such an extent as effectively to define different issues. The two cases are 'defend interests against the US and the USSR' versus 'defend interests against US, the Soviet Union and Japan'; and 'reduce regional differences' versus 'reduce regional differences within our country'. In these instances, the policy area is treated as two distinct issue areas.

In Table 11.2, the ranking of internationalized issues has been subdivided according to the average level of attributed internationalization shown in the right-hand column. Although this subdivision is necessarily somewhat arbitrary, the first six issues (from 'fight terrorism/crime' to 'ensure energy supplies') can be regarded as highly internationalized. The next ten issues (from 'fight rising prices' to 'reduce differences between regions in our country') can be seen as moderately internationalized, and the final three issues ('modernize education', 'more self-government for the regions', and 'provide housing') as weakly internationalized.

The remarkably comprehensive coverage of issues in the Eurobarometer attribution question means that in Table 11.3 we can present an attributed internationalization ranking for no less than thirty issues. Although, again, the cut-off points are somewhat arbitrary, these issues can be subdivided into three groups: ten issues show a high level of internationalization; ten show a moderate level; and ten show a low level. Where policies or issues are common to Tables 11.2 and 11.3, the assignment of the issue to a particular level of internationalization is generally confirmed.

However, as should be clear from the discusion so far, this kind of ordering and grouping of issues, while of some interest, does not get at the core of the problem. The key to the interpretation of these data lies in the relationship between attribution and the exogenous and endogenous dimensions of internationalization. Accordingly, we need to examine all three dimensions of internationalization in relation to each other. This can best be done in terms of the sub-sets defined in Figure 11.3.

The World According to Delors

Four issues fall fairly clearly within this particular subset: scientific research, development aid, environmental protection, and the fight against terrorism, drugs, and crime. The level of attributed

TABLE 11.3. *Attributed internationalization of policies in the European Community, 1989–93*

	1989	1989	1990	1990	1991	1991	1992	1992	1993	Average
Human rights									80	80
Fight cancer/AIDS									80	80
Fight against drugs									79	79
Citizens' rights									77	77
Scientific research	74	75	74	74	77	73	77	75	69	74
Third World	75	71	71	74	76	75	77	76	72	74
International co-operation									71	71
Environment	71	61	62	65	69	65	69	66	65	66
Foreign policy	65	61	61	65	69	66	68	69	66	66
Fight against poverty									65	65
Political asylum							54	55	56	55
Currency	52	54	50	56	58	53	54	55	56	55
Industrial policy							57	57	49	54
Immigration policy							54	54	54	54
VAT	52	51	48	50	51	48	52	52	46	50
Unemployment							49	50	48	49
Economic policy									49	49
Action for women									48	48
Action for young people									48	48
Security and defence	47	43	44	46	48	47	53	49	49	47

TABLE 11.3. *Cont.*

	1989	1989	1990	1990	1991	1991	1992	1992	1993	Average
Action for elderly									45	45
Workers' health and safety							47	45	42	45
Consumer protection									44	44
Action for families									43	43
Press standards	39	44	43	42	46	40	44	43	34	42
Cultural policy							45	37	34	39
Health welfare standards	43	36	38	36	40	34	40	37	36	38
Data protection	42	35	35	35	39	34	38	37	33	36
Educational standards	41	31	35	34	39	33	38	36	31	35
Workers co-determination	40	33	35	34	37	33	37	36	27	35
N	11,819	23,397	11,775	12,872	13,121	13,004	13,082	13,008	13,109	13,910

Note: Entries are percentages attributing responsibility for the policy to the European level.

Sources: Eurobarometer, Nos. 31*a*, 32–39.

internationalization is high in all cases, all are claimed as areas of competence by the Community,[5] and all are generally recognized as being appropriate to that level. Perhaps the most notable feature here is that, out of thirty issues, there are only four items in the set. The ideal world of perfect subsidiarity and (near) perfect information is far from realization.

To add to the problems of this particular ideal, we find (see Table 11.4) that one of the issues (development aid) is only moderately salient: 35 per cent consider it to be very important, compared to 77 per cent for environmental protection, 75 per cent for fighting unemployment, and 65 per cent for fighting poverty. The salience of environmental issues is further demonstrated in Table 11.5 which shows that 76 per cent believe that the protection of the environment and the struggle against pollution is urgent and immediate rather than a problem for the future or not really a problem at all. Moreover, despite the problems of unemployment and low economic growth, a mere 9 per cent think that the economy should take priority over the environment (Table 11.5). While one-third of European citizens feel that it is sometimes necessary to make a judgement between the two, 57 per cent chose the option 'protection of the environment is essential for economic development'.

The responses to a range of environmental problems at local, national, and global levels also show that the environmental problems people are concerned about are problems which, by their nature, are internationalized (Table 11.6). The local issues in this set show relatively low levels of concern, with only some 15–30 per cent of respondents indicating that they matter either a great deal or a fair amount. The issues defined in the question as global matters elicit concern from 75–80 per cent of respondents. It might be countered

TABLE 11.4. *Salience of four issues, 1989*

Issue	Very important	Important	Of little importance	Not important at all	N
Environmental protection	77.2	19.3	1.1	0.3	11,819
Development aid	34.4	40.5	16.5	4.6	11,819
Fight unemployment	74.8	21.1	1.8	0.3	11,819
Fight poverty	64.8	29.4	3.0	0.5	11,819

Note: Entries are percentages.

Source: Eurobarometer, No. 31*a*.

TABLE 11.5. *Salience of environmental issues, 1987*

	%
Many people are concerned about the protection of the environment and the struggle against pollution. How immediate do you consider this struggle to be?	
Urgent and immediate	76.1
A problem for the future	20.6
Not really a problem at all	3.3
$N = 11,223$	
I would like to give you some opinions which are often expressed about the problems of the environment. Which are you most in agreement with?	
The economy should take priority over the environment	9.0
It is sometimes necessary to make a judgement between the two	33.7
Protection of the environment is essential for economic development	57.3
$N = 10,540$	

Source: Eurobarometer, No. 28.

TABLE 11.6. *Salience of local, national, and global environmental issues, 1987*

	Matters a great deal	Matters a fair amount	N
Local issues			
Quality of drinking water	8.9	13.0	11,520
Noise	8.9	13.4	11,617
Air pollution	10.6	16.1	11,544
Rubbish disposal	10.4	14.5	11,534
Access to countryside	6.4	10.2	11,552
Loss of good farmland	8.2	13.3	10,895
Damage to landscape	13.0	17.8	11,338
National issues			
Pollution of rivers	45.9	35.9	11,550
Damage to sea life and beaches	48.4	34.1	11,466
Air pollution	44.3	34.1	11,538
Disposal of industrial waste	50.3	30.3	11,366
Global issues			
Extinction of plants and animals	42.8	35.5	11,485
Loss of natural resources	38.2	36.8	11,325
CO_2 damage to atmosphere and weather	44.3	33.2	11,202

Note: Entries are percentages.

Source: Eurobarometer, No. 28.

that Table 11.6 also shows that, since 'national environmental issues' elicit similar levels of concern, the definition of environmental problems as seen by the public does not have an inherently internationalized dimension. However, inspection of the individual items categorized under this heading suggests otherwise. With just one possible exception (disposal of industrial waste), these issues permeate borders in most member states of the Community. Certainly the issues of river pollution and damage to sea life and beaches do so, and they all elicit expressions of concern from some 80 per cent and more of respondents.

The Imperious Centre

Two issues seem to fit into this category: education or educational standards and workers' co-determination. Taking into account both Tables 11.2 and 11.3, the attributed internationalization of these two issues is very low. Moreover, it would be difficult to claim that, aside from the highly specific matters of mutual recognition of qualifications and social dumping, there is anything like a consensus that these are by nature internationalized issues. Yet the European Community has significant policy competence and has launched policy initiatives in both areas. It would appear, therefore, that these are areas where the perception of 'an overweening Brussels bureaucracy' may obtain. However, before drawing conclusions regarding the consequences of such perceptions for the legitimacy of the Community, we would need data on the salience of these issues. At this stage, and on the basis of the available data, it is worth noting that accounts which argue that the European public has been reacting against 'interference from Brussels', and that this explains the *malaise* regarding the Maastricht Treaty, may be somewhat exaggerated. There is some evidence of resistance to the imperious centre but it is limited in its scope and implications.

De Facto *Legitimacy*

Since the mid-1970s, the European Community has sought to develop a co-ordinated policy on energy supplies. In part, this policy is rooted in the origins of the Community in the ECSC and EURATOM. The major source of the policy has been the objective of secure supply and the relationship between this issue and several foreign policy issues. It seems from the data in Table 11.2 that a substantial section of the European public agrees that this is an internationalized issue. However, while the issue of energy supplies (as opposed to the issue of an internal market in energy) can be regarded as having fairly high attributed internationalization, it would seem difficult to argue that it is endogenously internationalized. Accordingly, the issue falls into the category of *de facto* legitimacy: the Community has the backing of the public in its pursuit of policies in this area, but its competence is vulnerable in that it is not based on considerations which are inherent in the nature of the problem. One might therefore anticipate that, as the principle of subsidiarity begins to be applied in a serious and systematic way, this particular policy competence will be curtailed and some effort will be required to re-orient public expectations in this area towards the nation state.

De-legitimizing Demand

This is the sub-set of issues where the public attributes competence to the agency of internationalized governance, yet without the agency in question claiming competence and without the existence of a cogent case for such competence. The de-legitimizing danger involved is that demands may be made on internationalized governance, and expectations of internationalized action created, which cannot be met. In early 1993, two out of every three respondents felt that the problem of fighting poverty ought to be tackled at a European rather than a national level. However, when the problem is defined as reducing inequalities between the rich and the poor, the level of internationalization falls to 57 per cent. In the category of moderately high internationalization, we also find the problem of unemployment (49 per cent in Table 11.3 but 58 per cent in Table 11.2).

The European Commission has had programmes and policies for fighting poverty and tackling unemployment over a considerable period. However, these measures are not capable of solving either problem; indeed, they are not designed to be the major means of solving them. Therefore, although there is a role for the Community in these policy areas, the most reasonable assumption would seem to be, on balance, that the issues are neither endogenously nor exogenously internationalized. Consequently, the Community is in the unenviable position of being expected to lead the battle against these twin problems without having adequate means with which to do so, and without any substantial evidence that either problem could be solved by action undertaken by the Community. The potential de-legitimizing consequences are underlined by the fact that these issues, especially unemployment, are highly salient (see Table 11. 4).

Fertile Ground

Since the inauguration of European Political Co-operation (EPC) in 1970, European élites have been inching their way towards a co-ordinated foreign policy. At the same time, they have jealously guarded the prerogatives of the state in this sensitive area of 'high politics'. While the Single European Act brought this activity within a treaty framework, it merely codified existing practice and did not represent any significant breakthrough in terms of claims to European competence. The Maastricht Treaty (Article J) has taken some steps in this direction, but the approach is still highly tentative and qualified. The issue, therefore, cannot be said to be clearly exogenously internationalized. Nevertheless, in a European context, a strong argument can be made that it is endogenously internationalized. Substantial sections of the European public seem to concur with this view. As Table 11.3 shows, an average of 66 per cent attribute competence for the policy area to the Community. Taking the Community as a whole, therefore, the issue falls into the category of 'fertile ground'.

As the issue of a common foreign policy belongs in the realm of high politics, and is therefore highly sensitive, one would hypothesize that there will be substantial contrasts between the attitudes of the public in different member states. In those member states in which the attribution of competence is noticeably lower, the issue may have to be regarded as belonging in the 'virgin territory' category; that is, as an issue requiring both an extension of the competence of the Union and persuasion of the public that such an extension is desirable. Accordingly, the hypothesis of national differentiation in attributed internationalization in this area will be taken up in dealing with the virgin territory category below.

Proceed and Persuade

In the information society, the issue of data protection transcends borders. The transnational nature of the issue is further enhanced by cross-border police co-operation in a system of open frontiers. Data protection is also an issue on which the European Community claims the right to set standards and to bring about harmonization. However, proceeding to do so will require considerable persuasion. As Table 11.2 shows, on average only a little over one-third of the European public sees the need for a benign European uncle to protect them from Big Brother.

It can, of course, be argued that many issues fall into the proceed and persuade category in so far as significant minorities withhold attributing competence to the Community on issues which are internationalized according to the other two dimensions. In the case of environmental protection, for example, there is the one-third minority who do not attribute competence in this area to the Community (see Table 11.3). So, why is it that environmental issues belong to 'the world according to Delors' for some and fall into the category of 'proceed and persuade' for others? Here, one of the relatively rare pieces of evidence on policy evaluation in the Eurobarometer surveys is of interest. The evaluation relates to national rather than European authorities, and is in response to the question 'Do you know if in (your country), the responsible authorities are concerned with the protection of the environment? If yes, do you think the authorities are doing an effective job or not?' In spring 1988, only one in four (23 per cent) of the citizens of Europe indicated that they believed that the national authorities were both concerned and effective. A clear majority, 57 per cent, believed that they were concerned but not effective; 20 per cent thought that they were not even concerned. This suggests that one source of the attributed internationalization of issues may be perceptions of policy-making failure at the national level. Unfortunately, it is not possible to test the relationship between the evaluation of national action and the attribution of competence to the Community as the attribution question was not asked in the Eurobarometer survey which carried the evaluation question.

Virgin Territory

As we saw above, foreign policy constitutes fertile ground where the Union can, in virtue of the combination of endogenous and attributed internationalization, confidently develop its capacity. However, we have speculated that in certain member states this policy area may belong to the category of issues which are endogenously transnational but which, were the Union to make major claims to competence, it would not be supported by public opinion. Figure 11.5 examines this question with data on the attribution of competence for foreign policy issues in 1989 and 1993. The countries are arranged from left to right in descending order of attributed internationalization in 1993. In the countries on the right-hand side of the figure—Greece, Portugal, and Denmark—this issue fell fairly clearly into the 'virgin territory' category in 1989 with relatively low attributed internationalization. Four years later, most member states showed increases in the attribution of competence for foreign policy to the Union, but the greatest increase occurred in those three same countries. Thus, there has been a

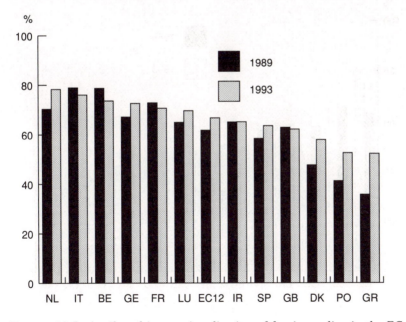

FIGURE 11.5. *Attributed internationalization of foreign policy in the EC by member states, 1989 and 1993.*

Sources: Eurobarometer, Nos. 32 and 39.

narrowing of the gap in the attributed internationalization of foreign policy; in other words, foreign policy is móre firmly within the fertile ground category than earlier. This development is all the more significant in that it occurred in a period during which, as demonstrated in Chapter 4, overall support for integration was in decline.

The Maastricht Treaty, however, has the stated aim of arriving not just at a common foreign policy but at a common foreign and security policy that would involve 'the eventual framing of a common defence policy, which might in time lead to a common defence' (Treaty on European Union, Art. J4 section 1). The circumspection of the treaty framers appears to be well justified in the light of data on the attributed internationalization of security and defence policy in 1989 and 1993, reported in Figure 11.6. With the exception of the Netherlands in 1993, no country reaches the levels of attributed internationalization evident in the case of foreign policy. More importantly, whereas the level of attributed internationalization on foreign policy was about two-thirds across the European Community as a whole, in the area of security and

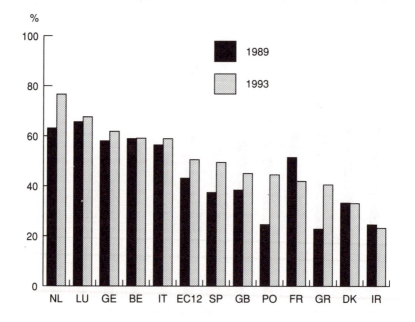

FIGURE 11.6. *Attributed internationalization of security and defence policy in the EC by member states, 1989 and 1993*

Sources: Eurobarometer, Nos. 32 and 39.

defence policy it was less than half. Finally, the spread of opinion across the member states, illustrated in Figure 11.6, is dramatic, ranging from a low of 23 per cent in Ireland and 33 per cent in Denmark to 77 per cent in the Netherlands. In short, if we make the assumption that, in a European context, security and defence policy is an endogenously internationalized issue, then in the Union as a whole, and in some member states in particular, it is virgin territory.

Conclusion

Our analysis suggests that the legitimacy of internationalized governance is a highly differentiated matter which varies from one policy area to another. It depends, moreover, on the relationship between public perceptions and expectations on the one hand, and, on the other, on the nature of the problems being confronted and the claims of the Community or other agency of internationalized governance.

Our analysis is limited in the sense that we examined certain policy areas for which we have evidence of attributed internationalization. Moreover, there are several issues which have not been considered here because we lack evidence about the degree of internationalization attributed to them. This suggests that the agenda of issues on which this kind of data is collected needs consideration. Even so, the analysis in this chapter adds weight to a recurring theme in this volume: that orientations towards internationalized governance are highly differentiated, by time and by country, and by institutional and policy sectors. This theme of the manifold nature of European public opinion and European publics is taken up again in the concluding chapter.

NOTES

1. For an introduction to the notation and its use, see Kemeny, Snell, and Thompson (1966: 45–57).
2. For example, the reference to Community action would have meant something quite different when the Luxembourg compromise was in operation from what it would have meant in the period following the Single European Act.
3. Note, however, that the wording used in Eurobarometer, Nos. 6 and 10, is substantially different. It will be necessary to return to this point in discussing the data.

4. The report contains a useful categorization of the competences of the Community in the context of the debate on subsidiarity. It lists issues which belong to the Community level according to the EEC treaty and the Single European Act and then goes on to apply the principle of subsidiarity to the powers which the Community envisages acquiring. It also lists a set of issues which should be entrusted mainly to the lower level (Giscard d'Estaing 1990: 8–11).

5. Differences between the ways in which two of these issues are handled at Community level illustrate the differences which can occur in the modes of exogenous internationalization. Environmental protection is very much a Commission bailiwick, whereas policy on terrorism, drugs, and crime has been kept well away from Commission intervention, being handled in the Trevi Group process and, now, in the third pillar developed under the Maastricht Treaty. But, despite the differences, both are forms of exogenous internationalization.

12

Democratic Legitimacy and the European Parliament

OSKAR NIEDERMAYER AND RICHARD SINNOTT

One of the underlying assumptions of this volume is that public opinion affects the legitimacy of internationalized governance—even in the absence of formal, institutional linkages. Accordingly, little attention has been paid, so far, to institutions, other than to note the general point that the relevance of public opinion is affected by variations in the institutional structure at the national level (see Chapter 1). However, we have now reached the stage at which it is necessary to deal with an aspect of internationalized governance with a strong institutional dimension: the issue of democratic representation and democratic legitimacy.

This issue is often discussed only in the context of the democratic deficit of the EC and often, even more narrowly, only in the context of the role and function of the European Parliament. But democratic theorists have been very alive to the wider dimensions of the problem. Thus Held (1993: 26) notes: 'decisions made by quasi-regional or quasi-supranational organizations such as the European Community, the North Atlantic Treaty Organization or the International Monetary Fund diminish the range of decisions open to given national "majorities"'. The result is that a core democratic principle, that of a self-governing community, is 'today deeply problematic'. Other key democratic notions become equally problematic 'as soon as the issue of national, regional and global inter-connectedness is considered . . . Whose consent is necessary and whose participation is justified in decisions concerning, for instance, AIDS, or acid rain, or the use of non-renewable resources. What is the relevant constituency: national, regional or international?' (Held 1993: 26–7). The two processes referred to by Held—decisions being made by agencies of internatio-nalized governance and the emergence of issues which transcend national boundaries—correspond quite precisely to the notions of exogenous and endogenous internationalization of issues discussed in the preceding chapter. This correspondence underlines the import-ance of public opinion and the democratic legitimacy of internationa-lized governance.

Although the question has wider implications, we concentrate on the European Community, in particular on one segment of the institutional structure of the Community—the European Parliament. Even so, the full significance of the problem of the 'democratic deficit' in the European Community and the role of the European Parliament can only be appreciated if it is set in the wider context of the history of democracy. The democratic deficit in the European Union is just one part of a broader scene on which a major historical process is being played out. As Held (1993: 45) concludes: 'if the history and practice of democracy has until now been centred on the idea of locality (the city-state, the community, the nation), it is likely that in the future it will be centred on the international or global domain.'

The Institutional Context

Given that the issue of democratic legitimacy is inseparable from the question of institutions, we start by considering the complex institu-tional mechanisms of the Community from the standpoint of mass democracy. Taking a summary and schematic approach, five mechan-isms can be considered on eight dimensions. As shown in Figure 12.1, the five mechanisms are the European Council, the Council of Minis-ters, the European Parliament, national parliamentary supervision of European policy and legislation, and, finally, referendums.[1] In assessing the implications of each of these institutions for democratic linkage, we consider eight dimensions. The *nature of linkage* refers to whether the link is direct or representational and, if representational, whether it is strong or weak. *Decisiveness* points to the impact of the institutions in the EC decision-making process. *Issue range* refers to the number and type of issues dealt with by the institution. The term *visibility* refers to the prominence of the institutional process in question in political life and to the amount of media attention generally devoted to it. *Transparency* deals with the extent to which the issues are debated in public rather than being negotiated behind closed doors, and the extent to which the process of decision-making is intelligible to the uninitiated. *Territorial coverage* describes variations in access to the particular institutional process between EU member-states. *Weighting* addresses the question of whether the linkage process translates individual opinion on a one-person-one-vote basis, as it were, or whether 'votes' are weighted in some way, and if so, in what way. Finally, *frequency* notes whether the linkage in question is available on a continuous, frequent, or an occasional basis.

A comprehensive account of the institutional aspects of mass democratic linkages would go through each of the institutions listed in Figure 12.1, tracing its development and role in detail, and assessing its rating on each dimension. However, our main interest is the European Parliament. Even so, as the role of the Parliament cannot be understood without reference to the Council of Ministers in particular, we comment briefly on the Council's ratings on these dimensions. But first we need to give a short account of the development of the European Parliament.

Given the élitist and functionalist tendencies in the origins of the European Communities, it is quite remarkable that the principle of representation in the decision-making process and a commitment to direct elections to the assembly were present from the very beginning. The Assembly of the European Coal and Steel Community, which first met in September 1952, consisted of 'delegates who shall be designated by the respective Parliaments from among their members in accordance with the procedure laid down by each Member State' (ECSC, Art. 21.1). However, it was also provided that 'The Assembly shall draw up proposals for elections by direct universal suffrage in accordance with a universal procedure in all member states' (ECSC, Art. 21.3). This provision was incorporated into the Treaty of Rome (EEC, Art. 138) but did not take effect for another twenty years or so because member states were given a veto over its implementation. During these years, members of the European Assembly were appointed from among the members of national legislatures. Thus, the status of the European Assembly (first of the ECSC and then of the EEC) was the same as that of the assemblies of considerably weaker forms of internationalized governance, such as the Council of Europe, the Western European Union, and NATO.

	Nature of linkage	Decisiveness	Issue range	Visibility	Transparency	Territorial coverage	Individual weighting	Frequency
European Council	Weak-moderate representational	High	Very wide	High	Low	Complete	Strong (small state)	Regular
Council of Ministers	Weak representational	High	Wide	Moderate	Zero	Complete	Moderate (small state)	Continuous
European Parliament	Strong representational	Low	Narrow	Low	Moderate	Complete	Slight (small state)	Continuous
National parliamentary supervision	Strong representational	Low	Wide	Low	Moderate	Variable	Equal	Variable
Referendums	Direct	High/low	Narrow	High	High	Very incomplete	Equal	Occasional

FIGURE 12.1. *Mass democratic linkages in the EC*

In the early years, the European Assembly had very limited powers. While its role in the Community legislative process was mandatory, its contribution was simply to be 'consulted', after which its 'opinion' could be accepted or rejected at the will of the Council of Ministers. Although, from the outset, the Assembly had the power to censure the Commission and thus force its resignation, this was a weapon so blunt as to be unusable and unused. In 1971 and 1975, the European Assembly acquired significant budgetary powers but these were confined to the non-compulsory elements of Community expenditure. However, the 1975 increase in the power of the Parliament included the power to reject the Community budget. The budgetary powers of the Parliament were further expanded in 1988.

A major change in the status of the Parliament occurred in 1979 with the first direct elections. The new Parliament immediately flexed its muscles. First, it used its delaying power—inherent in the requirement that the Parliament give an opinion on all legislation—as a means of extracting concessions from the Commission and the Council. Secondly, it launched a discussion of the next phase in the pursuit of European union and adopted the Draft Treaty Establishing the European Union in 1984. With the Single European Act in 1987, the Parliament acquired powers of second reading in the 'co-operation procedure'. However, these powers related only to measures having to do with the Single Market; moreover, the Council could still overrule the Parliament. The Single Act also conferred powers of 'assent', essentially a veto power, on the Parliament in regard to the accession of new members and the ratification of agreements with non-member states or international organizations.

Under the Maastricht Treaty, the Parliament's legislative role has been further enlarged to include a 'co-decision' procedure. This involves the creation of a Conciliation Committee to resolve legislative deadlock between the Parliament and the Council of Ministers and gives the Parliament a veto over some legislation. The qualifier 'some' is vital. As with the co-operation procedure, the Maastricht co-decision procedure applies to a limited range of policies. However, the Treaty also enlarged the powers of the Parliament in several other regards: the power of assent and initiative, the power to establish Committees of Inquiry, the right of citizens to petition the Parliament, the right to appoint an Ombudsman, and the right to be consulted on the choice of President of the Commission, and to vote approval of the President and the other members of the Commission as a body. The powers conferred by the Maastricht Treaty are, in the tradition of the development of the Parliament, incremental and do not amount to a radical refashioning of its role. Accordingly, while the ratings of the European Parliament on some of the dimensions in Figure 12.1 have strengthened somewhat with the passing of the Treaty on European Union, the general picture has changed little since the passing of the Single European Act in 1987.

This account allows us to assess the European Parliament on the eight dimensions shown in Figure 12.1. Since 1979, the nature of the linkage is strongly representational; the decisiveness of the Parliament, except in very limited policy areas, is low; the issue range is narrow; visibility varies between low and moderate—rising at election time but falling back in inter-election periods, as we shall see below. Transparency is, at best, moderate;[2] but territorial coverage is complete. There is a slight weighting in favour of individuals in small states; the frequency of the linkage is continuous.

The Council of Ministers is similar to the Parliament in just three respects: the completeness of territorial coverage, the continuous nature of the linkage, and the weighting of opinion in favour of the smaller states. After that the differences between Parliament and Council of Ministers become crucial: the issue range of the Parliament is narrow, that of the Council of Ministers is wide; the visibility of the Parliament is low, that of the Council of Ministers is moderate; the transparency of the Parliament may be moderate, but that of the Council of Ministers is poor to non-existent. Most important of all, whereas the decisiveness of the Parliament is low, that of the Council is high.

In light of these key differences, it is vital to note the nature of the linkage provided by each institution: strong representational linkage in the case of the generally weak Parliament; weak representational linkage in the case of the powerful Council. Against the background of this contrast between a politically powerful but representationally weak institution on the one hand, and a politically weak but representationally strong institution on the other, we now turn to the evidence of the orientations of the citizens of the European Community towards European democracy and the European Parliament.

Public Opinion and the Democratic Deficit

Data on the public's evaluations of the democratic quality of the European Community are available for three time points between June 1989 and spring 1993.[3] The circumstances at these time points were rather different. June 1989 was in the wake of European parliamentary elections and at a high point in expectations about the benefits from the forthcoming Single Market. Autumn 1992 was in the wake of the 'no' majority in the Danish referendum on the Maastricht Treaty, the very narrow 'yes' majority in the French referendum, and at a time of extensive media discussion of the democratic deficit. By spring 1993, public discussion about the democratic deficit was less prominent but anxiety about the problem had certainly not disappeared. To complicate further the assessment of the data, three different question wordings are involved.

The 1989 data on evaluations of the democratic character of the European Community shown in Table 12.1 present a mixed picture, leaving some room for interpretation. One interpretation might emphasize a rather negative picture. As few as 10 per cent of European citizens thought that the working of the Community is completely democratic, while 20 per cent said that the working of the Community shows very little or no democracy at all. A further 20 per cent had no clear view. But perhaps the criterion 'completely democratic' is too stringent. Is any political process ever 'completely democratic'? On this reading, one would focus on the fact that a substantial majority (58 per cent) thought that the working of the Community is either completely or to some extent democratic.

There is far less ambiguity about the autumn 1992 data in Table 12.1. The question asked: 'Do you think citizens have sufficient democratic influence in EC-decision making or not?' Respondents could answer 'yes', 'no', or 'don't know'. On this measure, only 15 per cent of EC citizens were satisfied with the degree of 'democratic influence' available to them. The overwhelming majority (71 per cent) answered 'no'; another small minority (14 per cent) did not know.

The 1992 data give us some yardstick by which to assess the 1989 data. If we assume for a moment that there was no shift in opinion between 1989 and 1992, we could note that while a majority of citizens think that the EC is at least to some extent democratic, an even larger majority think that 'to some extent democratic' is not good enough— that the Community is insufficiently democratic. Even though the

TABLE 12.1. *Satisfaction with democracy at EC and national levels, 1989–93*

	BE	DK	FR	GB	GE	GR	IR	IT	LU	NL	PO	SP	EC-12
Summer 1989: To what extent do you think the way the EC works is democratic?													
Completely	8	8	7	6	20	26	8	12	8	3	8	22	12
To some extent	44	46	47	46	51	31	43	54	43	36	45	35	46
Very little	19	23	23	15	15	11	11	16	21	29	11	6	16
Not at all	5	5	6	5	2	4	4	4	4	9	3	3	4
d.k./n.a.	24	18	17	28	12	28	34	14	23	22	32	34	21
N	1,028	1,000	1,040	957	1,202	1,000	1,016	1,011	301	970	1,000	1,003	11,819
Autumn 1992: Do you think citizens have sufficient democratic influence in EC decision-making or not?													
Yes	17	16	16	7	15	28	14	15	19	21	33	11	15
No	67	77	74	84	69	52	67	66	70	63	44	73	71
d.k./n.a.	16	7	9	9	16	21	19	19	11	16	23	16	14
N	1,040	1,000	1,005	1,058	1,013	1,006	1,008	1,052	500	1,003	1,000	1,004	11,993
Spring 1993: On the whole, are you very satisfied, fairly satisfied, not very satisfied, or not at all satisfied with the way democracy works in the EC?													
Very satisfied	3	4	2	2	3	8	11	1	4	1	3	4	3
Fairly satisfied	48	45	38	36	40	37	51	31	55	48	51	35	38
Not very satisfied	30	36	37	32	38	26	14	39	24	37	22	36	35
Not at all satisfied	9	12	13	15	10	11	7	15	3	6	8	10	12
d.k./n.a.	10	3	11	15	10	18	16	14	15	8	16	15	12
N	1,018	1,000	1,019	1,073	1,035	1,003	1,008	1,039	513	1,004	1,000	1,022	12,040
Spring 1993: On the whole, are you very satisfied, fairly satisfied, not very satisfied, or not at all satisfied with the way democracy works in your country?													
Very satisfied	4	21	3	7	6	6	15	1	10	9	3	3	5
Fairly satisfied	45	60	38	42	45	28	47	11	62	59	51	38	37
Not very satisfied	32	14	36	31	36	38	21	39	21	25	31	36	34
Not at all satisfied	14	4	20	17	10	27	11	49	3	5	12	20	21
d.k./n.a.	4	1	3	5	3	1	6	1	5	2	4	3	3
N	1,021	1,000	1,019	1,072	1,036	1,003	1,008	1,039	513	1,004	1,000	1,022	12,043

Note: Entries are percentages.

Sources: Eurobarometer, Nos. 31*a*, 38, and 39.

measures and the circumstances are not comparable, it is still possible to note a slight decline in assessments of the democratic quality of the Community between 1989 and 1992 in Spain and Germany. In both cases, there was a higher than average assessment that the EC was completely (and therefore, presumably, sufficiently) democratic in 1989. By 1992, the proportion of Germans saying that the Community was sufficiently democratic had dropped to 15 per cent (from 20 per cent completely democratic in 1989) and the proportion of Spaniards of that view had dropped from 22 per cent to 11 per cent. It is also worth noting that opinion in the Community as a whole had crystallized between the two dates: the 'don't knows' had dropped from 21 to 14 per cent. Assessments in 1992 also showed relatively little variation between member states. Only in Greece and Portugal was opinion substantially more positive than the average and only in Britain was opinion substantially less positive than in most of the other countries.

At first sight, the aspect of democratic quality being measured in 1993 seems quite close to the 1989 measure. As in 1989, the response categories constituted a scale. In 1989, the scale sought to measure the perceived extent of democracy in the way the EC works; in 1993, it sought to measure satisfaction with the working of democracy in the European Community. If we were to accept these data at face value, we might then conclude that satisfaction with the democratic quality of the European Community had declined fairly sharply, from 58 per cent giving a broadly positive response in 1989 to 41 per cent on the positive side of the scale (saying very or fairly satisfied) in 1993.

However, the object being evaluated in each case was quite different. In 1989, it was 'the way the European Community works'; in 1993, it was 'the way democracy works in the European Community'. The 1993 formulation is much less specific and could be seen to include the working of democracy not just at Community level but also at the national level of the member states. In fact, as the final set of figures in Table 12.1 shows, satisfaction with the way democracy works in the European Community and satisfaction with the way democracy works in the respondents' own countries show rather similar distributions across Europe as a whole in the spring of 1993. The major difference is that a somewhat larger proportion of Europeans were 'not at all satisfied' with democracy in their own country—notably in Italy and, to a lesser extent, in Greece.[4] In general, however, the closeness of the distribution of the two attitudes in 1993 increases the suspicion that the wording of the question about satisfaction with 'the way democracy works in the European Community' may have elicited a response which includes an assessment of the working of democracy in general rather than being limited to an assesment of 'the way the EC works'. This suspicion is strengthened when we note that the association between the Community-level assessment and the national-level assessment was considerably stronger in 1993 than in 1989 (correlations of 0.42 and 0.30 respectively).

In summary, trends in the assessment of the democratic quality of the European Community are very difficult to pin down. Instead, we are left with assessments which are specific to particular years and to particular aspects of the issue. However, no matter which way one looks at the data, it is evident that there is a persistent public sense of a democratic deficit in the European Community. In the light of the institutional aspects of the Community summarized in Figure 12.1, this is not surprising. European citizens perceive a democratic deficit at the Community level; and the simple fact is, there is one.

The European Parliament is specifically charged with representing the views of Community citizens and has a special responsibility, although not sole responsibility, for overcoming this democratic deficit (see Grabitz *et al.* 1988). This brings us to our central question: what are the cultural underpinnings of the institutional role of the Parliament? This involves examining how European citizens relate to the European Parliament in terms of awareness and psychological involvement, evaluation, and, ultimately, behaviour. Finally, we consider what this implies for the possibilities of overcoming the democratic deficit.

Awareness and Understanding of the European Parliament

One very telling fact about the relationship between the European Parliament and European publics is that the degree of media exposure of the Parliament in 1992 was the same as it had been in 1977 when the Parliament was not directly elected and when it had far less power than it has had since 1987. As we can see from Figure 12.2, the extent of exposure is affected by the cycle of European elections, although the 1989 elections did not have as strong an effect in this regard as the two previous elections. There was a pick-up in 1991, presumably related to media coverage of the Maastricht discussions, and then a more substantial increase in 1993 as the elections again appeared on the horizon. The significant point, however, is that there is no cumulation of

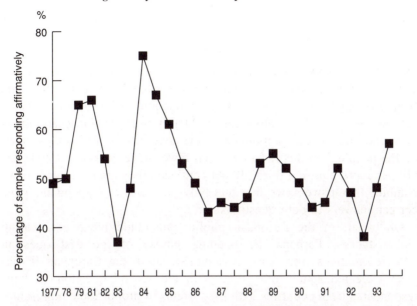

FIGURE 12.2. *Exposure to the European Parliament via the media, 1977–93*

Question: Have you recently seen or heard in the papers, or on the radio or TV, anything about the European Parliament, that is the parliamentary assembly of the European Community?

Sources: Eurobarometer, Nos. 8–39.

frequency of exposure commensurate with the increasing role of the Parliament.

Exposure to media coverage of the Parliament does not necessarily lead to increased understanding or knowledge of what the Parliament does.[5] Conversely, the absence of an increase in exposure does not imply that knowledge and understanding of the role of the Parliament have not increased. Indeed, we would expect such an increase to have taken place over the course of three direct elections to the European Parliament. Thus we would anticipate an increase in knowledge and understanding of the Parliament even in the absence of a cumulative increase in the exposure of citizens to media coverage of the institution.

People's knowledge and understanding of the Parliament have been measured on a number of occasions. Unfortunately, the questions in the surveys relate to different aspects of the role of the Parliament, hence it is not possible to measure growth or decline in knowledge and understanding in any rigorous way. Even so, the evidence is revealing. In spring 1983 only 55 per cent of European citizens correctly answered an elementary multiple choice question asking: 'Who sits in the European Parliament?' The choices presented and the distribution of responses were: 'Representatives from some but not all member states' (9 per cent); 'Representatives from all member states' (55 per cent); and 'Representatives from all the European countries' (10 per cent). A second question asked: 'How are the Members of the European Parliament chosen? Are they appointed by the government or directly elected by the people?' In this instance, even fewer gave the correct response (44 per cent); almost a third (30 per cent) said they are appointed. If we combine the answers, we find that only one-third of respondents gave correct answers to both questions.

On behalf of the European public, one could plead extenuating circumstances. Perhaps the opening phrase of the first question ('Representatives from various countries sit in the European Parliament') created some ambiguity. With the second question, perhaps respondents from countries with list systems of proportional representation had some difficulty distinguishing between the alternatives 'appointed by the government or directly elected by the people'. The excuses begin to look a bit thin, however, when one notes that ten years and two European parliamentary elections later, the correct response to a similar question ('Who elects the European Parliament?') was given by only 41 per cent of respondents.[6]

Even lower levels of knowledge and understanding of the European Parliament are indicated in responses to a question about the competences of the European Parliament which was asked in autumn 1988 and spring 1989. The question presented three statements about the competences of the Parliament: (1) 'The European Parliament has the power to pass laws that are binding in each member country of the European Community'; (2) 'The European Parliament has the power to refuse the European Community budget'; (3) 'The President of the Commission of the European Community is elected by the European Parliament'. Respondents were asked to indicate whether the statements were true or false. In autumn 1988, only 37 per cent gave the correct response to the first statement (false), and a mere 17 per cent gave the correct response to the third statement (false). In contrast, 61 per cent gave the correct response to the second statement (true). If we combine the responses to the three statements, we face the startling fact that only 4 per cent gave the correct responses to all three questions.

A striking feature of these responses is the contrast between the substantial proportion of correct answers on the budgetary powers of the Parliament on the one hand, and the low proportion of correct answers about the law-making power of the Parliament and the power to elect the President of the Commission on the other. This pattern might, of course, arise from an acquiescence response set, with respondents who have no opinion or are in doubt tending to agree with each statement. It is also possible, of course, that the more accurate perception of the budgetary powers is due to the considerable media coverage of the budgetary conflicts between the European Parliament and the Council of Ministers in previous years. A third, and perhaps the most likely, explanation is that many people project onto the European level the image of the role of parliament which they have formed on the basis of national experience. Thus, when faced with questions about the powers of a parliament they do not know much about, they answer in terms of what they think the national parliament does. In this sense, they have a stereotyped image (Niedermayer 1994) of the European Parliament which is manifest, in part, in a 'true–true–true' response set to the three questions. Such a response set is given by a plurality (30 per cent) of respondents.

Combining the responses allows us to calculate a European Parliament information index with a score for each respondent. Respondents score 1 for each correct answer; 0 for don't know; and score −1 for a wrong answer. This yields a scale from −3 to +3. In autumn 1988, something less than one-third of respondents scored 1 or higher; 20 per cent obtained zero; and the majority (50 per cent) scored −1 or less (see Table 12.2). There is some evidence that, as the third direct elections to the European Parliament (June 1989) drew near, public perception of the role of the Parliament became somewhat more accurate. The average score for the Community as a whole moved marginally from −0.25 to −0.2 on the seven-point scale. The proportion giving three correct answers actually remained the same, as did the tendency to project the image of the national parliament onto the European scene. However, there was a substantial increase (from 4 to 15 per cent) in the proportion giving a 'true–true–false' pattern of response. This group only erred in attributing an exaggerated law-making role to the Parliament. This is perhaps the most excusable error, particularly in the light of the emphasis in the Single European Act on increasing the Parliament's legislative role.

The most accurate perceptions were found, in both 1988 and 1989, in the Netherlands, Denmark, and Germany. The least accurate were in

TABLE 12.2. Accuracy of information about the European Parliament, 1988 and 1989

	BE	DK	FR	GB	GE	GR	IR	IT	LU	NL	PO	SP	EC-12
AUTUMN 1988													
Information index													
-3	8	4	6	7	6	6	3	16	5	5	8	3	7
-2	1	2	3	4	1	2	7	1	0	3	1	2	2
-1	50	31	47	40	46	40	40	47	42	38	45	28	41
0	9	22	18	21	4	28	33	9	14	14	30	32	20
+1	27	30	22	23	36	21	12	23	31	32	14	31	25
+2	1	3	2	3	1	0	2	1	2	3	1	2	2
+3	5	8	4	3	7	2	3	3	6	6	3	3	4
N	1,054	1,006	1,001	1,017	1,051	1,000	1,012	1,058	300	1,006	1,000	1,013	11,794
SPRING 1989													
Information index													
-3	4	5	5	4	5	5	4	5	8	4	3	3	5
-2	3	4	4	5	2	2	5	1	7	3	1	3	3
-1	44	32	46	37	43	56	39	48	44	39	52	48	44
0	14	23	10	18	9	16	23	10	12	10	20	21	16
+1	26	28	28	28	35	19	24	30	22	35	21	23	27
+2	3	4	3	3	2	1	3	2	3	3	1	1	3
+3	6	3	5	5	4	1	1	5	5	7	2	2	4
N	1,002	1,014	1,005	976	1,024	1,000	1,006	1,022	303	1,025	1,000	1,001	11,678

Note: Entries are distributions on the information index.

Sources: Eurobarometer, Nos. 30 and 31.

Greece and Portugal. Between 1988 and 1989 the accuracy of perception improved substantially in Britain, Belgium, Italy, and Ireland. Surprisingly, the accuracy of perception deteriorated in Denmark. It also deteriorated in Greece and especially in Spain; in both cases, there was a marked increase in the tendency to project the image of the national parliament on to the European level.

A third indicator of perceptions of the role of the Parliament is indirect and is available for 1992 and 1993. The question asked: 'Which of the following institutions of the European Community is, in your opinion, the most powerful in terms of having the final say on European Community legislation?' The response categories were the European Parliament, the Commission and the Council of Ministers. Only one respondent in four gave the correct answer (Council of Ministers). These correct responses were outnumbered by the 29 per cent who saw the European Parliament as the most powerful institution; and 17 per cent said the Commission has the final say. There were particularly high rates of 'don't know' in Spain (49 per cent) and Greece (40 per cent). The highest proportion of correct responses was in Denmark, Luxembourg, and the Netherlands; but the Danes were also inclined to exaggerate the role of the Commission, while the Dutch tended to exaggerate the role of the Parliament (see Table 12.3). The proportion identifying the Parliament as the most powerful institution in the European Community rose between 1992 and 1993. Overall, the rise was just 4 percentage points, but it was 10 points or more in France, Italy, and the Netherlands.

Putting together the evidence from these disparate indicators, it is apparent that only something between one-quarter and one-third of the citizens of Europe have even the most minimal grasp of the role of the European Parliament. This is the case whether we look at their knowledge of its composition or its legislative and other powers. Above all, it emerges that a major source of error is the tendency to exaggerate the power of the Parliament, presumably by projecting onto it a role similar to that played by national parliaments. Information about the European Parliament, and people's understanding of its role, are evidently biased by preferences and evaluations.

TABLE 12.3. *Perception of the most powerful institution in determining EC legislation, 1992–3*

	BE	DK	FR	GB	GE	GR	IR	IT	LU	NL	PO	SP	EC-12
Spring 1992													
Commission	14	27	24	25	14	13	23	16	19	15	14	7	17
Parliament	35	22	27	23	31	28	21	31	26	34	29	28	29
Council	25	38	27	23	26	19	26	19	37	34	22	17	24
d.k./n.a.	26	14	23	29	28	40	31	34	18	17	36	49	30
N	1,036	1,000	1,005	1,016	1,065	1,000	1,001	1,046	496	1,002	1,000	1,000	11,970
Spring 1993													
Commission	15	25	26	34	22	16	26	12	23	17	10	15	20
Parliament	40	26	38	31	33	33	27	42	17	44	26	36	33
Council	21	37	15	21	20	11	20	20	35	28	20	17	21
d.k./n.a.	24	12	22	14	26	40	28	26	25	11	44	33	26
N	1,016	1,000	1,019	1,069	1,033	1,003	1,008	1,039	512	1,004	1,000	1,022	12,031

Note: Entries are percentages.

Sources: Eurobarometer, Nos. 37 and 39.

Evaluations of the Role of the Parliament

Confirmation that conceptions of the role of the European Parliament are inflated is found in responses to a question about the importance of the Parliament asked on a regular basis since 1983. The proportions fluctuate but, in general, some 50–55 per cent of respondents thought the Parliament was either important or very important compared with an average of about 30 per cent who thought it was either not important or not at all important. The question had also been asked in 1977, and comparing the results shows a considerable rise in the perceived importance of the Parliament between 1977 and 1983. In 1977, prior to the first direct election (1979), 37 per cent had said the Parliament was important compared to 39 per cent who said it was not.

A net measure of the perceived importance of the Parliament can be obtained by subtracting the 'not important' responses and the 'don't knows' from the 'important' responses. Figure 12.3 presents the distributions on this measure for 1983 and 1992. It is immediately evident that there are very large discrepancies between the member states in their assessment of the role of the Parliament. Ranged at one end, and largely dismissive of the Parliament, are Britain, Denmark, France,

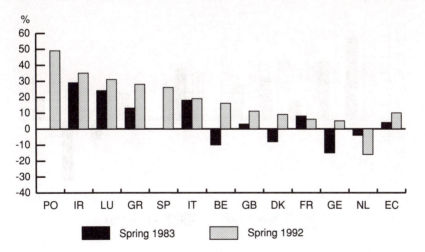

FIGURE 12.3. *Perceived current importance of the European Parliament, 1983 and 1992*

Note: The data are net responses: important − (not important + don't know).

Sources: Eurobarometer, Nos. 19 and 37.

Germany and, in particular, the Netherlands. At the other end are Spain, Greece, Luxembourg, Ireland, and Portugal. With the exception of Luxembourg, where the presence of some Parliament offices and functions makes a noticeable impact on a small society, Figure 12.3 presents a striking contrast between the more developed and less developed member states. The other notable feature of the graph is that, as the entry on the right side for each country indicates, the tendency has been for the perceived importance of the Parliament to increase over the decade. This is particularly true of Greece, Belgium, Denmark, and Germany. The main exception is the Netherlands.

Turning to the preferred future role of the Parliament, the differences between the member countries are less sharp, and the underlying contrast between them is not so much socio-economic as political. As is evident in Figure 12.4, the publics which are less enamoured of a more important role for the Parliament are found in Britain and Denmark, and to a lesser degree, in Ireland and Germany. The British and Danish reservations are not surprising, given what we know about their overall attitude to integration. However, the very substantial change in the view among the Danes between 1983 and 1992 is striking. The

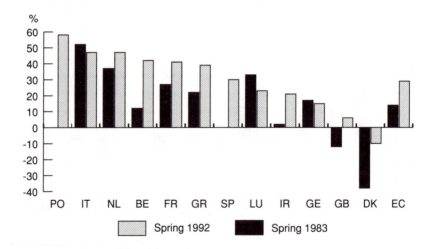

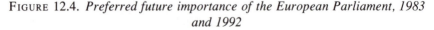

FIGURE 12.4. *Preferred future importance of the European Parliament, 1983 and 1992*

Note: The data are net responses: more important − (less important + don't know).

Sources: Eurobarometer, Nos. 19 and 37.

somewhat lower level of enthusiasm for the Parliament in Ireland can perhaps be explained by the view prevalent among Irish élites that, as a small state, Ireland can exercise more influence in the other Community institutions and that its influence would be weakened by a strengthening of the Parliament. However, support for a more important role for the Parliament is also relatively low in Germany, which runs directly counter to the view among the German political élites. The pro-Parliament end of the distribution is led by Portugal but also includes the Netherlands, Belgium, and France.

To understand the degree of importance attached to the role of the Parliament, we need to take into account, simultaneously, both current perceptions and future preferences. The problem is how to do so. One approach would be to treat perceived current importance as a cognitive variable similar to those discussed in the previous section. On this reading, there is a correct and an incorrect answer; the correct answer here being that the Parliament does not play an important role in the life of the European Community. One could then relate responses to this informational question to responses to the evaluative question measuring preferences regarding the future role of the Parliament. Combined in this way, the data could be used to assess the degree of realism and rationality underlying support for expanding the role of the Parliament.

This is the approach adopted by Hofrichter and Klein (1993: 29–32) in drawing up a typology of attitudes towards the Parliament between 1988 and 1992. In particular, they identify the ideal types of 'enthusiasts' and 'realists'. Enthusiasts are those who say the Parliament is important and should be more important; realists say it is unimportant and should be more important. The former are 'characterized by a positive affective pattern of orientation which is not influenced by any kind of information'. The latter, on the other hand, 'due to their knowledge of the European Community . . . have the intellectual capacity to draw conclusions from their perception of the European parliament as unimportant that are in favour of reducing the democratic deficit in European politics'. Hofrichter and Klein present the distributions for these and the other types of orientation by country and go on to examine the determinants of the various types in a sophisticated multivariate analysis.

Beguiling as this line of inquiry is, we do not pursue it here. This is because of the possibility, noted at the beginning of this section, that evaluations may be determining what are apparently cognitive judgements. Indeed, Hofrichter and Klein (1993: 21) acknowledge this

TABLE 12.4. *Relationship between perceived current importance of European Parliament and information index*

	BE	DK	FR	UK	GE	GR	IR	IT	LU	NL	PO	SP	EC-12
Autumn 1988	−0.15	−0.18	−0.19	−0.11	−0.23	−0.17	−0.15	−0.17	−0.18	−0.12	−0.07*	−0.12	−0.16
Spring 1989	−0.12	−0.12	−0.15	−0.10	−0.16	−0.08*	−0.09*	−0.13	−0.18	−0.11	−0.08*	−0.03	−0.13

Notes: Entries are correlation coefficients (Pearson's r). All correlations are significant at $p > 0.001$ except those marked * which are significant at $p > 0.05$.

Sources: Eurobarometer, Nos. 30 and 31.

problem: 'it can be assumed that the rather high level of perceived present importance reflects affective ties with the ideal of democracy and the corresponding institutions in general'. The force of these reservations can be tested empirically. If perception of importance is to be treated as a measure of the realism of respondents' views then it should be strongly and negatively correlated to the information score presented above: the higher the level of knowledge, the lower the perceived importance and vice versa. This relationship can be tested for autumn 1988 and spring 1989; our results are presented in Table 12.4.

The data show that the relationship is in the right direction. However, the relationship is hardly strong enough to justify using perceived importance as a cognitive measure of the realism of people's perceptions. Also damaging for the hypothesis is that the relationship is weaker in most countries in spring 1989 than in autumn 1988. If perceived importance is a cognitive measure, we would have expected a stronger relationship with the information index during a period when the campaigns for the June European Parliamentary elections should have been bringing the Parliament into sharper focus.

We can also use the 1988 and 1989 data to test the distinction between realists and enthusiasts. Realists should have 'a well-founded knowledge of European affairs', whereas 'the orientation of enthusiasts is not influenced by any kind of information'. Table 12.5 presents the frequencies of both groups on the seven-point information index. There was some tendency for realists, as defined by Hofrichter and Klein, to be better informed than enthusiasts in autumn 1988. Thus, 11 per cent of realists but only 3 per cent of enthusiasts scored +3; 60 per cent of enthusiasts scored −1 or less compared to 41 per cent of realists. However, the fact that 41 per cent of realists had a score of −1 or less, and a further 10 per cent scored zero, raises a question mark over the extent to which realists can be described as having a well-founded knowledge of European affairs. This question mark is reinforced when we look at the data for spring 1989 which show that the level of knowledge among realists showed little or no change at a time when, as argued above, it could be expected to have improved due to the increased attention to the Parliament. This suggests that, even in constructing 'ideal types', it is inadvisable to use judgements about the current importance of the European Parliament as a cognitive measure of the realism of citizens' perceptions.

Must we then abandon the idea of taking account of judgements of

TABLE 12.5. *European Parliament information index among 'enthusiasts' and 'realists'*

	Enthusiasts	Realists	Others
Autumn 1988			
−3	8	6	6
−2	3	2	2
−1	49	33	38
0	12	10	25
+1	23	36	23
+2	2	2	1
+3	3	11	4
N	3,418	1,350	7,026
Spring 1989			
	8	7	7
−3	2	2	2
−2	55	40	42
−1	10	7	23
0	21	33	25
+1	1	2	1
+2	3	10	3
+3			
N	3,708	1,350	6,620

Note: Entries are the percentage distribution of respondents on the scale values of the information index.

Sources: Eurobarometer, Nos. 30 and 31.

current importance when we examine preferences regarding the future role of the European Parliament? Our answer is: certainly not. In the first place, perceived current importance is a base line from which to assess preferences about the future role of the Parliament. Accordingly, the two variables must be seen in tandem. Secondly, this can be done without making assumptions about the degree of realism or knowledge involved in the perception of current importance. That is, the two 'importance' variables can be combined in an index which measures attitudes to the future role of the Parliament, taking into account the respondent's assessment of Parliament's current role. We can then assess the cognitive basis of attitudes towards the Parliament by relating this new index to the European Parliament information index described in the previous section.

The index is based on two ordinal scales: perceived importance of the European Parliament and attitude towards the future role of the

Parliament. The perceived importance scale runs from -2 to $+2$ ('don't knows' are scored zero), but the future role scale has only three points (more important, the same, and less important). These could be scored $+1$, 0, -1, and the 'don't knows' could also be assigned 0. Making the assumption about levels of measurement commonly made in the construction of Likert scales, we could add together the values on the two scales to produce an index. This is justified because the second scale is relative to the first: the second measures the preference for a more or less important role than the respondent currently ascribes to the Parliament. However, if we simply added together the scales scored in this way, the perception of current importance would predominate simply because it is a five-point scale. Whereas what we need is an index in which the preference for the future role of the Parliament is the dominant element. In order to achieve this, we rescored preferences regarding the future role of the Parliament, assigning a score of $+3$ to 'more important', 0 to the 'the same' or 'don't know', and -3 to 'less important'.[7] Summing the scales then produces an eleven-point index, ranging from $+5$ to -5, which measures preferences for the future role of the Parliament while taking account of perceptions of its current role.[8] The assignment of scores is illustrated in Figure 12.5.

Between 1983 and 1991, the proportion of respondents taking the view than the European Parliament should have a more important role ranged between 44 and 62 per cent. However, the distributions on the index, reported in Table 12.6, show a much more differentiated situation than is suggested by responses to the question on the 'preferred future role of the Parliament'. In autumn 1988,[9] for example, support for a significant role for the Parliament was both more widespread and more qualified than the 44 per cent figure registered by the future role question. Although two-thirds of respondents took a positive view of the role of the Parliament, less than a third envisaged a very strong role for the Parliament (points 4 and 5 on the scale). The plurality (38 per cent) had a moderately positive attitude (points 1 to 3), either taking the view that the Parliament is already important and should remain so or that it is currently unimportant but should become more important.

The scale also reveals more opposition to the role of the Parliament than indicated by the 10 per cent or so who thought it should become less important in the future. Thus, in 1988, 5 per cent envisaged an extremely weak role for the European Parliament, while a further 13 per cent expressed reservations, either thinking that the Parliament is

PERCEIVED CURRENT IMPORTANCE

| | | Very important | Important | Don't know | Not very important | Not at all important |
		2	1	0	−1	−2
PREFERRED FUTURE IMPORTANCE	More important 3	5	4	3	2	1
	Same/don't know 0	2	1	0	−1	−2
	Less important −3	−1	−2	−3	−4	−5

FIGURE 12.5. *Scoring of index of parliamentarization*

TABLE 12.6. *Attitude towards the role of the European Parliament by country, autumn 1988*

In favour of:	BE	DK	FR	GB	GE	GR	IR	IT	LU	NL	PO	SP	EC−12
Very weak role	3	7	2	13	10	1	3	1	2	7	1	2	5
Moderately weak role	21	21	10	19	18	7	11	4	14	17	4	10	13
Indifferent	12	18	13	14	14	14	10	13	14	15	25	21	15
Moderately strong role	39	43	43	32	38	34	42	41	44	40	32	36	38
Very strong role	26	11	32	22	20	44	34	41	24	21	39	32	29
N	1,024	1,006	1,001	1,017	1,051	1,000	1,012	1,058	300	1,006	1,000	1,013	11,794

Notes: Entries are percentages. The index values corresponding to the categories in the table are: −5 and −4, very weak role; −3 to −1, moderately weak role; 0, indifferent; 1 to 3, moderately strong role; 4 and 5, very strong role.

Source: Eurobarometer, No. 30.

unimportant and should remain so, or that it should become less important than it is. Significant pockets of outright opposition to the role of the Parliament were to be found in Britain (13 per cent) and Germany (10 per cent).

Combining all the groups with some degree of reservation about the role of the Parliament revealed considerable minorities opposed to any substantial role for the Parliament. Sizeable groups of this kind were to be found in Britain (32 per cent), Denmark (28 per cent), Germany (28 per cent), Belgium (24 per cent), and the Netherlands (24 per cent). Of course, all these countries—including Denmark and Britain—showed majorities in favour of a substantial role for the Parliament. None the less, it is noteworthy that 25 per cent or more of the citizens of some of the most developed states of the Community appear to have reservations about the European Parliament. At the other end of the scale, the largest majorities in favour of a substantial role for the Parliament were to be found in Italy, Greece, Ireland, France, and Portugal.

The index of attitudes towards the role of the Parliament leaves open the cognitive basis of these attitudes. But how realistic is the image of the Parliament held by both supporters and opponents? Are the generally positive attitudes towards the role of the Parliament a matter of rhetoric and vague aspiration, or are they grounded in a sober assessment of the actual powers of the Parliament. We have argued that the best way to examine this issue is, first, to create an index of attitudes towards the role of the Parliament, and then to relate this to our measure of information. The information index can be dichotomized into the more or less well informed (a score of 1 or more) and the uninformed (0 or less). The index of attitudes to the role of the Parliament can be divided three ways: positive, indifferent, and negative. The distribution of EC citizens in autumn 1988 across the six categories obtained by cross-classifying these two scales is shown in Figure 12.6.

A plurality (46 per cent) of EC citizens in 1988 had a positive attitude to the role of the Parliament, but one that lacked even minimal information or understanding. Informed support for the role of the Parliament amounted to less than half this proportion (21 per cent). On the opposition side, uninformed opponents outnumbered informed opponents by a small margin (11 to 7 per cent). The reservoir of the uninformed and indifferent was quite small (12 per cent). Thus, not only are there degrees of support and opposition, but, more importantly, positive attitudes towards the Parliament rest on varying cognitive foundations. In particular, even using our fairly generous definition of

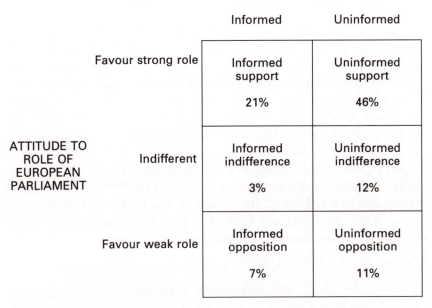

FIGURE 12.6. *Level of information and attitude towards the role of the European Parliament, 1988*

'informed', those whose support for the role of the Parliament rests on reasonably secure cognitive foundations constitute a distinct minority (one in five) of EC citizens.

What are the implications of all this for the legitimacy of the European Community? One could take the view that degrees of positive orientation, or the lack of a firm cognitive basis for such attitudes, do not particularly matter. In this argument, the vital fact is that a majority thinks that the Parliament is important. That such perceptions might be based on projecting the role of the national parliament on to the European level, or lack any firm basis in knowledge or understanding of the Parliament, is, in this view, neither here nor there. Legitimacy is enhanced in virtue of the positive orientations of European citizens towards the Parliament, irrespective of whether or not that view is adequately grounded in information and understanding.

There are several objections to this optimistic, even complacent interpretation. First of all, there are the public's doubts about the adequacy of democracy at the European level portrayed at the beginning of this chapter. The most unambiguous indicator of these doubts is the 71 per cent who, in autumn 1992, said that EC decision-making was not sufficiently democratic. The counter argument that there is also dissatisfaction with democracy at the national level carries little force. As demonstrated in Volume i, Chapter 11 of this series, dissatisfaction with democracy at the national level is not widespread in Western Europe. In any event, these nation states have enormous reservoirs of legitimacy on which to draw, and they are relatively settled political systems which are not engaged in the kind of constitution building that raises questions about legitimacy. That the European Union is so engaged means that the inadequacy of the informational basis of people's attitude towards the European Parliament cannot be lightly dismissed. Finally, the failure of the European Parliament to play a full legitimizing role in the European Union is confirmed when we turn from attitudes and orientations to behaviour.

The Behavioural Evidence

Behavioural orientations were identified as components of orientations towards internationalized governance in Chapter 2. Normally, we have to rely on reported or intended behaviour as evidence in this regard. But in this instance we can draw on the evidence of actual behaviour—that is, turnout in European parliamentary elections. Although these are aggregate-level data we can draw some inferences about individual-level behaviour.

At first sight, an average turnout of 63 per cent in the four European elections held during 1979–94 might be considered to be a reasonably acceptable level of involvement with the European Parliament on the part of its citizens. It compares favourably with turnout in presidential elections in the United States and might be considered acceptable for what is, afterall, a second-order election.

Looked at more closely, however, turnout in European parliamentary elections is far less satisfactory than the average figure suggests. In the first place, American turnout figures are based on eligible voters whereas European Parliament figures are based on registered voters. Secondly, while the concept of second-order elections is analytically useful (Reif and Schmitt, 1980), it should not be used as a yardstick by which to evaluate turnout (see Sinnott and Whelan, 1992). Thirdly, and more importantly, if we exclude the countries with compulsory voting

TABLE 12.7. *Turnout in European and national elections, 1979–94*

	European elections						Mean turnout in national elections
	1994	1989	1987	1984	1981	1979	1979–89
Belgium	90.7	90.7		92.1		91.4	93.8
Denmark	52.5	46.2		52.3		47.8	86.0
Britain	36.4	36.2		32.6		32.3	74.7
Germany	60.1	62.3		56.8		65.7	87.1
Greece	71.2	79.9		77.2	78.6	n.a.	82.8
France	82.7	48.7		56.7		60.7	71.6
Ireland	44.0	68.3		47.6		63.6	73.0
Italy	74.8	81.5		83.4		82.9	90.0
Luxembourg	86.6	87.4		88.8		88.9	88.4
Netherlands	35.6	47.2		50.6		57.8	83.4
Portugal	35.6	51.2	72.4	n.a.		n.a.	79.4
Spain	59.6	54.6	68.9	n.a.		n.a.	72.1
Mean							
All member states	60.8	62.9		63.8		65.7	
States with non-compulsory voting and without coinciding national elections	50.8	51.8		49.4		54.7	

Sources: Schmitt (1980); Office of the European Parliament (1984, 1989); European Parliament Directorate General for Information and Public Relations (1994); Mackie and Rose (1980–4); Mackie (1985–91).

(Belgium, Greece, and Luxembourg), or quasi-compulsory voting (Italy), and those instances in which European elections coincide with a general election, average turnout across the eight remaining countries in the four European elections to date has been only 52 per cent. Moreover, turnout has declined from 55 per cent in the 1979 elections to 51 per cent in the 1994 elections.

The implications of these average turnout figures can be seen by comparing turnout in European Parliament elections with turnout in national elections during the 1980s on a country by country basis. This comparison, shown in Table 12.7, reveals very substantial discrepancies between turnout in national elections and European elections in those countries which do not have either compulsory voting or parallel national elections. The countries with the highest percentage point differences in 1994 were the Netherlands (47 points), Portugal (43), and Britain (39). Denmark, Ireland, and Germany were in between, and the gap was noticeably less, although still quite substantial, in France and Spain. In short, the gap between the active national electorate and the active European electorate indicates substantial room for improvement by the European Parliament in its role as a link between the European Union and its citizens and as a means of cultivating the legitimacy of internationalized goverance.

Conclusion

That there is a democratic deficit in the European Community is widely accepted by political élites and commentators. The evidence we have considered shows that this deficit is widely perceived by mass publics. The evidence also suggests that the institution which ought to do most to make up that deficit—the European Parliament—is not succeeding in this task. Only something between one-quarter and one-third of European Community citizens have even the most minimal understanding of the role of the Parliament. The public tend to have an inflated conception of that role and to project the image of national parliaments on to the European body. It is true that there is widespread public support for the European Parliament, but these positive attitudes are quite graded and negative attitudes are somewhat more prevalent than might appear at first sight. Above all, positive attitudes are not rooted in a realistic conception of the Parliament; in autumn 1988 only 21 per cent of respondents across the Community as a whole could be described as informed supporters and this may be stretching the concept of informed. Uninformed support stood at over twice that level— 46 per cent.

All this is consistent with persistently low levels of participation in European elections. The result is a failure by the Parliament to make a substantial contribution to establishing the legitimacy of European integration. This is not to say that the European Community as a process of internationalized governance lacks popular support. Much of the evidence considered in this volume shows quite the contrary. But the European Parliament is not playing as large a role as it might in ensuring the institutionalization of legitimacy. If, as suggested in Chapter 2, European integration is making inroads on the functions of the nation state, then, in the light of the findings presented here, there is an urgent need to address the issue of institutionalized legitimacy. And if, as suggested at the outset of this chapter, the European Parliament is central to the wider issue of the democratization of internationalized governance, then the need assumes larger historical proportions and becomes all the more pressing.

NOTES

1. The list omits the Economic and Social Committee, the new Committee of the Regions, and the informal processes of lobbying which have a significant input into EC policy-making. On the following, see Sinnott (1994).
2. It could be argued that transparency in the post-Maastricht Parliament has deteriorated. The process of diplomatic negotiation that produced accretions to the power of the European Parliament led to so much qualification and complication that the procedures have become extremely obscure except to the initiated.
3. On the debate about the democratic quality of the EC, see Reif (1992).
4. See the discussion of the relationship between attitudes towards democracy at the national level and attitudes towards the European Community in Ch. 8.
5. Neither is media coverage necessarily positive. A follow-up question was put to those who indicated that they had read or heard something about the Parliament, asking whether the material had given a generally favourable or unfavourable impression of the Parliament. The results show considerable discrepancies in this respect between countries (Hofrichter and Klein 1993: 10).
6. The question was asked in Eurobarometer, No. 39. The alternative responses offered to respondents were: 'The national parliaments of the member states' (16%); 'Ourselves, by direct elections' (41%); 'The members of the European Council' (17%). There were 26% who did not know.
7. In this we follow Tufte's (1969: 642–6) advice about the 'wise assignment of numbers to ordered categories'. In particular he argues: 'The simple linear assignment of numbers to categories (e.g., 1, 2, 3, 4 to four ordered categories) usually won't do. Such a linear asignment is not in any way a sounder and more conservative choice than any other assignment. And the chances are that such an assignment is not consistent with the first principle of incorporating substantive information into the measurement.'
8. Thus a respondent who thinks that the Parliament is currently very important and thinks it should be more important obtains a score of 5; someone who thinks it is very unimportant and thinks it should be more important is given a score of 1; someone who thinks it is currently very important and that it should stay the same is scored 2; someone who thinks it is unimportant and should be less important is scored −4, and so on. However, there is a gap in our knowledge in so far as we do not know how far those who say the Parliament is currently unimportant and should be more important would be prepared to go in making it more important. This limitation follows from the three response categories—more important, the same, less important—for the future importance question. In the absence of evidence on degrees of

preferred future importance, we can only record that a respondent who says that the Parliament is currently very unimportant but should be more important has a positive attitude to the role of the Parliament. This is achieved by the scoring system displayed in Fig. 12.5.

9. This analysis focuses on the autumn 1988 data because for that year we can relate attitudes to the role of the Parliament to the information index presented in Table 12.2. Data from spring 1989 could also have been used but they might give exceptional results because of the imminence of the European Parliament elections.

PART IV

Enlarging the Scope of Internationalized Governance

13

The View from Within

BETTINA WESTLE

According to the Treaty of Rome, the EEC is defined as a political organization open to any European state which accepts its formal conventions and rules, has a democratic political system, and has its territory at least partly in Europe. Additional preconditions for membership, which are not regulated by treaty, are a competitive economy and economic power which is comparable to that of the member states. Although a number of countries wishing to join the EEC in the early 1960s met these preconditions, their applications were thwarted by the French veto of the British application in 1963. In 1967, Denmark, Ireland, Norway, and Britain again sought membership, and Sweden did so for the first time. However, no progress was made until De Gaulle retired in 1969, when moves towards enlargement as well as towards further internal integration were settled in principle at the Hague summit. In 1972 accession was ratified by Parliament in the British case, and by referendums in Ireland and Denmark. These three countries became members of the EEC in 1973. However, membership was rejected in the Norwegian referendum and the Swedish application went no further.

The second round of enlargement began in the mid-1970s, when Greece (1975), and Portugal and Spain (1977) applied for membership. There were intensive discussions between the governments of the EC member states concerning problems which might arise within the Community due to the lower level of economic development of these

My acknowledgements go to Brigit Zahn for preparing the data for this chapter.

applicants. However, the argument favouring support for the development of democracy in these countries carried more weight. Greece joined the EC in 1981. Spain and Portugal, after a somewhat longer period of economic adaptation, joined in 1986. This enlargement process was also accompanied by discussions about deepening integration which culminated in agreement, in principle, on the Single European Act (SEA) in December 1985.

The prospect of a single European market stimulated interest in joining the EC in several other countries. In 1987 Turkey and Morocco, Austria in 1989, Cyprus and Malta in 1990, Sweden in 1991, and Finland, Switzerland, and Norway in 1992 applied for membership. Negotiations with Austria, Finland, Norway, and Sweden led to accession agreements which, in 1994, were approved by referendums in Austria, Finland, and Sweden but rejected in Norway. With the collapse of the Soviet Union and the development of democratic political systems and market economies in Central and Eastern Europe, the issue of further enlargement came to the fore and remains at the top of the European Union's agenda.

The former GDR was fully integrated into the Community in 1990 after the unification of Germany. Hungary, Poland, the Czech Republic, and Slovakia have shown strong interest in EC membership. Since 1991 there has been a series of association agreements with these countries which envisage the possibility of their eventual accession. In early 1994, applications were received from Poland and Hungary. The prospect of enlargement beyond the present fifteen members considerably sharpens the persistent dilemma of 'deepening' versus 'widening', a dilemma which is accentuated by the imperatives of ensuring the economic and democratic development of the countries in Eastern and Central Europe and of establishing stability in the region.

It is clear that the process of enlargement is exclusively a matter for political élites. The citizens of the EC member states have never been asked by their governments whether or not they want other countries admitted.[1] Neither the prospective membership of a specific country nor the tension between deepening and widening have emerged as issues in public debate or as major differences among national political parties. This situation has a considerable effect on the theoretical expectations we might have in regard to attitudes towards the territorial dimension of the European Community.

Theoretical and Methodological Considerations

Our first expectation is that the knowledge of the territorial scope of the Community will be limited, and that there will be a high proportion of people without any opinion on the issue of territorial enlargement. Similarly, we expect that attitudes on this issue will be highly unstructured, and, to the extent that discernible influences are at work, that these will be derived from general evaluations of European integration rather than from socio-demographic variables or other political attitudes—and still less from attitudes towards detailed aspects of enlargement.

To test these assumptions, we examine the relationship between attitudes towards aspects of the enlargement issue and several individual-level variables. We look at gender, age, and place of residence as an indicator of closeness to a cosmopolitan way of life. We also consider satisfaction with life, satisfaction with democracy in one's own country, and overall attitudes to socio-political change. In addition, we take into account the impact of cognitive variables such as education, opinion leadership, political interest, and interest in the EC. Other factors which may contribute to the formation of attitudes in this area are reference group variables, such as left–right self-placement, materialism–postmaterialism, national and/or international political identity, and attitudes towards the peoples of the other EC member states or potential member states.

Previous research has shown that macro-level variables also influence the images of nations and the levels of mutual trust between nations (Deutsch *et al.* 1957; Buchanan and Cantril 1953; Nincic and Russett 1979). More recently, Inglehart (1991) found the level of economic development of countries to be a precondition of trust in their peoples. Level of economic development may have an even more direct effect on attitudes towards enlargement because economic considerations have always loomed large in elite discussions of the issue. These macro-level variables will be taken into account in interpreting the data and, where possible, the analysis will include indicators of economic perceptions and expectations at the individual level.

Before turning to the data, two additional methodological remarks are in order. First, the available data about which countries should or should not become members of the Community are based on two different types of indicators. One type is based on an open-ended, multiple response question which relies heavily on the respondent's active involvement in the issue and on the style of the interviewer. We treat responses to this type of question as *demands* for exclusion or inclusion. The second type uses a 'closed' question and focuses on those countries which had, at the time, already applied for membership. Responses to this type of question are regarded as *evaluations* of proposals for inclusion. The two types of questions will be examined separately because spontaneous demands for the inclusion or exclusion of countries may be shaped by quite different processes, particularly compared to reactions to the inclusion of countries whose application is on the table and whose admission has already been a matter of at least some public discussion.

The second methodological point is that almost none of the questions upon which the indicators are based have been asked in an identical form over time. In particular, explicit categories for respondents who have yet to make up their mind or who take a neutral position are not always provided. This problem is handled by assigning non-committal responses ('Do not know' and 'No answer') to a category of indifference—but with the caveat that the proportion of respondents who are indifferent is always higher when an explicitly neutral response category is provided.

Knowledge of Enlargement Issues

The knowledge of European citizens about a very basic aspect of the process of enlargement, that is, which countries have recently become members or are applicant members, can be examined for 1973, 1980, and 1985. The proportion of correct and incorrect answers given in 1973 is shown in Table 13.1. The striking contrast here is between the level of knowledge of Britain's membership and knowledge of the other two 1973 entrants: on average, three-quarters of respondents (77 per cent) could name Britain as a new member compared to only about a third (35 per cent) who could identify Ireland and a not much greater proportion (44 per cent) who could name Denmark.

In 1980 and 1985 the Eurobarometer survey asked a question about which countries had applied to join the EC. The responses, reported in Table 13.2, show a considerable knowledge 'jump' in that five-year period. In 1980, on average, half of the respondents could not name even one of the potential member countries, or named wrong ones. Only one-fifth were able to name all three. On the very eve of the Greek

TABLE 13.1. *Knowledge of the 1973 enlargement*

New members	Judging countries									EC
	BE	DK	FR	GB	GE	IR	IT	LU	NL	
Denmark	36	95	30	36	59	41	22	57	45	44
Ireland	21	56	16	44	36	89	16	46	19	35
Britain	67	88	74	82	83	80	59	79	85	77
Others	17	9	26	18	10	13	12	8	17	15
Mean	1.1	2.3	0.9	1.4	1.7	2.0	0.8	1.7	1.3	1.4

Notes: Entries are percentages and means. The means are based on a variable subtracting wrong answers from correct answers. The question was: 'As you know, several countries have recently joined the Common Market, i.e. the European Community. Can you tell me which countries they are? Any others?'

Source: European Community Study (1973).

accession, Spain's application, which was much farther back in the pipeline, was better known than the Greek application in a majority of the member states. This suggests that the size of a country and its prominence have an important effect on level of awareness. However, by 1985, just before the Spanish and Portuguese accession, knowledge of impending memberships had increased considerably in all countries. In fact, their impending accession was then considerably better known than had been the actual membership of either Denmark or Ireland in 1973.

The distributions in Tables 13.1 and 13.2 suggest that, apart from the size of a particular country, geographical propinquity and historical or cultural links also play some role in people's awareness. Thus, Germans were better informed than average about Danish membership in 1973, and the British were better informed about Irish membership. Likewise, the French were more aware of the Spanish and Portuguese applications in both 1980 and 1985. Even so, some constant contrasts are evident, with the Italians being consistently less well informed (except perhaps in relation to Greece) and people in Luxembourg being among the best informed.

At each of the three time points 1973, 1980, and 1985, and in each of the countries, the strongest influences on knowledge of the enlargement question are interest in EC problems, political opinion leadership, and education.[2] Moreover, in most countries, men's level of knowledge is higher than that of women; so is that of younger compared to older respondents. Controlling for the relative impact of these variables in a multiple regression analysis, interest in EC problems, opinion leadership and education retain their influence, whereas the effect of age disappears totally and the effect of gender is somewhat reduced—as the differential educational status of men and women would lead one to expect. However, all these variables taken together do not explain more than about 20 per cent of the variance. More comprehensive knowledge of EC membership, however, is clearly associated with a positive attitude to European integration. The same is true of those with a more international identity and those who believe that Europe's unification will bring opportunities rather than dangers for national identities and cultures.

TABLE 13.2. *Knowledge of applicant countries, 1980 and 1985*

Applicants	Judging countries										EC
	BE	DK	FR	GB	GE	IR	IT	LU	NL	GR	
1980											
Greece	33	57	43	20	49	29	34	52	42	—	37
Spain	36	60	57	36	51	36	33	60	54	—	45
Portugal	23	38	39	16	39	20	21	50	34	—	29
Others	8	11	5	7	2	4	4	11	12	—	5
Mean	0.8	1.4	1.3	0.7	1.4	0.8	0.8	1.5	1.2	—	1.1
1985											
Spain	69	75	80	58	77	66	58	88	77	59	69
Portugal	60	67	72	46	72	56	51	86	64	52	60
Others	4	7	3	10	4	0	4	0	8	1	5
Mean	1.3	1.4	1.5	0.9	1.4	1.2	1.1	1.7	1.3	1.1	1.2

Notes: Entries are percentages and means. The means are based on a variable subtracting respondent's wrong answers from correct answers. The 1980 question was: 'Three countries in Southern Europe have asked to join the European Community (Common Market). Can you remember which countries these are?' The 1985 question was: 'Two countries have asked to join the European Community (Common Market). Can you remember which countries these are?'

Sources: Eurobarometer, Nos. 13 and 23.

Demands for Exclusion

Before examining attitudes to enlargement in more detail, it is worth noting some evidence relating to the other side of the territorial dimension of the Community; that is, demands for the exclusion of particular countries which, at the time, were members. This issue was explored in 1976 and 1984 when respondents were asked if there were any countries which they would prefer not to be members of the Community. As the data in Table 13.3 demonstrate, in neither year were tensions in the EC countries such as to lead to a widespread demand for the exclusion of particular countries. Even so, some 30 per cent mentioned at least one country in 1976, and there was a perceptible increase in this kind of demand in 1984 when some 40 per cent pointed to at least one country they would prefer not to see in the Community.

In 1976, demands for exclusion were primarily concentrated on Italy and Britain and they emanated mainly from Germany, France, and Luxembourg. In 1984, however, animosities towards Italy were considerably reduced and demands for exclusion were directed almost exclusively against Britain. This demand came mostly from France, followed by Luxembourg, Germany, and Greece. Note, however, that just before the 1976 survey, Britain had been seriously considering leaving the EC and had held a referendum on the issue which probably contributed to Britain's already isolated position. That demands for the exclusion of Britain notably increased in 1984 may also reflect the heightened conflict with the Community under Prime Minister Margaret Thatcher and the controversy over the British budget rebate. Indeed, Britain, together with France, was mentioned most often as working against the unification of Europe in 1976. Across the EC as a whole, 45 per cent of respondents mentioned Britain and 36 per cent mentioned France as working against unification, whereas 50 per cent mentioned Germany as working hardest for unification, followed by 20 per cent mentioning France and the Netherlands.

The perception that a country is working against the unification of Europe shows some strong correlations with the demand for exclusion. However, the correlations are not particularly strong in the British or Italian cases. Neither socio-demographic characteristics, general political orientations, nor reference group membership make any significant difference to the level of demands for exclusion. A sense of international identification, the feeling of being a European, trust in the

TABLE 13.3. *Demands for exclusion of member countries, 1976 and 1984*

	Judging countries										
	BE	DK	FR	GB	GE	IR	IT	LU	NL	GR	EC
1976 exclude											
France	1	6	2	9	10	5	9	3	5		7
Belgium	0	2	1	1	2	1	2	2	0		1
Netherlands	1	2	1	1	1	1	3	0	0		1
Germany	2	3	4	3	1	3	6	3	2		3
Italy	6	9	11	9	27	5	1	16	13		12
Luxembourg	0	2	1	1	1	1	2	1	0		1
Denmark	1	15	1	1	1	2	9	2	0		1
Ireland	4	3	3	8	9	9	7	11	5		6
Britain	6	3	15	9	19	5	5	14	8		12
No. to be excluded											
0	84	73	73	70	57	77	77	68	76		70
1	12	21	20	26	23	19	16	19	19		21
2	3	3	6	4	15	3	4	10	4		7
3–9	1	2	2	1	5	1	3	3	2		3
1984 exclude											
France	1	2	0	25	4	2	5	2	3	5	6
Belgium	0	1	0	1	2	0	0	2	1	2	1
Netherlands	1	1	1	1	1	1	1	0	1	2	1
Germany		3	2	4	2	2	7	2	2	9	3
Italy	5	6	5	7	11	2	0	3	5	4	5
Luxembourg	0	1	0	1	1	0	1	0	1	2	1
Denmark	1	18	1	1	1	1	1	0	1	2	3
Ireland	4	3	2	8	5	5	1	6	8	2	4
Britain	20	15	41	12	33	14	18	38	23	27	22
Greece	7	9	4	8	13	2	3	9	7	13	7

TABLE 13.3. *Cont.*

No. to be excluded	Judging countries										EC
	BE	DK	FR	GB	GE	IR	IT	LU	NL	GR	
0	70	61	53	56	50	75	70	55	66	59	58
1	24	29	39	29	32	21	25	31	23	29	30
2	5	6	6	12	12	3	5	11	8	7	9
3–9	2	4	2	4	5	0	1	3	3	4	3

Notes: Entries are percentages. The 1976 question was: 'Among these countries of the Common Market, are there any that you would like not to be members of it?' The 1984 question was: 'This is a list of countries belonging to the European Community (Common Market). Among these countries of the European Community, are there any, including your own, you would prefer not to be in the Community? Which ones?'

Sources: Eurobarometer, Nos. 6 and 21.

peoples of other member states, and low ethnocentrism are linked to some degree to lower levels of demand for a country to be excluded, although the relationship is not uniform across all countries. Across the EC as a whole, the strongest relationships between feelings of identity and trust and a desire to exclude particular countries occur in relation to one or other of the four large countries—France, Germany, Italy, and Britain. This again bears out the observation about the impact of size on the salience of the territorial dimension of the Community. Even so, the multivariate analysis accounts for no more than 11 per cent of the variance in demands for the exclusion of Germany, 10 per cent with respect to Italy, and 8 per cent with respect to Britain and France. In fact, trust in a specific country is the only variable which retains an impact (beta about 0.27) when the simultaneous impact of all the other variables is taken into account (for details, see Westle 1992).

Demands for Enlargement

Almost half the respondents in the 1976 survey did not express any wish to see a further enlargement of the Community. But the relatively low level of demands for inclusion may indicate the low salience of the issue rather than opposition to extending the EC. Some 20 per cent mentioned just one country and 16 per cent mentioned two. As Table 13.4 shows, the desire for enlargement was somewhat more widespread in the older member countries than in the new ones. On average, Switzerland, Spain, and Austria were mentioned most often. Germans and Luxemburgers tended to refer to Switzerland and Austria, the Italians to Switzerland, and the French to Spain. These patterns suggest that linguistic or historical and cultural commonalities have some effect on attitudes towards enlargement.

Predictably, the number of countries mentioned for inclusion increases with cognitive involvement in politics; that is, with stronger interest in politics, interest in the EC and its problems, better education, and opinion leadership status. Internationalist attitudes, too, to some extent, are influential. However, a multivariate analysis accounts for only 13 per cent of the variance, reducing the independent impact of all variables near to insignificance except for interest in the EC (beta −0.20) and opinion leadership (beta −0.10). In sum, active demands for the exclusion or inclusion of countries are shaped to some degree by interest in EC issues. But when all the relevant variables are taken into

TABLE 13.4. *Demands for inclusion of particular countries, 1976*

| | \multicolumn{9}{c}{Judging countries} | | | | | | | | |
	BE	DK	FR	GB	GE	IR	IT	LU	NL
Include									
Greece	12	8	9	5	18	7	19	16	8
Spain	22	7	37	13	23	20	24	25	13
Portugal	12	6	14	5	13	5	18	17	10
Turkey	6	3	2	3	8	3	7	6	4
Switzerland	23	18	20	16	41	11	31	41	23
Austria	15	16	11	8	42	6	22	40	15
Others	10	4	14	19	5	11	15	7	31
No. to be included									
0	58	73	45	62	35	64	43	40	49
1	19	12	27	23	19	22	22	17	26
2	9	7	16	9	25	9	15	23	12
3–5	9	8	11	4	17	4	15	15	10
6+	5	3	2	2	4	2	5	5	3

Notes: Entries are percentages. The question was: 'Here is a list of countries that belong to the Common Market now. Are there any other countries in Europe that you would like to see joining the Common Market in the near future? Which ones?'

Source: Eurobarometer, No. 6.

account, such demands are largely unaffected either by socio-demographic characteristics, general political orientations, or by orientations towards the peoples of other states (Westle 1992).

Evaluations of Proposals for Enlargement

We distinguished earlier between demands for inclusion in the EC and evaluations of proposed new memberships. The distinction is both methodological and substantive. Methodologically, it is the difference between a spontaneous naming of a particular country as a desirable addition to the Community, as opposed to the more passive evaluation of a proposed new member listed by the interviewer. Substantively, demands are likely to reflect the salience of enlargement whereas the evaluations of proposed new memberships are likely to include responses from respondents for whom the issue is of little salience or interest. We now turn to evaluations of proposed new memberships, based on broad historical and geopolitical groupings of the applications.

First, the southern enlargement. When respondents were asked in 1979 which of the three southern countries—Greece, Spain, and Portugal—should be allowed to join the European Community, opinion was considerably more favourable than had appeared to be the case in 1976, based on spontaneous demands for inclusion. As we can see in Table 13.5, pluralities in most of the countries supported admission, although substantial proportions (20 to 30 per cent) were indifferent. Whereas most respondents would have allowed Spain to join, Greece and Portugal were somewhat less widely welcomed. Respondents from Italy and the Netherlands held the most positive view and respondents from France and Germany the least positive view on the issue.

In 1980, with the issue of Greek accession already decided, support for what had become official policy on the entry of Greece was clearly higher than opposition. But there were also substantial increases in the proportion of positive over negative responses for Portugal and Spain between 1979 and 1985. Again as with Greece, the Italians and respondents from the Benelux countries were most favourable towards these southern entries at both points in time, whereas respondents from Denmark, Greece, France, Britain, and Ireland were less favourable. Among those countries surveyed on this question in 1979 and 1985, the strongest positive change of opinion towards the southern extension took place in Germany, which had actually shown a balance of opinion against Portuguese entry and had been the least supportive in regard to Spanish entry in 1979.

By contrast, Turkish membership was clearly a low salience issue in most countries. This is evident from the high proportion of indifferent responses to a question asked in 1986, reported in Table 13.6. Whereas almost half of all Greek respondents were 'opposed' or 'very much opposed' to a Turkish application, in most instances—except France—there was a plurality of indifferent reponses, rising to almost 60 per cent in Britain. The overall balance of opinion in the Community as a whole was 21 per cent in favour, 30 per cent against, and 49 per cent indifferent. Given the Greek–Turkish conflict over Cyprus, it is not surprising that the lowest non-response rate and especially the highest rate of rejection of Turkey's admission came from Greece.[3]

The admission of former East Germany presents a very different situation. Early in 1990, Jacques Delors, President of the European Commission, in a speech to the European Parliament, emphasized

TABLE 13.5. *Evaluation of entry of Greece, Portugal, and Spain into the European Community*

	BE	DK	FR	GB	GE	IR	IT	LU	NL	GR	EC
					Judging countries						EC
GREECE											
1979											
Positive	45	—	38	44	37	—	61	—	55	—	
Indifferent	30	—	26	27	26	—	24	—	20	—	
Negative	25	—	37	29	37	—	15	—	25	—	
1980											
Positive	28	24	24	22	44	35	50	42	41	—	35
Indifferent	65	57	63	65	49	55	43	50	50	—	55
Negative	8	20	14	14	8	10	8	9	9	—	11
PORTUGAL											
1979											
Positive	46	—	40	44	25	—	59	—	52	—	
Indifferent	30	—	26	28	26	—	24	—	20	—	
Negative	24	—	34	28	49	—	17	—	28	—	
1985											
Positive	63	40	58	54	64	51	72	76	66	41	61
Indifferent	26	39	15	32	20	38	19	3	20	45	23
Negative	11	21	27	14	16	11	9	21	14	15	16
SPAIN											
1979											
Positive	51	—	51	48	41	—	62	—	58	—	
Indifferent	30	—	26	28	26	—	24	—	20	—	
Negative	19	—	24	24	33	—	14	—	22	—	
1985											
Positive	64	40	58	50	65	48	74	79	67	42	62
Indifferent	25	38	14	30	19	35	17	3	21	43	21
Negative	11	22	28	20	16	17	9	18	12	15	18

Notes: Entries are percentages. The 1979 question was: 'Three South European countries—Greece, Portugal, and Spain—are now being considered for membership in the European Community. Which of these do you think should be allowed to join the European Community—or do you think none of them should be allowed to join?' (multiple answers). The 1980 question was: 'Greece is due to join on 1 January 1981. In your opinion, is the entry of Greece into the European Community a good thing, a bad thing, or neither one nor the other?' The 1985 question was: 'Thinking about Spain joining the European Community, are you strongly for, somewhat for, somewhat against or strongly against? And thinking about Portugal joining the European Community, are you strongly for, somewhat for, somewhat against or strongly against?' The 1980 results for Greece are the average of the spring and autumn surveys.

Sources: Eurobarometer, Nos. 11, 13, 14, and 23.

TABLE 13.6. *Support for entry of Turkey into the European Community, 1986*

	Judging countries								EC
	BE	DK	FR	GB	GE	IT	NL	GR	
Positive	20	24	17	17	24	25	34	15	21
Indifferent	52	39	39	59	43	44	42	36	49
Negative	28	37	44	24	33	31	24	49	30

Notes: Entries are percentages. The question was: 'Supposing Turkey asked to be admitted as a member country of the European Community (Common Market), what would be your opinion? Would you be very favourable, opposed, very much opposed?' The question was not asked in Ireland and Luxembourg.

Source: Eurobarometer, No. 25.

that the East European countries would not be in a position to meet the political and economic preconditions for EC membership in the near future. However, he classified the GDR as a special case, following the decision of the European Council in favour of the German move to secure political unity. Thus, the integration of the GDR into the Community was mainly determined by the rapid progress of German unification.[4]

During the early phase of German unification, a plurality (roughly 45 per cent) in all EC countries except West Germany gave a higher priority to the completion of the Single European Market than to German unification. At the same time, a majority thought that the Germans themselves would give higher priority to unification. However, the proportion of Germans who were undecided (27 per cent), or even the proportion in favour of giving priority to the Single Market (20 per cent), may seem surprisingly high in the light of the level of support in West Germany for German unification (77 per cent). The explanation probably lies in the very controversial nature of the political debate and in far-reaching doubts about the speed of the unification process, which a considerable number of West Germans judged to be too fast (Westle 1992).

In the spring of 1990, when it was not yet clear if or when the two German states would unify, we find that a considerable proportion of European citizens (on average about 20 per cent) were uncertain about the issue of GDR membership of the Community and about the possible effects of German unification on the EC. Across a number of survey questions, respondents from Luxembourg, Denmark, the Netherlands,

Belgium, and Britain showed the lowest levels of support and the strongest opposition to GDR membership, whereas respondents from Greece, Spain, France, and Italy were more favourable disposed.

Between spring and autumn of 1990, German unification was supported in all EC countries by increasing majorities, rising to an EC average of 78 per cent. Strongest support came from those countries where relatively high numbers of respondents would have welcomed the GDR as an EC member. Opposition was again evident in Luxembourg, Denmark, the Netherlands, Belgium, Britain, and France. Although the French and British governments were the most sceptical about German unification, the people of these countries were not the most opposed. The stronger support evident in the southern EC countries than in the older EC countries may reflect fewer doubts about the possibility of regime transition in countries which had experienced transition to democracy in the recent past.

The data in Table 13.7 show a fairly rapid shift in opinion about the effects of German unification on European integration during 1990–1. In 1990, in most EC countries, optimism was not widespread, and in all EC countries, including Germany, one-third or more of citizens had no opinion on the question. One year later, after German unification had taken place, uncertainty about its effects had declined considerably and the balance of opinion had tilted towards positive expectations in all countries except Luxembourg. Even so, substantial minorities in Denmark, France, and the Benelux countries remained fearful, followed by the Belgians, the French, and the British. The Italians and the Spanish were the most optimistic, together with the citizens of the former GDR themselves, whereas the West Germans showed more scepticism. Essentially the same pattern is found, in 1991, in regard to the expected effects of German unification on the future of the respondent's own country.

With the collapse of Soviet domination, the inclusion of Central and East European countries in the EC rapidly became an urgent issue. In 1989, public opinion was divided on the priority to be given to the completion of the Single European Market versus an open approach towards Eastern Europe. Majorities in France, Belgium, Italy, Ireland, Greece, and Portugal gave priority to the completion of the Single Market, whereas in the other member countries 40–56 per cent favoured an open approach towards Eastern Europe. A year later, there was very little change in this situation.

When asked for a direct endorsement of specific policies towards

TABLE 13.7. *Perceived effects of German unification, 1990 and 1991*

							Judging countries								EC
	BE	DK	FR	GB	GE (W)	GE (E)	IR	IT	LU	NL	GR	PO	SP		
1990															
Integration															
No problem	32	29	32	35	50		31	53	30	34	40	33	53		43
Indifferent	36	33	38	37	33		46	27	39	33	35	47	32		34
Interfere	32	38	30	28	17		23	20	31	33	25	20	15		23
1991															
EC															
Hopeful	57	51	55	60	63	79	68	78	44	62	51	66	68		62
Indifferent	11	11	10	8	9	6	14	12	18	8	21	19	21		13
Fearful	32	38	35	32	28	15	18	10	38	30	28	15	11		25
Nation															
Hopeful	51	58	46	53	62	77	61	70	46	60	47	59	64		58
Indifferent	18	9	12	16	5	4	19	17	23	14	23	23	26		15
Fearful	31	33	42	31	33	19	20	13	31	26	30	18	10		27

Notes: Entries are percentages. The 1990 question was: 'Thinking of the possible effects of political developments in Germany on European integration, which of the following statements comes closest to your opinion? (1) A unified Germany can be integrated into the European Community without any problems. (2) German unification will interfere with the process of European integration.' The 1991 question was: 'Germany has become bigger since the unification of its two states. (a) Would you say that a unified Germany personally makes you very hopeful about the European Community and its future, rather hopeful, or very fearful? (b) And would you say that a unified Germany personally makes you very hopeful about the [nation] and its future, rather hopeful, rather fearful or very fearful?'

Sources: Eurobarometer, Nos. 33 and 35.

Eastern Europe, some 60–70 per cent of the European public expressed approval across a range of policies. This approval covered speeding up internal integration, the participation of Eastern countries in EC resources, the offer of association treaties without membership, and future membership. The data on future membership, shown in Table 13.8, suggest that the inclusion of Central and East European countries was fairly widely endorsed across the EC as a whole.

Other data (not shown here), however, indicate that for most citizens, the prospect of closer co-operation with Central and Eastern Europe was an issue of modest salience, resting on incomplete understanding of its implications—both for the EC and their own country. Respondents tend to agree with every policy, even a budget increase, so long as these policies are not highlighted as affecting their own resources. The only survey question which points to the possibility of conflicting aims and limited resources—whether the EC should reduce subsidies for less developed regions within the EC in order to help East European countries—produced considerably less favourable responses (50 per cent against, 20 per cent indifferent, and 30 per cent in favour). This suggests that support for the European Union's policies in Central and Eastern Europe may come under considerable pressure once the real costs come to the public's attention (Westle 1992).

There is, of course, more to the question of enlargement than subsidies and transfer payments, in particular the issue of 'widening versus deepening'. This issue was put directly to respondents for the first time in 1988. The question asked whether the EC should be expanded in the next five years at the cost of maintaining its present form, or, alternatively, whether current EC membership should be maintained with the benefit of enhancing political integration among the existing twelve member countries. Across the EC as a whole, 40 per cent of respondents preferred deepening, another 40 per cent preferred widening, and 20 per cent were without an opinion. The preference for deepening was somewhat more frequent in most of the older member countries, especially in France and Luxembourg, whereas the preference for widening was more frequent in Italy and in the newer member countries.

In 1988 the issue of enlargement was still fairly remote. Only Turkey had actually applied to join the Community and it was the least likely candidate. By 1992, however, the five EFTA countries had either applied or were about to apply for membership and several other countries had been added to the list of applicants. The full list and

TABLE 13.8. *Orientations towards the inclusion of Central and East European countries, 1990*

	Judging countries													EC
	BE	DK	FR	GB	GE (W)	GE (E)	IR	IT	LU	NL	GR	PO	SP	
1990 spring														
Agree	61	54	59	62	57	72	59	76	42	54	67	51	72	63
Indifferent	19	28	24	21	21	16	30	15	26	15	23	34	23	21
Disagree	20	18	17	17	22	12	12	9	34	31	10	15	5	16
1990 autumn														
Agree	60	57	62	68	65	72	62	74	55	60	69	59	65	64
Indifferent	20	12	17	18	17	16	25	16	15	14	20	25	29	19
Disagree	20	31	21	14	18	12	13	10	30	26	11	16	6	17

Notes: Entries are percentages. The question was: 'We are currently witnessing rapid changes in Central and Eastern Europe. In your opinion, what should the European Community do about this? [Should it] prepare itself for each of the countries of Central and Eastern Europe that requests it to join the EC, as soon as it has established democracy and an open economy?'

Sources: Eurobarometer, Nos. 33 and 34.

the distribution of responses are shown in Table 13.9. Support for the inclusion of Sweden, Norway, Finland, Switzerland, and Austria was overwhelming, averaging about 78 per cent. Support for Iceland (which was not contemplating an application for membership), averaging 72 per cent, was only slightly lower. However, support for Malta and Cyprus, whose applications were on the table, was notably lower (averaging 62 per cent) but still comfortably favourable. The only country to encounter substantial opposition was Russia, but even then the balance of opinion was in favour of entry.

The patterns in the data again point to the importance of geographic or cultural proximity as a determinant of attitudes towards the inclusion of additional countries in the Community. Thus, support for the membership of the Scandinavian countries was highest in Denmark and the Netherlands, and support for Malta and Cyprus was strongest in the four southern EC countries. The effect of earlier political ties and current conflicts shows up particularly in the extraordinarily high support for Cypriot membership among the Greeks. The prospect of Russian membership was most strongly supported by Spanish and Italian respondents, while the strongest opposition was expressed by respondents in Denmark, Luxembourg, and France.

The question about admission of these additional countries was followed by questions on what would be the effects on the current member states. The distribution of positive and negative expectations is quite similar to the distribution of support for membership. However, as has been observed before in regard to earlier candidate countries, uncertainty about possible effects is far more widespread than uncertainty regarding support.

Sources of Attitudes to Enlargement

We noted earlier that neither socio-structural characteristics (gender, age, or place of residence) nor general social and political orientations (satisfaction with life, attitude towards socio-political change, satisfaction with democracy) show strong and significant effects on attitudes towards the admission of new members. This is a regular pattern across countries and time points. The few effects these variables have in some of the EC countries are mainly due to traditional social roles and variations in cognitive skills, and seem to vanish with the modernization of those countries between the early 1970s and the early 1990s.[5]

TABLE 13.9. *Support for the inclusion of EFTA and other countries, 1992*

	Judging countries													EC
	BE	DK	FR	GB	GE (W)	GE (E)	IR	IT	LU	NL	GR	PO	SP	
Austria														
Positive	75	89	73	80	79	90	69	78	80	81	71	69	72	77
Indifferent	17	5	10	13	9	8	22	13	10	9	19	20	23	14
Negative	8	6	17	7	12	2	9	9	10	10	10	11	5	9
Sweden														
Positive	77	92	77	81	79	90	71	83	80	91	76	74	74	80
Indifferent	17	3	10	12	10	8	21	12	10	6	17	19	22	13
Negative	6	5	13	7	11	2	8	5	10	3	7	7	4	7
Finland														
Positive	73	90	73	79	76	86	70	80	78	87	73	69	72	77
Indifferent	19	4	12	14	12	10	22	13	10	9	21	22	23	15
Negative	8	6	13	7	12	3	8	7	12	4	7	9	5	7
Norway														
Positive	75	93	75	80	79	87	71	80	80	92	72	69	73	79
Indifferent	18	2	12	13	11	10	21	13	10	6	21	21	22	14
Negative	7	5	13	7	10	3	8	7	10	2	7	10	5	7
Iceland														
Positive	66	90	68	74	69	74	65	74	74	78	68	63	71	72
Indifferent	21	4	13	15	15	17	24	13	11	14	23	24	23	16
Negative	13	6	19	11	16	9	11	13	15	8	9	13	6	12
Switzerland														
Positive	76	88	74	81	79	88	73	79	80	86	76	77	75	79
Indifferent	17	6	9	11	10	8	20	10	9	9	16	16	21	12
Negative	7	6	17	8	11	4	7	11	11	6	8	7	4	9

TABLE 13.9. *Cont.*

					Judging countries										EC
	BE	DK	FR	GB	GE (W)	GE (E)	IR	IT	LU	NL	GR	PO	SP	
Malta															
Positive	53	56	52	71	46	55	63	74	51	62	66	57	65	64
Indifferent	26	19	18	15	21	25	24	16	19	21	22	25	25	19
Negative	21	25	30	14	39	20	13	10	30	17	12	18	10	17
Cyprus															
Positive	50	47	49	62	40	52	59	67	47	51	86	55	64	60
Indifferent	26	17	18	17	21	25	24	18	17	20	9	26	24	19
Negative	24	36	33	21	33	23	17	15	36	29	5	19	12	21
Russia															
Positive	33	31	34	47	41	47	43	60	33	42	55	48	61	48
Indifferent	26	12	14	17	21	20	26	16	15	21	19	22	24	18
Negative	41	57	52	36	38	33	31	24	52	37	26	30	15	34
Mean (0–9)															
Positive	5.8	6.7	5.7	6.5	5.9	6.7	5.8	6.8	6.0	6.7	6.4	5.8	6.2	6.4
Indifferent	1.9	0.7	1.2	1.3	1.3	1.2	2.1	1.2	1.1	1.1	1.7	1.9	2.1	1.4
Negative	1.3	1.6	2.1	1.2	1.8	1.1	1.1	1.0	1.9	1.2	0.9	1.2	0.7	1.2

Notes: Entries are percentages and means. The column means are based on counts of positive, indifferent, and negative evaluation of countries. The question was: 'For each of the following countries, are you in favour or not of their becoming part of the European Community in the near future? And for Russia?'

Source: Eurobarometer, No. 37.

There are just a few exceptions to this pattern. In almost all countries, and especially in the earlier years of the EC, the better educated, the cognitively mobilized, and those interested in EC problems show somewhat stronger support for enlargement. Also a more positive orientation towards the inclusion of additional countries can be observed among postmaterialists in the 1970s and early 1980s. However, this effect, which was weak to begin with, declines over time and is even reversed in the 1990s. Indeed, in the early 1990s postmaterialists were less supportive of enlargement than materialists. The data also reveal country-specific differences in the effects of left–right self-placement which mainly reflect the stances of the political parties towards the EC. In most cases, however, these effects are very small.

Respondents with low trust in peoples from countries outside the EC showed less support for the southern enlargement. Trust in other peoples, whether inside or outside the Community, had an effect, in particular, on attitudes towards the admission of Turkey. Moreover, the general level of trust in others and a sense of European identity were clearly related to support for the entry of former East Germany, for German unification, for a policy of closer co-operation with Eastern European countries, and for the admission of the EFTA countries. Even so, in all these cases trust and identity explain less than 10 per cent of the variance in a multivariate analysis, except for the entry of Turkey (Westle 1992).

In the case of Turkey, a more generalized ethnocentrism surfaced as a factor in Germany, Denmark, the Netherlands, Belgium, and France. However, if trust in the Turkish people as well as ethnocentrism is taken into account, the impact of ethnocentrism vanishes in every country except Greece. In brief, the variance explained by ethnocentrism and trust is strongest in Germany ($r^2 = 0.38$), followed by Greece ($r^2 = 0.17$), France ($r^2 = 0.16$), the Netherlands ($r^2 = 0.14$), Denmark ($r^2 = 0.13$), and Belgium ($r^2 = 0.11$). Except for France, this result shows that in those countries with a high proportion of Turkish people, trust in Turkish people contributes considerably to a positive evaluation of the entry of Turkey into the EC. In countries lacking direct experience of Turkish people, determinants of opinions on Turkey's membership remain an open question. However, research results from other Eurobarometer surveys show some evidence that Turkey itself is not perceived as fully European, but as oriental and differing widely from European countries with respect to religion, value orientations, and culture (Hofrichter 1992).

For the most part, we do not have extensive data on the expected effects of the accession of any particular country on attitudes to that country's application for membership. However, questions have been asked at intervals in the Eurobarometer surveys about the expected effects of Spain's entry into the Community. Although the questions tended to attract a particularly high abstention rate (about 40 per cent on average), the positive answers outweighed the negative ones in all countries except Denmark (data not shown here). While élite discussions about the southern extension centred mainly on the principle of supporting the new democratic regimes as against expectations of possible negative economic effects, this controversy was virtually undetectable in public opinion. Across the EC as a whole, about 70 per cent judged the Spanish entry as a good thing for Spain, but about 50 per cent did not expect any effects on their own country. This holds in 1977, 1978, and 1985, again indicating both the low salience of enlargement as a political issue and the gap between élite and mass thinking.

In 1977, while the effects of Spanish accession were the most positively evaluated (38 per cent in favour), one third of respondents also expected positive effects on their own country from the entry of Greece and Portugal, whereas only about 16 per cent expected negative effects from these two entries. Respondents in Italy, Germany, and Ireland held the most positive expectations; respondents from Denmark and the Netherlands held the most negative. Thus, at the aggregate level, the economic affluence of the judging countries showed no systematic relationship to expectations about the entries of these economically less advanced countries.

As the year of Spanish accession was approaching, we might have expected a decline in the rate of non-responses, on the assumption that there would have been increasing public discussion of the issue. Comparing the data for 1977 and 1985, this is indeed the case for most EC countries, but the changes are often quite small and there are wide variations in the associated changes in positive and negative expectations. In fact, changes in expectations regarding the effects of Spanish entry were even greater in some of the countries which had not witnessed a strong decline in non-responses.

The questions asked about Spanish entry in 1985 can be used to build an index of perceived benefits and disadvantages arising from Spain's entry. The distributions on this index, reported in Table 13.10, show that relatively few respondents expected their own country to benefit more than Spain, and relatively few thought that the entry of Spain would be disadvantageous for both their own country and Spain (or would have no effect on Spain). However, there were considerable differences between countries in regard to positive expectations for both their own country and Spain. Respondents in Italy, Belgium, Luxembourg, and Germany were the most optimistic about the outlook for both countries. In contrast, the expectation of disadvantages stemming from the entry of Spain was relatively high in France, Ireland, and Denmark.

Looking at the 1977 and 1985 data more closely, it appears that negative expectations about the entry of Spain were due mainly to the anticipation of problems in the agricultural sector. Examining the means of responses, shown in Table 13.11, in 1977 it was only in Luxembourg, France, the Netherlands, Belgium, and Italy that respondents representing the agricultural sector had more negative expectations than respondents not in contact with the agricultural sector. By 1985 the situation had changed considerably. In every EC country the expectations of respondents involved in the agricultural sector were more negative than the expectations of those in other sectors.

Also shown in Table 13.11 are differences in positive and negative expectations according to different levels of opinion leadership. As in earlier chapters, we follow Inglehart (1990) in regarding people who often discuss politics and attempt to persuade others to their views as opinion leaders. Such opinion leaders usually hold the most positive orientations towards the EC (see Chapter 9). In 1977, the perceived effects of Spanish accession generally conformed to this pattern. However, in 1985, in almost all countries, opinion leaders were the ones with the most negative expectations regarding the effects on their own country of Spain's entry into the EC. Moreover, in those countries with the strongest overall increase of negative expectations—France, Germany, and Ireland—it was the opinion leaders who changed most drastically to a negative view in 1985. Thus, on the assumption that opinion leaders function as opinion multipliers, this helps to explain the different country-specific change in attitudes as well as the strong change from positive towards negative expectations among the general public in Ireland, France, and Germany.

TABLE 13.10. *Expected benefits and disadvantages from entry of Spain, 1985*

	BE	DK	FR	GB	GE	IR	IT	LU	NL	GR	EC
						Judging countries					
Bad for own nation + good for Spain	8	16	30	14	11	21	14	13	12	11	16
Bad for own nation + bad/no effect for Spain	3	6	6	8	4	12	2	3	2	14	5
No effect for own nation + all responses for Spain	48	62	35	48	49	41	40	42	57	52	45
Good for own nation + bad/no effect for Spain	3	3	3	3	3	2	2	4	2	4	3
Good for own nation + good for Spain	38	13	26	27	33	24	42	38	27	19	31

Notes: Entries are percentages. The questions were: 'If Spain joins the European Community, do think it would be a good thing for Spain's future, a bad thing, or neither good nor bad?'; 'And for [respondents' country], in particular, would it be a good thing, a bad thing, or neither good nor bad?'

Source: Eurobarometer, No. 23.

TABLE 13.11. *Anticipated effects from entry of Spain by sector and opinion leadership, 1977 and 1985*

					Judging countries						EC
	BE	DK	FR	GB	GE	IR	IT	LU	NL	GR	
HOUSEHOLD OCCUPATION											
1977											
Agricultural	1.85	1.99	2.13	1.67	1.60	1.63	1.80	2.25	2.04	—	1.80
Non-agricultural	1.82	2.04	1.86	1.90	1.61	1.74	1.71	1.77	1.90	—	1.89
1985											
Agricultural	1.80	2.20	2.19	2.08	1.86	2.19	2.04	2.25	2.12	2.12	2.13
Non-agricultural	1.70	2.04	2.07	1.91	1.83	2.04	1.71	1.74	1.84	2.00	1.89
OPINION LEADERSHIP											
1977											
Opinion leadership	1.56	1.98	1.90	1.86	1.47	1.77	1.75	1.70	1.75	—	1.77
Intermediate	1.78	2.03	1.83	1.89	1.58	1.67	1.67	1.77	1.88	—	1.79
Non-leadership	1.87	2.06	1.90	1.92	1.68	1.76	1.75	1.82	1.95	—	1.86
1985											
Opinion leadership	1.67	2.04	2.15	2.00	1.95	2.06	1.78	1.93	1.92	2.16	2.02
Intermediate	1.70	2.08	2.05	1.87	1.81	2.14	1.70	1.68	1.81	2.01	1.89
Non-leadership	1.72	2.03	2.09	1.94	1.86	2.00	1.72	1.83	1.83	1.98	1.91

Notes: Entries are means. The means range from 1 (good) to 3 (bad).

Sources: Eurobarometer, Nos. 8 and 23.

Attitudes to Integration and Enlargement

Turning to the question of the relationship between attitudes to integration and attitudes towards enlargement, we can anticipate three approaches. The first is to give priority to enlargement as a means of diluting integration. Implicitly if not explicitly, this is the rationale behind the 'widening before deepening' option. The second is to give priority to deepening, even at the expense of widening. The third and probably the 'official' view is that both must be done together; that is, the European Union must be widened and deepened simultaneously. Note that, in the first two perspectives, attitudes towards integration and attitudes towards enlargement are inversely related. In the first, a negative attitude towards integration entails a positive attitude towards enlargement; in the second, a positive attitude towards integration entails a negative attitude towards enlargement. In the third view, the two attitudes are positively related.

While it is clear that the subtleties behind these arguments do not percolate down to the mass of the population, public opinion corresponds more closely to the third, official, view than to either of the other two. In all countries and at all time points, positive attitudes towards the EC, as measured by the membership, unification, benefits, and dissolution indicators discussed in Chapter 4, go along with support for the inclusion of new member states. For the most part, attitudes measured by these four variables are more closely associated with attitudes towards the expansion of the EC than socio-structural characteristics, general political orientations, identity, and trust between people of different countries. Even so, there are considerable differences in the bivariate relationships between countries and within countries over time (see Westle 1992).

The interesting questions, however, relate not just to the impact of attitudes towards integration but to their impact relative to the other variables which, in our analyses so far, have shown some relationship with attitudes towards the territorial scope of the Community. These include socio-structural characteristics, general political orientations, identity, and trust between people of different countries. They also include measures of the perceived change in the level of agreement between EC member states, expectations concerning the Single European Market, interest in the EC, and the expected effects of accession of a particular country; that is, the effects on the country in question, on the respondent's own country, or on the EC as a whole. We examined these effects using multivariate analysis. Several models, using different combinations of variables, were tested (for details, see Westle 1992), although, unfortunately, the entire set of independent variables is not available for each of the dependent variables we wished to consider. The final equations are reported in Table 13.12.

Trust reveals moderate and fairly consistent effects but, in most cases, it is overshadowed by the effect of general attitudes towards integration. In the case of the admission of Greece, in most member states, respondents' attitudes towards membership of their own country in the EC is more important than trust in the Greeks. Likewise, in regard to the possible future inclusion of countries from Central and Eastern Europe, general attitudes towards integration have a greater impact than trust in the peoples of these countries. However, in the case of the Turkish application, trust in the Turks is a more important influence than overall attitudes towards European integration. In the case of attitudes to the admission of the EFTA countries, expectations concerning the impact of the Single European Market ('SEM effect') and the combined effect of the basic indicators of attitudes towards integration (EC-index)[6] are the dominant influences. Even so, the level of explained variance remains very low.

In the case of Spain, we are in a position to include in the analysis all the variables measuring the perceived effects of an enlargement of the EC on the candidate country, on the respondent's own country, and on the EC as a whole. In this instance, the level of variance explained increases considerably. The more specific 'effect' variables show the greatest impact, while the influence of general attitudes towards integration and the influence of trust are substantially reduced. It is notable that the perceived effect on Spain itself has a consistently weaker impact than perceptions of the effect on the respondent's own country or perceptions of the effect on the EC. Of the latter two variables, the perceived effect on the EC tends to be somewhat stronger except in Germany and France where the impact of each variable is much the same. In Luxembourg and Greece the perceived effect on the respondent's own country predominates.

TABLE 13.12. *Multiple regression analyses of attitudes towards enlargements*

	BE	DK	FR	GB	GE (W)	IR	IT	LU	NL	GR	PO	SP	EC
1985: Inclusion of Spain													
Unification	*	0.07	*	0.05	0.09	0.07	0.12	*	0.10	0.11			0.06
Dissolution	*	*	0.08	0.12	*	*	*	*	*	*			0.06
Membership	0.10	*	*	*	0.08	*	0.12	*	*	*			0.07
Agreement	*	*	*	*	*	*	*	*	0.07	*			*
Effect on EC	0.41	0.27	0.33	0.33	0.34	0.37	0.32	0.20	0.32	0.11			0.30
Effect on nation	0.14	0.20	0.35	0.26	0.33	0.18	0.21	0.32	0.22	0.30			0.28
Effect on Spain	0.13	0.08	0.06	0.06	*	0.07	*	*	0.08	0.22			0.08
R^2	0.39	0.26	0.45	0.40	0.48	0.33	0.35	0.27	0.33	0.37			0.38
1980: Inclusion of Greece													
Unification	0.12	0.18	0.14	0.09	*	*	0.10	*	0.11				0.09
Membership	0.32	0.26	0.40	0.40	0.44	0.54	0.28	0.30	0.32				0.38
Trust in Greeks	0.11	0.21	0.14	0.16	0.15	*	0.15	0.27	0.26				0.07
R^2	0.18	0.20	0.25	0.23	0.25	0.31	0.15	0.20	0.23				0.19
1986: Inclusion of Turkey													
EC-index	0.13	0.20	0.12	0.16	0.19	—	0.09	—	0.15	*	0.14	0.15	0.14
Trust in Turks	0.29	0.44	0.40	0.32	0.54	—	0.26	—	0.35	0.30	0.24	*	0.35
R^2	0.11	0.23	0.19	0.15	0.38	—	0.08	—	0.15	0.09	0.08	0.02	0.15
1990: Prepare for membership of East European countries													
EC-index	0.16	0.15	0.30	0.15	0.22	0.19	0.10	0.24	0.11	0.27	0.14	0.12	0.19
European identity	*	*	*	*	*	*	*	*	*	*	*	*	0.05
Interest in EC	*	*	*	*	*	*	*	*	*	*	*	0.17	*
Trust in Eastern countries	0.19	0.11	0.14	0.17	0.13	*	*	*	0.15	*	0.18	*	0.10
R^2	0.11	0.04	0.15	0.09	0.14	0.10	0.02	0.15	0.05	0.08	0.06	0.09	0.07

1992: Inclusion of EFTA and other countries

EC index	0.15	0.19	0.16	0.14	0.29	0.12	0.09	0.11	0.12	0.14	*	0.16	0.11
European identity	*	*	*	*	*	0.09	0.09	*	*	*	0.07	*	0.04
SEM effect and country	0.09	*	*	*	0.07	0.07	0.10	*	0.11	0.09	0.14	*	0.07
SEM effect and EC	*	0.09	0.15	0.12	0.09	0.13	0.11	0.15	0.11	0.24	0.14	0.12	0.13
R^2	0.08	0.07	0.13	0.05	0.19	0.09	0.11	0.06	0.11	0.11	0.09	0.12	0.08

Notes: Entries are multiple regression coefficients (beta) and multiple correlation coefficients (R^2). Starred cells indicate non-significant relationships. Dashes have been entered where data are not available. Cells are left blank if a country was not a member of the EC during the year in question.

Sources: Eurobarometer, Nos. 13, 23, 25, 33, and 37.

Conclusions

Our initial assumption that attitudes towards the territorial dimension of the European Community have relatively low salience is confirmed. If the EC itself is a remote political object with low salience, its territorial aspect is even more obscure for most citizens. In particular, knowledge about actual or impending changes to the territorial dimension is quite poor. In this situation of little knowledge and scant interest, it is difficult for citizens to respond to survey questions about the inclusion or exclusion of particular countries. This is demonstrated by the high proportions of indifferent responses in each country and at all time points. Moreover, it is likely that expressed 'opinions' also conceal a number of haphazard or random responses and thus reflect non-attitudes.

This view is supported by the highly unstructured nature of the attitudes observed and the weak impact of many of the independent variables and the low proportions of variance explained. However, where we have more specific evidence about perceived advantages and disadvantages arising from the accession of a particular country—in this instance, Spain—the proportion of variance explained notably increases. Furthermore, the main effects come from the perceived impact on the EC as a whole and on the respondent's own country rather than the perceived impact on the applicant country.

In addition to individual-level effects, macro-level factors appear to have some influence. The size and prominence of a country, together with its positive or negative interactions with other countries, influence awareness of the country in question and levels of support for it remaining or becoming an EC member. These effects were observable in the case of Spain in 1980, with its greater familiarity among EC citizens compared to Portugal and Greece, and in the case of Danish preferences regarding enlargement. They were also evident in the case of Greek–Turkish antagonism. The influence of negative interactions, presumably arising from controversies within the EC, shows up in the considerable opposition in several countries—especially France—in the mid-1980s to Britain remaining a member of the Community.

In the 'normal' situation of the non-politicization and low salience of the issue, lack of media coverage, and few interactions between countries, respondents' views on enlargement are largely influenced by their general attitudes towards European integration. This was the dominant pattern in the analyses. Even in the 1990s, with all the discussion about the Single European Market and the applications or aspirations for membership on the part of several EFTA and Central and East European countries, the élite debate about deepening versus widening the EC was virtually non-existent in public opinion. If citizens hold positive attitudes towards their own country's membership in the EC and towards the EC as a whole, they also tend to favour widening the Community or Union. Thus, paradoxically, the 'logic' of attitude formation in regard to the territorial scope of internationalized governance works in the same direction as the official discourse about the intrinsic relationship between deepening and widening.

NOTES

1. The only exception, the French referendum on De Gaulle's rejection of Britain's application for EC membership, was not a constitutional requirement
2. The results of analyses carried out in preparing this chapter are sometimes cited without presenting the tables. An exhaustive set of tables is contained in Westle (1992).
3. For a more detailed description of orientations towards an application by Turkey to enter the EC, see Hofrichter (1992).
4. For a detailed description of EC policy concerning the former GDR, see Kohler-Koch (1991).
5. For a discussion of the significance of the decline in the structuring of attitudes towards integration, see Ch. 6.
6. The more general EC orientations were included in the analyses, first, as separate variables and, secondly, as an EC index. The results do not differ greatly regarding either the explanation of variance or the remaining impact of the other variables. Therefore, we show the EC index in those cases where all four variables are available.

14

The View From EFTA

FRANK AAREBROT, STEN BERGLUND, AND THOMAS WENINGER

For much of the post-war period, the separation of the five European Free Trade Association (EFTA) countries of Austria, Finland, Norway, Sweden, and Switzerland from the European Community had a certain air of historical inevitability. In the north, there was a virtual Nordic island, separated by the dynamics of the 'Nordic balance' and integrated by a common historical, cultural, and political legacy, with close contemporary ties of trade and communication. It is true that Norway had contemplated membership of the European Economic Community on a number of occasions but rejected that option in a popular referendum in 1972. It is also the case that another member of the Nordic club—Denmark—did join, but, as is evident from many chapters in this book, its degree of 'attitudinal integration' has been limited and problematic.[1] The EFTA 'ring' on the borders of the European Community was completed on the south side by Austria with its 'permanent' neutrality and Switzerland with a neutrality which, although not declared to be permanent in principle, was deeply rooted both historically and in current political assumptions.

The *raison d'être* of the EFTA as a political community was eroded in two stages. Prior to 1972, EFTA's existence was based on two pillars, one positive and one negative: the positive need for Britain to retain a European trading foothold, and the negative pressures exerted by the Soviet Union on dependent and semi-dependent West European countries to prevent them joining the EEC. After 1972, the British interest in EFTA disappeared; and with the fall of the Berlin Wall and the subsequent dissolution of the Soviet empire, the second constraint was also removed. Thus EFTA lost much of its purpose, leaving the remaining member states to redefine its role in Europe.

Through the European Economic Space Agreement (EESA), the EFTA countries sought a new definition of themselves as non-members with a 'special relationship' to the European Union. Two factors were not foreseen, however. The collapse of the Soviet Union turned out to be more fundamental than expected, and Switzerland rejected the European Economic Space Agreement in a referendum in December 1992. Thus, by the early 1990s, EFTA's new status had been undermined, leaving EFTA not as one entity but rather as two separate spheres of economic interest—the four Nordic countries and the two Alpine German border countries of Austria and Switzerland—joined together only by their non-membership of the European Union. The final blow to EFTA's *raison d'être* was of course the expansion of the European Union from twelve to fifteen members in 1995 and the ambiguity of Switzerland's status. What remains today is really a set of somewhat elaborate trade agreements between Norway, Iceland, and the European Union within the framework of the European Economic Space agreement. Switzerland and Liechtenstein, while still EFTA members, are not part of this main body politic. While this chapter deals primarily with attitudes towards European integration within the framework of the EU, it is also about the disintegration of EFTA.

Austria applied for membership of the European Union in 1989, Sweden in 1991, Finland and Norway in 1992. They were all accepted as applicants; they all successfully completed their negotiation with the Commission of the European Community; and they all decided to refer the membership issue to the electorate in consultative referendums. The results were popular acceptance in Austria, Finland, and Sweden: all three countries were formally admitted to the European Union on 1 January 1995. In Norway, however, the referendum went against the Union. Meanwhile, the Danish electorate rejected the Maastricht Treaty in a compulsory referendum in March 1992 only to accept it in a somewhat modified form in a referendum a year later. By contrast, at a very early stage in the process, the Swiss rejected the European Economic Space Agreement in a compulsory referendum in December 1992. Thus, in the match between the popular will of the Nordic and Alpine peoples and the idea of European integration the score is currently 5–3 in favour of Brussels.[2]

Similarities and Differences

Geographical propinquity and cultural and linguistic affinities might seem to suggest that these five countries should be treated in two separate sub-sets—the three Nordic countries on the one hand and Austria and Switzerland on the other. However, consideration of their position in the international political economy, of their political culture, and of their geo-political situation points to underlying parallels and similarities which argue for treating the five countries as one group when investigating attitudes to internationalized governance. All five states are small open economies in which strategies of adjustment to international economic developments have loomed very large on the domestic agenda. In all cases, the response has been to emphasize internal solidarity and consensus. This response has built upon historical traditions of accommodation or on precedents set by major compromises which overcame deep cleavages in the country's past. It has also been buttressed to a greater or lesser extent by neo-corporatist and/or consociational arrangements and practices and by a strengthening of solidaristic aspects of the political culture. These similarities have developed despite quite radical differences in formal political structure, which extend from Finland's pronounced presidentialism, through fairly standard parliamentary systems in Norway and Sweden, to Austrian *proporz* and Switzerland's unique form of federalism.

Neutrality is another issue cutting across the two sub-sets of EFTA. Sweden and Switzerland have long-standing traditions of self-imposed neutrality, while Finland and Austria are cases of imposed neutrality *vis-à-vis* the Soviet Union. It is tempting to suggest that the relatively high support for EU membership in Finland and Austria in the wake of the demise of the Soviet empire may be interpreted in this light. However, the three Atlantic EFTA members—Denmark, Iceland, Norway—have never been neutral, but rather staunch supporters of NATO. Despite these historical differences, in the world of the 1990s the Nordic as well as the Alpine countries all enjoy considerable freedom of decision in terms of geo-political security. But this degree of freedom, now shared by the EFTA countries, is of recent vintage and, indeed, was instrumental in bringing about the demise of EFTA.

The final element common to all five countries is their shared experience of limited forms of internationalized governance. In the first place, EFTA became increasingly important to the Nordic countries, while losing its significance as a European instrument. Before

1972, EFTA was an association of countries with heavy trade links to the UK; after 1972, it functioned mainly as a trade network for the Nordic countries within the Nordic area and in facilitating bilateral trade between Austria and Switzerland. The original conception of the EFTA as an association limited to economic relations, without the political overtones and institutional structures of the EC, was particularly well suited to the interests of Finland, Austria, and Switzerland. Secondly, the Nordic Council represented the limited institutionalization of Nordic co-operation. Sometimes ridiculed as merely a body of parliamentarians kept busy granting cultural awards, the Nordic Council was not allowed to discuss important foreign policy issues largely because of the Finnish predicament. Nevertheless, the Nordic Council can point to some notable achievements. In particular, full passport freedom for inter-Nordic travel and a free labour market were achieved in the Nordic area at a time when these were still only items on some agenda in Brussels.

Attitudes towards European Integration in 1992

First, we investigate whether there is a 'Nordic profile' in attitudes towards European integration. The main similarities and differences, in 1992, in response to key questions about attitudes towards integration and the EC[3] among the five EFTA countries are summarized in Table 14.1, which also includes, for the reasons outlined above, Denmark.

In all six countries about half the respondents express a general sympathy towards European integration. However, the EFTA peoples were considerably cooler on the general idea of European integration than EC citizens on the whole. Two observations are particularly noteworthy. The Swiss are definitely most in favour of integration as a general concept, while the Danes seem unaffected by the fact that Denmark has been a member of the EC for some twenty years or by the Finnish and Swedish *rapprochement* towards the European Union. The other half of the respondents in these samples mention national identity as the only salient identity—which is considerably higher than the EC average. The proportion of 'true' Europeans, mentioning only a European identity, is almost non-existent in the six countries, albeit that these birds are altogether rather rare in the EC. It is seemingly paradoxical that Austria has the highest score on national identity, given Austria's historical, economic, and cultural ties with the German sphere

TABLE 14.1. *Attitudes towards European integration in five EFTA countries and Denmark, 1992*

	Attitudes towards:					
	European integration			EC membership		
	'Unification' (in favour)	National identity predominant	European identity predominant	'Dissolution' (regret)	'Membership' (a good thing)	'Benefit' (benefited)
Finland	47.6	53.7	0.9	21.9	39.2	59.8
Norway	53.8	49.4	0.9	20.1	32.9	30.5
Sweden	48.6	50.8	1.7	15.4	35.9	38.7
Austria	50.7	60.8	0.8	24.5	34.8	43.1
Switzerland	58.3	49.2	2.0	29.5	39.3	49.5
Denmark	51.2	48.4	1.3	36.8	56.5	66.9
EC-12	76.4	37.6	4.0	48.1	65.0	53.2

Notes: Entries are percentages. For question wording, see n. 3 in text.

Source: European Integration Survey (1992).

in Europe. We would be inclined to account for this paradox in terms of Austria's unique and rather recent process of nation building which did not gain impetus until well after the Second World War, following the severing of ties with Germany.

It would be a mistake, however, to assume that the peoples are divided into 'Europeans' and 'nationalists'. At a general level, an individual may have a positive attitude towards European integration along with a predominantly national identity. But the real conflict of identity is not brought out on this level of generality: it is as easy to be in favour of European integration in general and to express a general sense of nationality as to love little birds and favour world peace in general. In the Nordic countries it has been almost something of a ritual, certainly not controversial, for governments to express positive ideas in general about such issues as human rights, the United Nations, disarmament, and the general desirability of European integration. In other words, most opponents of Norway's membership of the EC membership are probably in favour of German membership; and most proponents of Norwegian national self-determination would probably agree that EC membership has been a positive development in curtailing French and German national self-determination.

Responses to direct questions about EC membership reveal an altogether different pattern, however. As we can see from Table 14.1, the importance of membership increases both in terms of expressing regret about the hypothetical demise of the EC and in terms of expressing general, diffuse, support for the EC. Even so, respondents in Austria, Switzerland, Finland, Sweden, and Norway are less sorry about the hypothetical breakdown of the EC, and less supportive of the EC, than respondents in Denmark or respondents across the EC as a whole. When asked about the perceived utility in terms of benefits to themselves, Finns and Danes are more instrumentally supportive than citizens of the EC in general, Austrians and Swiss somewhat less supportive, while Swedes and Norwegians express considerably less belief in the instrumental utility of the EC than EC citizens in general.

The overall impression from the table is that the homogeneity of public opinion across the various countries is strongest for the most diffuse attitude towards unification. The more specific the question at issue, the less homogeneous are people's attitudes. For the most specific evaluation of potential benefits of EC membership, Norway and Sweden clearly belong to a class of countries whose populations are more sceptical about concrete benefits from membership than the average EC citizen, whereas Danes and Finns were more optimistic about benefiting specifically from EC membership than the EC average. Something of a middle-ground position is evident amongst the Austrians and the Swiss on this issue.

Two questions may be posed on the basis of this observation, one simple and another somewhat more complex. First, is the tendency among the EFTA countries towards similarity with respect to diffuse evaluations but towards dissimilarity with respect to specific support accounted for by the more immediate concern among Danish voters about the implications of the Maastricht Treaty and among Finnish voters about the impact of the dramatic changes in the Soviet Union? Secondly, to what extent can the similarity of diffuse evaluations and the dissimilarity of specific support be accounted for in terms of structural differences and similarities?

Diffuse Euro-Scepticism: Danish Rebellion or Nordic Identity?

Due to their geographical proximity and cultural similarities, our answer to the two questions about the Danish rebellion over the Maastricht Treaty is sought mainly in the Nordic arena. The apparent unity of the Nordic countries in a common negative diffuse evaluation of European integration needs to be examined in the light of political events current at the time when the relevant survey (Eurobarometer, No. 37) was conducted. Denmark was then heavily involved with the referendum campaign on the European Union. Thus, it is possible that the similarity between opinion in Denmark and her Nordic neighbours was only temporary, an artefact of the campaign process in Denmark.

In Figure 14.1 we compare the results from two Eurobarometer, Nos. 37 (spring 1992) and 38 (autumn 1992), for Denmark, Norway, and Finland.[4] We can see immediately that after the referendum, Danish voters expressed more supportive attitudes towards the EC and

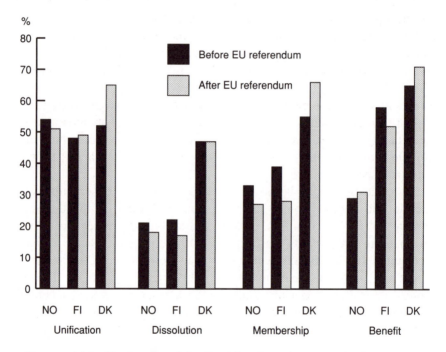

FIGURE 14.1. *The impact of the Danish referendum on attitudes towards European integration*

Notes: The entries are: *Unification*, proportion in favour of efforts being made to unify Western Europe'; *Dissolution*, proportion who would be 'very sorry' if told that the European Community had 'been scrapped'; *Membership*, proportion who think that their own country's membership of the EC is/would be a 'good thing'; *Benefit*, proportion who said that, on balance, their own country has benefited/would benefit from being a member of the EC. For question wording, see n. 3 in text.

Sources: Eurobarometer, Nos. 37 and 38.

European integration in general. Conversely, Finnish and Norwegian voters tended to become even more sceptical towards European integration, both in diffuse as well as specific terms. In all, after the Maastricht referendum, Danish opinion takes on a more continental, or European character—certainly more positive in mood than in either Finland or Norway.

We may, therefore, conclude that some of the similarities between the countries evident in Table 14.1 may be accounted for by the specific circumstances of the Danish referendum campaign. Moreover, there seems to be a somewhat closer Danish adaptation to the evaluation pattern of the EC average than is the case for Norway or Finland. But despite this modification, Euro-scepticism still seems generally stronger in the Nordic region than in the rest of Europe. Even if the Danes evaluate Europe and the EC somewhat more positively than their Scandinavian neighbours, they are still less positive in their general, diffuse evaluation than their EC neighbours. However, in terms of evaluating specific benefits from the EC, the Danes are evidently considerably more pro-European. We can think of this as bread-and-butter Europeanism—or 'bacon-and-butter' Europeanism as the case may be.

Analysis of the impact of the Maastricht referendum in Denmark on the neighbouring Nordic countries can be generalized in two ways. First, by extending the scope of our enquiry to include all five of our EFTA countries, and, secondly, by investigating the impact of the approaching referendum in each country rather than focusing on a Danish 'contagion effect' as we have done here.

Euro-Scepticism and EU Referendums

In discussing Table 14.1, we made the point that there are marked variations between the countries in specific evaluations of the European Union, but that in terms of general, affective, or diffuse evaluations of the EU there is not necessarily a relationship between a strong national identity and a strong European identity. We hold this to be true in general, but we may legitimately ask if this remains true as the reality of a referendum approaches. During the period of negotiations with the European Commission, in particular, the agenda set by the media in all countries seems to have been dominated by specific issues. In Switzerland and Austria, there was debate focusing on heavy transit traffic through the Alps; in Norway and Finland, the impact of the Common Agricultural Policy was discussed in terms of its consequences for heavily subsidized peripheral smallholders; in Norway, EU fisheries policy was very much an issue. Even in Sweden, the EU ban on 'wet' snuff excited normally complacent citizens—the terms of evaluation could hardly be more specific than that.

We suggest that our findings from the first Danish referendum on the Maastricht Treaty can be generalized in the following way. Prior to a referendum, public debate over specific issues tends to influence general evaluations of the EU. The population tends to become more sceptical towards the EU as a function of such debates. In the last phase of the referendum campaign, however, the governing élites of each country spend a great deal of time and effort in restoring—or re-mobilizing—general, diffuse, support which has been disrupted by the debates about specific issues during the negotiation process. To highlight the dynamics of this process, we have compiled time series from pre-referendum polls in Austria, Finland, Sweden, and Norway. The questions in the polls ask about voting intentions in the upcoming EU referendum, which we interpret as a general evaluation of the EU on a par with the Eurobarometer question about EU membership.

In Figure 14.2 the time series is presented in the form of the percentage of electors who report that they intend to vote 'yes' in the forthcoming referendum in the four countries which had negotiated for full membership. The country-specific time series include the actual referendum results presented in terms of eligible voters, not the percentage turnout. This results in an overall deflation of the figures familiar from the official statistics. Thus, the 66.6 per cent of Austrian voters who voted 'yes' to the European Union (12 June 1994) correspond to 54.8 per cent of the Austrian electorate. When viewed in this light, the majorities of 56 per cent in Finland (16 October 1994) and 52.6 per cent in Sweden (13 November 1994) for the European Union are in fact transformed into respectable and sizeable minorities of 44.4 per cent in Finland and 43.9 per cent in Sweden. With a turnout close to 90 per cent, the 47.8 per cent of the Norwegian electorate who voted 'yes' to the Union in the referendum (28 November 1994) corresponds to 44.4 per cent of the electorate—or slightly more than the level of mobilization which took Finland and Sweden safely into the EU.

It is readily seen from Figure 14.2 that support for EU membership produces a U-curve with higher levels prior to the negotiations, lower levels during and immediately after the negotiation process, but a

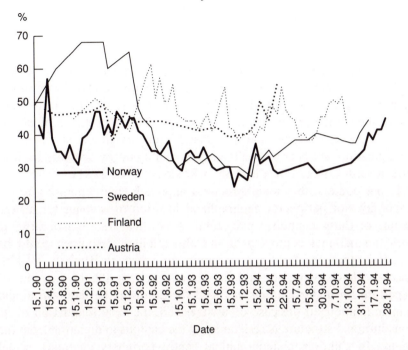

FIGURE 14.2. *'Yes' voting intention and actual vote (as percentage of electorate) in EU referendums in Norway, Sweden, Finland, and Austria*

Notes: The data on which this graph is based have been supplied by the following polling companies: Austria 1991: Fessel and GFK, Plasser and Ulram and Lammel; Austria 1992: Fessel and GFK/IFES (*N* = 1,500–2,000 per survey) and Ulram; Austria 1993–4: Ulram; Finland 1991–4: Suomen Gallup; Sweden 1991–4: SIFO; Norway 1991–4: Opinion.

regaining of strength as the referendum date approaches and the impact of élite mobilization comes to be felt. Tactical considerations both in terms of media impact during the negotiation process and in terms of élite mobilization are obviously present.

We now turn to analyse some of the structural determinants of support and opposition to integration. Here, we have to bear in mind that both the climate and the context of contemporary public opinion is far from stable in this part of the world.[5] Indeed, we have already seen in Figure 14.1 that evaluation patterns are subject to the volatility of the world of political events.

Determinants of Support for Integration

Three sets of hypotheses may be distinguished to explain different aspects of the determinants accounting for variations in the evaluation of European integration. First, there are hypotheses about the importance of variations in socio-geographical structure. This is a well-established tradition in political sociology. The importance of differences between centres and peripheries for variations in territorial identification has been underlined time and again by scholars such as Erik Allardt (1964, 1981) and Stein Rokkan (1967, 1981).

In our context, this socio-structural approach entails pointing to the importance of peripheral geographical location to account for a high degree of Euro-scepticism in general. A political tradition of struggle with the national centres over the allocation of resources could be translated into fear for a similar future struggle with Brussels. Experiences with Oslo or Helsinki as centres are not the best points of departure for understanding the need for European harmonization and standardization. In the case of Switzerland, the very foundation of its constitutional structure is resistance by the cantons to dictation from the centre. In addition to geographical centre–periphery contrasts, social status, gender, and age structure may, of course, play a role in accounting for variation.

Secondly, there are hypotheses about the importance of information and cultural integration. This is more than a class of social science theories: it is also a set of widespread strategic political beliefs. It seems that many proponents and opponents of EU membership share a common belief that, through information, people can be 'taught' to accept EC membership or 'saved' from the great mistake of joining. In the Nordic context, this can be accounted for, to some extent, by the strong historical relationship between the structuring of mass politics and the development of the elementary school system, as well as the establishment of the adult education movement known as 'People's High Schools', dating from the second half of the nineteenth century.

Political mobilization theory also emphasizes the importance of access to information to account for integration in general. This has been emphasized by both Daniel Lerner (1958) and Karl Deutsch (1953, 1961) in their attempts to analyse national identity as a vehicle for social mobilization and political development. In our context, this means that we would expect people with access to information about European integration, or who express satisfaction with their information level about European affairs, to be more inclined to evaluate European integration in a positive light.

Thirdly, there are hypotheses about the importance of the relationship between the established cleavage structure in the national political system and the European issue. Following Rokkan (1967), it would be crucial to establish the extent to which variations in evaluations of European integration correlate with those political divisions which are well established within the structure of social cleavages in each country. In particular, is Euro-scepticism part of the traditional left–right division in Scandinavian politics, or is it a new, and essentially independent, phenomenon?

Moving beyond traditional cleavages, the concept of 'protest voting' has often been employed in recent years to account for unexpected and relatively strong support for new parties in the electoral arena. The emergence of the Progress Party in Denmark and Norway, the Greens and the New Democrats in Sweden, the Finnish Vennamo movement, and the restructuring of the Austrian right by Jürg Haider are all cases in point. If resistance to EU membership and European integration can be compared to these phenomena through the concept of 'protest voting', we would expect a negative correlation between pro-European attitudes and evaluation of the way democracy works in each of these countries.

We can now proceed to test these several hypotheses—to the extent that secondary analysis of Eurobarometer data allow us to do so.[6] Hypotheses about the importance of variations in socio-geographical structure have been operationalized through a set of four demographic indicators: urbanization, education, gender, and age groups.[7] Hypotheses about the importance of information and cultural integration have been operationalized through a set of three cognitive indicators: the extent to which respondents have heard about the EC at all;[8] respondents' knowledge of the Maastricht Treaty;[9] and whether or not respondents feel informed about the EC.[10] Hypotheses about the importance of the relationship between the established cleavage structure and attitudes about the European issue have been operationalized through two indicators of political attitudes: left–right voting;[11] and respondents' satisfaction with democracy in their own country.[12]

Using correlational analysis, we examine the impact of each of the three sets of indicators on our four measures of European integration: unification, dissolution, membership, and benefit. Our results are reported and discussed in the next section.

Correlates of Support

The demographic correlates of attitudes towards European integration, reported in Table 14.2, allow us to assess the importance of variations in socio-geographical structure. The centre–periphery polarity, indicated by the urbanization variable, does indeed have an impact in Switzerland, Finland, and Norway irrespective of the specificity of the attitudinal measure. In Finland and Norway, respondents living in rural areas and small towns tend to be generally more negative towards European integration than people living in urban centres; they tend to be less concerned about the fate of the EC, to be less enthusiastic about membership, and to be more sceptical about the potential benefits of their country's entry into the EC. In Denmark and Austria, however, this factor seems not to be important. In general, in the three countries where geography is of any topographical importance, there seem to be clear indications that attitudes towards European integration are, indeed, associated with centre–periphery geographical location. In Austria and Denmark, however, the dominant capitals of Vienna and Copenhagen seem to reduce the impact of urbanization on attitudes towards integration. In these metropolitan areas there is a tendency towards an urban, radical Euro-sceptical milieu.

The level, or length, of education seems to be conducive to a positive view of Europe in all countries. This is evident, too, in the three Nordic countries for which we have data: higher levels of education seem to promote pro-European attitudes. This ties in with the impression that social élites in most European countries tend to be more favourable towards European integration. It also emphasizes the importance of cognitive factors in general. Unfortunately the Swiss and Austrian data do not include education.

As for the effects of gender, Danish and Norwegian women are considerably less favourably inclined towards European integration than men. But gender does not seem to be as important in Finland, Austria, and Switzerland. For the two more diffuse questions about European integration, there is even a tendency for Finnish men to be less European minded than women. Finally, with respect to the demographic correlates, age group and generational effects are almost absent. The only exception is a tendency among Finnish youth to be more optimistic about the potential benefits of EC membership than their older compatriots.

Cognitive correlates are, of course, also related to education. But here

TABLE 14.2. *Demographic correlates of support for European integration in four EFTA countries and Denmark, 1992*

	Urbanization	Education	Gender	Age group	N
Unification					
Denmark	n.s.	−0.10*	0.15*	n.s.	984
Finland	−0.24*	−0.27*	−0.09	0.08	977
Norway	−0.16*	−0.19*	0.15*	n.s.	995
Austria	n.s.	n.d.	0.09*	n.s.	1,054
Switzerland	−0.37*	n.d.	n.s.	n.s.	885
Dissolution					
Denmark	n.s.	−0.13*	0.15*	n.s.	984
Finland	−0.16*	−0.18*	−0.11*	n.s.	977
Norway	−0.14*	−0.14*	0.14*	n.s.	995
Austria	n.s.	n.d.	n.s.	n.s.	1,054
Switzerland	−0.27*	n.d.	n.s.	n.s.	885
Membership					
Denmark	n.s.	−0.10	0.15*	n.s.	984
Finland	−0.21*	−0.21*	n.s.	n.s.	977
Norway	−0.15*	−0.11*	0.10	0.07	995
Austria	n.s.	n.d.	n.s.	n.s.	1,054
Switzerland	−0.35*	n.d.	n.s.	n.s.	885
Benefit					
Denmark	n.s.	−0.11*	0.13*	n.s.	984
Finland	−0.16*	−0.14*	n.s.	0.13*	977
Norway	−0.13*	−0.12*	0.16*	n.s.	995
Austria	n.s.	n.d.	n.s.	n.s.	1,054
Switzerland	−0.25*	n.d.	0.10*	n.s.	885

Notes: Entries are correlation coefficients (Pearson's *r*). Coefficients marked * are significant at 0.001 level; all other correlation.s. are significant at 0.01 level; 'n.s.' = 'not significant'; n.d. = no data.

Source: European Integration Survey (1992).

we are more concerned with perceived information levels. In general, the results shown in Table 14.3 indicate positive, even strong, relationships between all the evaluative questions about European integration and the perceived knowledge of respondents. People who feel informed about various aspects of the institutions and policies of the EC tend to take a positive view of European integration. Only responses to the question about having heard of the EC recently are an exception. However, we suspect that this question is overly simplistic.[13] The weak Danish and Norwegian correlations between 'having heard about the EC' and the unification and the dissolution questions are due to the fact that the very few Danes and Norwegians who have never heard of the EC are less concerned with Europe in general than the rest of the population.

In Denmark, Finland, Austria, and Switzerland, feeling informed about the EC seems to be strongly related to a positive assessment of things European. This is also the case for Norway, but not to the same degree as in the other four countries. In Norway, as many opponents of membership feel well informed about membership as do the supporters.

TABLE 14.3. *Cognitive correlates of support for European integration in five EFTA countries, 1992*

	Heard about EC	Feel informed about EC	Know about Maastricht Treaty	N
Unification				
Denmark	0.09	0.23*	0.22*	984
Finland	n.s.	0.22*	0.29*	977
Norway	0.11*	0.12*	0.20*	995
Austria	n.d.	0.28*	n.d.	1,054
Switzerland	n.d.	0.31*	n.d.	885
Dissolution				
Denmark	0.11*	0.20*	0.15*	984
Finland	n.s.	0.17*	0.16*	977
Norway	0.10*	0.10*	0.15*	995
Austria	n.d.	0.20*	n.d.	1,054
Switzerland	n.d.	0.22*	n.d.	885
Membership				
Denmark	0.09	0.22*	0.18*	984
Finland	n.s.	0.19*	0.22*	977
Norway	n.s.	n.s.	0.15*	995
Austria	n.d.	0.28*	n.d.	1,054
Switzerland	n.d.	0.22*	n.d.	885
Benefit				
Denmark	n.s.	0.18*	0.12*	984
Finland	n.s.	0.12*	0.20*	977
Norway	n.s.	0.12*	0.17*	995
Austria	n.d.	0.25*	n.d.	1,054
Switzerland	n.d.	0.25*	n.d.	885

Notes: Entries are correlation coefficients (Pearson's *r*). Coefficients marked * are significant at 0.001 level. Other correlations are significant at 0.01 level. 'n.s.' = 'not significant'; 'n.d.' = 'no data'.

Source: European Integration Survey (1992).

This is a testimony to the activities of the very strong and well-organized mass movement against Norwegian membership. But in terms of a more general assessment of European integration, as well as in term of respondents' own analysis of the potential benefits of membership, Norwegians, too, seem to be swayed by their knowledge of the EC. Knowledge about the Maastricht Treaty, in particular, seems to have a positive impact across the board in the three Nordic countries. In general, diffuse identification with European integration tends to be most heavily influenced by information, hope for specific benefits the least influenced. But, taken all together, there is confirmatory evidence here for Deutsch's postulate that access to information is a prerequisite for social integration and political mobilization.

The correlates of the political cleavage structure, reported in Table 14.4, provide insights into the importance of the politicization of the

TABLE 14.4. *Political correlates of support for European integration in Denmark, Finland, and Norway, 1992*

	Satisfaction with democracy in own country	Left–right trichotomy based on respondent's vote in the last election	N
Unification			
Denmark	0.24*	−0.31*	984
Finland	0.11*	−0.24*	977
Norway	0.20*	−0.17*	995
Dissolution			
Denmark	0.27*	−0.36*	984
Finland	0.08	n.s.	977
Norway	0.21*	−0.22*	995
Membership			
Denmark	0.28*	−0.36*	984
Finland	0.16*	−0.19*	977
Norway	0.17*	−0.29*	995
Benefit			
Denmark	0.30*	−0.25*	984
Finland	0.14*	−0.15*	977
Norway	0.15*	−0.19*	995

Notes: Entries are correlation coefficients (Pearson's *r*). Coefficients marked * are significant at 0.001 level using a one-tailed *t*-test. Other correlations are significant at 0.01 level. The coefficients for respondents' vote in last election are based on respondents who indicated a rankable party preference (Denmark, *n* = 792; Finland, *n* = 661; Norway, *n* = 710).

Source: European Integration Survey (1992).

European issue in the Nordic countries. Unfortunately, such data are not available for Switzerland and Austria.

In all Nordic countries, those satisfied with their own democracies tend to be more pro-European, irrespective of the specificity of the attitude in question. This tendency is strong, and particularly strong in Denmark. Thus, the European issue can hardly be considered a ripe fruit in the fertile garden of Scandinavian 'protest voting'. Indeed, our findings cast some doubt on the currently popular interpretation of the Danish 'no' result in the first of the Maastricht referendums as predominantly an expression of dissatisfaction with their political system among Danish electors.

European integration is definitely not a 'new' issue in the Nordic cleavage structure, in the sense that this issue is unrelated to traditional politics. On the contrary, positive assessment of European integration and the EC is rather strongly associated with having voted to the right in the most recent general elections. This is particularly true in Denmark. Parties of the right, favouring European integration and supporting EC membership, are generally more in tune with their voters than those parties of the left which hold the same positive positions. This is particularly a problem for the Social Democrats, one of the traditional ruling parties in Scandinavian countries.

We should note one deviation from the general pattern. Left-inclined Finns and Finns dissatisfied with the working of democracy in their country are as worried about a possible dissolution of the EC as their satisfied and right-leaning compatriots. The former are generally more opposed to Finnish membership and less positive about general European integration, but they still want to see the EC remain in place with other countries as members. Here we catch a glimpse of a unique aspect of the Finnish position: the common concern with security policies irrespective of people's views about the European issue or domestic issues. We should also note that the relationship between the four indicators of European integration and national political cleavages are less pronounced in Finland than in Denmark and Norway.

These findings explain, in some measure, the longevity of the EC issue in Norway and Denmark. As long as the European issue remains associated with the main domestic cleavages of the two countries, Denmark will remain an uneasy EC member and Norwegian political leaders will have a hard time convincing electors of a glorious common future in Europe. The very cleavage structure which supports and sustains the present political system incorporates the European issue.

In traditional Danish and Norwegian politics, European integration is neither a new nor a neutral issue.

Explaining Attitudes towards Internationalized Governance

The bivariate analyses presented in the previous section point to some of the basic similarities and differences between the EFTA countries in relation to European integration. In an attenpt to sort through these relationships and gain an insight into the mental landscape of voters, we present the results from a multiple regression analysis taking into account all the indicators operationalized in our three main hypotheses. The limitations on the data available from the European Integration Study mean that our analysis is confined to the three Nordic countries. Even so, it may give us some grasp of what kind of creature the EC is in the voter's mind.

In Table 14.5, we present the standardized regression coefficients, by country, as a way of assigning weights to all our determinants simultaneously. Comparing these different weights reveals some clear patterns which can be related to the three sets of hypotheses discussed earlier.

Examining the significant beta weights for Denmark clearly shows that this is a country in which the questions relating to European integration have been thoroughly politicized. Being in favour of European integration is predominantly associated with conservative voting behaviour and satisfaction with the way democracy works in Denmark. There is a weak element of cognition as well, with a slight tendency for better-informed citizens to be pro-European. The primacy of domestic partisan association over social distinctiveness indicates that social differences exert very little direct influence on Danish attitudes towards European integration. The direct influence of gender and education on Europeanism observed earlier (see Table 14.2) is absorbed through the regular electoral process in ordinary general elections.

Norway is similar to Denmark in that the parties seem to have absorbed the European issue on the left–right dimension, albeit to a somewhat lesser extent than in Denmark. Unfortunately for some parties, many supporters seem to have taken a stand on the issue more or less independently of the leadership. Even if the Labour Party is in favour of EC membership, many voters seem to expect a party of the left to oppose membership. Indeed, 35 per cent of Labour voters

TABLE 14.5. *Multiple regression analysis of support for European integration*

Determinants	Denmark	Finland	Norway
Unification			
Left–right vote	−0.24*	−0.14*	−0.12*
Satisfied with democracy	0.18*	0.07	0.12*
Feel informed about EC	0.10*	0.16*	−0.02*
Feel informed about Maastricht	0.11*	0.17*	0.10
Heard about EC	0.03	−0.05	0.09
Education	−0.01	−0.11	−0.07
Urbanization	0.01	−0.14*	−0.12*
Gender	0.06	−0.06	0.11*
Age group	−0.07	0.07	0.03
R^2	0.18	0.20	0.13
Dissolution			
Left–right vote	−0.30*	−0.03	−0.17*
Satisfied with democracy	0.20*	0.07	0.18*
Feel informed about EC	0.10*	0.13*	0.02*
Feel informed about Maastricht	−0.02	0.10	0.06
Heard about EC	0.06	−0.03	0.04
Education	−0.05	−0.10	−0.02
Urbanization	0.01	−0.12*	−0.11
Gender	0.08	−0.11	0.09
Age group	−0.07	0.00	0.03
R^2	0.21	0.10	0.13
Membership			
Left–right vote	−0.30*	−0.09	−0.26*
Satisfied with democracy	0.19*	0.14*	0.16*
Feel informed about EC	0.12*	0.15*	−0.06
Feel informed about Maastricht	0.03	0.10	0.09
Heard about EC	0.02	0.01	0.04
Education	0.01	−0.13*	0.03
Urbanization	0.05	−0.06	−0.11*
Gender	0.07	−0.07	0.04
Age group	−0.01	−0.06	0.06
R^2	0.20	0.16	0.14
Benefit			
Left–right vote	−0.18*	−0.06	−0.14*
Satisfied with democracy	0.23*	0.14*	0.14*
Feel informed about EC	0.12*	0.10	0.03
Feel informed about Maastricht	0.01	0.13*	0.07
Heard about EC	0.05	−0.05	0.02
Education	−0.03	−0.15*	0.00
Urbanization	0.04	0.03	−0.09
Gender	0.09	−0.03	0.12*
Age group	0.03	0.04	0.03
R^2	0.16	0.14	0.10
N	792	661	710

p< 0.001

Note: Entries are beta weights and multiple correlations (R^2).

Source: European Integration Survey (1992).

voted against their own government in the referendum. But urbanization seems to play an independent role in Norway. Norwegians in sparsely populated areas are more sceptical about Europeanism than city dwellers. Such scepticism follows in a long tradition of peripheral protest; first against Copenhagen, then against Stockholm, finally against Oslo, and, quite likely, now and in the future, against Brussels. In assessing the concrete benefits of EC membership, Norwegian women are more negative than men. This may be accounted for by the relatively high proportion of women employed in the public service sector. Employees in protected sectors tend to take a rather lighthearted view of possible benefits for those working in the maelstrom of international competition in the competitive private sector, who are disproportionately male.

In Finland, cognitive processes reign supreme as explanatory factors when we take account of variation in the other determinants. Feeling informed about the EC and the Maastricht Treaty seems to account for a positive assessment of European integration at all levels. High education level is another positive determinant which further enhances this impression. Diffuse desires for unification are somewhat stronger among voters for parties of the right, whilst satisfaction with Finnish democracy is of some importance for positive specific evaluations of membership and benefits.

Despite these variations, the main image remains that of the Nordic countries in a historical theatre queue moving slowly towards Europe. Denmark is already inside the theatre and her citizens' evaluation of European integration is thoroughly ingrained into the fabric of day-to-day domestic politics. The adaptation of the cleavage structure goes a long way towards accounting for the Danes' evaluation of Europe. Norway hesitates as she approaches the door, which she has done before, and decides at the last moment not to enter. The Norwegian political cleavage structure is somewhat adapted to the European issue, but old socio-geographical identities and interests persist to the detriment of Europeanism. Finland, last in line, having only recently received enough money to go to the theatre, is trying to figure out what is on. Those who know about the play want to see it, but many do not yet know enough about it to be sure. In this instance, information as a prerequisite for integration seems to be the relevant model; those best educated have already obtained and processed a great deal of relevant information. In the end, many Finns who did not know what the play was about still decided to enter the theatre because they trusted someone who said he did know.

Using the same analogy, it is tempting to speculate that people living in Central Europe generally have a more sophisticated approach to the theatre. The Austrians decided to go in despite some nasty rumours about the play; and the Swiss knew about the play but simply were not interested—maybe because they suspected that the performance would be in French.[14]

Conclusion

It is easy to point to immediate and striking differences of experience with European integration. Denmark has been a member of the EC since 1972, whereas Norway has tried to become a member three times since 1961. Nevertheless, Norway has most definitely been a member of the Western club—through membership of NATO and growing economic dependence on the EC. Finland is the newcomer to this issue: before the fall of the Berlin Wall, opportunities for integration were not even a distant dream. Austria belongs to the same class as Finland. Thinking seriously about membership was problematic until after 1989; and neutrality remained an issue in Austria as late as 1992.

Switzerland, of course, is a truly deviant case. The rejection of the European Economic Space Agreement by Swiss voters in December 1992 stands out as less surprising when we consider that Swiss voters have rejected even membership of the United Nations and that Swiss governments consistently refuse to take part in peace-keeping operations anywhere in the world. This does not necessarily mean that Swiss governments are not concerned about European integration. It is noteworthy that the Swiss government—in contrast to Austria—did not include a neutrality clause when filing its application for full membership in 1992. Indeed, the relative isolationism of Norway and Switzerland seems to be a creature of the electorates rather than an expression of government wishes.

After the referendums of 1994, it is clear that the integration of the EFTA countries into the European Union was not an unconditional victory for internationalized governance. A rump EFTA, consisting of Norway, Iceland, Switzerland, and Liechtenstein, still exists. Moreover, in contrast to Austria, neither the Finnish nor the Swedish referendum results reflect overwhelming support for the idea of European integration. Furthermore, one of the major findings of this chapter remains valid after the referendums. In general, attitudes towards European integration in the five EFTA countries examined—those which are now members of the European Union as well as those which are not—reflect less enthusiasm for internationalized governance than is the case among EU citizens at large. We have related this to structural determinants, and we feel vindicated in doing so when comparing the EFTA countries to Denmark—a country with more than twenty years experience as an EU member but sharing most of the characteristics of the EFTA countries. Indeed, to this day the Danish level of support for integration is closer to that found in the EFTA countries than to that in most EU member states. However, this finding should not be interpreted to indicate that Denmark is less adapted to the European Union than other member countries. Our structural analysis shows that Danish attitudes are more integrated with common political beliefs within the EU than similar attitudes in the EFTA countries.

In the small and relatively rich countries examined in this chapter, people express a good deal of scepticism towards internationalized governance. None the less, once admitted as members, they seem to adapt to such governance. In general, in terms of popular attitudes, the similarities between the Nordic and the Alpine EFTA countries are more striking than the differences between them. The main source of variation is at the geopolitical macro level in terms of self-imposed and external constraints. The vast macro-level changes in Europe in recent years made it possible for Austria, Finland, and Sweden to join the European Union. Indeed, the changes in the strategic options open to these countries probably enhanced the willingness of voters to join, most of whom are moderately enthusiastic. Norway, the only country whose strategic options were not influenced by the turmoil of 1989–90, decided not to join; whilst Denmark, also safely removed from the impact of geopolitical reshuffling, came out one step ahead on Euro-scepticism by initially rejecting the Maastricht Treaty.

We are left, then, with a paradox. The small countries we have considered are still heavily influenced by European macro-politics, but in a quite different way compared to the days of the Cold War. Thus, the lesson for those eager to promote internationalized govern-ance is double-edged. On the one side, there is the positive endorsement of European integration reflected in the search for support and protec-tion within Europe by Austria, Finland, and Sweden. On the other side, there is the negative assessment of the European Union implied by the rejection of internationalized governance by Switzerland and Norway. Thus, developments in these five EFTA countries drive home that the impact of centre–periphery location is complex. Morever, as the Norwegian and Swiss cases indicate, the centre–periphery cleavage within countries is as relevant as the centre–periphery cleavage between countries in understanding the advance of internationalized governance.

NOTES

1. Although this chapter concentrates on the five EFTA countries and, consequently, on only three of the Nordic countries, special attention is occasionally drawn to Denmark as one of the original Nordic members of EFTA.
2. The Swiss referendum on the European Economic Space Agreement, in December 1992, is here treated as a vote on European integration and as a proxy for a referendum on EC/EU membership. The negative outcome to the EESA referendum led to the suspension but not withdrawal of the Swiss application for full membership submitted in May 1992.
3. The questions in the European Integration Study are virtually identical to the main indicators used in this volume: *Unification*—'In general, are you for or against efforts being made to unify Western Europe?' *Dissolution*—'If you were told tomorrow that the European Union had been scrapped, would you be very sorry about it, indifferent, or very relieved?' *Membership*—'Generally speaking, do you think that [own country's] membership of the European Community [EC countries/ EFTA countries] is/would be a good thing, a bad thing or neither good nor bad?' *Benefit*—'Taking everything into consideration, would you say that [own country] has on balance benefited/could on balance benefit (EC countries/EFTA countries) or not from being a member of the European Community?' The question 'In the near future, do you see yourself as (own nation) only, (own nation) and European, European and (own nation), or European only?' is treated as an indicator of political identity.
4. Sweden is not included in the rest of the analysis, much to our regret, due to severe limitations in the Swedish data. Notably, the Swedish sample is only half of the Eurobarometer standard ($N = 1,000$) for Eurobarometer, No. 37. This makes it impossible to use the Swedish data for any analytic purpose beyond the presentation of simple marginals, as in Table 14.1.
5. Eurobarometer surveys have only been conducted outside the EU countries in the last few years, in most instances as part of the European Integration Study. Therefore, it was not possible to establish long-term trends, which would have enabled us to assess the degree of volatility involved.
6. This analysis is entirely based, for Finland, Norway, Switzerland, and Austria on the European Integration Study which was co-ordinated with Eurobarometer, No. 38, and included Denmark. The Swiss, Austrian, Danish, and Norwegian data were made

available by the Norwegian Social Science Data Services and the Finnish data through the good offices of Suomen Gallup.

7. Urbanization is based on respondents' area of residence: (1) rural area or village; (2) small- or medium-sized town; (3) large town or city. The data for Switzerland do not distinguish between city and town. The education variable for Denmark and Norway is based on respondents' recall of their age when their full-time schooling ended: (1) 13–16 years of age; (2) 17–21 years of age; (3) older than 22 years of age. The education variable for Finland is based on a classification of the highest completed level of schooling: (1) elementary school; (2) O-levels; (3) A-levels and higher. There are no education data for Switzerland and Austria. Gender is coded (1) female, (2) male. Age groups are based on the age of the respondent: (1) 15–24; (2) 25–39; (3) 40–59; (4) More than 60 years of age.

8. The question wording is: 'Have you recently heard or read anything about the European Community (EC), its policies, its institutions?' Responses: 'Yes'; 'No'; 'Don't know'. No data on this question are available for Switzerland and Austria.

9. The question wording is: 'How much do you feel you know about the Maastricht Treaty?' Responses: 'A great deal'; 'A fair amount'; 'Know just a little'; 'Heard of, know nothing else'; 'Never heard of it before today'; 'Don't know'. No data for Switzerland and Austria.

10. The question wording is: 'All things considered, how well informed do you feel you are about the European Community, its policies, its institutions?' Responses: 'Very well'; 'Quite well'; 'Not very well'; 'Neutral/don't know'; 'Not at all well'.

11. Based on respondents' recall of which party they voted for in the last general election. These responses were classified into left parties, centre parties, and right parties. Respondents voting for 'other', minor, parties, or did not reply have been omitted from the analyses for this variable. Left–right self-placement might have been a better indicator but this indicator was missing from the Finnish, Austrian, and Swiss data.

12. The question wording is: 'On the whole, are you very satisfied, fairly satisfied, not very satisfied or not at all satisfied with the way democracy works in own country?' No data for Austria and Switzerland.

13. The questions about having heard about the EC and having heard about the Maastricht Treaty are simplistic to the point of being insulting to a Nordic audience. No doubt the Swiss and the Austrians would feel much the same about these questions.

14. In the EESA referendum, the majority of the people in the French cantons and the two cantons of Basil voted for EESA accession; in the other cantons the majority decided against participation.

15

The View from Central and Eastern Europe

STEN BERGLUND AND FRANK AAREBROT WITH JADWIGA
KORALEWICZ

That part of Europe nowadays referred to as Eastern Europe is not—and never was—a homogeneous area, neither in historical, cultural, religious, nor political terms. The current map of Eastern Europe is a by-product of the breakdown of the Russian and Austro-Hungarian empires in the wake of the First World War. The borders between the countries of Eastern and Central Europe were subsequently revised to the benefit of the Soviet Union and the detriment of Germany and its allies in the Second World War (Urwin 1991).

The three Baltic states—Estonia, Latvia, and Lithuania—were incorporated into the Soviet Union and Germany was divided into two separate states. Apart from these major exceptions, however, the number of national actors in Europe remained roughly the same from one war to the other. Culturally, Eastern Europe has always been marked by tensions among linguistically and historically distinct ethnic groups. Romanians and Hungarians speak languages and represent cultures as far apart as French and Russian, but Romania with its large Hungarian minority has to accommodate both of them. Similar comments apply to the Turks of Bulgaria, the Poles of Lithuania, and the Ukrainians of Poland—to say nothing of the ethnic strife within Russia.

With the persecution and large-scale extermination of East European Jews during the German occupation, the deportation of millions of ethnic Germans from East Germany (Prussia, Pommerania, and Silesia), and millions of ethnic Poles from Eastern Poland after the war, Eastern Europe has had more than its fair share of what is nowadays known as 'ethnic cleansing'. Even so, the states of Eastern Europe are far from being homogeneous nation states.

In terms of religion, Eastern Europe remains about as heterogeneous as it ever was. There are still Jewish minorities scattered all over Eastern Europe, many of whom are Mosaic believers. There are Muslim minorities in countries like Bulgaria and Yugoslavia (particularly in Bosnia and Hercegovina), and there is the whole range of Christian religions—Roman Catholic, Lutheran, Russian and Greek Orthodox—along with the standard variety of free churches. Some countries are religiously more homogeneous than others, but they all share a certain religious diversity. The socialist system of government imposed on Eastern Europe by the Soviet Union in the wake of the Second World War produced an impression of underlying similarities, but this was largely spurious. The countries of Eastern Europe would not have adopted the Soviet model of government if it had not been for the heavy-handed policies of the victorious Red Army. They would not have formed a military alliance with the Soviet Union and its socialist allies in Eastern Europe, including some of their own historical enemies, if it had not been for strong Soviet pressure. Nor would they have entered into economic co-operation with the Soviet Union on terms that severely curtailed their competitiveness in international markets.

This is not to say that the Soviet system of government was upheld by force and violence alone. It enjoyed a certain amount of popular support throughout Eastern Europe. Pro-socialist and pro-Soviet sentiments probably culminated in the early days of popular democracy in the late 1940s and early 1950s. But with the governing Marxist-Leninist parties counting their members in millions and with the ruthless, but seemingly efficient, repression of political dissent in Eastern Europe, few, if any, observers of Eastern Europe expected the Stalinist and neo-Stalinist regimes to crumble under the impact of a largely peaceful revolution. Yet this is precisely what happened in the autumn of 1989 and the winter and spring of 1990.

The post-communist regimes in Eastern Europe and the former Soviet Union all claim allegiance to capitalism as well as democracy. They have a genuine interest in European co-operation. Several of the former Eastern bloc countries have signed treaties of co-operation with the EC; many of them would like to join the EC as full members and, in a dramatic historic turnabout, some of them have expressed an interest in joining the former ideological arch-enemy, the North Atlantic Treaty

Organization (NATO). But they are also new democracies with uncertain prospects for pluralism and European integration.

In line with these observations, we begin our analysis by applying a macro-level perspective for the purpose of identifying salient cleavages in Eastern Europe. We then turn to a micro-level perspective and prod the survey data at hand for clues to answer three questions. First, what do the East Europeans think about European integration in general and EC membership in particular? Secondly, which groups favour or oppose EC membership? And, thirdly, what is the extent of nationalism and xenophobia in Eastern Europe, and how do they influence support for European integration?

The Revolution that Changed the World

On 4 June 1989 Poland held its first free or almost free elections in over forty years. The election resulted in a landslide victory for Solidarity and paved the way for the first non-communist government in Poland since the end of the Second World War. Less than six months later, the Stalinist and neo-Stalinist regimes of Eastern Europe were virtually all dead and gone. The transition was smooth and peaceful in Poland and Hungary which had a tradition of dialogue and negotiations; it was peaceful but painful in East Germany, Czechoslovakia, and Bulgaria; and it was painful and violent in Romania which was on the verge of civil war by Christmas 1989. The initial changes in the Baltic republics were peaceful, but resulted in increasingly tense relations with Moscow.

The revolution was a by-product of a long-standing and deeply felt legitimacy crisis in Eastern Europe, including the Baltic states. The crisis was permanent and built into the Stalinist and neo-Stalinist system of government which ruled out the possibility that the Marxist-Leninist party might be completely out of touch with the people it was supposed to represent. By the late 1980s, the crisis was compounded by a series of serious political and economic mistakes. The strategy of confrontation and oppression adopted by the communist parties of East Germany, Bulgaria, Czechoslovakia, and Romania had not worked. The strategy of appeasement which had been applied by the rulers of Hungary and Poland had done little to boost the authority and popularity of their respective communist parties. And, as if this were not enough, it had become glaringly apparent that the planned economies of Eastern Europe and the Soviet Union had exhausted most of their potential. In Estonia, Latvia, and Lithuania, it became apparent that the prevailing pattern of development merely led to a *cul de sac* and that alternative strategies had to be sought.

The partially free elections in Poland served as an outlet for the grievances of the Polish people and as a source of inspiration for the rest of Eastern Europe. If the political transition in Poland could take place without provoking any negative reactions from the Soviet Union, there were good reasons to believe that Moscow had given up the standard military response to political change within the traditional Soviet sphere of interest. In fact, Moscow had given up entirely on the hibernating Stalinist and neo-Stalinist regimes of East Germany, Bulgaria, Czechoslovakia, and Romania which were openly critical of Gorbachev's political and economic reforms. The full extent of Soviet rejection did not become apparent until the autumn of 1989 when Gorbachev and the Soviet media lashed out against Honecker, Zhivkov, Jakes, and Ceauşescu while they were still in office in Berlin, Sofia, Prague, and Bucharest. When this became public knowledge, it served as a starting signal for reform communists and anti-system dissidents alike all over Eastern Europe.

The movement towards political and economic reform in the Baltic states paralleled that of Eastern Europe. Reform communists played an important role, particularly at the outset of the democratization process, but the problems were of a different order from those confronting the political leaders of the other East European countries. If the Baltic republics were allowed to break out of the Soviet Union, it might jeopardize the very existence of the Soviet Union. In the final analysis, the government in Moscow resigned itself to the fact that Eastern Europe would go its own way, but it was reluctant to accept the erosion of the Soviet power base which Baltic independence would entail.

The three Baltic republics were not officially recognized by the Soviet government until late August 1991. The decision to resolve the issue in favour of the Baltic independence movements was clearly a by-product of the complete moral and political bankruptcy of the Soviet Communist Party in the wake of the aborted coup by neo-Stalinist hardliners on 19 August 1991. A few months later, on 31 December 1991, after having given birth to twelve new independent states, the Soviet Union ceased to exist.

The twelve motherless children of the former Soviet Union have pledged themselves to political and economic co-operation within the framework of a Commonwealth of Independent States (CIS). They favour a market economy and democracy of the Western variety and have a favourable opinion of West European institutions, such as the European Community and the North Atlantic Treaty Organization, which some of them would like to join—just like the new democracies in Eastern Europe. But, all things considered, there is a gap of at least ten years of economic and political reforms between the twelve Soviet republics which remained within the union until the bitter end in December 1991 and most of the recently liberated states in Eastern Europe, including Estonia, Latvia, and Lithuania.

The New Democracies of Eastern Europe

With communism on the way out, some of the old cleavages reasserted themselves in Eastern Europe. The competitive multi-party systems which emerged in the autumn of 1989 included a number of parties with ideological and organizational roots in the 1920s and 1930s, and to some extent even further back. There are agrarian parties, social democratic parties, left-socialist or communist parties, Christian democratic parties, and ethnic parties. As a rule, however, they were not among the big winners in the process of democratization.

The electoral wind favoured the politically heterogeneous 'catch-all' umbrella organizations such as Solidarity in Poland, Democratic Forum in Hungary, and Civic Forum in Czechoslovakia, which had been part of the struggle for democracy and against communism. But there are exceptions to this rule. In East Germany it was an old bloc party —the Christian Democrats—which benefited from the profound anti-communist backlash. In Bulgaria and Romania there was an electoral backlash against communism, but the old power structures remained intact under somewhat modified labels.

In the Baltic republics, the popular fronts gradually took over power. In the 1990 elections they gained parliamentary majorities in their own right in Latvia and Lithuania. In Estonia, a popular front emerged as the single most important political formation and formed a government with the support of some small parties. But the popular fronts of the Baltic countries are also socially and politically heterogeneous organizations which face a number of difficulties in the current transition period. The recent November 1992 elections in Lithuania—which spelled defeat for the Sajudis movement and victory for the reformed

Lithuanian Communist Party—testify to the fluidity of Baltic party politics.

The distinction between East and West made good sense at the height of the Cold War, but the traditional diversity is now re-emerging in Eastern Europe. There are Central European countries such as Poland, Hungary, and the Czech and Slovak Republics; there are the Baltic countries; and there are Balkan countries such as Bulgaria and Romania. The prospects for democracy are perhaps bleakest in the Balkan countries. They are developing rather than developed countries; they do not have much of a democratic record before communism; and, with the exception of Yugoslavia which was excommunicated from the Soviet bloc in 1948, they have only recently emerged from a communist system of government which was totalitarian rather than authoritarian. But this is not to say that the Baltic states and the Central European countries are already safe for democracy.

Prospects for Democracy

Any discussion of prospects is bound to have an element of speculation attached to it and our discussion of the potential for democracy in Central Europe and the Baltic states is no exception. But it does not have to be normative. Our analysis starts from the simple notion that there have been stable and unstable democracies over the past century of European history. Most of the stable democracies like Britain, West Germany, and in the Scandinavian countries have a long-standing tradition of what Sartori (1966, 1976) would call 'moderate pluralism'. Most of the unstable democracies, by contrast, such the German Weimar Republic (1919–33), the Third and Fourth Republic in France, Spain before and immediately after Franco, Italy before and after the Second World War, were or are plagued by what Sartori refers to as 'extreme pluralism'.

Moderate pluralism is equated with a bell-shaped distribution of voter preferences, and extreme pluralism with deviations from a statistically normal distribution of party preferences. A variety of deviations are possible. The preference curve could, for example, have two peaks—one on the far left and one on the far right—and flatten out as we move towards the centre. The dynamics of such a party system will be centrifugal rather than centripetal. The parties of the extremes will have little incentive to move towards the centre, and the parties in the middle are also likely to defend their positions in the party space. In such a political climate, the process of government formation is likely to prove difficult, with the country running the risk of succumbing to the kind of political immobilism which toppled the Third and Fourth Republic in France.

Democracy under conditions of moderate pluralism is entirely different. The political parties will try to position themselves somewhere in the middle of the bell-shaped political spectrum where the majority of the voters are located. The drive of the party system will be centripetal, with the parties trying to carve out niches for themselves by a process of marginal differentiation which might eventually end up in the proverbial Tweedledum and Tweedledee of American two-party politics. In these circumstances, polarization is theoretically impossible and the process of government formation is likely to run smoothly.

The cleavage structures of the East European countries have not settled yet (Berglund and Dellenbrant 1993). There is overwhelming evidence of an anti-communist backlash throughout Eastern Europe and the Baltic states, but this cleavage is bound to lose salience with the passage of time. The fate of Solidarity in Poland is a good case in point. It was always a heterogeneous coalition of workers and intellectuals, believers and non-believers, radicals and conservatives. The common struggle against the communist regime provided the glue which held it together for more than ten years of both legality and illegality, but the latent tensions became manifest as soon as it was apparent that communism was defeated. The presidential election of November and December 1990, which pitted the two leading Solidarity leaders Walesa and Mazowiecki against one another, put an abrupt end to the myth of unity.

There were early intimations of a latent left–right cleavage within Solidarity, as might be expected of a heterogeneous umbrella organization committed to developing a market economy without broad consensus about the methods. Similar comments apply to Civic Forum in Czechoslovakia, Democratic Forum in Hungary, and the popular fronts of the Baltic states. The political parties which staged a comeback on the basis of past performance in the 1920s and 1930s were in a sense reborn only to be rejected (Lindström 1991). Many of them, particularly the social democratic parties and the old bloc parties, were hurt by the anti-communist backlash. More to the point, all the parties with ideological and historical roots in a distant but glorious past returned to find their constituencies changed almost beyond recognition by more than half a century of 'real socialism'. The policies of extensive industrialization and collectivized agriculture adopted by almost all the Soviet bloc countries throughout the 1950s had a profound impact on the social structure. They were designed to break up the rural way of life and to promote industrialization and urbanization. Thus, by the 1980s, the core groups of the pre-war parties either no longer existed, or, to the extent that they did exist, they no longer represented the same thing. The agricultural sector is a good case in point. The interests of an independent farmer in the rural economy of Eastern Europe in the 1920s and 1930s were not likely to be identical with those of his son or grandson in the semi-industrial collectivized rural economy of the 1980s and 1990s. In so far as the reformed agrarian parties failed to take this into account, they were doomed to failure.

With the benefit of hindsight, this kind of insensitivity seems to have been rather typical of the pre-war parties. The party organization and the party ideology had survived in the hearts and minds of old men and women—few of whom were younger than 65—with personal experience of political work in the heyday of democracy; they failed to realize that while they waited in the wings to perform a play written well over forty years ago, the audience had all but vanished.

This is not to say that the potential of the old cleavages is exhausted in the contemporary East European political landscape. The political parties with roots in pre-war parliamentary democracy may yet carve out viable electoral niches for themselves; and old cleavages based on religion, ethnicity, and nationalism may find new outlets. Industrialization, urbanization, and migration from the countryside have reduced the impact of religion, but the religious factor should not be discounted. It remains a potential line of demarcation throughout Eastern Europe.

Ethnicity and nationalism, by contrast, represent potentially the most explosive and divisive cleavages. The collapse of the Stalinist and neo-Stalinist system of government has provided the oppressed ethnic minorities of Eastern Europe and the former Soviet Union with an opportunity to voice their grievances and to improve their situation. But it has also resulted in a revival of nationalism and a heightening of ethnic tensions which had been repressed for almost half a century. The situation is particularly severe in Yugoslavia, which has fallen apart under the impact of a bloody civil war along ethnic lines, and in the former Soviet Union with its serious local ethnic conflicts.

Ethnic cleavages, however, are by no means unique to those two countries. Romania and Bulgaria have large minorities of ethnic

Hungarians and Turks. Poland has small but vocal German and Silesian minorities, and a stake in the Polish settlements in Lithuania and other parts of the former Soviet Union. Czechoslovakia had a long-standing tradition of tensions between Czechs and Slovaks, the two dominant nationalities in a federal republic which was formally dissolved on 1 January 1993. There is a substantial Hungarian minority in the Slovak Republic and a small German-speaking minority in the Czech Republic. Again, there are places in the three Baltic states where the Russian-speaking minority constitutes a solid majority of the local population.

In addition to all this, there is the spectre of anti-Semitism with its deep historical roots in Eastern Europe, Russia, Ukraine, and other parts of the old Soviet Empire. It has reappeared as a prominent part of the official rhetoric of a variety of right-wing movements, particularly in Poland and Russia. Moreover, anti-Semitism clearly strikes a chord in political settings where there is a premium on easy answers to the question of whom to blame for the political, moral, and economic bankruptcy of entire nations.

Anything is still possible in Eastern Europe. The extreme multi-partism of the early days of democracy will not necessarily carry over into the future. With the passage of time, the cleavage structure may settle into the British and Nordic mould with one dominant cleavage; and the distribution of party preferences may come to comply increasingly with the precepts of moderate pluralism (cf. Downs 1957). On the face of it, however, such a development does not seem very likely. The stage is set for extreme pluralism, and the problem with that kind of democracy is that it tends to be unstable. The Third and Fourth Republic in France, the Weimar Republic, and Spain before Franco do not count among the most successful experiments in democracy. It would clearly be premature to rule out such a scenario even in the most promising of the new democracies in Eastern Europe.

The market economy has no doubt come back to stay, but Eastern Europe is not yet safe for democracy. The rough transition to a market economy may help the reformed communists in their bid for a return to power and add additional fuel to underlying ethnic resentments; and authoritarianism has never been alien to Central Europe and the Baltic states. The democratic traditions of the 1920s and 1930s did not produce stable democratic regimes in the past, and may turn out to be of little avail in the face of socio-economic unrest and nationalistic revival.

Within a New Europe?

Many East Europeans count on Western Europe to help their countries out of their present economic and political predicament. The gradual integration of Eastern Europe into the European Community, and possibly into NATO, is not likely to solve all the problems of Eastern Europe, but it might help strengthen the East European economies and increase the odds of democracy in Eastern Europe. And whatever the future may hold in store, it is a question of no small interest how the East Europeans themselves perceive their role in the Europe of the 1990s. Are they primarily preoccupied with the process of nation building or the process of European integration—with all which that entails by way of economic and political co-operation with the EC? The two perspectives are not mutually exclusive, but they are distinct enough to produce two rather different kinds of world view.

To the extent that the East Europeans are preoccupied by problems of nation building, we would expect them to be nationalists first and foremost and Europeans in, at best, second, third, or fourth place. We should not be surprised to find that they focus on ethnic tensions at home, and their relations with neighbouring countries. Nor should we be surprised to find that they approach the EC in a strictly instrumental fashion—as a saviour from distress. To the extent that East Europeans are preoccupied by the process of European integration, we would not expect them to be Europeanists first and nationalists in second, third, or fourth place. Indeed, few EC citizens fulfil that requirement! But we would certainly expect them to have a European, rather than a nationalist, orientation and to approach the EC in terms which are not purely instrumental.

The survey data we use were gathered in 1990 and in the summer of 1992. They reflect the post-revolutionary euphoria in Eastern Europe and high hopes for the future in three Baltic republics before and shortly after formal independence from Moscow. In Bulgaria, Czechoslovakia, Hungary, and Poland—the four East European countries for which we have roughly comparable data—there was widespread satisfaction with the transition from communism to democracy, and from a socialist command economy to capitalism. In the three Baltic republics, the popular fronts which had set out to implement such a programme enjoyed overwhelming support among Estonians, Latvians, and Lithuanians.[1]

The popular fronts of Estonia, Latvia, and Lithuania fought an up-hill battle for independence in the negotiations with Moscow, until the situation changed, literally overnight, after the aborted coup in August 1991. Few expected the Baltic countries to gain independence as quickly as they did. Had the architects of the impressive Baltic surveys suspected as much, they would probably have included a couple of explicit questions about the European Community in the questionnaire. But they did not, and we do not know for sure how people in these countries felt, in 1990, about the prospect of closer co-operation with the EC.

This was the very topic, however, of the Eurobarometer surveys in Eastern Europe in 1990 and in the Baltic countries in 1992. The wording of the questions varies somewhat from one questionnaire to the other, but the responses are broadly comparable as indicators of attitudes towards the EC. On some indicators, we also have data for the European Free Trade Area (EFTA) countries—Austria, Switzerland, Finland, Sweden, and Norway—which were then preparing to apply for EC membership. We include some reference to these countries as a form of comparative baseline.

As is evident from Table 15.1, there is no doubt that the former communist countries were under the sway of a pro-European, post-revolutionary mood. The overwhelming majority of people in Czechoslovakia, Hungary, and Poland favoured membership in the European Community at least within the next five years. The level of support is more modest in Bulgaria, but none the less a comfortable majority favoured EC membership. Favourable attitudes are at a more modest

TABLE 15.1. *Attitudes towards EC membership in East European countries and the Baltic republics, 1990 and 1992*

1990	Bulgaria	Czechoslovakia	Hungary	Poland
EC membership immediately or at least within next five years	57	62	75	72
N	1,492	1,490	989	1,014
1992	Estonia	Latvia	Lithuania	EFTA average
EC membership is a 'good thing'	53	50	54	36
N	1,000	1,000	1,000	4,500

Note: Entries are percentages.

Sources: Eurobarometer, Nos. 37 and 38; European Integration Study (1992).

level again in the Baltic states, but still the balance of opinion is in favour of membership.

To the extent that there is a pattern in the East European data, support for the EC would seem to be related to a country's economic performance. It is on the low side in economically backward Bulgaria and at its highest in relatively more advanced Hungary and Poland.[2] The Baltic data, however, show little variation between the three countries. Should it be thought that levels of support are lower than might be expected in the Baltic states, it is worth noting that the EFTA countries approach the EC with much more scepticism.

Those in favour of a quick and successful deal with the EC are not always that different from those who opt for a more cautious or even negative approach to the EC. On the whole, however, as is evident from Figures 15.1 and 15.2, those who favour the idea of EC membership seem much the same as those who advocate a quick transition to capitalism. This is one piece of corroborative evidence supporting the notion of the EC as a friend in times of economic distress upon which we shall elaborate later. But, first, we take a closer look at the new Europeans.

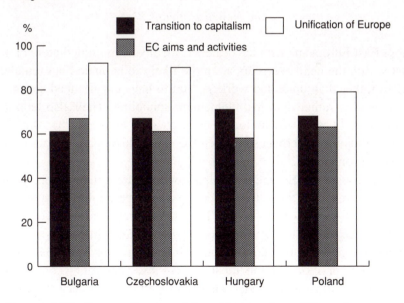

FIGURE 15.1. *Support for a market economy and pro-EC sentiments among EC sympathizers*

Source: *East European Eurobarometer* (1990).

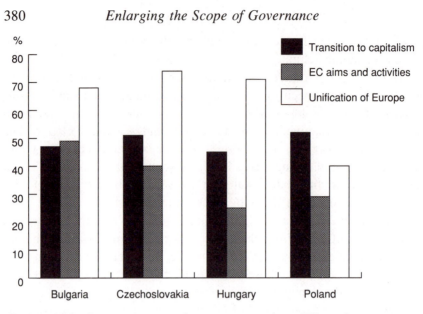

Figure 15.2. *Support for a market economy and pro-EC sentiments among EC sceptics*

Source: *East European Eurobarometer* (1990).

The New Europeans

Those East Europeans who advocate EC membership immediately or at least within the next five years are more likely to be male than female, skilled rather than unskilled workers, and to have experienced secondary education rather than just elementary schooling. They also tend to be moderately well off, although not rich (see Figure 15.3). But, in social terms, the differences between EC sympathizers and sceptics are not very pronounced.[3]

The advocates of EC membership, however, are notably more politically aware than their fellow countrymen, particularly those set against the EC. As we can see in Table 15.2, they tend to be opinion leaders in the sense that they are keen on discussing politics and they try to persuade friends and acquaintances to support their opinions. Fully 80 per cent or more of the most fervent EC supporters confess to discussing politics on a regular basis, and well over 50 per cent claim that they try to persuade friends and acquaintances to share their political views.

Moreover, the advocates of EC membership are largely in favour of a

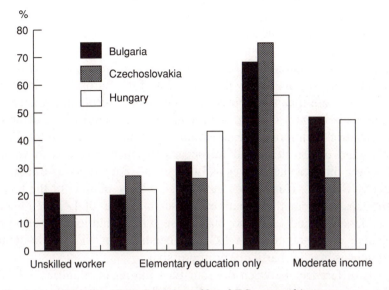

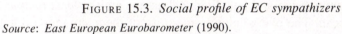

FIGURE 15.3. *Social profile of EC sympathizers*

Source: *East European Eurobarometer* (1990).

market economy, and high proportions have a positive opinion of the EC's aims and activities. Even more to the point, they are overwhelmingly—although not exclusively—in favour of the unification of Europe, including their own countries, in 'a United States of Europe'. And they are almost unanimously in favour of closer co-operation between their respective countries and the European Community (see Figure 15.1 above).

TABLE 15.2. *Political discussion, knowledge, and European identity among EC supporters, 1990*

	Bulgaria	Czechoslovakia	Hungary	Poland
Discuss politics on regular basis	88	92	—	83
Regularly try to persuade friends	57	70	—	65
Can identify Jacques Delors as President of EC Commission	27	27	—	16
Heard of EC economic assistance	64	66	71	36
Think of themselves as Europeans	28	62	73	57
N	845	924	744	729

Note: Entries are percentages.

Source: Eurobarometer, No. 37.

However, supporters of EC membership in the East European countries do not seem to be particularly knowledgeable about the EC and, judging from the Baltic surveys, do not feel particularly well informed about it.[4] Less than a third of EC supporters in Bulgaria, Czechoslovakia, and Poland can identify the President of the European Commission by name; more than two-thirds of respondents in Bulgaria, Czechoslovakia, and Hungary claim that they have never heard of the efforts by EC countries to improve the economic situation of their country. Nor do they stand out as dedicated Europeans: when prodded as to whether they ever think of themselves as Europeans—not simply as Bulgarians, Czechs, Slovaks, Hungarian, and Poles—a large number of the respondents answered in the negative. Those in favour of EC membership were less inclined to do so than those with a cautious or outrightly negative approach towards EC membership, but the within-country differences are not particularly impressive.

The differences between the four East European countries are, thus, all the more impressive and puzzling. Bulgarians are the least inclined to feel European. The overwhelming majority of them say they do not know whether they feel Bulgarian or European; and among those who do give a substantive answer, only a minority confess to feeling European most of the time. Similar comments apply to the Poles, although they are somewhat less inclined to say that they do not know.[5] The Czechoslovaks and the Hungarians are less likely to dodge the question and more likely to provide substantive answers, a large number of which qualify as pro-European.

To some extent this outcome makes good sense, and to some extent it seems counter-intuitive. It is hardly surprising that the vast majority of the Bulgarians are Bulgarians first and Europeans in the second, third or fourth place. Within an East European context, Bulgaria is underdeveloped in socio-economic terms, and within the socialist system of states, Bulgaria was one of the most faithful allies of the Soviet Union engaging in only minimal contacts with Western Europe. The position of the other three countries makes good sense in terms of economic but not political development. In the East European context, Poland qualifies as a developing country, rather than as an industrial country, but politically it has a long and impressive tradition of pluralism and openness which surpasses that of the other former communist countries in Eastern Europe, including Hungary and Czechoslovakia.

Turning to the Baltic countries, we draw on data from the 1990 World Values Study.[6] Representative samples of Estonians, Latvians, and Lithuanians were asked which of the following they identified with in the first place and which in the second place: the locality or city where they live, the republic where they live, the Soviet Union, Europe, or the whole world. The vast majority of them, including the ethnic Russians, did not opt for anything beyond the republic. Europe only drew a handful of votes in the first round and 5–10 per cent in the second round. The details are reported in Table 15.3.

Baltic Europeans tend to be well educated and well off. They also tend to stand out as politically active and they are strongly in favour of independence, which quite a few of them believed could be achieved with the aid of the West (see Figure 15.4). The most striking feature about the Baltic data, however, is the evidence of ethnic cleavages. The

TABLE 15.3. *Primary and secondary identification among major ethnic groups in Baltic countries, 1990*

	Object of identification					N
	Locality	Republic	USSR	Europe	World	
ESTONIA						
Estonian						
Primary object	31	66	1	1	1	612
Secondary object	51	31	3	12	4	603
Russian						
Primary object	31	36	24	2	7	306
Secondary object	29	38	21	4	9	301
LATVIA						
Latvian						
Primary object	27	72	1	—	1	447
Secondary object	53	26	2	11	8	429
Russian						
Primary object	41	38	12	1	9	319
Secondary object	24	40	18	5	13	296
LITHUANIA						
Lithuanian						
Primary object	22	73	—	1	3	764
Secondary object	51	24	1	13	11	745
Russian						
Primary Object	30	43	19	1	7	89
Secondary Object	33	26	21	6	15	88

Note: Entries are row percentages.

Source: Baltic World Values Study (1990).

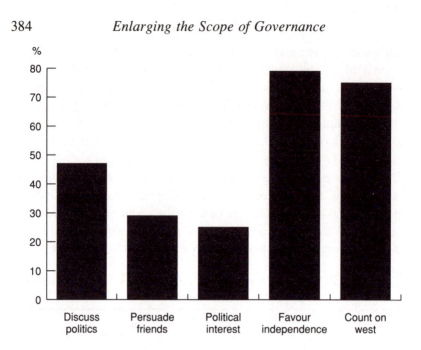

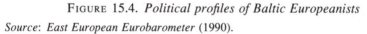

FIGURE 15.4. *Political profiles of Baltic Europeanists*
Source: *East European Eurobarometer* (1990).

ethnic Russians are integrated into the Baltic societies, but only partly so. They are less likely than the Estonians, the Latvians, and the Lithuanians to identify with Europe and considerably more likely to identify with the Soviet Union.

The Baltic states have since gained the independence which probably was not thought to be imminent in 1990. But they are now up against a nation-building crisis, the contours of which were intimated in the 1990 Baltic surveys. In all likelihood, this nation-building crisis will have to be successfully resolved by the Baltic states before the people are prepared to commit themselves to integration with a distant entity such as Europe. Nevertheless, the prevailing mood is strongly pro-European. In all, as shown in Table 15.4, although rather less likely to think of themselves as European, people in the Baltic republics were considerably more likely than people in the EFTA countries to be positive about the EC and to perceive EC membership as a solution to at least some of the problems they were facing.

There are some indications in the 1990 East European data that the commitment to European integration is genuine and well considered. Respondents were asked how rapidly their country should become a

TABLE 15.4. *European identity and attitudes towards European integration in the Baltic and EFTA countries, 1992*

	Estonia	Latvia	Lithuania	EFTA
Think of themselves as Europeans	42	57	36	45
Would be very sorry if EC were to be scrapped	36	41	39	22
Perceive EC membership as beneficial	57	53	57	43
N	1,000	1,000	1,000	4,500

Notes: Entries are percentages. The wording of the question for the first item is not identical with that used in the early Eurobarometer studies, but close enough for functional equivalence.

Source: European Integration Study (1992).

member of the EC and in what sectors they would welcome or oppose closer European integration. Their answers suggest an underlying conflict of two, and possibly three, dimensions. This is evident from a factor analysis of the data for Czechoslovakia and Poland, reported in Table 15.5.

The economic implications of closer co-operation with the EC are separated from the defence and foreign policy implications; and the cultural aspects of co-operation with the EC, including professional training and youth exchange, tend to be distinguished from the explicitly materialistic implications in the industrial and agricultural sectors. And there is a high degree of attitudinal consistency. Those favouring EC membership immediately or at least within the next five years tend to welcome closer co-operation with the EC across the board. Those who advocate a more cautious and outright negative approach towards EC membership tend to be somewhat less open to closer co-operation with the EC in general, and particularly within the fields of foreign policy and defence (see Figure 15.5).

Although not particularly rich in information about social cleavages, our data include some potentially disturbing evidence of the prevailing mood in the East European and Baltic countries. They do not trust their fellow countrymen and they do not trust their neighbours. Neighbouring (West) Germans fare considerably better than neighbouring Russians, Poles, Czechs, Slovaks, Ukrainians, and Lithuanians, but less well than geographically distant members of NATO such as the United States, Britain, and France (data not shown here).[7]

Anti-Jewish sentiments in the three Baltic states testify to the resilience of traditional ethnic tensions (see Table 15.6). The anti-Jewish feelings of the Russian speakers are hardly surprising considering the

TABLE 15.5. *Structure of attitudes towards co-operation with the EC in Czechoslovakia and Poland, 1990*

	Factor 1	Factor 2	Factor 3
CZECHOSLOVAKIA			
When should Czechoslovakia become EC member?	−0.003	0.213	0.357
Welcome closer co-operation in:			
Culture	0.365	0.447	0.014
Agriculture	0.019	0.149	0.585
Industry	0.227	0.101	0.673
Higher education	0.351	0.146	0.478
Defence	0.106	0.552	0.206
Foreign policy	0.179	0.687	0.172
Environment	0.724	0.194	0.061
Human rights	0.069	0.534	0.167
Professional training	0.886	0.153	0.251
Youth exchange	0.248	0.337	0.263
Proportion of variance explained	28.2	7.8	6.3
POLAND			
When should Poland become EC member?	0.283	0.167	
Welcome closer co-operation in:			
Culture	0.550	0.191	
Agriculture	0.225	0.687	
Industry	0.224	0.832	
Education	0.559	0.229	
Defence	0.547	0.164	
Foreign policy	0.603	0.159	
Environment	0.472	0.370	
Human rights	0.510	0.294	
Professional training	0.655	0.203	
Youth exchange	0.594	0.143	
Proportion of variance explained	33	6.5	

Note: Entries are loadings on rotated factor matrix.

long-standing tradition of anti-Semitism in Russia (Parland 1993). Anti-Semitism among the Estonians, the Latvians, and the Lithuanians may be accounted for in similar terms.[8]

Suspicion of their next-door neighbours throughout Eastern Europe, along with anti-Jewish sentiments in the Baltic countries, suggest that these countries may have a long way to go in progressing towards European integration. The low turnout in recent East European elections, the rough transition to a market economy throughout Eastern

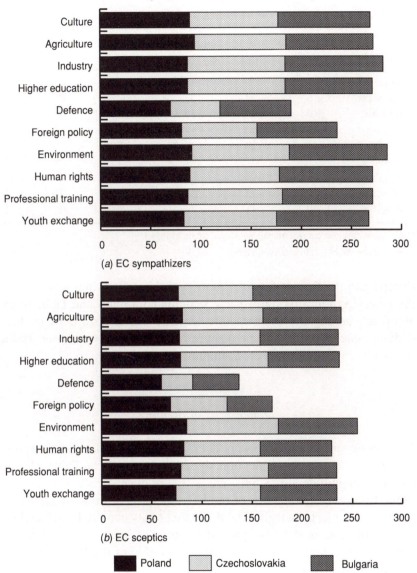

FIGURE 15.5. *Favourable attitudes towards closer co-operation with EC by policy area among EC sympathizers and sceptics in Bulgaria, Poland, and Czechoslovakia, 1990*

Source: Eurobarometer, No. 37.

TABLE 15.6. *Degree of trust in Jews in the Baltic countries, 1990*

	Complete trust	A little trust	Neither trust nor distrust	Not particularly	No trust at all	N
Estonia						
Estonians	5	29	33	22	12	467
Russians	10	50	16	14	10	234
Latvia						
Latvians	11	28	34	18	9	334
Russians	17	37	21	12	13	254
Lithuania						
Lithuanians	9	33	35	15	9	697
Russians	20	41	22	8	10	74

Note: Entries are percentages among the major ethnic groups.

Source: Baltic World Values Survey (1990).

Europe and the former Soviet Union, and the underlying instability of the emerging pluralist multi-party systems (Berglund and Dellenbrant 1993) are among the other factors which make it hazardous to draw definite conclusions about the posture of the East European and Baltic states *vis-à-vis* the European Community.

Dimensions of Support

The Baltic and East European data indicate high levels of diffuse support for European unification. Indeed, as shown in Table 15.7, it attains a magnitude almost on a par with—or even slightly above—that in the twelve member states of the EC and surpasses that of the EFTA countries by a large margin. The differences between the EC-12 and the EFTA countries may be interpreted in terms of integration effects, but that cannot account for the pro-European profile of the Baltic and East European countries.

These favourable evaluations could be dismissed as simply part and parcel of the post-communist and pro-European euphoria in the Baltic and East European countries. However, there are notable differences between the countries. The Baltic countries are more favourably disposed towards European integration than the EFTA countries as a whole, but not by very much. Opinion in Bulgaria comes somewhere between the overall levels in the EC and the EFTA countries. Poland

TABLE 15.7. *Evaluation of European unification in Central and Eastern Europe, 1990 and 1992*

	For, very much	For, to some extent	Total
1990			
Poland	28	41	69
Czechoslovakia	33	46	79
Hungary	41	40	81
Bulgaria	47	24	71
1992			
Estonia	29	34	63
Latvia	26	35	61
Lithuania	28	35	63
EC-12	31	46	76
EFTA average	17	39	55

Notes: Entries are percentages. In the 1990 survey, the question probed attitudes towards the unification of Europe leading to the formation of a 'United States of Europe'. The question wording was simplified in the 1992 survey, with respondents asked whether or not they were in favour of 'efforts made to unify Western Europe'.

Sources: Eurobarometer, No. 38; European Integration Study (1992).

comes rather close to the EC level, while Czechoslovakia and Hungary surpass it. Clearly, a closer analysis is called for.

Our analysis is confined to the 1990 data for Bulgaria, Czechoslovakia, Hungary, and Poland, and explores the determinants of EC support. In particular, the analysis is designed to address three questions. First, to what extent is the pro-European and pro-EC mood in Eastern Europe a product of individual-level perceptions of self and society? Here we focus on respondents' evaluation of societal change (assessments of the economic situation and relative satisfaction with the development of democracy); respondents' self-evaluation (perceived political competence and self-placement on a left–right scale); and respondents' personal resources (subjective level of information about the EC and actual knowledge about the EC). Secondly, to what extent is there a direct relationship between standard sociological variables such as gender, age, and education on the one hand, and different kinds of EC support on the other? Thirdly, to what extent is the relationship between perceptions of self and society and support for the EC spurious in the sense that it disappears after controlling for gender, age, and education?[9]

Attitudes towards the EC and European integration may be seen to break down into two categories—diffuse and specific. The East European Eurobarometers have at least three items tapping diffuse or general orientations in this area: European identity, support for European unification, and evaluation of the aims and activities of the EC. Only one item—evaluation of EC assistance programmes for each country—taps specific, or *quid pro quo*, support for the EC. Thus, we have four dependent variables and nine independent variables. The variables and the questions used to measure them are listed in the appendix to this chapter.

Perceptions of Self and Society

The correlations between the four dependent variables and the six variables measuring perceptions of self and society are presented in Table 15.8. The general pattern is fairly consistent. Personal resources with respect to information about the EC, whether subjective or objective, show the strongest correlations for all four dependent variables in all four countries. Generally speaking, respondents' self-evaluation seems to be more important than their evaluations of the development of their society as a whole in accounting for their propensity to feel European. There are, however, some substantially interesting exceptions to this pattern—including the possibility of what might be described as an 'Albanian syndrome' in Bulgaria.[10]

Personal resources also stand out as the single most important determinants of EC support, regardless of specificity. Except in Bulgaria, the two personal resource items correlate with the European identity questions at the 0.20 level or above. Except in Poland, the correlation coefficients for European unification fall within the range 0.14–0.20. Note, however, that all correlations involving the unification variable are lower than for the other three support variables—which is due, partly, to the restrictive wording of the question which refers to the formation of a 'United States of Europe', and partly to our restrictive recoding of the variable. Even so, the correlations for the unification question are in line with the results for the other dependent variables. The aims and activities of the EC correlate with the two resource items in the 0.26–0.49 range for all four countries, while the coefficients for the salience of help from the EC fall within the range 0.21–0.29.

The two indicators of self-evaluation correlate more modestly with the four dimensions of support for the EC. The coefficients between

TABLE 15.8. *Correlations between perceptions of self and society and European orientations in four East–Central European countries, 1990*

	European identity				European unification				Aims and activities of EC				Salience of EC assistance			
	POL	HUN	CZ	BUL	POL	HUN	CZ	BUL	POL	HUN	CZ	BUL	POL	HUN	CZ	BUL
Information about EC	0.25	0.26	0.28	0.16	0.12	0.19	0.20	0.15	0.39	0.26	0.34	0.47	0.29	0.25	0.29	0.24
Knowledge about EC	0.20	—	0.24	0.12	0.13	—	0.16	0.14	0.39	—	0.32	0.49	0.26	—	0.29	0.21
Political competence	0.20	—	0.25	0.12	n.s.	—	0.11	0.09	0.17	—	0.23	0.30	0.12	n.s.	0.19	0.21
Left–right self-placement	n.s.	n.s.	-0.19	n.s.	n.s.	n.s.	-0.19	-0.23	n.s.	n.s.	-0.19	-0.14	n.s.	—	-0.14	n.s.
Economic situation	0.14	n.s.	n.s.	0.13	n.s.	n.s.	n.s.	n.s.	0.16	n.s.	n.s.	n.s.	0.09*	n.s.	0.08*	n.s.
Satisfaction with democracy	0.09*	0.13	0.12	0.09	0.12	0.11	0.12	n.s.	0.12	n.s.	0.10	0.12	n.s.	0.16	0.10	0.08*

Notes: Entries are correlation coefficients (Pearson's r). All correlations are significant at the 0.001 level except those marked * which are significant at the 0.01 level; 'n.s.' = 'not significant'.

Source: East European Eurobarometer (1990).

TABLE 15.9. *Correlations between social structure and European orientations for four East–Central European countries, 1990*

	European identity				European unification				Aims and activities of EC				Salience of EC assistance			
	POL	HUN	CZ	BUL	POL	HUN	CZ	BUL	POL	HUN	CZ	BUL	POL	HUN	CZ	BUL
Gender	0.14	0.10	0.10	0.12	0.09*	0.14	0.14	0.10	0.22	0.16	0.19	0.17	0.14	0.10*	0.12	0.10
Age	—	n.s.	n.s.	n.s.	—	-0.09	n.s.	n.s.	—	n.s.	0.08*	0.13	—	n.s.	n.s.	0.07*
Education	—	-0.22	-0.16	-0.13	—	n.s.	0.08*	-0.07*	—	0.23	-0.21	-0.32	—	-0.13	-0.14	-0.12

Notes: Entries are correlation coefficients (Pearson's r). All correlations are significant at the 0.001 level except those marked * which are significant at the 0.01 level; 'n.s.' = 'not significant'.

Source: East European Eurobarometer (1990).

European identity and subjective level of political competence range between 0.12 and 0.25, while in Poland, Hungary, and Bulgaria there are no significant correlations for left–right self-placement. In Czechoslovakia, however, with a coefficient of -0.19, there is evidence of a politicization of the question of European identity. Thus, the Czechoslovak data point to a fairly direct relationship between the political right and European identity. This may reflect the fact that the notion of European identity was part and parcel of Czech politics, particularly Czech rhetoric, in the aftermath of the 'Velvet Revolution'.[11] But it may also be an indication that factors other than left–right self-placement have more influence on European identity in the other three countries.

The relationship between European unification and the two self-evaluation items is relatively weak and stands out as only slightly more important than the largely insignificant correlations produced by European unification and the social change variables. For self-perceived political competence the correlations are around 0.10. But left–right self-placement displays an interesting pattern. Here, too, Czechoslovakia shows a correlation of -0.19 indicating that the political right tends to be in favour of European unification. Bulgaria shows an even higher correlation coefficient of -0.23. Poland and Hungary display no significant correlations at all. In other words, the issue of European unification is politicized in Czechoslovakia and Bulgaria, but not in Hungary and Poland.

With correlations in the range of 0.17–0.30, self-perceived political competence is a relatively strong determinant of attitudes towards the aims and activities of the EC. However, there are no significant relationships for left–right self-placement in Poland and Hungary, although Czechoslovakia (-0.19) and Bulgaria (-0.14) are moderately politicized on this issue as well. The item tapping specific support—the salience of help from the EC—does not produce any relationships worth mentioning with left–right self-placement except in Czechoslovakia (-0.14). Self-perceived political competence results in correlations between 0.12 and 0.21.

The two indicators evaluating societal change are the least important in accounting for support for the EC. Generally speaking, the correlations are low or insignificant, but there are some exceptions. Bulgaria and Poland show modest correlations of around 0.14 between European identity and economic evaluations. In these two countries, there seems to be some relationship between the way people perceive the country's economic situation and their propensity to think of themselves as

European. The optimists tend to do so; the pessimists tend not. As for satisfaction with democracy, there are weak but significant relationships with European identity in all countries, ranging from 0.09 to 0.13. Perceptions of the economic situation have no significant impact on attitudes towards European unification in any of the four countries. Satisfaction with democracy has a weak but significant relationship of around 0.12 in Poland, Czechoslovakia, and Hungary. In Bulgaria, satisfaction with democracy has no significant impact on attitudes towards European unification.

The only country with a significant correlation between evaluations of the economic situation and assessments of the aims and activities of the EC is Poland (0.16). Polish economic optimists tend to be supportive of the EC's aims and activities. With correlations around 0.11, those satisfied with democracy in Poland, Czechoslovakia, and Bulgaria also tend to support the aims and activities of the EC. In Hungary, evaluation of societal change seems to have little impact on assessments of the aims and activities of the EC.

With regard to the instrumental aspect of support for integration, there is a weak—although statistically significant—relationship between the salience of the EC to their country and evaluations of the economic situation among Czechoslovaks and Poles. Hungarians (0.16) and Czechoslovaks (0.10) who are satisfied with democracy in their own countries tend to perceive assistance co-ordinated by the European Commission as important to their respective countries. There is a similar, but weaker, correlation for Bulgaria (0.08).

Generally speaking, among the variables measuring perceptions of self and society, knowledge and information level stand out as the most important. People's sense of themselves as opinion leaders also shows some interesting relationships with levels of support. But respondents' evaluation of the economic and political situation in their country constitutes the weakest of the three sub-sets of explanatory factors.

Social Structure

In general, the social background variables display weaker relationships with attitudes towards the EC than perceptions of self and society. This is particularly true in contrast to subjective and objective knowledge about the EC. Among the three social background variables, gender and educational level have a modest to strong impact on the four indicators of European orientation. Our results are presented in Table 15.9.

The relationship between European identity and gender is evident in all four countries. The correlations, in the narrow range 0.10–0.14, indicate a certain tendency for men to be more committed to Europe than women. Age has almost no direct impact on European identity. In Hungary, Czechoslovakia, and Bulgaria, the correlation between education and European identity ranges from −0.13 to −0.22, indicating a modestly strong relationship between high education and a European orientation.

As to the unification of Europe possibly leading to the formation of a 'United States of Europe', gender has some effect in that men are slightly more in favour of unification than women in all four countries. This effect is rather stronger in Hungary and Czechoslovakia (0.14) than in Poland (0.09) and Bulgaria (0.10). But age and education have either little effect, or relatively weak effects, in all four countries on attitudes towards unification. However, analysis of this question is marred by its restrictive formulation.

By contrast, evaluation of the aims and activities of the EC is the one dependent variable which is directly affected by variations in social background. Better educated people have a strong tendency to take a more favourable view, particularly in Bulgaria (−0.32) but only rather less so in Hungary (−0.23) and Czechoslovakia (−0.21). Men show the more positive evaluation of the EC in all four countries, with coefficients ranging from 0.16 to 0.22. In Bulgaria there is a modest tendency (0.13) for young people to be more favourable towards the aims and activities of the EC than others. But age has no significant impact in Hungary and a relatively weak impact in Czechoslovakia (0.08), thus following the general pattern.

The correlates of the perceived salience of EC assistance are similar to those for European identity. The modest coefficients for increasing education levels (−0.12 to −0.14) and for men (0.10 to 0.14) complete the picture. Age has no direct effects on the salience of EC aid in Hungary and Czechoslovakia. A minor but nevertheless interesting observation is that young Bulgarians display a weak but significant tendency to attach more weight to EC assistance than older people (0.07). Indeed, Bulgaria stands out as the only country where age is of some significance in accounting for positive orientations towards the EC.

Nowhere and for none of the four dependent variables have we observed one instance where the direct impact of a social background variable is stronger than either subjective and objective knowledge about the EC. The four countries seem to fall into two groups, since Bulgaria stands out from the rest as a society where the social background variables play a more important direct role. But it is feasible to imagine the Balkans as an area where societal divisions—relative to political attitudes—are more important than in Central Europe. And probably not only in regard to attitudes towards Europe and the EC.

The role of knowledge and education suggested by this analysis is by no means coincidental, and it is tempting to refer to the traditional role of the intelligentsia in East European politics—in the pre-communist, communist and, apparently, post-communist periods. But before drawing any broader inferences, we need to examine possible interactions between social background and the perceptual and attitudinal indicators.

Interaction Effects

In Table 15.10, we present the standardized regression coefficients for all the predictors examined above for two countries: Czechoslovakia and Bulgaria. These are the only two countries for which we have a complete set of indicators.

Beginning at the highest level of generality—the sense of European identity—we observe some interesting differences between Czechoslovakia, a Central European country, and Bulgaria, a Balkan country. In Czechoslovakia, a syndrome constituted by knowledge, information, self-evaluation of political competence, left–right self-placement, and satisfaction with democracy in their own country, seems to have an impact on European identity. We may refer to this syndrome as 'politicized knowledge'. Individual belief and confidence in one's own resources seem to be important here. By contrast, in Bulgaria the position of respondents in the social structure seems to be more important than their beliefs. Thus, a set of variables including gender, education, evaluation of the country's economic performance, and feeling well informed are more decisive predictors. In short, this syndrome is rooted in the social structure and economic evaluations.

Thus, on the one hand, it is the more individualistic Czechs and Slovaks, confident of their personal potential and resources, who favour European integration. On the other hand, in Bulgaria, a demographically

TABLE 15.10. *Determinants of attitudes towards the EC in Czechoslovakia and Bulgaria, 1990*

	European identity		European unification		Aims and activities of EC		Salience of EC assistance	
	CZ	BUL	CZ	BUL	CZ	BUL	CZ	BUL
Information about EC	0.18	0.09	0.11	0.09	0.21	0.26	0.17	0.14
Knowledge about EC	0.11	0.02	0.05	0.05	0.17	0.30	0.19	0.11
Political competence	0.17	0.06	0.04	0.02	0.10	0.11	0.10	0.13
Left–right self-placement	−0.15	0.02	−0.15	−0.20	−0.14	−0.07	−0.11	0.03
Economic situation	0.01	0.13	0.00	−0.01	0.03	−0.01	0.06	−0.03
Satisfaction with democracy	0.07	0.06	0.11	0.03	0.04	0.07	0.04	0.06
Gender	−0.01	0.09	0.07	0.06	0.05	0.07	0.00	0.06
Age	0.01	0.00	0.01	−0.05	0.03	−0.02	0.01	0.01
Education	−0.05	−0.10	0.00	−0.03	−0.08	−0.08	−0.03	−0.03
R^2	0.16	0.07	0.08	0.08	0.21	0.39	0.16	0.12

Note: Entries are standardized regression coefficients.

Source: *East European Eurobarometer* (1990).

more segmented society, it is men, the better educated, and the economic optimists who favour Europe. Indeed, it is easy to imagine Bulgaria as a mosaic of collective subcultures, including a subculture of intermediary social élites or semi-élites of well-educated men. Note, however, that our analysis yields a better account of variations in personal commitment to the EC in Czechoslovakia than in Bulgaria.

The results for the unification question are rather poor. This is probably due to the strong wording of this question. None the less, in both Bulgaria and Czechoslovakia, this rather radical call for European unification—to the point of creating a 'United States of Europe'—strikes a chord among sympathizers with the political right and among people who feel well informed about the EC. But the most conspicuous feature of this item is the low proportion of variance explained.

Our set of independent variables provides a much better account of evaluations of the aims and activities of the EC. In Czechoslovakia and in Bulgaria, knowledge and information are prominent explanatory factors in accounting for positive assessments of the EC. Political competence and left–right self-placement are equally important in both countries. So is the level of education. Additionally, in Bulgaria, gender and satisfaction with democracy show some impact. Assessment of the aims and activities of the EC is influenced by respondents' beliefs in their own personal resources as well as by their place in society as given by their educational level. Individualism and social stratification tend to reinforce one another in both societies. Thus, on this aspect of diffuse support for the EC, the two countries are rather alike.

Turning to the perceived salience of EC aid programmes, it seems that social stratification has virtually no impact at all. It is personal resources such as knowledge, information, and political competence which influence perceptions and assessments of the EC aid programmes. And they do so irrespective of respondents' social position. The impact of education is picked up through variations in knowledge and information. The population of Czechoslovakia is evidently the more politicized, in the sense that people on the right are more positive in their evaluation of EC aid programmes.

To summarize. With respect to European identity, the most diffuse of our four measures, there is an interesting contrast between the individualistic Czechs and Slovaks on the one hand and, on the other hand, the Bulgarians who seem to be more under the sway of social cleavages. But the unification question yields uninteresting results, probably due to the wording of the question, with its mention of a 'United States of Europe'. As for the two other measures of support for European integration, Czechoslovakia and Bulgaria are basically similar. In particular, in both countries, education has a direct impact on evaluations of the EC's aims and activities but not on evaluations of the salience of EC aid.

Conclusion

The EC is currently assimilating the 'EFTA enlargement', and when it will be ready for a new wave of applications from the former Warsaw Pact countries is a moot question. The current mood in Eastern Europe, and in the Baltic countries, clearly favours such a step; and in a sense, the East Europeans are ready for the EC. They are favourably disposed towards the European Community, and they definitely seem to have been won over to capitalism and a market economy. The East Europeans of today have a higher level and a broader scope in education than ever before. And, as we have demonstrated, knowledge and education have a clear bearing on attitudes towards European integration in general, and the EC in particular. But it is an open question how they will feel about the EC after a few more years of a market economy with all that that entails by way of privatization and dismantling of the welfare state. This question may apply to masses and élites alike, even though findings based on data from 1990 suggest rather significant differences between the better educated and the rest of the people.

At present, East Europeans generally approach European integration and the EC in positive terms. In this chapter, we have tried to highlight some of the obstacles which this optimism may encounter. Our evidence suggests that an overwhelming majority of East Europeans expect full integration into the European Community to take place at least within the next five years. If this does not happen, which is likely, several problems may occur. Even in a data set marked by the postcommunist Euro-phoria of the early 1990s, our analyses point to at least two such problems.

First, there is the challenge of nationalism. We noted the considerable degree of xenophobia which exists in these countries, as evidenced by low trust in the peoples of neighbouring East European countries. The low level of integration of the sizeable Russian minorities in the three Baltic countries constitutes further evidence. Low trust in Jews enhances this impression. So far these attitudes co-exist with a strong desire for European integration. But when we consider the relatively high level of trust between member countries of the EC (see Chapter 10), it is clear that problems of trust among and between the East European peoples will have to be resolved if integration is to be achieved. This, of course, raises a difficult question for the EC-12 countries: should the integration of the East European countries be accelerated in order to prevent these countries from sliding into nationalist dictatorships—which was central to the decision to admit Spain, Portugal, and Greece—or should the EC insist upon successful transition to a market economy and clear evidence of democratic stability before welcoming the East European countries into the EC? The latter seems to be the current thinking.

Secondly, there is the panacea syndrome. It is very tempting to interpret positive attitudes towards European integration and the EC at face value. This is especially true since this eagerness to join the Western sphere also constitutes a compliment to the West European way of life. Our analysis provides substantial evidence that there is, indeed, a genuine desire on the part of East Europeans to take part in the process of European integration. However, we have also found evidence that peoples in countries outside Central Europe, such as Bulgaria, tend to rely on collective mechanisms of identification such as social cleavages, while Central Europeans, such as the Czechs and the Slovaks, identify with Europe in individualistic terms. Moreover, negative assessments of the performance of domestic economies by no means preclude being generally in favour of European integration (Haas and Schmitter 1964). From this perspective, support for European integration may, in itself, constitute a problem in so far as well-qualified individuals from Eastern Europe may vote with their feet, as was dramatically demonstrated by the Albanian exodus in 1990.

In our data, the panacea syndrome seems to follow a clear north–south pattern. In Central Europe, trust in the domestic economy and belief in democracy are clearly associated with pan-Europeanism. Evidence from the Balkan countries suggests otherwise. This implies that the EC may be well advised to adopt different policies towards the integration of different parts of Eastern Europe.

APPENDIX

Variables and Questions Used in the Analysis of European Orientations

(1) *European identity*: 'Do you ever think of yourself as not only (Bulgarian, Czech/Slovak, Hungarian or Pole), but also European? Does this happen often, sometimes, never?'

(2) *European unification*: 'In general, to what extent are you for or against the unification of Europe, leading to the formation of a "United States of Europe", including (Bulgaria, Czechoslovakia, Hungary or Poland)? Are you for, very much; for, to some extent; against, to some extent; against very much?'

(3) *Aims and activities of EC*: 'Would you say that your impressions of the aims and activities of the European Community are generally positive, neutral or negative?'

(4) *Salience of EC assistance*: 'Have you heard about assistance to help improve the (Bulgarian, Czechoslovak, Hungarian or Polish) economy being provided by 23 industrialised nations and co-ordinated by the Commission of the European Communities?' [If yes] Do you feel that this assistance programme is having a major impact, a minor impact or no real impact at all in helping improve the (Bulgarian, Czechoslovak, Hungarian or Polish) economy?'

(5) *Economic situation*: 'Over the next 12 months, do you think the general economic situation in (Bulgaria, Czechoslovakia, Hungary or Poland)

will get a lot better, get a little better, stay the same, get a little worse, get a lot worse?'

(6) *Satisfaction with democracy*: 'On the whole, are you very satisfied, satisfied, not very satisfied or not satisfied at all with the way democracy is developing in (Bulgaria, Czechslovakia, Hungary or Poland)?'

(7) *Subjective political competence*: 'When you hold a strong opinion, do you ever find yourself persuading your friends, relatives or fellow workers to share your views? Does this happen often, from time to time, rarely, never?'

(8) *Left–right self-placement*: The left–right item for Czechoslovakia, Hungary, and Poland was recoded to comply with a three-point self-placement scale used in Bulgaria (left, middle, and right).

(9) *Subjective level of information*: 'Taking into account all you know about the European Community, how well informed do you feel about its aims and activities, very informed, quite informed, not very well informed, not at all informed?'

(10) *Knowledge about the EC*: This variable combines data from two items, one asking whether or not the respondent knows about the EC, and one tapping respondent's knowledge about the EC by asking them to identify the President of the Commission of European Communities from a list of five politicians. Those who have heard about the EC and identified Jacques Delors as President of the Commission were counted as very knowledgeable about the EC; those who had heard about the EC but identified one of the other EC politicians as President were counted as a little less knowledgeable; those who had heard about the EC but failed to mention one of the five EC leaders were seen as somewhat less knowledgeable; and those who had not heard about the EC and did not know whom to identify as President of the European Commission were counted as not knowledgeable at all.

(11) *Gender*: male (1); female (2).

(12) *Age*: 15–24 (1); 25–39 (2); 40–59 (3); over 60 (4).

(13) *Education*: elementary (1); vocational (2); secondary (3); higher (4).

NOTES

1. The large Russian minorities in Estonia and Latvia (40% and 50%, respectively) and the sizeable Russian minority in Lithuania (10%) were understandably more cautious in their approach to the Popular Fronts with their call for secession from the Soviet Union. See Berglund and Dellenbrant (1993).

2. The subsequent Eurobarometer survey (autumn 1991) testifies to the continued salience of the EC option in East European political thinking. Between 60% and

70% of respondents, including the Bulgarians, said they were in favour of joining the EC immediately or at least within the next five years.

3. Whether an urban–rural cleavage prevails could not be tested as the wording of the questions differed from one country to another. The Hungarian survey recorded whether the respondent was from Budapest, other cities, or the countryside. Running this variable against the preferred timetable for EC membership revealed no evidence of an urban–rural cleavage.

4. When asked how well informed they felt about the EC, less than 25% of Baltic respondents claimed to be well informed. The average for the EFTA countries was well over 30%. The data were collected in the Eurobarometer surveys in the spring and summer of 1992.

5. Details of a Polish case study, which deals with this aspect based on 1992 public opinion data, are available from Jadwiga Koralewicz.

6. We are indebted to Hans-Dieter Klingemann and his associates in the Baltic World Values Study for making available to us the rich interview data (summer 1990) for these four Baltic countries.

7. The trust items in the Baltic World Values Study and the Eurobarometer survey are not comparable.

8. It has been insinuated, for example, that Baltic Jews were instrumental in engineering the Soviet take-over in 1940, and again in 1945, and many Baltic Jews were portrayed as war criminals.

9. There are missing data for Hungary on some of the perceptual and attitudinal variables, and missing data for Poland on age and education.

10. In the 1992 East European Eurobarometer survey, 91% of Albanian respondents said they were in favour of the EC; 44% believed that Albania should become a full member immediately or at least within the next five years; and 54% said they had seriously considered going to work in Western Europe. These data testify to a widespread and deeply felt desire to work outside Albania as well a genuine wish for Albania to be integrated into Western Europe.

11. The Czechoslovak sample is representative of the proportional distribution of the two peoples in the federation; thus, Czech respondents outweigh Slovaks by 2 to 1.

16

NATO, the European Community, and the United Nations

PHILIP EVERTS

❖

Analysing attitudes towards the North Atlantic Treaty Organization (NATO) and, in so far as the data permit, towards the United Nations enable us to address two key questions concerning public opinion and internationalized governance. First: can public support for an agency of internationalized governance withstand fundamental contextual change, even changes in the very mission of the agency? Is public opinion, in other words, a resource which a regime can draw on during a period of transition? The second question is more theoretical. Is there a single continuum of attitudes corresponding to the continuum of internationalized governance—that is, corresponding to the degree to which authority is transferred to international institutions? Or, on the contrary, are attitudes and orientations multi-dimensional, depending on the nature of the issues involved? Building on the distinction between 'militant internationalism' and 'cooperative internationalism' (Wittkopf 1986; 1991; Wittkopf and Maggiotto 1983), and on Ziegler's study of the dimensionality of attitudes in this area (Ziegler 1987), this chapter examines whether attitudes towards the EC, NATO, and the United Nations (UN) belong to one and the same dimension of attitudes towards internationalized governance, or represent distinct and separate dimensions.

Why Study NATO Now?

In one view, NATO could conclude that its task has been completed and thus could dissolve itself, close the offices, and go home. In this view, NATO is at best an organization in search of a mission. Yet one could argue that NATO's task is by no means over and its continued existence is as essential as before. In fact, in a situation in which everything has become possible and Europe is threatened by new, manifest, and latent instabilities, it is often argued that NATO represents the only functioning international security institution in Europe. Its possible roles include providing the physical and organizational framework for the involvement of the United States in the security of Europe; acting as the framework in which German power can be embedded, or 'neutralized'; preventing a 'renationalization' of military power in Europe; constituting a counterweight to what is still the most powerful state in the area, Russia;[1] and, finally, providing the organizational framework for conflict management on behalf of the Conference on Security and Co-operation in Europe (CSCE)—more recently the Organization for Security and Co-operation in Europe (OSCE). Even if one allows for a degree of self-perpetuation and self-interest underlying such arguments, it is hard to deny the validity of some of these considerations. However, the circumstances under which NATO will have to function in the coming years will be very different indeed, including first and foremost the absence of a clearly defined threat and a much reduced American presence.

The outcome of these developments will be decided, in the main, by traditional foreign policy and strategic considerations. But even successful political institutions with considerable bureaucratic momentum cannot survive in a democracy without public support. Hence, the question whether, and to what extent, the public support given to NATO in the past will also be forthcoming in the different circumstances of the future is crucial. On the one hand, we might argue that support for NATO (except in a few countries) has generally been high in the past. Indeed, there was support to such a degree that, notwithstanding recurring doubts about its effectiveness and often strong disagreement about some of its policies, the conclusion seems warranted that the institution was taken for granted. To the extent that this support has fluctuated over time, these fluctuations seem to have little to do with specific policies, nor with fear of an aggressive Soviet Union (Feld and Wildgen 1982) but, rather, with domestic affairs on the one hand, and attitudes towards the United States and its policies on the other (Munton 1990; Wecke 1987). This would mean that 'belief in NATO' is somehow divorced from considerations drawn from concrete historical situations; consequently, one might expect that the degree of support in the past will be carried over into the future as a matter of course. This is one hypothesis to be tested.

It is quite conceivable, however, that, with the disappearance of Cold War certainties, the stability and continuity in orientations with respect to NATO and security policies more generally (Eichenberg 1989; Russett, 1990) will also disappear. This is the alternative hypothesis. In fact, the allegedly greater sophistication of the general public with respect to international affairs[2] may well have been an artefact of a basically stable international environment. If this were true, there would be little we could say on the likely evolution of public orientations towards NATO as an institution. Examining the available data should therefore help to establish the confidence we may have in extrapolating from the past to the future in regard to public support for NATO.

If the question 'Why study NATO now?' has at least to be posed, the equivalent question for the United Nations seems otiose. The UN has been freed from the constraints imposed by the pervasive bipolar confrontation which characterized the Cold War and can now concentrate on the functions assigned to it in the UN Charter. The organization may have many problems but they are not problems of relevance. However, from the point of view of our interest in public opinion and political culture, there are two difficulties in studying attitudes to the United Nations. The first arises from the remoteness of the object and the lack of detailed knowledge of it. This is not so much a methodological problem as a characteristic of the attitude domain in question and a challenge to research. To the limited extent that the data permit, it will be taken up again below. But this brings us to the second problem, which is methodological and which arises from the scarcity of data on attitudes to the UN. This is best considered in the context of a general consideration of data availability.

Sources and Data

Our examination of orientations towards NATO focuses mainly on diffuse evaluations of NATO membership rather than on specific evaluations of NATO policies (see Chapter 3). Although the available data vary considerably from country to country, time series data on evaluations of NATO membership can be constructed for several countries. Aiming for full coverage of policy evaluations, however, would force us to deal with a large variety of defence policy matters in which it is often difficult to separate the domestic from the international aspects. Moreover, these questions have been dealt with extensively by others and there is little to be added to their findings; for example, in regard to the deployment of new nuclear missiles in Europe in the late 1970s and early 1980s (de Boer 1985; Eichenberg 1989; Flickinger 1983; 1984; Flynn and Rattinger 1985; Mortensen 1983; Russett and Deluca 1983).

The data on attitudes to NATO examined in this chapter have been collected from many different sources.[3] First, there are data from the numerous polls conducted on an *ad hoc* or single country basis for the media or other organizations. Secondly, there is the regular biannual Eurobarometer series. Unfortunately, unlike the problems of integration and international institution-building in general, questions of defence and international security get less attention in these surveys. Thirdly, there are the frequent but irregular surveys conducted on behalf of the United States Information Agency (USIA). Although preoccupied with US standing in world affairs, these surveys provide useful information for our purposes. Unfortunately, these data are difficult to get hold of and are not easily available for further inspection (Eichenberg 1989: 244–45).[4] In general, we have rather abundant information on Germany and the Netherlands and hardly anything on Greece, Spain, or Portugal. This is only partly due to difficulties in accessing data sources: in most instances the data simply do not exist. The available data are also unevenly distributed over time and are of uneven quality. These considerations will be taken into account when they impinge on interpretations of attitudes towards NATO.

Public opinion data on the United Nations and its activities are almost non-existent. While a search of available sources yielded more than 1,300 questions on NATO as an international institution, less than 150 questions were asked about the UN, including many which are hardly useful.[5] Only a few surveys permit comparisons over time and across countries. One of the most useful is Eurobarometer, No. 32 (1989), which repeated questions from two earlier Gallup International surveys and included some additional questions.[6] While the paucity of public opinion data on one of the most important international institutions is appalling, the data which are available enable us to include the United

Nations in examining the dimensionality of attitudes to internationalized governance.

Attitudes Towards NATO

Figure 16.1 shows 'net support' for NATO in the five countries for
which a reasonably long time series can be constructed. The level of net
support is calculated as the proportion of proponents of NATO membership minus the proportion of opponents. With the exception of Spain,
support for membership in these countries has generally been high
throughout the period of NATO's existence, with, in fact, some tendency for the level of support to increase over time. Looking at

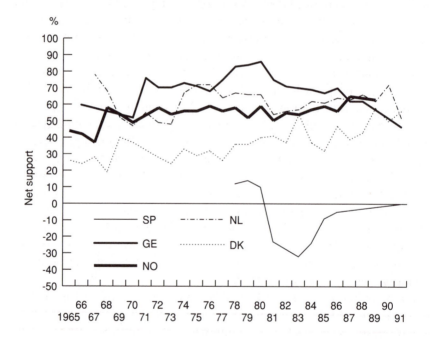

FIGURE 16.1. *Net support for NATO membership, 1965–91*

Sources: Data Bank Institute for International Studies, Leiden University; Sørensen
(1990); Everts (1983; 1984–90); Flynn and Rattinger (1985); Capitanchik and Eichenberg (1983); Noelle-Neuman (1983); Rattinger (1987; 1991); Rattinger and Heinlein
(1986); Reports Civilian Affairs Committee, North Atlantic Assembly (1985; 1986;
1988); EMNID, *Meinungskilma sur wehrpolitischen Lage, 1970–89*; Santamaría and
Alcover (1987).

countries for which only more limited data on this question are available suggests that this increase also occurred in Belgium and Britain. It is also evident that the level of support for membership has traditionally been lower in the southern European countries generally, not just in Spain.

Apart from these general trends there have also been fluctuations in particular countries which call for explanation. However, the fact that the fluctuations do not coincide in time makes it difficult to discover common causes. For example, it is tempting to explain the clear dip in Dutch support in the period 1968–73 by pointing to prevailing critical attitudes towards US policies in Vietnam. If this were the cause, it remains to be explained why a similar dip cannot be observed in comparable countries like Norway and Denmark.

The view that fluctuations in popular support for NATO stem primarily from domestic sources and the peculiarities of national situations is reinforced when we turn to net support based on a question about whether 'NATO is still essential', reported in Figure 16.2. However, there are three periods during which, with just a few exceptions, support for NATO dips down at more or less the same time in all seven countries considered in Figure 16.2. The first is a slight fall around 1971. The second occurs around 1980–2, years of extensive protest against the new generation of INF weapons. In this case, France was the exception. This is also true with respect to the third commonality: the downturn in the perceived need for NATO which starts around 1984 in almost all the countries and lasts until 1989. In France the opposite occurred, with NATO being gradually seen by more people than before as 'still essential'. Since 1989, although still below the average, France follows the general pattern of steadily recovering support for the notion that, even in the post-Cold War circumstances, NATO is 'still essential'.[7]

When we compare attitudes towards membership with attitudes to the 'still essential' role of NATO in the countries for which data on both are available (Denmark, Germany, and the Netherlands), it is clear that in recent years more people subscribed to the desirability of membership than to the notion that NATO is essential. This trend is most marked in the Netherlands. The general upswing in the belief that NATO is essential which occurred during 1989–91 reduces these gaps. It also brings us directly to the question of whether attitudes to NATO have been fundamentally changed by the 'events' of autumn 1989.

The data in Figure 16.2 certainly suggest that the fall of the Berlin

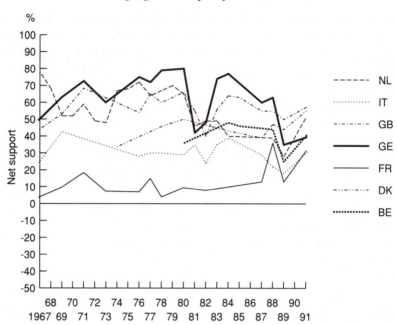

FIGURE 16.2. *Is NATO still essential?*

Sources: USIA; Eurobarometer, Nos. 14, 30, 32, and 35; NIPO (1967–84); Eichenberg (1989); *Public Opinion*, 12 (1989: 21); Sabin (1990); Sørensen (1990); Szabo (1989); Treverton (1985).

wall had a dramatic effect on attitudes. The data for 1989 are from Eurobarometer, No. 32, for which the fieldwork was carried out in October and November 1989. As measured in this set of surveys, belief that NATO is essential fell in all countries and fell precipitously in some. Figure 16.2 also indicates, however, that by 1991 NATO had recovered most of the ground it had lost.[8] This lends support to the hypothesis that NATO is largely seen as a successful organization, with support having become more or less divorced from specific situations and policies.

The shifts in attitudes on the need for NATO correlate with shifting expectations concerning the likelihood of a new world war. However, as we can see from Figure 16.3, fluctuations in the fear of war show much stronger uniformity cross-nationally than fluctuations in support for NATO. The correlation takes two quite different forms, one of which is rather surprising if one reasons that a high degree of war fever should correlate with more support for NATO. As fear of a world war declined in the early 1980s, after a sudden rise, the degree to which NATO was seen as 'still essential' declined as well. However, in the period up to 1981, rising fear of a world war was accompanied by declining support for NATO. An explanation could be that many then saw NATO as part of the problem rather than as part of the solution.[9] Finally, before leaving Figure 16.3, it is worth noting the sudden re-emergence of fear of war in 1990, a fear which is clearly a consequence of the conflict in the Persian Gulf.

So far we have focused on general attitudes towards NATO. The extent of such support does not, however, imply equal levels of support for NATO policies.[10] Indeed, it is often alleged or feared that, because of a primitive sort of 'domino effect', opposition to NATO policies would inescapably lead to reduced support for NATO as such. The available evidence does not support this conclusion.[11] That a favourable

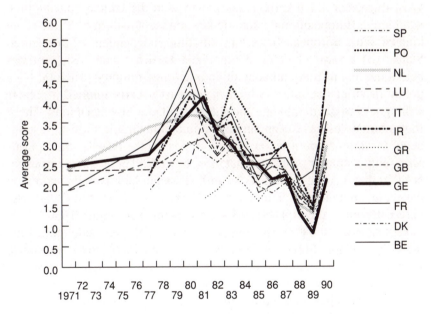

FIGURE 16.3. *Perceived danger of a new world war*

Note: The question wording is: 'Would you, with the help of this card, tell me how you assess the chance of a world war breaking out in the next 10 years?' Respondents could choose their response from a scale ranging from 'No danger at all' to 'World war certain'. The figure shows average scores per country on a 1–10 scale.

Sources: Eurobarometer, Nos. 0, 8, 13, 16, 18, 20, 22, 26, 28, 30, and 34.

orientation towards NATO in general need not always be accompanied by confidence in NATO's policies appears, for instance, from a comparison between Tables 16.1 and 16.2. With the exception of Germany and Portugal, fewer people were confident that NATO's policies are in the best interest of their country (Table 16.2) compared to those who exhibit a favourable orientation towards NATO (Table 16.1). At the same time, however, there is a strong correlation between these two dimensions (tau-c = 0.51 for the EC as a whole).

NATO and Some Alternatives

While today a wider range of alternatives comes to mind, over the years basically four alternatives for the organization of collective security in Western Europe can be distinguished: (1) a unified separate collective West European defence force associated with the United States which would give Europeans considerable say and responsibility; (2) the same kind of West European force, but this time independent of the United States; (3) a form of defence organized on a national basis, without belonging to a military alliance or an integrated military structure; (4) a policy of strict neutrality (which in the past usually implied a greater willingness to accommodate the interests of the Soviet Union). These four alternatives have been submitted in a comparable form to respondents in various countries at various times. Since each of the options represents a greater or lesser 'distance' from NATO or some variant of NATO, they can be treated as an ordinal scale, and average scores on the scale calculated.[12] 'Support for NATO over alternatives' can thus vary between 0 and 1. The results are presented in Figure 16.4.

Whether we look at the average scores for the scale or at the individual items, three patterns are evident. First, there is strong support for NATO compared to alternative forms of organizing security. Secondly, support has risen considerably since the end of the 1950s when it was first measured. Thirdly, in the 1980s support varied relatively little over time and across countries.[13] As might be expected, the French were much more likely to favour other forms of organizing security, either nationally or on a separate West European basis, although French support for NATO has been increasing over time.

The question of whether NATO represents the best way of organizing European security has also been measured in other ways. Moreover,

TABLE 16.1. *Overall opinion of NATO, 1989*

	BE	DK	FR	GE	GB	GR	IR	IT	NL	PO	SP
Very favourable	11	28	7	16	25	10	14	14	13	8	8
Somewhat favourable	48	40	38	45	44	29	31	42	52	34	25
Somewhat unfavourable	14	14	12	15	7	20	8	17	14	6	19
Very unfavourable	5	6	3	6	3	19	4	5	3	2	21
Has not heard enough to say	18	11	28	11	15	8	23	12	12	29	15
No reply	5	1	12	7	7	15	20	10	7	21	12
Average scores	22	35	15	23	38	-4	17	19	27	16	-9
N	826	893	721	1,015	807	925	751	906	913	709	839

Notes: Entries are percentages. Question wording: 'What is your overall opinion of NATO, that is, the North Atlantic Treaty Organization of Western Europe, the United States, and Canada? Is your opinion of NATO very favourable, somewhat favourable, somewhat unfavourable, or very unfavourable, or have you not heard enough about NATO to say?' Average scores can vary between 100 and −100. The question was not asked in Luxembourg.

Source: Eurobarometer, No. 32.

TABLE 16.2. *Confidence in NATO, 1989*

	BE	DK	FR	GE	GB	GR	IR	IT	NL	PO	SP
Great deal of confidence	9	20	5	12	14	7	9	7	7	8	5
Fair amount of confidence	44	39	37	42	48	15	33	33	43	36	23
Not very much confidence	26	26	22	29	19	28	15	36	34	12	30
No confidence at all	8	8	5	8	6	30	12	8	7	5	20
No reply	13	7	31	7	14	20	31	17	10	40	22
Average scores	17	27	5	9	19	−24	4	−2	4	19	−14
N	1,000	997	997	1,106	960	1,013	968	1,033	1,042	998	984

Notes: Entries are percentages. Question wording: 'How much confidence do you have that decisions made by NATO will be in the best interest of [your country]? Do you have a great deal of confidence, a fair amount of confidence, not very much confidence, no confidence at all?' Average scores can vary between 100 and −100. The question was not asked in Luxembourg.

Source: Eurobarometer, No. 32.

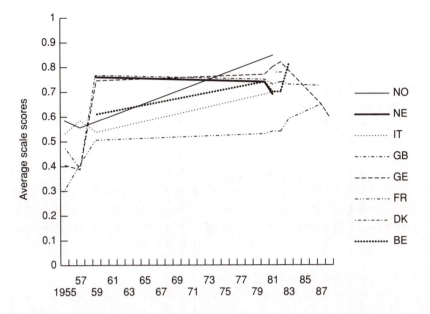

FIGURE 16.4. *Support for NATO over alternative security arrangements, 1955–88*

Sources: Databank Institute for International Studies, Leiden University; USIA (1955, 1957, 1981); Eurobarometer, Nos. 11 and 13; GIRI (1982); Panorama-IMR (Belgium); Louis Harris (France); DOXA (Italy); SOFRIES (France). See also Erskine (1969); Eichenberg (1989), Flynn and Rattinger (1985).

with the deepening of European integration and the challenge to the *raison d'être* of NATO, the issue of NATO versus the European Community as the locus for European collective security has become more salient. Public attitudes on this issue in November 1989 are presented in Table 16.3. It is only in Denmark, Germany, Britain, and the Netherlands that pluralities (in Denmark a clear majority) expressed themselves in favour of NATO. In Belgium, Ireland, and Portugal opinion was divided, and in France, Greece, Italy, and Spain the European Community emerges as the preferred vehicle for common defence. This is roughly reflected in the positions taken by the respective governments in recent debates on this issue.

TABLE 16.3. *Best forum for making decisions about West European security, 1989*

	BE	DK	FR	GE	GB	GR	IR	IT	NL	PO	SP
NATO	36	60	21	45	42	8	21	19	41	24	12
European Community	33	11	43	28	30	49	35	45	37	23	42
West European Union	5	1	3	2	1	5	1	15	2	3	2
Other organizations	5	9	1	3	5	5	4	1	3	1	4
Nobody: we should make our own decisions spontaneous	8	8	6	10	6	9	8	3	4	8	14
No reply	13	12	25	13	17	23	31	16	13	41	26
N	993	1,004	1,009	1,131	958	1,012	965	1,033	1,032	1,005	988

Notes: Entries are percentages. Question wording: 'In your opinion should NATO [in France, the 'Atlantic Alliance'] continue to be the most important forum for making decisions about the security of Western Europe in the future, or should the European Community make these decisions, or should some other organization make these decisions?' The question was not asked in Luxembourg.

Source: Eurobarometer, No. 32.

Geopolitics of Attitudes Towards NATO

In dealing with general trends in attitudes towards NATO, we have encountered evidence of considerable differences between countries—both in attitudes on particular issues and in fluctuations over time (see Tables 16.1–16.3). To probe more systematically into these differences, we dichotomized and summed the scores for each of five measures of commitment to NATO. Table 16.4 presents the correlations among the original five indicators and between these and the overall index. The results give sufficient confidence that this measure is a reliable indicator of overall attitudes.

The aggregate scores on this NATO index by country are presented in Figure 16.5. They suggest a geopolitical division at the level of mass opinion between north and south, with the Germanic north looking towards the Atlantic and the Mediterranean south looking inward towards Europe. Opinion in France shows a somewhat mixed perspective. Portugal, however, is a strong exception to any generalization we might make about southern countries, but this can be accounted for in geopolitical and historical terms.

These differences between countries suggest that we need to examine the distribution of opinion in each country across the full range of the NATO index. We do this in Table 16.5. Figure 16.6 supplements these data by presenting the profile for each country. The profiles are based on the scores for each of the five constituent variables of the NATO index, to which have been added the scores on the separate dimension 'need for a strong defence'.

TABLE 16.4. *Relationship between the constituent variables of the NATO index, 1989*

	1	2	3	4	5
1. Favourable opinion of NATO	—				
2. NATO essential for security	0.61	—			
3. Confidence in NATO decisions	0.51	0.59	—		
4. NATO or EC best forum for defence	0.25	0.51	0.29	—	
5. US military presence necessary	0.33	0.52	0.32	0.23	—

Notes: Entries are correlation scores (Cramer's *V*). Pooled data.

Source: Eurobarometer, No. 32.

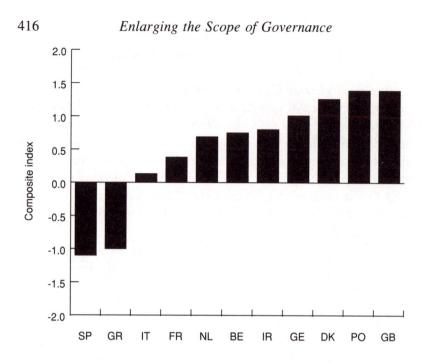

FIGURE 16.5. *Composite index of commitment to NATO by country, 1989*
Source: Eurobarometer, No. 32.

In Belgium and the Netherlands we see comparable profiles: a relatively favourable orientation towards NATO, and widespread belief that NATO is still necessary and that NATO decisions are in the best interests of the country. However, these attitudes are combined with a relatively low degree of belief in the effectiveness of NATO and in the need for strong defence. Greece represents the very opposite case. While there is widespread belief in the need for strong defence, NATO enjoys relatively little sympathy and trust. Together with Spain, but quite unlike Portugal, Greece is to be found at the lower end of the scale of general commitment to NATO. The profiles of Denmark and Germany also have many elements in common. They share a relatively high degree of support for NATO on all dimensions, but a low degree of belief in the necessity of strong defence. The Danes in particular are not highly supportive of an EC role in defence policy. The view that the EC, rather than NATO, constitutes the best forum for defence is relatively favoured in France, a view faithfully reflected in the country's policies.

TABLE 16.5. *Index of commitment to NATO by country, 1989*

	BE	DK	FR	GE	GB	GR	IR	IT	NL	PO	SP	Mean
Very strongly pro-NATO	30	42	16	42	37	8	23	19	25	41	7	27
Strongly pro-NATO	22	25	26	21	27	16	28	20	24	28	16	23
Somewhat pro-NATO	15	8	19	8	16	13	20	18	17	10	10	14
Somewhat anti-NATO	11	6	15	6	8	10	10	13	11	6	8	9
Strongly anti-NATO	7	5	10	7	6	11	9	9	10	5	12	8
Very strongly anti-NATO	15	14	15	17	6	41	10	21	14	10	47	19
N	654	734	451	760	631	572	402	598	668	408	539	

Note: Entries are percentages.

Source: Eurobarometer, No. 32.

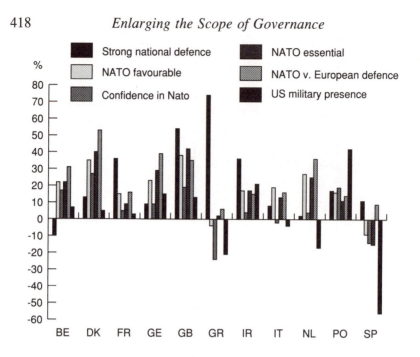

FIGURE 16.6. *Country profiles of attitudes towards NATO and national defence, 1989*

Source: Eurobarometer, No. 32.

On the other dimensions, the French do not stand out for their strong opinions but fall into the middle group. With the British, the Greeks, and the Irish, the French tend to believe in the need of a strong defence. Germans are most outspoken with respect to the question of whether NATO has been effective as a defence organization. Many of them also favour NATO as the forum for collective defence policy. Italy clusters towards the lower end of the scale because opinions are less outspoken on most dimensions than in the other countries. There is less support for strong national defence than for NATO, but confidence in NATO as an effective organization is low. In this matter of confidence, opinion in Italy is surpassed only by Spain and Greece.

The significance of these variations between countries is highlighted by the fact that only one of the several socio-demographic and political variables tested shows a substantial relationship to the NATO index. This is the relationship with left–right self-placement, a finding which is in line with earlier research (Eichenberg 1989; Flynn and Rattinger 1985; McIntosh and MacIver 1994). This result brings us directly to the second question raised at the outset of this chapter: do attitudes towards international governance constitute one single dimension, perhaps one closely aligned with the left–right dimension, or are attitudes multidimensional and dependent on particular issues and particular institutions?

Structure of Attitudes towards Internationalized Governance

The unidimensional view could also be thought of as the federalist view: that attitudes towards internationalized governance can be arranged on a single nationalism–internationalism scale, with all pre-ferences for international co-operation being part of a general orienta-tion. In this view, support for European co-operation would go together with support for NATO, the UN, and so on. The other hypothesis, which one might label the functionalist view, contends that people make distinctions between various issue areas and may subscribe to inter-nationalization in some areas but not in others.

An early attempt to probe this issue was made by Ziegler (1987), who analysed data from eleven questions in Eurobarometer, No. 14 (1980). The factor analysis produced two independent dimensions—or sets of orientations. The first was 'military co-operation' consisting of (*a*) defence expenditure, (*b*) the necessity of NATO for peace, (*c*) the rejection of alternatives to NATO, (*d*) the priority for defence, and (*e*) the reliability of the United States. The second was 'non-military co-operation' consisting of (*a*) the unification of Europe, (*b*) the desirability of a common European–American foreign policy, and (*c*) the desirability of a common economic policy on the part of Japan, the European Community, and the United States. A third factor (expecta-tion with respect to future stability) was unrelated to any other and was left out of consideration. This research suggests that two separate attitudes on internationalized governance exist side by side, one con-cerning military matters, the other concerning foreign policy co-opera-tion in general. Combining the two dimensions produced four groups with the following labels and distributions in the four countries included in the analysis: 'military allies' (21 per cent); 'Atlanticists' (34 per cent); 'dovish partners' (20 per cent), and 'isolationists' (25 per cent). An Atlanticist attitude prevailed in Germany, the French were relatively the most isolationist, most of the British were 'military allies', and among the Italians there was a preference for being 'dovish partners'.

Was this structure of attitudes peculiar to 1980 and the onset of the 'new Cold War'? What happens if we add data about attitudes to the United Nations? How do attitudes in these areas vary and co-vary over time? To address these questions we performed a principal components factor analysis of survey items dealing with the EC, NATO, and the UN contained in Eurobarometer, No. 32 (1989). Our findings are reported in Table 16.6.

The analysis yielded three factors with eigen-values greater than 1.00. Together, the three factors accounted for 54 per cent of the variance. The factor loadings suggest that the first factor consists of attitudes related to European integration. The second factor relates to military co-operation and defence matters in an Atlantic framework and can be labelled 'military integration'. The third factor, which is also an independent dimension, refers to the United Nations.[14] The distribution of high and low loadings on each of the factors and, in particular, the lack of any substantial overlap created by the same questions having substantial loadings on more than one factor, indicate that we are, indeed, dealing with independent attitudinal dimensions. It seems

TABLE 16.6. *Structure of attitudes towards EC, NATO, and UN, 1989*

Variables	Orthogonally rotated factors		
	I	II	III
EC membership	0.76	0.06	0.03
Unification of Europe favoured	0.69	0.00	−0.02
Benefit of European integration	0.69	0.04	0.12
Regret if EC were dissolved	0.62	0.02	−0.16
Confidence in EC decisions	0.50	0.26	0.32
US military presence in Europe	0.03	0.75	−0.07
Opinion on NATO	0.05	0.83	0.09
NATO still essential	0.03	0.79	0.03
EC or NATO responsible for defence	0.09	0.59	0.19
Strong national defence	0.05	0.54	−0.39
UN doing a good job	0.02	0.16	0.82
Variance explained	28.9%	16.8%	8.4%

Notes: Entries are factor loadings; pooled data.

Source: Eurobarometer, No. 32.

safe, therefore, to conclude that attitudes on internationalized governance do constitute a multi-dimensional structure as far as the EC,
NATO, and the UN are concerned. What prevails are the ends rather
than the means of international co-operation—the functionalist rather
than the federalist view.

With this multidimensional structure in mind, it is worth looking
again at the distribution of attitudes towards internationalized governance over time. Attitudes towards the United Nations will be dealt with
first, both because of the finding that attitudes towards the UN constitute a separate dimension and because, as emphasized already, data in
this area are neither as plentiful nor as revealing as one would wish. The
other two dimensions of attitudes towards internationalized governance
will then be examined in combination.

Knowledge and Evaluation of the United Nations

In 1989, on average, 88 per cent of the populations of EC countries had
heard about the United Nations. The actual proportions vary between 99
per cent in Denmark and 72 per cent in Portugal. This level of
awareness, which was just as high in 1974, seems related to whether
or not students are taught about the United Nations in school. Knowledge does not seem to go very deep, however. Only 26 per cent of all
respondents were able to mention a UN agency or body—about half the
figure for the same question in 1974. Among the bodies mentioned,
UNESCO and UNICEF came out on top. From a list of all secretaries
general, 41 per cent were able to name correctly the Secretary General
at the time (Mr Perez de Cuellar). Respondents displayed a lively
interest in the issues dealt with by the United Nations with the environment, human rights, international peace and security, and drug abuse
heading the list.

Uncertainty and lack of knowledge also seem at play in the high
proportion of respondents (36 per cent) who did not answer the question
about whether the UN is 'doing a good job or a poor job in trying to
solve the problems it has to face' (see Table 16.7). It is also quite
possible, however, to attribute this to the vagueness of the question. To
the extent that people were willing to make a judgement on the
performance of the UN, that judgement was largely positive: 51 per
cent of all respondents (80 per cent of those who gave an answer) said

TABLE 16.7. *Ratings of the performance of the United Nations, 1985 and 1989*

	1985			1989			
	Good	Poor	d.k./n.a.	Good	Poor	d.k./n.a.	N
Belgium	34	17	49	52	14	34	1,000
Denmark	—	—	—	73	10	17	1,000
Britain	26	47	27	50	24	26	947
France	—	—	—	46	13	41	999
Germany	25	31	44	47	8	44	1,129
Greece	31	36	33	45	20	35	1,007
Ireland	—	—	—	58	10	32	965
Italy	—	—	—	43	9	48	1,085
Netherlands	66	23	12	50	14	36	1,045
Portugal	17	14	69	44	3	53	998
Spain	—	—	—	53	8	39	986
Mean	33	28	39	51	13	36	

Notes: Entries are percentages. *N* are not available for the 1985 data. Question wording: 'In general, do you think that the United Nations is doing a good job or a poor job in trying to solve the problems it has to face?' 'd.k.' = 'don't know'; 'n.a.' = 'not available'.

Sources: Gallup International (1985); Eurobarometer, No. 32.

that the UN was doing 'a good job'. This was a slight increase on the 1974 figure of 45 per cent.

In addition to the results for 1989, Table 16.7 shows results for 1985 for six countries for which comparable figures are available. Taking the simple arithmetic mean of the figures in the first column (other measures not being available), in 1985, on average, only 33 per cent of the people in these six countries thought the UN was 'doing a good job'. In each of these six countries except one, the rating of the UN improved significantly in 1989. The exception was the Netherlands where its rating in 1985 (66 per cent) was unusually high.

In summarizing the findings on attitudes towards the United Nations, the point to be emphasized is the inadequacy of the available data. The UN is a highly important institution of internationalized governance, and the data which do exist suggest that attitudes towards it constitute a separate dimension of attitudes towards internationalized governance. However, even this finding must remain tentative, given the limited data on which it is based. In terms of the substance of attitudes, all we know is that there is a high level of awareness of the United Nations, a low level of knowledge about some of its component elements, a high degree of interest in several of the key problems it tackles, and an overall positive evaluation of the institution itself. All this, however, is accompanied by a very high level of 'don't knows'. These findings relate to 1989. Given the growth in the importance of this institution since then, a comprehensive study of attitudes towards the United Nations is imperative.

Attitudes Towards Non-Military Co-operation

Earlier we examined attitudes towards military co-operation in international relations. Attitudes towards various forms of non-military—largely economic—co-operation and integration are dealt with elsewhere in this volume. This division of labour is justified by the results of our factor analysis showing that these two areas do indeed constitute separate attitudinal dimensions.[15] However, it is now time to consider the two sets of attitudes in tandem.[16]

Concentrating on the two dimensions of 'European integration' and 'military integration' we can identify four main groups, which, partly following Ziegler,[17] can be labelled as follows: (1) integrationists, who favour both military (NATO) and civilian (EC) co-operation; (2) non-military partners, favouring co-operation within the EC but opposed to NATO; (3) military allies, favouring co-operation with NATO but opposed to European integration; and (4) isolationists, who oppose co-operation with both the EC and NATO. However, the full set of variables on which the factor analysis is based is available only for 1989. Accordingly, in analysing developments in these attitudes, we have had to rely on single items. The European integration dimension has been measured by the 'unification' question in 1957, but by the membership question in 1980, 1989, and 1991. The military co-operation dimension has been measured by the question about confidence in NATO in 1957 but, for subsequent years, by the question on whether NATO is essential.

The question about EC membership allows respondents to take a middle position, 'neither for nor against'. Non-respondents on this question can be included in this middle category. By doing the same with the unification and the NATO questions, we obtain a 3 × 3 table. This can be reduced to more manageable proportions by concentrating on the four main groups identified above, together with those who give a neutral or 'don't know' response on both questions (here labelled simply 'don't knows') plus those who take a middle or 'don't know' position on only one of the two dimensions. The latter are here labelled 'doubters'. The distributions of these six groups over time—for the countries for which data are available—are given in Table 16.8.

Perhaps the most remarkable feature of the evolution of these attitudes is the increasing outspokenness of the European public. This is evident, first, in the drop in the numbers who decline to state their views on both questions. While some 20–30 per cent of national populations were 'don't knows' in the late 1950s, by 1991 the proportion approached zero in most countries. The acronyms EC and NATO have become household words, and questions about them seldom elicit a non-response. Moreover, the public has become considerably more polarized in the sense that the proportion of doubters, those who take a middle position on one of the dimensions, has declined consistently since 1980.

With one or two exceptions (such as Spain in 1989) 'integrationists' have always carried the day over those who are either committed to more limited forms of integration or co-operation, or who are sceptical. By and large, integrationists have gradually become the majority in Belgium, the Netherlands, Denmark, Germany, Italy, and Portugal. The Danish case represents a dramatic change since 1980. Although in 1991 integrationists remained short of a majority in France and Britain, they were not all that far short, and the evolution of attitudes in both these countries since 1957 is very striking. A considerable shift towards the integrationist position took place between 1989 and 1991, although this should be seen in the light of the fact, noted above, that 1989 was a fairly bad year for NATO. The proportion of 'non-military partners'— the second largest group in all countries—has varied over time, but has generally tended to decline, at least in the most recent period. It is the only group which has not profited from the polarization process we noted. The two other groups have always been small. With the exception of Denmark in 1989, the 'isolationists' have never numbered more than 10 per cent in any country. More recently, however, there has been some increase in the size of this group. Also the proportion of 'military allies'—those who endorse military integration but reject integration in other areas—has increased somewhat in most countries since 1980.

Analysis of these attitudes in the EC as a whole in 1989 and 1991 reveals a substantial increase in support for the combination of economic (EC) and military (NATO) integration, or co-operation, to the

TABLE 16.8. *Orientations towards military and non-military international governance, various years*

	Integrationists	Economic partners	Military allies	Isolationists	Doubters	Don't know
France						
1957	14	12	1	5	38	30
1980	20	12	2	3	41	21
1989	30	20	2	3	35	11
1991	46	16	9	5	23	2
Germany						
1957	49	17	2	4	21	7
1980	55	3	4	1	29	8
1989	44	15	4	3	27	7
1991	56	13	10	6	15	1
Italy						
1957	35	13	1	5	27	20
1980	41	14	1	2	31	11
1989	38	22	1	4	29	8
1991	51	21	6	4	19	—
Britain						
1957	27	18	4	5	27	20
1980	22	1	31	7	35	5
1989	39	9	10	4	32	7
1991	46	8	18	4	22	2
Belgium						
1980	32	8	2	2	31	25
1989	44	20	2	3	26	5
1991	52	17	9	4	17	1
Denmark						
1980	3	5	3	6	55	28
1989	34	5	13	12	33	4
1991	53	8	13	4	21	1
Netherlands						
1980	52	16	2	3	23	5
1989	51	24	2	1	20	3
1991	67	18	5	3	9	—
Ireland						
1989	35	13	2	2	33	14
1991	42	17	6	2	31	1
Greece						
1989	35	23	—	4	29	9
1991	47	19	3	7	23	1
Portugal						
1989	32	10	—	2	33	23
1991	57	8	6	2	26	1
Spain						
1989	18	31	1	3	33	14
1991	37	33	5	7	18	1
All						
1989	36	18	7	4	33	10
1991	49	18	8	5	20	1

Note: Entries are percentages.

Sources: USIA (1957); Eurobarometer, Nos. 14, 32, and 35.

point where it constitutes almost a majority position (49 per cent). This increase appears to have taken place at the expense of the doubters and the 'don't knows' while the other three groups stayed at more or less the same size.

Conclusion

However we measure commitment, it is evident that NATO has enjoyed a great deal of loyalty and commitment in most member countries throughout its existence. This commitment appears to have survived the momentous international changes in recent years. These observations should not cause us to overlook the fluctuations of support over time in particular countries, nor the sometimes major differences in support levels among the countries concerned. The fluctuations over time show no recognizable pattern, with the exception of a slight secular trend towards increasing support and confidence in the effectiveness of the organization. There are, however, considerable differences in levels of support for NATO along a north–south dividing line in Europe. Moreover, that the need for NATO is subscribed to by large numbers in most countries of Western Europe does not at all imply that support for NATO's policies can be taken for granted.

It is noteworthy also that many perceive a role for other organizations in the realm of security, the EC and NATO in particular being in potential competition in this regard. There seems to be a generally shared notion that, no matter how one thinks about the need for strong military forces, countries can no longer find security outside the framework of international organizations. In northern Europe, NATO remains the preferred forum; among southern EC states (with the exception of Portugal), there is much more sympathy for the idea of dealing with security issues primarily via the European Community.

These conclusions must be seen in light of our finding that attitudes towards the internationalization of governance are clearly multi-dimensional. They cannot be arrayed simply on a general continuum from 'nationalism' to 'federalism' or 'internationalism', but are heavily influenced by responses to specific issues. This is underscored by the finding reported in Chapter 11, that support for internationalized governance is more extensive in some policy areas than in others. In sum, orientations towards internationalized governance can be best described in terms of functionalist categories. Issue dependence also implies, however, that if there is such a thing as a spill-over effect, which is central to neo-functionalist theory, it is neither general nor automatic in the case of public opinion.

NOTES

1. Although it has become far-fetched to imagine a large-scale military confrontation of the kind NATO has traditionally prepared for, Russia could yet evolve into a threat as a highly nationalistic revanchist power.
2. This is in contrast to earlier authors who stressed the volatility and 'moodiness' of public opinion (see Everts and Faber 1990)
3. An inventory of available Eurobarometer data on matters of defence, international security, and related issues has been drawn up by Phillipe Manigart, Royale Militaire Belge, Brussels. Useful general secondary sources are the regular summaries in *Public Opinion*, *Public Opinion Quarterly*, and the annual *Index to Public Opinion* (ed. E. H. and P. K. Hastings). The *SIPRI Yearbook on World Armaments and Disarmament* contains a useful annual section on public opinion in the period 1984–1986 (den Oudsten 1984, 1985, 1986). General studies of available data covering several countries include Adler (1986; Adler and Wertman 1981); De Boer (1981, 1985); Capitanchik and Eichenberg (1983); Eichenberg (1989); Erskine (1969); Feld and Wildgen (1982); Flynn (1985); Flynn and Rattinger (1985); Listhaug (1986); Manigart and Marlier (1991*b*); Merritt and Puchala (1965); Russett and Deluca (1983); Zoll (1979, 1981).

   Among the available single country studies and data sources are: Desmet (1990), Dumoulin (1985), Manigart and Marlier (1991*a*) for Belgium; Sorensen (1990, 1991) for Denmark: CEVIPOF, Paris (data bank), Rozès (1989) for France; Noelle-Neumann (1983), Rattinger (1987, 1991*a*), Rattinger and Heilein (1986), and Allensbach Institut für Demoskopie yearbooks (ed. Noelle-Neumann) for Germany; British Social Attitudes (annually), Marsh and Fraser (1989); Sabin 1986–7, 1988*a*, 1988*b*) for Britain; Dimitras (1983) for Greece; Hardarson (1985) for Iceland; databank held by P. Isernia, Rome; Battistelli and Isernia (1990) for Italy; Everts (1983, 1984–90), Roschar (1975), Rebel (1985), Vaneker and Everts (eds) 1985, and the Databank of Institute for International Studies, Leiden University for the Netherlands; Mortensen (1983) for Norway.

   Several colleagues in other countries have been consulted in collecting data for this project. I am indebted in particular to Luc Desmet, Pierangelo Isernia, Jaime Pastor, Hans Rattinger, Philip Sabin, Henning Sorensen, and Pascal Vennesson for their assistance and suggestions about data sources. I am particularly grateful to Sef Janssen for his assistance in analysing the USIA and Eurobarometer data. I am also much indebted to Arthur Faber and Ralph van Haren for their assiduous assistance with data collection, which has resulted in a set of some 1,250 individual questions concerning orientations towards NATO with aggregated responses; about 800 of these questions are from polls held in more than one country at the same time or repeatedly. The databank at the Institute of International Studies, Leiden University can be consulted through the author. A summary listing of the currently available data, as well as the full set of marginals can be obtained from the author.

4. A specially constructed USIA data set was made available for the BiG project but it contained very few questions on NATO.

5. The sources consulted include *Public Opinion and Public Opinion Quarterly*, and Hastings and Hastings, *Index to International Public Opinion*. Requests for information to the relevant department of the UN secretariat produced no useful results.

6. Gallup International conducted two surveys, one in 1974 and one in 1985, in six European countries. The data from the 1974 survey could not be located. The available data from the 1985 survey are probably incomplete.

7. This trend continued up to 1993 in those countries for which data are available.

8. See Everts (1992) for details.

9. Some further light can be thrown on this issue by considering to what extent NATO is believed to be responsible for the non-occurrence of war in Europe. Combining the few available data from various sources shows not only that confidence increased between 1957 and 1982, but also that in 1989 confidence in NATO had increased considerably in most countries. See Everts (1992) for details.

10. On the relationship between diffuse and specific orientations, and on policies as an object of orientation, see Ch. 3.

11. See Everts (1992) for details.

12. Strictly speaking, adding the scores requires equal intervals between the scores for all respondents. While caution should therefore be exercised in interpreting the results, such treatment of ordinal scores is quite a standard practice.

13. This has to be qualified by noting that we lack appropriate data for the 1983–7 period.

14. Only 'strong defence' loaded (negatively) on this dimension as well as on factor 2, but its loading on the UN factor was just below the conventional 0.40 cut-off point.

15. This is in line with Hurwitz and Peffley's assumption that the public engages in two basic foreign-policy decisions in formulating attitudes towards specific foreign-policy issues: whether or not to become involved with other countries, and whether or not to employ force (Hurwitz and Peffley 1987: 1107, as summarized by McIntosh and McIver 1994: 12).

16. See Everts (1993) for a more detailed analysis.

17. Ziegler's labels refer to political–geographic terms but it seems more appropriate, considering the variables in question, to refer to the issues concerned. What distinguishes the first group is not their 'Atlantic' orientation (which should then be contrasted to a 'European' orientation), but a favourable attitude towards both military (NATO) and civilian (EC) co-operation. Hence the terms 'integrationist' and its opposite 'isolationist'.

PART V

Conclusion

17

Conclusion: European Publics and the Legitimacy of Internationalized Governance

PHILIP EVERTS AND RICHARD SINNOTT

Much of the analysis in this volume has focused on attitudes to various aspects of European integration. But integration is only one instance, albeit the most important, of a more general process; it is one point on the continuum of internationalized governance. The European experiment provides more than forty years of experience of varying degrees of internationalized governance. For more than twenty of those years the Eurobarometer surveys have provided regular and detailed evidence of the reactions and attitudes of European publics. And while the original laboratory, as it were, in which the experiment was conducted was relatively small, comprising six states, it has since extended to nine, to twelve, and now to fifteen. Beyond these fifteen, either through attempted accession or aspiration, it has become a focus for almost all European states.

In addition to the European Community, or Union, Europe has been the main site of another experiment in international co-operation—NATO. Although frequently known simply as 'the Alliance', NATO has been much more than a traditional alliance and constitutes another point on the continuum for which we have public opinion data. Finally, we have at least some minimal data on attitudes to the United Nations, a third important institution of internationalized governance. In sum, we have to hand the means of analysing responses to the internationalization of governance over a substantial period of time and across a wide and diverse range of publics.

The cross-time dimension is significant because it enables us to get at the question of change. The change we are interested in is not just a matter of the evolution of attitudes; change also occurs in the object of attitudes, as the process of integration has matured and deepened. In the case of NATO, a regime has encountered a fundamental transformation in its environment, requiring it to adjust and adapt.

The possibility of cross-national comparison is equally important. The study of politics is necessarily comparative. The reasons are simple. Nation states are systems. Systems have effects on what occurs within them, particularly on patterns of behaviour and attitudes. In order to analyse such effects, research must be cross-systemic, that is, cross-national. Thus, our commitment to comparison is partly a matter of following the advice of Przeworski and Teune (1970) to 'substitute variables for the proper names of systems'. However, in our case, it is more than that. The national political systems which present us with different patterns of attitudes are not just sources of methodological puzzles; they are central to the very object we are seeking to analyse, namely, the attitudes European publics adopt in response to the interplay between national and international levels of governance.

Why should we imagine that public opinion has anything to do with the internationalization of governance? Certainly, that might have been the stock reaction a few years ago, but no historian looking back at the year 1992 as a moment in the evolution of the European Community is likely to dismiss the significance of public opinion. The rejection of the Maastricht Treaty in the Danish referendum of June 1992, the narrowness of its passage in the French referendum three months later, and the rejection of the European Economic Area agreement in the Swiss referendum in December of that year all testify to the need to take into account mass opinion. The referendums of 1994 confirmed the point, with particular emphasis in the case of Norway. Moreover, governments in many other countries began to show signs of recognizing a restiveness in public opinion *vis-à-vis* the process of international integration— whether European political integration or monetary integration, or international co-operation in new UN peace and security tasks.

There is a sound basis underlying the message of referendums and the hunches of politicians. The theory of political integration, as documented in Chapter 2, almost always regarded political culture and public opinion as important factors in the integration process. In particular, it was anticipated that mass attitudes would really matter when the process of internationalization began to make inroads on the functions of states. These insights are found also in theories of disintegration and theories of the obstinacy of the nation state. Moreover, theories of international relations have lifted the lid off the 'black box' of domestic politics, exploring how developments in the international environment affect the attitudes of national actors and publics and how international co-operation is facilitated or constrained by domestic factors, including public opinion.

Both events and theory, therefore, highlight that the legitimacy of internationalized governance is at issue. Public opinion affects and is affected by internationalization. In this volume we have argued for the former proposition as a starting assumption and concentrated our empirical analysis on public attitudes as consequences either of the process of internationalization or of the changing economic, social, and cultural environment of Europe in the last quarter of the twentieth century.

As well as demonstrating the relevance of public opinion, the review of theory in Chapters 2 and 3 identified the dimensions of attitudes and some of the hypotheses and variables which would be central to the inquiry. Functionalism and neo-functionalism provide an essentially utilitarian or rationalist account of the transfer of loyalty to the supranational level. Transactionalism also involves a calculus of sorts, as do core–periphery theories. However, the main emphasis in transactionalism is on communication and learning; and not just across societies but also within them. Recurrent co-operative interactions shade into regimes and regimes shade into institutions. Institutions can be regarded as causes, as in federalist theories of integration. Well short of such ambitious thinking, regime theory still ascribes a significant role to 'principles, rules, and decision-making procedures'. However, a moment's reflection on the impact of institutions or decision-making procedures reminds us that the state is the dominant institution and that, therefore, analysis of the relationship between attitudes towards the state and attitudes towards integration is essential. The first task in our study, however, was to identify the overall trends in attitudes towards European integration among the publics of the member states.

Trends in Attitudes towards Integration

Support for European integration can be measured by responses to four Eurobarometer questions which are labelled according to the aspect of integration on which they focus: 'unification', 'membership', 'benefits' and 'dissolution'. The differences between the proportion of positive and negative responses to each of these questions provide net evaluation indices varying between -1 and $+1$. All four indices are positive over the period examined and the overall trend in support between 1973 and 1990 is upwards. However, more detailed inspection of the data shows some variation within this period.

In order to summarize complex trends, Chapter 4 talked of the 'Europeanization' and 'nationalization' of public opinion to describe an increase or a decline in the value of one or more of these indices. European public opinion underwent a degree of 'nationalization' during 1978–80. The following five years, 1981–5, saw an almost uniform 'Europeanization' of opinion, noteworthy for the fact that it preceded the launching of the Single Market. Then, just as the Single Market initiative was getting off the ground, divergent trends emerged, with net support in the original six member states remaining unchanged and all the growth in pro-European sentiment occurring in the member states which had joined the Community in or after 1973.

This picture might suggest an underlying evolutionary growth, with latecomers gradually catching up on countries which had already reached the ceiling of support. While such a process would indeed seem to be at work (and evidence in subsequent chapters confirms this), it is not the whole story. The analysis of country differences, including attitudes to unification in Germany, Britain, France, and Italy from as early as 1952, suggests a substantially more complex pattern. In the 1950s, the balance was highly positive in all four countries, implying that support for integration did not require any initial learning process. From the outset, it was seen as a good thing, even in Britain. The danger was unlearning and this is what happened in the British case. In the early 1960s, net support in Britain fell well below that in the three large countries which had signed up to the Treaty of Rome in 1957. Presumably the source of the decline was the politicization of the issue which took place when it became evident that this unification of Europe might involve Britain, or, for those who would have wanted Britain involved, that there were some in the Community who wanted to keep her out.

Partly as a result of the change in British attitudes, the first enlargement of the Community some ten years later introduced considerable variation in opinion within the Community. However, the differences were created not just by Britain but by Denmark, and, to a lesser extent,

Ireland. Meanwhile, public opinion in the countries of the southern enlargement (Greece, Spain, and Portugal) showed a very different pattern, suggesting that the prospects of economic benefits and the stabilization of the new democratic regimes may override any evolutionary tendencies or learning processes. Niedermayer suggests that analogous arguments may help to account for the exceptionally high support for integration in Germany in the 1950s. Such considerations relate essentially to the national situations of particular states. In this vein, Chapter 4 points to Britain's imperial legacy and Denmark's ties to other Nordic countries and its apprehensions about domination by a large neighbour as rather better explanations of continued resistance to integration than late entry to the learning curve.

Given the differences between countries, there is a remarkable uniformity to the downturn or 'nationalization' of opinion which occurred in 1991 and has continued to the time of writing. Chapter 4 showed that this trend pre-dated the signing of the Maastricht Treaty. Apart from its immediate political implications, this development raises the issue of the solidity of prevailing pro-integration attitudes in the face of what appears to have been, in part at least, a general politicization of the issue of integration. The question of the solidity of attitudes towards integration can be clarified to some extent by examining their causes and correlates.

Economic Benefits and European Integration

In Chapter 5, Newton and Bosch's investigation of the cost–benefit explanation of support for integration established that substantial numbers of EC citizens do attach economic significance to the Community. It would be extraordinary if they did not: for much of its early life it was known as the European Economic Communities, or simply as the Common Market. However, from there on the evidence for an economic explanation of support goes mostly downhill. A country's net budgetary receipts from the Community between 1982 and 1984 appear unrelated to the level of support for integration among its citizens; neither the level of wealth nor the rate of economic growth in a country shows a consistent relationship with attitudes to European integration. There is some marginal association between the benefits indicator and net receipts but the relationship is weak and conditional.

Perhaps economic factors affect fluctuations in support rather than absolute levels of support? However, a multivariate time series analysis for the nine countries which were members of the Community for the entire period 1973–90 indicates that there are different effects in different countries in different years. Even more to the point, after controlling for other factors, economic variables played little or no role in the equations. On the contrary, support for the Community is more strongly associated with social and attitudinal variables of a non-economic kind, such as optimism or pessimism regarding next year, left–right orientation, education, and satisfaction with life in general. Even then, the amount of variance explained is very small. In fact, the only variable showing a substantial effect is length of EC membership: up to 1990, each year seemed to add something between one-fifth and one-quarter of 1 per cent to approval of European unification and EC membership.

Analysis of individual-level data confirms that, at best, economic variables have a marginal impact on support for integration. To the extent that economic factors had any effects, they tended to be weak and randomly distributed in different countries in different years. It is notable that age did not play a role, suggesting that, if, in the period 1973–90, growing support was a function of the passage of time, it was due to greater familiarity with the EC rather than any process associated with cohort replacement.

Finally, Chapter 5 examined some test cases for an economic inter-pretation of support. One focused on farmers among whom, it was anticipated, levels of support would be different from other sectors of the population—either because of the tangible benefits they receive from the EC or because of dissatisfaction with the implementation of policy or with outcomes which did not match their expectations. As it turns out, during the 1970s, farmers and their dependants across the Community were significantly more supportive of membership than were those in non-agricultural sectors. However, that difference had disappeared by 1981 and, in 1986, farmers were slightly but signifi-cantly less supportive of their country's membership of the Community. These general tendencies mask considerable differences among the member states. From the mid-1970s onwards, farmers in France, Germany, and Italy tended to be more negative than their fellow citizens. At the opposite end of the scale, Danish farmers were sub-stantially more positive than other Danes throughout the period 1973–92, although with some tailing off in the early 1990s. Irish farmers fall in between; from the mid-1970s to the mid-1980s they were more positive but, from 1986 on, they were no different from the rest of their society. In sum, support for the EC among farmers varies by country and by time period—and does so in a way which suggests that support from this sector responds in at least some degree to policy changes affecting farmers' livelihoods.

The lack of evidence that, except perhaps in the case of farmers, economic considerations have much influence on support for integration leads to the accretion thesis, or, as Bosch and Newton put it, 'familiarity breeds content'. But how solid is the support generated in this way? If inertia, custom, and tradition maintain support for integration and even produce some growth in support, that support may well be quite flimsy and vulnerable to a sharp gust of politicization. Perhaps, as Bosch and Newton speculate, things will return to normal and the pre-1991 trends will reappear. Obviously, any assessment of the probability of this outcome must take account of other possible sources of general pro-integration attitudes.

Diffusion versus Replacement

Taking up where the economic analysis leaves off and casting the aphorism 'familiarity breeds content' into the language of diffusion theory, Chapter 6 investigated the accretion of support for integration. Previous research has tended to focus on the notions of 'cognitive mobilization', generational or cohort differences, and differences in political outlook between materialists (earlier generations) and post-materialists (later generations) and on the underlying assumption that the bulk of the growth in support for integration would be due to processes of replacement. An important corollary was that attitudinal differences between cohorts and between social and political strata should persist. In this view, it is the changing composition of society that brings about change in the overall level of support for integration. The implication of the diffusion model is quite the opposite. As diffusion takes place, differences between cohorts and between various social, educational, and political strata actually decline. As its implications are quite at odds with the expectations raised by previous research, the diffusion model is eminently testable. Furthermore, although borrowed from another field of research, the approach touches on causal mechanisms identified in theories of political integration; for example,

Deutsch's notion of 'increased communication across strata' and Haas's concept of 'social learning'.

Dealing first with European awareness or, more precisely, the accessibility of European Community issues, Wessels shows that, while education and political involvement have significant effects, 'differences between respondents of varying levels of political involvement regarding their ability to develop an attitude towards the EC are disappearing'. More importantly, diffusion is shown to be at work also in the case of pro-integration attitudes. Social, educational, and political stratification, and a number of political cleavages, do affect such attitudes, but the crucial finding is that, in the overwhelming majority of member states, these effects are less significant in the period 1983–91 compared with the preceding period 1973–82. Denmark is a striking exception to this rule. But even then the exception is only partial; the impact of social stratification in Denmark declines but the impact of political cleavage variables increases. This shows that diffusion has its limits and the limits are reached when the process meets the countervailing force of politicization.

These findings suggest the need to examine the relationship between the views of party supporters and the policy positions of the parties themselves. In Chapter 6, parties were grouped into broad party families and the position of parties *vis-à-vis* integration assessed on the basis of the existing literature. Analysis of the attitudinal data shows that there is a good deal of consistency between the positions of the parties and the views of their followers. The findings clarify the nature of the polarization of attitudes in Denmark by showing that it is not just a polarization between different parties but also a polarization within parties. Similar levels of party polarization on EC issues are found in Greece.

The correspondence between party positions on integration and the attitudes of their supporters raised the questions about élite–mass linkages and the direction of influence. Do party and other élites 'pull' mass attitudes towards their own position or do mass attitudes 'push' élites in either a pro- or anti-integration direction?

Élite–Mass Linkages

Having confirmed, on the basis of the attitudes of élites and mass publics in the late 1950s and mid-1970s, that there is a systematic and strong relationship between élite and mass opinion, Chapter 7 asks whether this relationship fits the 'cascade model' of attitude formation suggested by Deutsch. According to the model, political stratification gives rise to five interconnected opinion pools: the opinions of the top socio-economic élite, of political élites, of the media, of opinion leaders and, finally, of the politically relevant strata of society. Other models of opinion flow envisage fewer levels but all agree that opinion cascades, flows, or trickles from top to bottom.

The evidence shows considerable support for this conception of the process of opinion formation. First, there is the simple fact of higher levels of support for European integration at higher levels of opinion leadership. Then there is the linear decline in the strength of time-series correlations as one moves down the scale of opinion leadership. The real test comes, however, in a detailed examination of the linkage between party followers and political parties. In this test, party views are identified more systematically and on a party-by-party basis through the analysis of party manifestos. When these data are combined with the Eurobarometer data, the link between party positions and the attitudes of party supporters over time can be analysed. In Chapter 7, this is done by taling all elections in all member states between 1973 and 1991, focusing on three periods in the electoral cycle: when party manifestos are produced, during the elections, and during the formation and presentation of the government programme.

The findings indicate that the views of party followers have some influence on the formulation of the manifestos but that, once formed, party platforms have a 'remarkable influence' on the opinion of party followers during the election campaign and in the post-election period. Of course, the basic factor accounting for the position adopted by a particular party's followers at any given time is their position at a previous point in time. However, even when this continuity is taken into account, party platforms can be shown to have an impact on party follower opinion at election time. This is further borne out by Wessels's demonstration that, in two-thirds of the cases in which parties are out of line with the views of their supporters, the parties succeed in reducing the gap at election time. However, the evidence also indicates that the effect is not permanent or cumulative, therefore parties and political élites must continuously work at the task of moving their followers in their preferred direction. This suggests that in identifying transnational parties as important for generating support for integration, some of the early theories may have been right in focusing on parties but wrong in thinking that only transnational parties could have the desired effect.

Parties, however, are not the only—or even the chief—institution influencing mass attitudes. The state is not a neutral arena in which parties and other groups compete and thereby influence the attitudes of the citizens. The state itself is a focus of attitudes and loyalties. One view is that this is a zero-sum situation: the stronger the hold of the state on the loyalties and affections of its citizens, the lower the probability of integrative attitudes developing. The alternative view is that successful integration at the national level is a precondition of integration at the supranational level (see Chapter 2). Chapter 8 set out to examine a central aspect of this issue by analysing the relationship between attitudes to the national political system, as measured by satisfaction with democracy, and attitudes to supranational integration, as measured by the 'membership' indicator.

Six countries—Denmark, Ireland, Luxembourg, the Netherlands, Portugal, and Britain—show an increase in satisfaction with democracy over the period considered. In the other six member states, satisfaction with democracy either remained stable or showed an overall decline; the tendency to decline being particularly evident between 1990 and 1993. In the countries showing increasing satisfaction with democracy, there was a net increase in support for membership of the Community; in the countries with stable or declining satisfaction with democracy, there was an overall decline in support, especially in the period 1990 to 1993.

After identifying these differences between countries, Martinotti and Stefanizzi went on to develop a typology of orientations at the individual level by combining the two variables, satisfaction with democracy and attitudes towards EC membership. This produced four basic types: the 'integrated' who are positive on both dimensions; the 'alienated' who are negative on both; the 'nation statists' who are positive about democracy in their own country but negative about EC membership; and the 'innovators' or 'escapists' who are negative towards democracy at the national level but positive towards EC membership.

The findings reveal substantial differences between four groups of states. First, there are the predominantly integrated states; that is, countries characterized by an absolute majority in the integrated category and relatively few people in any of the other three categories. This group consists of Luxembourg, the Netherlands, Ireland, and Portugal. Secondly, there is a group of countries which lack an integrated majority and have relatively high levels of innovator-escapists. France, Belgium, and Spain make up this group. The third group is the integrated plus nation statist countries, of which West Germany is the best example but to which Denmark and Britain also belong. Finally, there is the predominantly innovator-escapist group in which Italy is virtually in a class of its own. However, if we allow for the clear plurality of innovator-escapists in Greece in 1992, that country joins Italy in this fourth group. Apart from the country-specific circumstances which these patterns might suggest, analysis showed that right–left orientation had a significant effect in almost all countries but that the direction of the effects varied by country. Specifically, being right wing was associated with an integrated orientation in Greece and Denmark but with nation-statist orientations in West Germany, Spain, and Britain.

Thus, there are countries in which positive attitudes towards integration are combined with a sense of failure at the level of the nation state. But such a syndrome is predominant only in Italy and prevalent without being predominant only in Greece. A majority across the Community as a whole, and at least a clear plurality in all member states except Italy and Greece, combine positive attitudes towards the nation state with positive attitudes towards integration. None the less, significant proportions of nation statists and the alienated are to be found in various countries at different times. More importantly, the coexistence of positive attitudes towards the nation state and positive attitudes towards EC membership does not rule out the possibility of conflict or the dominance of one set of attitudes over the other when political orientations at each level have to compete for space and attention. In any such competition internationalized governance faces an entrenched force. The outcome can be considered in relation to identity, trust, policy competences, and democracy.

Nation States versus Europe: Identity and Trust

The available data provide two quite different measures of identity. The first, used in the late 1970s, measures identification with place. The words 'geographical unit' are specifically used in the question and, on this basis, the question probes for people's sense of belonging to a locality or town, region, country, Europe, and the world. According to this measure, the primary spatial or geographical identification throughout most of the member states of the European Community is the locality or town in which the individual lives. Europe comes in a poor fourth. Adding together the first and second choices of respondents only brings the European 'score' up to an average of less than 10 per cent.

The second measure of sense of identity is much more political, and is available at fairly regular intervals between 1982 and 1992. It asks whether it ever occurs to individuals that they are not only French or Irish or whatever but also European, with a reference to being a citizen of the particular country or of Europe sometimes being added to the question (see Chapter 9). According to this measure, the southern European countries (France, Italy, Greece, Spain, and Portugal) are the most European; in contrast, in Britain, Denmark, Ireland, and— somewhat surprisingly—the Netherlands, we find majorities denying ever having a sense of European identity. European identity has tended to increase in Ireland and Britain but has declined fairly consistently in Germany: in 1992, Germany was in the group of countries with the lowest sense of European identity.

Taken together, the national trends do not support the view that European identity increases with the passage of time: an increase between 1982 and 1986 was followed by a decline in the years 1986– 90, then a short-lived recovery in 1991 which was abruptly terminated by a general decline in 1992. Duchesne and Frognier argue that there is some evidence here of a 'notoriety' effect: European identity is accentuated when Europe is in the news, as in 1986 with the discussion of the Single European Act, and in 1991, in the run-up to the Maastricht Treaty. However, it seems that such gains are neither stable nor cumulative, and may be counteracted by developments such as those contained in the Maastricht Treaty which confront people with the implications of common citizenship before the sense of European citizenship has been consolidated.

As with most other aspects of attitudes towards integration, education is the most important influence on the development of a sense of European identity across all countries. However, Chapter 9 shows that this and other relationships between identity and the socio-economic characteristics of individuals are noticeably stronger in the economically less-developed member states. Duchesne and Frognier emphasize that European identity is unrelated to national pride. This considerably qualifies the notion that European identity is necessarily in competition with national identity. Or, perhaps more accurately, it confirms that, if there is competition between the two, it is a competition for attention and salience between potentially compatible affiliations, not a competition between mutually exclusive allegiances. However, the weight of the evidence considered in Chapter 9 indicates that Europe is far from winning the battle even for attention and salience. The development of either Schmitter's 'distinctive regional identity and its wide distribution across classes and corporate groups' or Deutsch's more modest 'partial identifications in terms of self images' still lies in the future.

But what of the sense of trust, the other main aspect of community identified by Deutsch? This can be readily measured using Eurobarometer data. The evidence in Chapter 10 again suggests that the nation state is still the primary locus of trust; in 1990, on a scale running from 0 to 3, citizens of the Community scored an average of 2.39 for trust in people of their own nationality and, on average, 1.75 for trust in the peoples of all of the other member states. Moreover, in terms of trust as part of the underpinning of a security community in the sense outlined by Deutsch, the four most trusted nationalities in the European Community are from four small states which are among the least threatening: Luxembourg, Denmark, the Netherlands, and Belgium. The large countries, whose size alone puts them in a potentially more threatening position, are mostly in the middle of the trust-in-people ranking, although the British stand with the Portuguese and the Greeks on the lowest rungs of the scale. That the position of the British probably reflects current tensions over Community policy is indicated by the fact that the British were the only nationality subject to a decline in trust over the decade 1980–90. However, trust varies depending on both the nationality being assessed and the nationality of the individual expressing the judgement. Danes, Dutch, and Belgians are not only more frequently objects of trust on the part of the people of other member states, they also have higher levels of trust in the people of the other member states. The Spanish and the Italians are considerably less positive on this latter count.

Although trust among the peoples of the Community may not be as high as trust in the people of one's own country, Niedermayer shows that trust within the Community has developed substantially since the mid-1970s, rising from 1.55 in 1976 (barely above the mid-point on the scale) to 1.75 in 1990 (weighted averages). Moreover, the level of European citizens' overall trust in each of the member states was higher in 1990 than it had been in 1976. In some cases the difference between 1976 and 1986 is small but in all cases it is positive; trust in certain nationalities grew substantially. The most notable jumps were in trust in the French and the Spanish between 1986 and 1990, in the Italians between 1980 and 1986, and in the Irish between 1976 and 1980. In the latter case, however, it is difficult to disentangle the possibly adverse effects of the Northern Ireland conflict on the 1976 data from the positive effect of becoming a member of the Community which might have been expected to have become evident by 1980, since the question wording changed from 'the Irish' in 1976 to 'people of the Republic of Ireland' in 1980. One other notable development is that the capacity of European citizens to form a judgement about the smaller member states increased by about 10 percentage points between 1986 and 1990.

States are not only important because they establish the main boundaries of identity and give rise to different levels of mutual trust. Even more fundamental is their range of policy competence. Here, however, the challenge to the state is stronger because it arises not just from the setting up of supranational institutions or various other attempts to promote integration. It stems also from the emergence of problems which can only be solved by internationalized governance. Has this resulted in a decline in the perceived comprehensiveness of the state? And are we beginning to see the emergence of those 'transnational political issues of interest to all political forces and publics across boundary lines' identified by Hoffmann as a precondition for integration. If this were the case, the implications for the legitimacy of internationalized governance would be considerable. This suggests the need to explore the relationship between public perceptions and expectations on the one hand and the nature of the problems being confronted and the claims of the Community or other agencies of internationalized governance on the other.

Nation States versus Europe: Policy Competences

Chapter 11 argues that discrepancies between public perception, subsidiarity, and institutional ambition or, in the terms used by Sinnott, between attributed, endogenous, and exogenous internationalization, create considerable potential either for the enhancement of legitimacy or for substantial challenges to it. Both the opportunities and the challenges can be explored by examining the seven sets of issues arising from the different possible combinations of attributed, exogenous, and endogenous internationalization. This suggests that the set of issues in which the legitimacy of internationalized governance has been achieved—labelled 'the world according to Delors' in Chapter 11—comprises relatively few issues, the most notable being the environment. The considerably less salient issues of development aid and scientific research are also in this set. Beyond this limited set of issues, three further sets show some potential for the enhancement of legitimacy. These are, in increasing order of difficulty, foreign policy, characterized as 'fertile ground'; data protection in the 'proceed and persuade' set; and common defence, identified as 'virgin territory'. On the negative side, the legitimacy of the Union could be seen to be under threat in the two areas described as 'the imperious centre' (educational issues and workers' co-determination) and 'delegitimizing demand' (poverty and unemployment).

Of course the assessment in Chapter 11 relates to the situation in the Community or Union as a whole. When we descend to the national level we find that an issue, for example foreign policy, which is 'fertile ground' in one country may be 'virgin territory' in another. Moreover, internationalized issues do not automatically undermine the nation state or lead to an upward transfer of legitimacy. Sinnott concludes that the implications for the legitimacy of internationalized governance vary from one set of issues to another and from one country to another depending on three factors: the nature of the issue or problem, the action or inaction of an agency of internationalized governance, and the public's reaction to both of these.

Nation State versus Europe: Democracy

There can be no doubt that democratic life in Western Europe is centred on the nation state. Certainly, there are institutionalized democratic linkages above the national level but a review of these linkages in Chapter 12 concluded that their main feature is a contrast between a politically powerful but representationally weak institution (the Council of Ministers) on the one hand and a politically weak but representationally strong institution (the European Parliament) on the other.

Against this background, it is not surprising that there is a perceived democratic deficit. How great one judges that deficit to be depends on definitions, yardsticks, and question wordings. In 1992, only one-sixth of the EC's citizens thought they had 'sufficient democratic influence on EC decision-making'. The fact that in 1989, in the immediate aftermath of European elections, only one in ten Europeans took the view that the 'way the European Community works' is 'completely democratic' may appear to be even more damning. However, adding in the next response category shows that 58 per cent thought that the working of the Community is either 'completely' or 'to some extent' democratic, compared to 20 per cent who thought that it was largely undemocratic, being characterized by either 'very little democracy' or 'none at all'. When we put these findings alongside the fact that over the years some 50–55 per cent of EC citizens have expressed the view that the European Parliament plays an important role, and that more substantial majorities express the wish that the Parliament should play a more important role in the future, we might be tempted to conclude that the Parliament is making a significant contribution to the democratic functioning and the legitimacy of the Community.

However, further analysis in Chapter 12 reveals that such a conclusion would be based on rather shaky foundations. Other than at European election time, less than half of the EC's population claim to have 'recently' heard, seen, or read anything about the Parliament in the media. More importantly, accurate knowledge of the European Parliament, of its composition and powers, is rare, while a comprehensive knowledge of the Parliament and its powers is almost non-existent. Niedermayer and Sinnott argue that the most common tendency seems to be to project the powers of national parliaments on to the European Parliament, greatly exaggerating its power. One manifestation of this tendency to inflate the role of the European Parliament is that, in spring 1993, a plurality of respondents (33 per cent) considered the European Parliament the most powerful institution in determining EC legislation.

What this adds up to is that, on the basis of even the most minimal criterion, informed support for the role of the European Parliament was in the region of only 20 per cent. By contrast, a plurality of citizens (46 per cent) fell into the category of uninformed supporters of the Parliament. Of course, it could be argued that the weak informational base can be ignored, that what is significant is that the public believes in the role of the Parliament and that this contributes to the legitimization of Community decision-making. Against this Bagehot-style view, there is, first, the fact that the public does perceive a democratic deficit. Secondly, given the constitution-building challenges facing the Union in the coming years, its democratic legitimacy needs to be grounded in more than a myth of an influential Parliament based on the projection of an ideal conception of national parliaments. Thirdly, the behavioural evidence exposes the weakness underlying the apparently positive image of the Parliament: only some 50 per cent of voters in the Community turn out to vote in European elections, except where voting is compulsory or the European elections coincide with national elections.

This account of attitudes towards the European Parliament reinforces a message which comes through from most of the analyses reported in Part III of this volume: while general support for integration is widespread, the legitimacy of internationalized governance looks considerably weaker when we examine specific attitudes. We return to this problem at the end of the chapter, but note here that the problem is made all the more acute by the challenges facing the Union as it seeks to extend the scope of internationalized governance. This includes both territorial extension and the extension of scope entailed in the Maastricht Treaty's commitment to 'the eventual framing of a common defence policy, which might in time lead to a common defence'.

Enlarging the Territorial Scope: The View from Within

For nation states, matters of territorial extent, territorial boundaries, and territorial integrity are, in most cases, fixed and highly salient. The Community's territorial scope has always been open in principle, evolutionary in practice and, with one exception, relatively non-controversial and non-salient. The exception is the highly particular case of the French veto of Britain's attempts to join the European Economic Communities in the 1960s.

The issue of the territorial scope of the Community is clearly of low salience as far as public opinion is concerned. Chapter 13 showed that, while the size and prominence of Britain and, presumably, its long-running and well-publicized on/off relationship with the Community prior to entry, meant that 77 per cent could name it as one of the three new members in 1973, far fewer (44 per cent) could name Denmark as a new member, and fewer still (33 per cent) could name Ireland. Similarly, in 1980, on the eve of Greek accession, only 37 per cent could name Greece as an applicant country. However, knowledge of the Spanish and Portuguese applications increased considerably just prior to accession: figures of 45 and 29 per cent in 1980 rose, respectively, to

69 and 60 per cent in 1985. Westle shows that geographical propinquity and historical or cultural links play a role both in levels of awareness of particular enlargement issues and in levels of support for the admission of particular countries. Controversy, too, seems to affect attitudes towards the membership of particular countries. Thus, in 1976, just after the British referendum on remaining in the Community, 19 per cent in Germany and 15 per cent in France identified Britain as a country which they 'would prefer not to be in the Community'. Eight years later, these figures had risen to 33 per cent in Germany, 41 per cent in France, and these critics of British membership were joined by 38 per cent in Luxembourg, 27 per cent in Greece, 23 per cent in the Netherlands, and 20 per cent in Belgium.

Economic assessments, too, appear to be relevant to attitudes towards territorial enlargement. Some 60–70 per cent of the European public approved a range of policies relating to Central and East European countries which included preparing for their future accession. However, a direct question on whether the EC should reduce subsidies for less-developed regions within the EC in order to help East European countries produced reactions which were considerably less favourable (50 per cent against, 20 per cent indifferent, and only 30 per cent in favour). Further evidence of at least an awareness of cost–benefit issues in this area comes from perceptions of the impact of Spanish entry on the respondent's own country. In 1977, a generally negative assessment of Spanish entry among farmers was confined to a few countries; by 1985 this pessimism had spread to almost all countries. Moreover, between 1977 and 1985 expectations became more pessimistic among opinion leaders, a factor which may have accounted for growing negative expectations among the general public.

However, economic expectations regarding the effect on one's own country do not determine attitudes towards enlargement. For one thing, support for Spanish membership increased between 1977 and 1985 in most of the countries for which we have data. Secondly, the multivariate analysis in Chapter 13 shows that, in several member states, people's expectation of the effect of a particular accession on the Community as a whole is a more powerful consideration than expected effects on the respondent's own country. General attitudes towards integration are also relevant. Indeed, the overall impression which emerges is that weakly formed positive attitudes towards enlargement seem to go along with positive attitudes to integration. Westle argues that, in the perceptions of the public, widening and deepening are not in conflict. However, she also shows that the issue is capable of being politicized either by economic considerations, or, in rare cases, by more directly political conflict. In general, however, it would seem that the Union can proceed to expand secure in the knowledge that a fairly apathetic public opinion will follow. Whether public opinion will follow if major developments in institutional or policy integration become preconditions of enlargement is another question, to which we return below.

Enlarging the Territorial Scope: The View from EFTA

The combined effects of moves towards the Single Market and the crumbling of strategic constraints symbolized by the fall of the Berlin Wall meant that the issue of European integration would sooner or later confront the main European Free Trade Area (EFTA) countries. Trends in public opinion in the four countries which held referendums on membership of the Union lead Aarebrot, Berglund, and Weninger to argue that that there is dynamic which gives rise to a U-shaped curve in the graph of voting intentions. Voting intentions are relatively favourable to entry prior to the onset of detailed negotiations, waver in the middle as negotiations and debate get under way, and rise again as the referendum nears and political we élites throw their weight behind the campaign. Apart from such overall trends, attitudes to integration are clearly affected by centre–periphery factors in Switzerland, Finland, and Norway but not in Denmark or Austria. In all countries, feeling well informed about the EC is associated with favourable attitudes towards integration, although this relationship is less strong in Norway, reflecting the well-organized 'no' campaign in the 1994 referendum.

In the event, three countries voted to enter the European Union while Norway voted to remain outside and Switzerland had already voted against the European Economic Area in 1992. However, even the positive outcome in three out of the five countries could lead to an exaggerated impression of the extent of support for integration. The pro-membership majority was extremely narrow in Sweden, narrow enough in Finland, and generous only in Austria. Moreover, Chapter 13 shows that, in 1992, support for the general idea of European unity was at about the level found in Denmark, and membership was only endorsed as 'a good thing' by little over one-third of respondents in all the countries concerned. This suggests that the decisions in favour of entry were made grudgingly, and that these countries may bring with them into the Union a less enthusiastic attitude towards integration.

Enlarging the Territorial Scope: The View from Central and Eastern Europe

In 1992, the publics of Central and East European countries were much more enthusiastic about integration than those in the EFTA countries. Opinion in Hungary and Poland was most favourable, followed by Czechoslovakia, then Bulgaria. The Baltic countries registered the lowest levels of support but were still well ahead of the five EFTA countries considered above. Chapter 15 also shows that European identity was more prevalent in Poland, Czechoslovakia, and Latvia than in the European Community as a whole; in fact, a sense of European identity was as prevalent as in those member states (generally the southern states) which scored highest on this measure.

But how robust are such attitudes? If the shallowness of attitudes within the European Union seems to be a problem, it is likely that what Berglund, Aarebrot, and Koralewicz refer to as postcommunist Europhoria, and the tendency to reach for panaceas, may create higher but flimsier support in East European countries. We might also question whether such attitudes would survive the shock of entry into the European Union. Developments in the former East Germany are not encouraging. Between 1990 and 1993, the proportion of positive responses in the former GDR fell on each of our four measures of support: from 88 to 61 per cent on 'unification'; from 87 to 52 per cent on 'membership'; from 78 to 38 per cent on 'benefit'; and from 71 to 32 per cent on 'dissolution'.

Chapter 15 indicates further grounds for concern about the legitimacy problems which may follow from entry into the Union of the states of Central and Eastern Europe. These are not well-integrated societies, either internally or *vis-à-vis* their neighbours. Thus, in Poland the level of trust in the peoples of Western Europe is considerably higher than trust in the peoples of neighbouring East European states. This obtains also in Czechoslovakia, although in this case the contrast is not as strong. It is particularly notable that people in both countries, but especially Czechoslovakia, showed greater trust in Germans than in their fellow East Europeans. The extent of potential ethnic conflict between indigenous and Russian nationalities is also apparent in

Estonia and Latvia, and in all three Baltic states one finds substantial minorities with distrustful attitudes towards Jewish people.

The dilemma arising from these findings is clear. Should integration proceed in the belief that institutionalized co-operation will solve the economic problems and ensure political pluralism and political stability, or should the process be put on hold pending the achievement of the economic, political, and cultural preconditions of integration? The dilemma is all the more acute given what many see as the mission of European integration; that is, having succeeded in creating a 'security community' in Western Europe, the Union must now rise to the challenge of extending this to Central and Eastern Europe. But this challenge immediately raises the issue of extending not only the territorial scope of integration but also its policy scope into the area of security and defence. This brings us to our last substantive topic.

Extending Internationalized Governance: Security and Defence

The European Union is not the only agency of internationalized governance with a potential role in strengthening and extending Europe's security community. In pursuing this goal, therefore, the Union has to sort out its relationship with the North Atlantic Treaty Organization (NATO). Accordingly, any discussion of the implications of this issue must take account of attitudes towards NATO and, in particular, how these attitudes may have changed since 1989. As well as raising the question of whether public support endures through a process of regime change, consideration of attitudes towards NATO raises more directly a question hinted at in Chapter 16: do attitudes towards internationalized governance constitute a single dimension or are there different sets of attitudes for different sets of issues and different policy areas?

Chapter 16 shows that, notwithstanding fluctuations in some countries which seem to have been due largely to domestic politics, support for NATO membership has never been in serious doubt in NATO member states. In fact there is some evidence that support has increased over time, despite some faltering in support for the view that 'NATO is essential' in 1971, in 1980–2, and between 1984 and 1989. Then, in autumn 1989, belief that NATO is still essential fell in all countries and fell quite dramatically in some. By 1991, however, NATO had recovered most of the lost ground. This suggests that an international regime can undergo transformation, even transformation related to the very purposes for which it was founded, and still maintain a high level of public support.

It is also apparent, however, that there has been a persistent contrast between the countries of northern and southern Europe in levels of support for NATO. This was particularly evident in 1989 when respondents were asked to choose between NATO and the European Community as the best way of organizing European security. On this there was a clear discrepancy between opinion in Denmark, Germany, Britain, and the Netherlands on the one hand, and France, Greece, Italy, and Spain on the other. Belgium, Ireland and Portugal took an intermediate position.

The only other variable showing a consistent relationship with attitudes towards NATO is left–right self-placement. This contrasts with analyses in other chapters which have tended to show a varying relationship between left–right location and attitudes towards the economic and political aspects of European integration. Does this suggest that attitudes towards integration and attitudes towards military co-operation are separate dimensions rather than different points on a single dimension determined by a single set of considerations? Everts argues that functionalist theory could be thought to imply the first view and federalist theory the second.

The question was tackled in Chapter 16 by a factor analysis of attitudes towards European integration, NATO, and the United Nations. This showed a three-dimensional structure, indicating that attitudes to internationalization are functionally differentiated. Using the first two dimensions revealed by the factor analysis ('European integration' and 'military integration') leads to the identification of four main positions: military and economic integrationists, economic partners, military allies, and isolationists. There have been two principal trends in the evolution of these attitudes over time. The first is a polarization of attitudes, with noticeable declines in the proportions of 'Don't knows' and doubters. The second has been an increase in military and economic integrationists to the point, in 1991, that they constituted almost a majority (49 per cent) of the citizens of the European Community. Moreover, they were either a majority or a substantial plurality in all member states except Spain, where the proportion of military and economic integrationists (37 per cent) was almost matched by the proportion of 'economic partners' (33 per cent). Not surprisingly, the greatest changes occurred in Britain, Denmark, and France and the changes in these (and other countries) tended to be concentrated in the period 1980–91.

The existence of a virtual majority of 'military and economic integrationists' does not guarantee the safe passage of a common foreign and security policy for the European Union. Military integration here means integration in the framework of NATO and Atlanticism in general. Moreover, we have seen that the issue of the European Union as a forum for military and defence co-operation divides member states between north and south. The third reason why this distribution of attitudes does not give *carte blanche* for a common defence policy is that, as Everts shows, the connection between support for military integration and support for economic and political integration is contingent. Attitudes in these different areas of internationalization are compatible but, although there may be evidence of a transfer of support from NATO Mark I to NATO Mark II, this does not necessarily mean that a legacy of support for NATO could be handed on to a European Union in full pursuit of a common foreign and security policy. The policy implication is that relations between different security institutions will have to be carefully managed if the current moderately widespread consensus in favour of both kinds of integration or internationalization is to be maintained.

Conclusions: Implications for Internationalized Governance

How, then, does the balance sheet for the legitimacy of internationalized governance turn out? On the credit side, there are several points to note. First, there are the high levels of support for European integration among the established member states. This support shows a tendency to appreciate over time and to appreciate faster in those countries which have been most sceptical in the past. That support is not determined by economic considerations alone might also be regarded as a positive factor. This makes European integration less subject to economic downturns and less vulnerable to adverse developments in the balance of what countries get out of the Union which might result from further enlargement. Moreover, since support has spread by diffusion in the past, it may do so again in the future. There is even evidence to suggest that élites, particularly party élites, can, if they are so committed, give this process a helping hand.

Over and above this widespread general support for integration, there is some evidence of a sense of European identity and of a growth in trust between the nationalities which make up the Community or Union. There is also evidence of a willingness on the part of citizens to transfer certain policy responsibilities to the supranational level and of considerable support for the role of the European Parliament. On the question of enlargement, attitudes have, in the past, been permissive and continue to be so. Looking at enlargement from the outside, voters in three EFTA countries have endorsed membership, and majorities in all of the Central and East European states examined aspire to immediate or early incorporation. The final positive consideration is that attitudes which are supportive of internationl governance are not confined to the economic and political aspects of the European Union, but extend to military co-operation and to NATO. In particular, support for the latter seems to have survived the challenge of regime transformation.

What about the debit side? The first factor is that support for integration has been in decline in the European Union as a whole since 1991. This suggests a certain lack of solidity in the widespread support which obtained up to 1991. That supportive attitudes are not rooted in either economic calculations or in longer-term processes of structural change but in a process of diffusion also suggests that they may be built on somewhat flimsy foundations. A certain superficiality also becomes apparent when one looks for signs of European identity. Moreover, mutual trust within the Community may have grown but it is still well short of the levels of trust which obtain within national boundaries. For sure, there is evidence of the attribution of policy competences and policy responsibility to the supranational level but it is also apparent that this involves a double risk: that internationalized governance is saddled with responsibility for policy problems which it can do little about and that the competences required for effective governance may not be the ones attributed to it.

Then there is the debit in terms of democracy, a legitimacy problem so obvious that it has entered common parlance as 'the democratic deficit'. Here, the evidence is that positive attitudes towards the role of the European Parliament are quite superficial. They are based on an unwarranted projection of images and expectations from the national to the supranational level; and they are not backed either by information and understanding or by habits of participation and involvement. To which we might add that enlargement may exacerbate these problems of legitimacy by bringing in more sceptical publics from Scandinavia and Austria. Finally, if enlargement were to include countries in Central and

Eastern Europe, our evidence suggests that their high levels of enthu-siasm may have even less firm foundations than those underlying support among the publics of established member states.

But the balance sheet cannot be assessed by simply adding up two columns. There are systematic variations in attitudes underlying the balance sheet and these variations are paramount in evaluating the overall picture. First, there are considerable variations in attitudes across the political strata which divide European publics into the mobilized and non-mobilized, or into opinion leaders and followers, and across the related divide created by different levels of education. In other words, there are different European publics. There are pro-integrationists and anti-integrationists. But there is also the silent majority and the mobilized minority—the former being either a poten-tially mobilizable resource or an inhibiting constraint. Thus, although permissive consensus may be the dominant characterization of public opinion in this area, it is not the only characterization. The crucial point here is that integration is an ongoing process. As integration intensifies and the politicization of the issues increases, there is the likelihood of a movement out of permissive consensus. Some of the movement will be into active support for integration, but some will be into negative attitudes which remain latent and some into active opposition.

Any assessment of how this movement will develop needs to take into account that attitudes towards internationalized governance vary by issue area. This is partly a matter of taking the analysis beyond the level of general support for the unification of Europe or membership of the European Union to consider attitudes sector by sector, even issue by issue. One of the principal variations is between attitudes towards economic and political co-operation on the one hand and military co-operation on the other. At present attitudes to both are positive and, for the bulk of the European public, the two are seen as compatible. Even so, the evidence is that the one does not imply the other, still less that they should be embodied in a single institutional form.

Over and above this distinction, it is also evident that support for the internationalization of policy competences varies from issue to issue. This might seem to create the possibility of a match between the principle of subsidiarity and what is regarded as legitimate by the public. However, we have seen that public opinion does not always match the requirements of subsidiarity, and the mismatch between them, and between them and the actual and claimed competences of the European Union, lead to a variety of challenges to the legitimacy of internationalized governance.

The third variation which must be taken into account is variation by country. Almost every aspect of the attitudes we have examined varies to a significant degree as between countries, or between groups of countries. While theories of integration suggest that this is no bad thing, provided that the differences remain moderate and non-cumulative, it makes arriving at an overall balance sheet difficult. One might envisage drawing up a country-by-country balance sheet but that is beyond our task here. Instead, we focus on two general implications of the differences between countries.

The first stems from the methodological imperative, noted at the outset of this chapter, of searching for the systemic factors giving rise to the observed differences. To do this in a thorough fashion would be to map out a future research agenda. However, one pattern is clear: variations in support for integration, and other more specific attitudes, are rooted in national situations which are a combination of domestic political considerations and international circumstances. These, rather than the fact of joining some developmental processes at different times, are the source of persisting differences between countries. In concrete terms, the 1973 entrants were not different from the original six because they arrived later. Rather, they arrived later because they were different—in geopolitical and historical terms. This applies not just to the 1973 enlargement but to the different reactions of the entrants and potential entrants to the process since its inception. Thus, it applies to the enthusiasm of the original entrants, particularly the Germans, to the reluctance of the British, the Danes and, to a lesser extent, the Irish, to the enthusiasm of the Spaniards and the Portuguese, to the reticence of the Scandinavians, and to the eagerness of the Central and Eastern Europeans.

Differences in national circumstances and experiences also account for differing attitudes towards NATO between the publics of northern and southern European countries. That these differences might also be related to a stronger sense of European identity in southern Europe must, given the data to hand, remain a more speculative point. However, while historical, cultural, and geographical circumstances make the lower incidence of European identity in Britain, Ireland, and Denmark understandable, there remains the puzzle about the low incidence of European identity in the Netherlands and its decline in Germany. More specific illustrations of the proposition that the national situations of states are fundamental to understanding the attitudes of their populations could be multiplied, as, for example, with the innovator-escapist syndrome in Italy and more recently in Greece, or the distinctive and changing reactions to European integration on the part of Danish and Irish farmers. What is of interest here is the general point: attitudes towards integration are moulded by national experience.

This is more than an observation typical of comparative politics. It is a forceful reminder that the political processes underlying internationalized governance are primarily national. This applies both to the circumstances which determine initial levels of support for integration and, as the analysis of élite–mass linkages showed, to the processes which foster or undermine such support. This points to a dilemma at the centre of the integration or internationalization process which affects our assessment of the balance sheet. The process of transcending the nation state depends on state agents to initiate—or at least to acquiesce in—and implement the necessary measures, and depends on national political actors and processes to persuade national publics to legitimize them. All this might be fine if European integration had all the time in the world and if it were about to enter a period of consolidation and repose. But that does not seem to be in the offing. The 1996 Inter-Governmental Conference and, above and beyond that, the task of reshaping and redefining internationalized governance in Europe, will give rise to increased rather than diminished politicization. The dilemma will therefore intensify, as will the significance of European public opinion and the impact of the processes of attitude formation and differentiation identified in our research.

REFERENCES

Adler, K. P. (1986). 'West-European and American Public Opinion on Peace, Defence and Arms Control in a Cross-national Perspective'. *International Social Science* 38, 4: 589–600.

———— and Wertman D. A. (1981). 'Is NATO in Trouble? A Survey of European Attitudes'. *Public Opinion* 4 (4): 8–12 and 50.

Aldrich, J. H., Sullivan, J. L., and Borgida, E. (1989). 'Foreign Affairs and Issue Voting: Do Presidential Candidates "Waltz Before a Blind Audience"?' *American Political Science Review* 83: 123–41.

Allardt, E. (1964). 'Patterns of Class Conflict and Working Class Consciousness in Finnish Politics'. In *Cleavages, Ideologies and Party Systems: Contributions to Comparative Political Sociology*, ed. E. Allardt and Y. Littunen. Helsinki: Transactions of the Westermarck Society.

———— (1981). *Att ha, att älska, att vara*. Lund: Argos.

Almond, G. A. (1980). 'The Intellectual History of the Civic Culture Concept'. In *The Civic Culture Revisited*, ed. G. A. Almond and S. Verba. Boston: Little, Brown.

———— and Verba, S. (1963). *The Civic Culture*. Boston: Little, Brown.

———— ———— (1980). *The Civic Culture Revisited*. Boston: Little, Brown.

American Institute of Public Opinion (1972). *The Gallup Poll: Public Opinion, 1935–1971*. New York: Random House.

Ardy, B. (1988). 'The National Incidence of the European Community Budget'. *Journal of Common Market Studies* 26: 401–29.

Bardes, B. A., and Oldendick, R. W. (1990). 'Public Opinion and Foreign Policy: A Field in Search of Theory'. *Research in Micropolitics* 3: 227–47.

Battistelli, F., and Isernia, P. (1990). 'What Happens when you Open Pandora's Box? The Peace Movement and its Impact on the Political System'. Paper presented at the ECPR Joint Sessions of Workshops, Bochum.

Berglund, S., and Dellenbrant, J.-Å. (eds.) (1993). *The New Democracies in Eastern Europe: Party Systems and Political Cleavages*. Aldershot: Edward Elgar.

Boer, C. de. (1981). 'The Polls: Our Commitment to World War III'. *Public Opinion Quarterly* 45: 126–34.

———— (1985). 'The Polls: The European Peace Movement and the Deployment of Nuclear Missiles'. *Public Opinion Quarterly* 49: 119–32.

Bonfadelli, H. (1987). 'Wissenskluftforschung'. In *Medienwirkungsforschung*, ed. M. Schenk. Tübingen: Mohr.

Bosch, A. (1992). 'Economic Well-being and Support for the EC'. Barcelona: Institut Ciencies Politiques Sociales Working Papers.

—— (1993). 'Tres Models per a l'Estudi de les Actituds Envers la CE a Espanya'. Doctoral dissertation, Universitat Autonoma de Barcelona.

Buchanan, W., and Cantril, H. (1953). *How Nations See Each Other: A Study in Public Opinion*. Urbana: University of Illinois Press.

Capitanchik, D., and Eichenberg, R. (1983). *Defence and Public Opinion*. Boston: Routledge & Kegan Paul.

Caporaso, J. A. (1973). 'The Development of System Linkages in the European Community'. In *Quasi-Experimental Approaches: Testing Theory and Evaluating Policy*, ed. J. A. Caporaso and L. L. Roos. Evanston, Ill.: Northwestern University Press.

—— (1974). *The Structure and Function of European Integration*. Pacific Palisades, Calif.: Goodyear.

—— and Keeler, J. T. S. (1993). 'The European Community and Regional Integration Theory'. Paper prepared for the Third Biennial International Conference of the European Community Studies Association. Washington.

Cayroll, R. (1983). 'Media Use and Campaign Evaluations: Social and Political Stratification of the European Electorate'. In *Communicating to Voters*, ed. J. G. Blumler. London: Sage.

Commission of the European Communities (1987). *Eurobarometer: Public Opinion in the European Community*, 27.

—— (1989). *Eurobarometer: Public Opinion in the European Community*, 32.

Converse, P. E. (1964). 'The Nature of Belief Systems among Mass Publics'. In *Ideology and Discontent*, ed. D. A. Apter. New York: Free Press.

Dalton, R. J. (1988). *Citizen Politics in Western Democracies*. Chatham, NJ: Chatham House.

—— and Duval, R. (1986). 'The Political Environment and Foreign Policy Opinions: British Attitudes toward European Integration, 1972–1979'. *British Journal of Political Science* 16: 113–34.

—— and Eichenberg, R. C. (1991). 'Economic Evaluations and Citizen Support for European Integration'. Paper presented to the Annual Congress of the American Political Science Association, Washington.

Davidson, A. R., and Thomson, E. (1980). 'Cross-cultural Studies of Attitudes and Beliefs'. In *Handbook of Cross-Cultural Psychology*, v, ed. H. Triandis and R. Brislin. Boston: Allyn & Bacon.

Dawes, R. M., and Smith, T. L. (1985). 'Attitude and Opinion Measurement'. In *Handbook of Social Psychology*, i, ed. G. Lindzey and E. Aronson. New York: Random House.

Delors, J. (1991). 'The Principle of Subsidiarity: Contribution to the Debate'. In *Subsidiarity: the Challenge of Change—Proceedings of the Jacques Delors Colloquium*. Maastricht: European Institute of Public Administration.

Desmet, L. (1990). 'Belgian Peace Movement Polled: A Review of Public Opinion Poll Results on the Issues of War and Peace, Security and Defense,

Armament and Disarmament in Belgium between 1979 and 1985'. In *Towards a Comparative Analysis of Peace Movements*, ed. K. Kodama and U. Vesa. Aldershot: Dartmouth.

D'Estaing, Giscard V. (1990). *The Principle of Subsidiarity*. European Parliament Committee on Institutional Affairs.

Deutsch, K. W. (1953). *Nationalism and Social Communication*. New York: John Wiley.

—— (1961). 'Social Mobilization and Political Development'. *American Political Science Review* 55: 493–514.

—— (1968). *Analysis of International Relations*. Englewood Cliffs, NJ: Prentice-Hall.

—— and Merritt, R. L. (1965). 'Effects of Events on National and International Images'. In *International Behavior: A Social-Psychological Analysis*, ed. H. C. Kelman. New York: Holt, Rinehart & Winston.

—— Burrell, S. A., Kann, R. A., Lee, M. Jr., Lichtermann, M., Loewenheim, F. L., and Van Wagenen, R. W. (1957). *Political Community and the North Atlantic Area*. Princeton, NJ: Princeton University Press.

Dimitras, P. (1983). 'Greece's New Isolationism?' *Public Opinion* 6 (1): 14–15 and 20.

Downs, A. (1957). *An Economic Theory of Democracy*. New York: Harper & Row.

Draft Treaty Establishing the European Union (1984). European Parliament, February.

Duchesne, S. (1994). *Citoyenneté à la française*. Paris: Institute d'Études Politiques.

Dumoulin, M. (1985). 'Opinion Publique et Politique Extérieure en Belgique de 1945 à 1962: Orientation des Etudes et Perspectives de la Recherches en Belgique'. *Res Publica* 27 (1): 3–29.

Easton, D. (1965) (1979 2nd edn.). *A Systems Analysis of Political Life*. New York: John Wiley.

—— (1975a). 'A Re-assessment of the Concept of Political Support'. *British Journal of Political Science* 5: 435–57.

—— (1975b). *A Framework for Political Analysis*. Englewood Cliffs, NJ: Prentice-Hall.

Eco, U. (1964). *Apocalittici a integrati*. Milan: Bompiani.

Eichenberg, R. (1989). *Public Opinion and National Security in Western Europe*. London: Macmillan.

Erskine, H. (1969). 'The Polls: Some Recent Opinions on NATO'. *Public Opinion Quarterly* 3: 487–99.

European Parliament Directorate General for Information and Public Relations (1994). *Europe Elections 1994: Results and Elected Members Provisional Edition*. Brussels: EP DG for Information and Public Relations, 15 June.

Everts, P. P. (1983). *Public Opinion, the Churches and Foreign Policy: Studies of Domestic Factors in Dutch Foreign Policy*. Leiden: Institute for International Studies.

—— 1984–7. *Jaarboek Vrede en Veiligheid*. Alphen aan den Rjin, Amsterdam: Samsom.

—— (1988–90). *Jaarboek Vrede en Veiligheid*. Amsterdam: VU-uitgeverij/ Jan Mets.

—— (1992). 'Belief in NATO as an International Institution: A Comparative Trend Analysis'. In *The Future of Security in Europe: A Comparative Analysis of European Public Opinion*, ed. P. Manigart. Brussels: Royal Military School.

—— (1993). 'General or Specific? Orientations towards Internationalized Governance'. In *International Relations and Pan-Europe*, ed. F. R. Pfetsch. Münster: LIT Verlag.

—— and Faber, A. (1990). 'Public Opinion, Foreign Policy and Democracy'. Paper presented at ECPR Joint Sessions, Bochum.

Featherstone, K. (1988). *Socialist Parties and European Integration: A Comparative History*. Manchester: Manchester University Press.

Feld, W. J., and Wildgen, J. K. (1976). *Domestic Political Realities and European Unification: A Study of Mass Publics and Elites in the European Community Countries*. Boulder, Col.: Westview Press.

—— —— (1982). *NATO and the Atlantic Defense: Perceptions and Illusions*. New York: Praeger.

Ferrera, M. (ed.) (1991) *Le dodici europe: I paesi della comunità di fronte ai cambiamenti del 1989–1990*. Bologne: Il Mulino.

Festinger, L. (1957). *A Theory of Cognitive Dissonance*. Stanford, Calif.: Stanford University Press.

Ficker, H. C., Fischer-Dieskau, C., and Krenzler, H. G. (1976). 'Die Zusammenarbeit der liberalen Parteien in Westeuropa: Auf dem Wege zur Föderation?' In *Zusammenarbeit der Parteien in Westeuropa*. Bonn: Europa Union Verlag.

Fischer, C. S. (1978). 'Urban-to-Rural Diffusion of Opinions in Contemporary America'. *American Journal of Sociology* 84: 151–9.

Fishbein, M., and Ajzen, I. (1975). *Belief, Attitude, Intention and Behavior*. Reading, Mass.: Addison-Wesley.

Flickinger, R. (1983). 'The Peace Movement and Nato Missile Deployment'. *Peace and Change* 9: 17–30.

—— (1984). 'Responses to Protest: Western European Governments and Public Opposition to INF Deployment'. Paper presented to International Studies Association Convention, Atlanta, Ga.

Flynn, G. (ed.) (1985). *NATO's Northern Allies: the National Security Policies of Belgium, the Netherlands, Denmark, and Norway*. Totowa. NJ.: Rowman & Allanheldt.

Flynn, G., and Rattinger, H. (eds.) (1985). *The Public and Atlantic Defence.* London: Croom Helm.

Free, L. A. (1976). *How Others See Us: Critical Choices for Americans*, iii. Lexington, Mass: Lexington Books.

Fuchs, D. and Klingemann, H.-D. (1989). 'The Left–Right Schema'. In *Continuities in Political Action*, ed. M. K. Jennings, J. W. van Deth, *et al.* Berlin: Walter de Gruyter.

Gabriel, O. W. (1992). *Die EG-Staaten im Vergleich: Strukturen, Prozesse, Politikinhalte.* Opladen: Westdeutscher Verlag.

Gamson, W. A., and Modigliani, A. (1966). 'Knowledge and Foreign Policy Opinions: Some Models for Consideration'. *Public Opinion Quarterly* 30: 187–99.

Gellner, E. (1964). *Thought and Change.* London: Weidenfeld & Nicolson.

Genova, B. K., and Greenberg, B. S. (1979). 'Interest in News and the Knowledge Gap'. *Public Opinion Quarterly* 43: 79–91.

Grabitz, E., Schmuck, O., Steppat, S., and Wessels, W. (1988). *Direktwahl und Demokratisierung: Eine Funktionenbilanz des Europäischen Parlaments nach der ersten Wahlperiode.* Bonn: Europa Union Verlag.

Greven, M. T. (1977). *Parteien und politische Herrschaft.* Meisenheim am Glan: Anton Hain.

Haas, E. B. (1958). *The Uniting of Europe.* Stanford, Calif.: Stanford University Press.

———— (1971). 'The Study of Regional Integration: Reflections on the Joy and Anguish of Pre-theorizing'. In *Regional Integration: Theory and Research*, ed. L. Lindberg and S. Scheingold. Cambridge, Mass.: Harvard University Press.

———— (1976.) *The Obsolescence of Regional Integration Theory.* Berkeley, Calif.: Institute of International Studies.

———— and Schmitter, P. (1964). 'Economics and Differential Patterns of Political Integration: Projections about Unity in Latin America.' *International Organization* 18: 705–37.

Hägerstrand, T. (1968). 'The Diffusion of Innovations'. In *International Encyclopedia of the Social Sciences*, ed. D. L. Sills. New York: Free Press.

Haggard, S., and Simmons, B. A. (1987). 'Theories of International Regimes'. In *International Organization* 41: 491–517.

Handley, D. H. (1981a). 'Public Opinion and European Integration: The Crisis of the 1970s'. *European Journal of Political Research* 9: 335–64.

—— (1981b). 'Public Opinion and the European Community'. *Journal of Common Market Studies* 2: 101–26.

Hardarson, O. T. (1985). *Icelandic Attitudes towards Security and Foreign Affairs*, Reykjavik: Icelandic Commission on Security and International Affairs. Occasional Paper no. 2.

Harrop, M., and Miller, W. L. (1987). *Elections and Voters: A Comparative Introduction*. London: Macmillan.

Hastings, E. H., and Hastings P. K. (eds). (1978–79 to 1987–88). *Index to International Public Opinion*. Westport, Conn.: Greenwood Press/Survey Research Consultants International.

Hechter, M. (1975). *Internal Colonialism: The Celtic Fringe in British National Development*. London: Routledge & Kegan Paul.

Heine-Geldern, R. (1968). 'Cultural Diffusion'. In *International Encyclopedia of the Social Sciences*, ed. D. L. Sills. New York: Free Press.

Held, D. (ed.) (1993). *Prospects for Democracy: North, South, East, West*. Cambridge: Polity Press.

Hewstone, M. (1986). *Understanding Attitudes to the European Community: A Social-Psychological Study in Four Member States*. Cambridge: Cambridge University Press.

—— (1991). 'Public Opinion and Public Information Campaigns: The Value of the Eurobarometer'. In *Eurobarometer: The Dynamics of European Opinion*, ed. K. Reif and R. Inglehart. Basingstoke: Macmillan.

Hoffmann, S. (1966). 'Obstinate or Obsolete? The Fate of the Nation State and the Case of Western Europe'. *Daedalus* 95: 862–915.

Hofrichter, J. (1992). 'Public Opinion on EC Membership of Turkey in the Countries of the European Community'. Paper presented at the Conference on European Political Co-operation and Turkey: Divergence and Convergence in Foreign Policy. Istanbul, March.

—— and Klein, M. (1993). *The European Parliament in the Eyes of EC Citizens*. Report on behalf of the European Parliament, Directorate General III, Information and Public Relations. Mannheim: ZEUS.

—— and Niedermayer, O. (1991). *Cross-Border Social European Integration: Trust between the Peoples of the EC Member States and its Evolution over Time*. Report prepared on behalf of DG-X of the Commission of the European Communities. Mannheim: ZEUS.

Hurwitz, J., and Peffley, M. (1987). 'How Are Foreign Policy Attitudes Structured? A Hierarchical Model'. *American Political Science Review* 81: 1099–120.

Hyman, H. H., Wright, C. R., and Reed, J. S. (1975). *The Enduring Effects of Education*. Chicago: University of Chicago Press.

ICPSR (1980). *Codebook for Eurobarometer 1980*, 9 (Ann Arbor: ICPSR).

Inglehart, R. (1967). 'An End to European Integration?' *American Political Science Review* 61: 91–105.

—— (1970*a*). 'Cognitive Mobilization and European Identity'. *Comparative Politics* 3: 45–70.

—— (1970*b*). 'Public Opinion and Regional Integration'. *International Organization* 24: 764–95.

Inglehart, R. (1971a). 'Changing Value Priorities and European Integration'. *Journal of Common Market Studies* 10: 1–36.

——— (1971b). 'The Silent Revolution in Europe: Intergenerational Change in Post-Industrial Societies'. *American Political Science Review* 65: 991–1017.

——— (1977a). 'Long-Term Trends in Mass Support for European Unification'. *Government and Opposition* 12: 150–77.

——— (1977b). *The Silent Revolution: Changing Values and Political Styles among Western Publics*. Princeton: Princeton University Press.

——— (1990). *Culture Shift in Advanced Industrial Societies*. Princeton: Princeton University Press.

———(1991). 'Trust between Nations: Primordial Ties, Societal Learning and Economic Development'. In *Eurobarometer: The Dynamics of European Public Opinion*, ed. R. Inglehart and K. Reif. London: Macmillan.

——— and Rabier, J.-R. (1978). 'Economic Uncertainty and European Solidarity: Public Opinion Trends'. *Annals of the American Academy of Social and Political Science* 440: 66–97.

——— ——— (1984). 'La confiance entre les peuples: déterminants et conséquences'. *Revue Francaise de Science Politique* 34: 5–47.

——— and Reif, K. (1991). 'Analysing Trends in West European Opinion: The Role of Eurobarometer Surveys'. In *Eurobarometer: The Dynamics of European Public Opinion*, ed. K. Reif and R. Inglehart. Basingstoke: Macmillan.

——— Rabier, J.-R., and Reif, K. (1987). 'The Evolution of Public Attitudes toward European Integration, 1970–1986'. *Journal of European Integration* 10: 135–55.

Jacobs, F. (1989). *Western European Political Parties: A Comprehensive Guide*. Harlow: Longman.

Janning, J. (1991). 'Germania: il delicato cammino verso l'unificazione'. In *Le dodici europe: I paesi della comunità di fronte ai cambiamenti del 1989–1990*, ed. M. Ferrera. Bologne: Il Mulino.

Janssen, J. I. (1991). 'Postmaterialism, Cognitive Mobilization and Public Support for European Integration'. *British Journal of Political Science* 21: 443–68.

Jowell, R., and Hoinville, G. (eds). (1977). *Britain into Europe*. London: Croom Helm.

Katz, E., Levin, M. L., and Hamilton, H. (1963). 'Traditions of Research on the Diffusion of Innovation'. *American Sociological Review* 28: 237–52.

Kelman, H. C. (1965). 'Social-Psychological Approaches to the Study of International Relations: Definition of Scope'. In *International Behavior: A Social-Psychological Analysis*, ed. H. C. Kelman. New York: Holt, Rinehart & Winston.

Kemeny, J. G., Snell, J. L., and Thompson, G. L. (1966). *Introduction to Finite Mathematics*. Englewood Cliffs, NJ.: Prentice-Hall.

Keohane, R. O., and Hoffmann, S. (1990). 'Conclusions: Community Politics and Institutional Change'. In *The Dynamics of European Integration*, ed. W. Wallace. London: Pinter.

—— —— (1991). 'Institutional Change in Europe in the 1980s'. In *The New European Community: Decision Making and Institutional Change*, ed. R. O. Keohane and S. Hoffmann. Boulder, Colo.: Westview Press.

—— and Nye, J. S. (1977). *Power and Interdependence: World Politics in Transition*. Boston: Little, Brown.

—— —— (1987). 'Power and Interdependence Revisited'. *International Organization* 41 (4): 725–53.

Key, V. O. (1961). *Public Opinion and American Democracy*. New York: Knopf.

Klingemann, H.-D. (1990). 'Party Families: An Effort to Compare Political Parties across Countries'. Unpublished manuscript.

Kohler-Koch, B. (1991). 'Die Politik der Integration der DDR in die EG'. In *Die Osterweiterung der EG: Die Einbeziehung der ehemaligen DDR in die Gemeinschaft*, ed. B. Kohler-Koch. Baden-Baden: Nomos.

Krasner, S. D. (ed.) (1983). *International Regimes*. Ithaca, NY: Cornell University Press.

Kratochwil, F., and Ruggie, J. G. (1986). 'International Organization: State of the Art on an Art of the State'. *International Organization* 40: 753–75.

Larsen, O. N. (1962). 'Innovators and Early Adopters of Televison'. *Sociological Inquiry* 32: 16–33.

Lasswell, H. (1936). *Politics: Who Gets What, When, How*. New York: McGraw-Hill.

Lazarsfeld, P. F., Berelson, B. R., and Gaudet, H. (1944). *The People's Choice*. New York: Duell, Sloan & Pearce.

Lerner, D. (1958). *The Passing of Traditional Society*. Glencoe, Ill.: Free Press.

—— and Gordon, M. (1969). *Euroatlantica: Changing Perspectives of the European Elites*. Cambridge, Mass.: MIT Press.

Lewin, L. (1991). *Self-Interest and Public Interest in Western Politics*. Oxford: Oxford University Press.

Lewis-Beck, M. (1986a). 'Comparative Economic Voting: Britain, France, Germany, Italy'. *American Journal of Political Science* 30: 315–46.

—— (1986b). *Economics and Elections*. Ann Arbor: University of Michigan Press.

Lindberg, L. N., and Scheingold, S. A. (1970). *Europe's Would-Be Polity: Patterns of Change in the European Community*. Englewood Cliffs, NJ: Prentice-Hall.

Lindberg, L. N., and Scheingold, S. A. (eds.) (1971). *Regional Integration: Theory and Research*. Cambridge, Mass.: Harvard University Press.

Lindström, U. (1991). 'East European Social Democracy: Reborn to be Rejected'. In *Social Democracy in Transition*, ed. L. Karvonen and J. Sundberg. Aldershot: Dartmouth.

Lionberger, H. F. (1960). *Adoption of New Ideas and Practices*. Ames: Iowa State University Press.

Listhaug, O. (1986). 'War and Defence Attitudes: A First Look at Survey Data from Fourteen Countries'. *Journal of Peace Research* 23: 69–76.

Lodge, J. (1978). 'Loyalty and the EEC: The Limitations of the Functionalist Approach'. *Political Studies* 26: 232–48.

—— (1983). 'Integration Theory'. In *The European Community: Bibliographic Excursions*, ed. J. Lodge. London: Pinter.

Lohmoeller, J.-B. (1984). *LVPLS 1.6. Program Manual: Latent Variables Path Analysis with Partial Least-squares Estimation*. Cologne: Zentralarchiv für empirische Sozialforschung.

Manigart. P., and Marlier, E. (1991*a*). 'Belgians and Security Issues: A Trend Analysis (1970–1990)'. *Res Publica* 33,: 503–22.

—— —— (1991*b*). 'The Future of Security in Europe: Civilian Opinions'. Paper for International Symposium on The Future of the Military in Europe, Marburg.

Marsh, C., and Fraser, C. (eds.) (1989). *Public Opinion and Nuclear Weapons*. London: Macmillan.

Massari, O. (1991). 'Gran Bretagna: il dopo Thatcher'. In *Le dodici europe: I paesi della comunità di fronte ai cambiamenti del 1989–1990*, ed. M. Ferrera. Bologne: Il Mulino.

McClosky, H. (1967). 'Personality and Attitude Correlates of Foreign Policy Orientation'. In *Domestic Sources of Foreign Policy*, ed. J. N. Rosenau. New York: Free Press.

McDonald, R. (1989). 'Greece's Year of Political Turbulence'. *World Today* 45: 194–7.

McIntosh, M. E., and MacIver, M. A. (1994). 'The Structure of Foreign Policy Attitudes in East and West Europe: Does the American Model Apply?' Paper presented at the 35th Annual Convention of the International Studies Association, Washington DC.

McKenna, P., and Niedermayer, O. (1990). *European Attitudes of Women*. Report prepared on behalf of the DG X of the Commission the EC.

Mackie, T. T. (1985–9, 1991). 'General Elections in Western Nations'. *European Journal of Political Research* 13–17, 19.

—— and Rose, R. (1980–4). 'General Elections in Western Nations.' *European Journal of Political Research* 8–12.

Merritt, R. L. (1968). 'Visual Representation of Mutual Friendliness'. In

Western European Perspectives on International Affairs, ed. R. L. Merritt and D. Puchala. New York: Praeger.

—— and Puchala, D. (eds.) (1968). *Western European Perspectives on International Affairs*. New York: Praeger.

Merten, K. (1988). 'Aufstieg und Fall des "Two-Step-Flow of Communication" '. *Politische Vierteljahresschrift* 29: 600–35.

Michelat, G., and Thomas, J.-P. (1966). *Dimensions du Nationalisme*. Cahiers de la Fondation Paris: Nationale des Sciences Politiques/Armand Colin.

Michelmann, H. J., and Soldatos, P. (1994). *European Integration: Theories and Approaches*. Lanham, Md.: University Press of America.

Mitrany, D. (1943). *A Working Peace System: An Argument for the Functional Development of International Organization*. Oxford: Oxford University Press.

Modigliani, A. (1972). 'Hawks and Doves, Isolationism and Political Distrust: An Analysis of Public Opinion on Military Policy'. *American Political Science Review* 66: 960–78.

Mortensen, M. S. (1983). 'NATO's dobbeltvedtak: Folkeopinionen i Norge 1979–1980'. *Internasjonal Politikks* 3: 397–440.

Munton, D. (1990). 'NATO up against the Wall: Changing Security Attitudes in Germany, Britain and Canada, 1960s to the 1980s'. Paper presented at International Studies Association, Washington.

Namer, G. (1993). *Memorie d'Europa: Identità europea a memoria collettiva*. Messina: Rubettino.

Niedermayer, O. (1989). *Innerparteiliche Partizipation*. Opladen: Westdeutscher Verlag.

—— (1991). 'Bevölkerungsorientierungen gegenüber dem politischen System der Europäischen Gemeinschaft'. In *Staatswerdung Europas?* ed. R. Wildenmann. Baden-Baden: Nomos.

—— (1994). 'Europäisches Parlament und öffentliche Meinung'. In *Wahlen und Europäische Einigung*, ed. O. Niedermayer and H. Schmitt. Opladen: Westdeutscher Verlag.

Nincic, M., and Russett, B. (1979). 'The Effect of Similarity and Interest on Attitudes toward Foreign Countries'. *Public Opinion Quarterly* 43: 68–78.

Noel, E. (1991). 'The Political Prospects for Europe in the Wake of the Single European Act: A Response to Public Expectations'. In *Eurobarometer: The Dynamics of European Public Opinion*, ed. K. Reif and R. Inglehart. Basingstoke, Hants: Macmillan.

Noelle-Neumann, E. (ed.) (1950s–1990s). Allensbach Institut für Demoskopie, *Jahrbuch der öffentlichen Meinung*. Allensbach and Bonn: Verlag für Demoskopie (early volumes); Munich, New York, London, Paris: K.G. Saur (later volumes).

—— (1983). 'The Missile-Gap: the German Press and Public Opinion'. *Public Opinion* 6: 45–9.

North Atlantic Assembly, (1984–91). Reports of the Civilian Affairs Committee and Subcommittee on Public Information on Defence and Security.

Nye, J. S. (1971). (1987 2nd edn.). *Peace in Parts: Integration and Conflict in Regional Organization.* Boston, Mass.: Little, Brown.

Office for the Official Publications of the European Communities (1991). *The Community Budget: The Facts in Figures.* Luxembourg.

Office of the European Parliament (1984). *European Parliament Election Results Ireland, June 1984.* Dublin: European Parliament Office.

—— (1989). *European Parliament Election Results Ireland, June 1989.* Dublin: European Parliament Office.

Oskamp, S. (1977). *Attitudes and Opinions.* Englewood Cliffs, NJ.: Prentice-Hall.

Oudsten, E. den (1984). 'Public Opinion and Nuclear Weapons'. In *SIPRI Yearbook, World Armaments and Disarmament 1984*: 15–20.

—— (1985). 'Public Opinion'. In *SIPRI-Yearbook 1985*: 31–38.

—— (1986). 'Public Opinion on Peace and War'. In *SIPRI-Yearbook 1986*: 17–35.

Parland, T. (1993). *The Rejection of Totalitarian Socialism and Liberal Democracy: A Study of the Russian New Right.* Helsinki: Suomen Tiedeseura.

Pentland, C. (1973). *International Theory and European Integration.* London: Faber & Faber.

Percheron, A. (1991). 'Les Français et l'Europe: Acquiescement de façade ou véritable adhésion?' *Revue Française de Science Politique* 41: 382–406.

Peterson, S. (1972). 'Events, Mass Opinion, and Elite Attitudes'. In *Communications in International Politics*, ed. R. L. Merritt. Urbana: University of Illinois Press.

Pool, I. de Sola (1965). 'Effects of Cross-National Contact on National and International Images'. In *International Behavior: A Social-Psychological Analysis*, ed. H. C. Kelman. New York: Holt, Rinehart & Winston.

Przeworski, A. and Teune, H. (1970). *The Logic of Comparative Social Inquiry.* New York and Chichester: Wiley-Interscience.

Puchala, D. J. (1970). 'The Common Market and Political Federation in Western European Public Opinion'. *International Studies Quarterly* 14: 32–59.

—— (1984). 'The Integration Theorists and the Study of International Relations'. In *The Global Agenda: Issues and Perspectives*, 2nd edn., ed. C. W. Kegley and E. Wittkopf. New York: Random House.

—— and Hopkins, R. F. (1983). 'International Regimes: Lessons from Inductive Analysis'. In *International Regimes*, ed. S. D. Krasner. Ithaca, NY: Cornell University Press.

Putnam, R. D. (1976). *The Comparative Study of Political Elites.* Englewood Cliffs, NJ: Prentice-Hall.

—————— —————— (1988). 'Diplomacy and Domestic Politics: The Logic of Two-Level Games'. *International Organization*, 42 (3): 427–69.

Rabier, J.-R. (1965). *L'Information des Européens et l'intégration de l'Europe*. Brussels: Institut d'Études européennes de l'Université de Bruxelles.

Rattinger, H. (1987). 'Change versus Continuity in West German Attitudes on National Security and Nuclear Weapons in the Early 1980s'. *Public Opinion Quarterly* 51: 495–521.

—————— (1990). 'Domestic and Foreign Policy Issues in the 1988 Presidential Election'. In *European Journal of Political Research* 18: 623–43.

—————— (1991*a*). 'The Development and Structure of West German Public Opinion on Security since the Late 1970s'. In *Debating National Security: the Public Dimension*, ed. H. Rattinger and D. Munton. Frankfurt: Verlag Peter Lang.

—————— (1991*b*). 'Unemployment and Elections in West Germany'. In *Economy and Politics: The Calculus of Support*, ed. H. Norpoth, M. S. Lewis-Beck, and J.-D. Lafay. Ann Arbor: University of Michigan Press.

—————— and Heinlein, P. (1986). *Sicherheitspolitik in der Öffentlichen Meinung: Umfrageergebnisse für die Bundesrepublik Deutschland bis zum Heißen Herbst 1983*. Berlin: Wissenschaftlicher Autorenverlag.

Rebel, H. J. C. (1985). *Defensie in Nederland: Opinieonderzoek 1978–1982*. The Hague: Ministry of Defence.

Reif, K. (ed.) (1978). *Die mittlere Führungsschicht politischer Parteien in der Bundesrepublik Deutschland*. Mannheim: Institut für Sozialwissenschaften der Universität Mannheim.

—————— (1992). 'Wahlen, Wähler und Demokratie in der EG'. *Aus Politik und Zeitgeschichte. 19: 43–52.*

—————— (1993). 'Ein Ende des "Permissive Consensus"? Zum Wandel europapolitischer Einstellungen in der öffentlichen Meinung der EG-Mitgliedstaaten'. In *Der Vertrag von Maastricht in der wissenschaftlichen Kontroverse*, ed. R. Hrbek. Baden-Baden: Nomos.

—————— and Inglehart, R. (eds). (1991). *Eurobarometer: The Dynamics of Public Opinion*. Basingstoke: Macmillan.

—————— and Schmitt, H. (1980). 'Nine Second Order National Elections: A Conceptual Framework for the Analysis of European Election Results'. *European Journal of Political Research* 8: 3–4.

Reimann, H. (1973). 'Bedeutung der Kommunikation für Innovationsprozesse'. In *Soziologie: Sprache–Bezug zur Praxis–Verhältnis zu anderen Wissenschaften: René König zum 65. Geburtstag*, ed. G. Albrecht, H. Daheim, and F. Sack. Opladen: Westdeutscher Verlag.

Robinson, J. P. (1976). 'Interpersonal Influence in Election Campaigns: Two Step-Flow Hypotheses'. *Public Opinion Quarterly* 40: 304–19.

Rogers, E. M. (1962). *Diffusion of Innovations*. New York: Free Press.

—————— and Eveland, J. D. (1978). 'Diffusion of Innovations Perspective on

National R and D Assessment: Communication and Innovation in Organizations'. In *Technological Innovation: A Critical Review of Current Knowledge*, ed. P. Kelly and M. Kranzberg. San Francisco: San Francisco Press.

Rogers, E. M., and Shoemaker, F. F. (1971). *Communication of Innovations: A Cross-cultural Approach*, 2nd edn. New York: Free Press.

Rokkan, S. (1966). 'Electoral Mobilization, Party Competition and National Integration'. In *Political Parties and Political Development*, ed. J. LaPalombara and M. Weiner. Princeton: Princeton University Press.

—— (1967). 'Geography, Religion and Social Class: Cross-Cutting Cleavages in Norwegian Politics'. In *Party Systems and Voter Alignments*, ed. S. M. Lipset and S. Rokkan. New York: Free Press.

—— (1981). 'The Growth and Structuring of Mass Politics in the Nordic Countries'. In *Nordic Democracy*, ed. F. Vesti. Copenhagen: Det Danske Selskab.

Roschar, F. M. (ed.) (1975). 'For Nederlands Instituut voor Vredesvraagstukken'. *Buitenlandse politiek in de Nederlandse publieke opinie, 1960–1975*. The Hague.

Rosenau, J. N. (1961). *Public Opinion and Foreign Policy: An Operational Formulation*. New York: Random House.

—— (1992a). 'Governance, Order, and Change in World Politics'. In *Governance Without Government: Order and Change in World Politics*, ed. J. N. Rosenau and E. O. Czempiel. Cambridge: Cambridge University Press.

—— (1992b). 'Citizenship in a Changing Global Order'. In *Governance without Government: Order and Change in World Politics*, ed. J. N. Rosenau and E. O. Czempiel. Cambridge: Cambridge University Press.

Rosenberg, M. J., and Hovland, C. I. (1960). 'Cognitive, Affective and Behavioral Components of Attitudes'. In *Attitude Organization and Change*, ed. C. I. Hovland and M. J. Rosenberg. New Haven: Yale University Press.

Rozès, S. (1989). *Politique exterieure et opinion publique*. Contribution aux journées d'étude de l'Association Française de Science Politique, December.

Russett, B. (1990). *Controlling the Sword: The Democratic Governance of National Security*. Cambridge, Mass.: Harvard University Press

—— and DeLuca, D. R. (1983). 'Theater Nuclear Forces: Public Opinion in Western Europe'. *Political Science Quarterly* 98: 179–96.

Sabin, P. A. G. (1986–7). 'Proposals and Propaganda: Arms Control and British Public Opinion in the 1980s'. *International Affairs* 63: 49–63.

—— (1988a). *British Perceptions of the USA and USSR: The Limits of Comparative Opinion Polling*. London: Department of War Studies, King's College.

—— (1988b). 'Assessing a Peace Offensive: The Impact of Gorbachev on

British Public Opinion'. In *Defence Yearbook*. London: Royal United Services Institute and Brassey.

———— (1990). 'Western European Public Opinion and "Defence without the Threat"'. Unpublished manuscript.

Santamaría, J., and Alcover, M. (1987). *Actitudes de los Españoles ante la OTAN*. Series Estudios y Encuestas no. 6. Madrid: Centro de Investigaciones Sociológicas.

Sartori, G. (1966). 'European Political Parties: The Case of Polarized Pluralism'. In *Political Parties and Political Development*, ed. J. LaPalombara and M. Weiner. Princeton: Princeton University Press.

———— (1976). *Parties and Party Systems: A Framework for Analysis*. Cambridge: Cambridge University Press.

Schmitt, H. (1980). 'Appendix: The First European Parliament Direct Elections, 7–10 June 1979; Results Compared with National Election Results'. *European Journal of Political Research* 8: 145–58.

Schmitter, P. C. (1971). 'A Revised Theory of Regional Integration'. In *Regional Integration: Theory and Research*, ed. L. N. Lindberg and S. A. Scheingold. Cambridge, Mass.: Harvard University Press.

———— (1992). 'Interests, Powers and Functions: Emergent Properties and Unintended Consequences in the European Polity'. Draft paper for Center for Advanced Study in the Behavioral Sciences.

Schneider, W. (1983). 'Elite and Public Opinion: The Alliance's New Fissure?' *Public Opinion* 6 (1): 5–8 and 51.

Scott, W. A. (1965). 'Psychological and Social Correlates of International Images'. In *International Behavior: A Social-Psychological Analysis*, ed. H. C. Kelman. New York: Holt, Rinehart & Winston.

Shepherd, R. J. (1975). *Public Opinion and European Integration*. Farnborough: Saxon House.

Sigelman, L., and Conover, P. J. (1981). 'Knowledge and Opinions about the Iranian Crisis: A Reconsideration of Three Models'. In *Public Opinion Quarterly* 45: 477–91.

Silberer, G. (1983). 'Einstellungen und Werthaltungen'. In *Marktpsychologie als Sozialwissenschaft, Enzyklopädie der Psychologie*, iv, ed. M. Irle and W. Bussmann. Göttingen: Hogrefe.

Sinnott, R. and Whelan, B. J. (1992). 'Turnout in Second Order Elections: The Case of EP Elections in Dublin 1984 and 1989'. *Economic and Social Review* 23: 147–66.

Sørensen, H. (1990). 'Danish Public Opinion of Security Issues over the Last Forty Years in an International Perspective'. Copenhagen: Institute for Peace and Conflict Research, Working Paper 13.

———— (1991). 'Danish Public Opinion of Foreign Policy Issues after World War II: A Stable Distribution'. Unpublished manuscript.

Stavridis, S. (1992). 'The Forgotten Question of the European Parliament's Current Lack of Legitimacy'. *Oxford International Review* 3(2): 27–9.

Strange, S. (1983). 'Cave! Hic Dragones: A Critique of Regime Analysis'. In *International Regimes*, ed. S. D. Krasner. Ithaca, NY: Cornell University Press.

Stroebe, W., Hewstone, M., Codol, J.-P., and Stephenson, G. M. (eds.) (1990). *Sozialpsychologie. Eine Einführung*. Berlin: Springer.

Szabo, F. (1989). 'Public Opinion and the Alliance: European and American Perspectives on NATO and European Security'. In *NATO in the 1990's*, ed. S. R. Sloan. Washington, DC: Pergamon-Brassey.

Taft, R. (1959). 'Ethnic Stereotypes, Attitudes, and Familiarity: Australia'. *Journal of Social Psychology* 49: 177–86.

Timmermann, H. (1976). 'Zwischen Weltbewegung und regionaler Kooperation: Die Zusammenarbeit der kommunistischen Parteien'. In *Zusammenarbeit der Parteien in Westeuropa*. Bonn: Europa Union Verlag.

Tönnies, F. (1922). *Gemeinschaft und Gesellschaft*, 4th edn. Berlin: Curtius.

Treiber-Reif, H. and Schmitt, H. (1990). *Structure in European Attitudes*. Report prepared on behalf of the Cellule de Prospective of the Commission of the European Communities ZEUS, University of Mannheim.

Treverton, G. (1985). 'Images of Allies: From Total Dependency to Uneven Partners'. In *Public Images of Western Security*, ed. G. Flynn. Paris: Atlantic Institute for International Affairs.

Troeltsch, E. (1928) (5th edn). *Die Bedeutung des Protestantismus für die Entstehung der modernen Welt*. Berlin: Oldenbourg.

Tufte, E. R. (1969). 'Improving Data Analysis in Political Science'. *World Politics* 21: 642–54.

—— (1978). *Political Control of the Economy*. Princeton: Princeton University Press.

Urwin, D. (1991). *The Community of Europe: A History of European Integration since 1945*. London: Longman.

Vaneker, C. H. J.. and Everts, P. P. (eds.) (1985). *Buitenlandse politiek in de Nederlandse publieke opinie, 1975–1984*. The Hague: Instituut Clingendael.

Volkens, A. (1989). 'Parteiprogrammatik und Einstellungen politischer Eliten'. In *Konfliktpotentiale und Konsensstrategien*, ed. D. Herzog and B. Wessels. Opladen: Westdeutscher Verlag.

—— and Klingemann, H. -D. (1991). *Documentation for the Data Sets on Election Programmes in Contemporary Democracies*. Berlin: Wissenschaftszentrum.

Walker, J. L. (1973). 'Comment: Problems in Research on the Diffusion of Policy Innovations'. *American Political Science Review* 67: 1186–91.

Wallace, H. (1991). 'Gran Bretagna: i rischi dell'isolamento'. In *Le dodici europe: I paesi della comunità di fronte ai cambiamenti del 1989–1990*, ed. M. Ferrera. Bologne: Il Mulino.

—————— (1990*a*). 'Introduction: The Dynamics of European Integration'. In *The Dynamics of European Integration*, ed. W. Wallace. London: Pinter.

—————— (1990*b*). *The Transformation of Western Europe*. London: Pinter.

Webb, W. (1983). 'Theoretical Perspectives and Problems'. In *Policy Making in the European Community*, 2nd edn., ed. W. Wallace, H. Wallace, and W. Webb. Chichester: John Wiley.

Weber, M. (1968). *Economy and Society*. New York: Bedminster.

—————— (1972). *Wirtschaft und Gesellschaft*. Tübingen: Siebeck.

Wecke, L. (1987). 'Enemy Images and Public Opinion'. In *Friends, Foes and Values*, ed. H.-J. Rebel and L. Wecke. Amsterdam: Jan Mets.

Weiler, J., and Wessels, W. (1988). 'EPC and the Challenge of Theory'. In *European Political Cooperation in the 1980s: A Common Foreign Policy for Western Europe?* ed. A. Pijpers, E. Regelsberger, and W. Wessels. Dordrecht: Martinus Nijhoff.

Westle, B. (1989). *Politische Legitimität: Theorien, Konzepte, empirische Befunde*. Baden-Baden: Nomos.

—————— (1990). 'Unterstützung der politischen Gemeinschaft in der Bundesrepublik Deutschland der achtziger Jahre'. Sonderforschungsbereich 3, Arbeitspapier no. 311, 'Mikroanalytische Grundlagen der Gesellschaftspolitik'. Frankfurt.

—————— (1991). 'Documentation and Classification of Eurobarometer Variables'. Paper presented to the BiG Conference, Essex. May.

—————— (1992). 'Orientations towards the Territorial Dimension of the European Community: An Empty Landscape?' Paper prepared for Group 2 meeting, Beliefs in Government Project, Paris.

—————— and Niedermayer, O. (1991). 'Die Europäische Gemeinschaft im Urteil ihrer Bürger: ein sozialwissenschaftlicher Untersuchungsansatz'. *Integration* 14: 177–86.

Wilke, M., and Wallace, H. (1990). 'Subsidiarity: Approaches to Power-sharing in the European Community'. Royal Institute of International Affairs Discussion Paper no. 27.

Wittkopf, E. R. (1986). 'On the Foreign Policy Beliefs of the American People: A Critique and Some Evidence'. *International Studies Quarterly* 30: 425–45.

—————— (1991). 'Public Attitudes toward American Foreign and National Security Policy since Vietnam'. In *Debating National Security: The Public Dimension*, ed. H. Rattinger and D. Munton. Frankfurt: Verlag Peter Lang.

—————— and Maggiotto, M. A. (1983). 'The Two Faces of Internationalism: Public Attitudes toward American Foreign Policy in the 1970s—And Beyond?' *Social Science Quarterly* 64: 288–304.

Worre, T. (1988). 'Denmark at the Crossroads: The Danish Referendum of 28 February 1986 on the EC Reform Package'. *Journal of Common Market Studies* 26: 361–88.

Ziegler Jr, A. H. (1987). 'The Structure of Western European Attitues towards Atlantic Cooperation: Implications for the Western Alliance'. *British Journal of Political Science* 17: 457–77.

Zoll, R. (1979). 'Public Opinion and Security Policy: The West German Experience'. *Armed Forces and Society* 5, 4: 590–605.

——— (1981). *Public Opinion on Security Policy and Armed Forces in the USA and the FRG: A Comparative Study*. Sozialwissenschaftliches Institut der Bundeswehr, Munich. Paper for Fourth Annual Scientific Meeting of the International Society for Political Psychology (ISPP), Mannheim.

AUTHOR INDEX

SUBJECT INDEX

accession 334–5, 338, 342, 447–8
affects 33–6, 44–7
age 93–7, 102, 106, 109, 112–15, 121–4,
   183–7, 209–13, 223, 238, 241–2,
   354–7, 389, 394, 400
Agency of Internationalized
   Governance 248–9, 251, 253–4,
   259–60, 270, 275, 278
agriculture 97–9, 263, 335, 375, 436
AIDS 277
Albania 399, 401
alienated 176–88, 440
Alpine countries 345–6, 365
American party system 374
anti-semitism 376, 386
Atlanticists 419, 453
attitudes, *see* orientations; public opinion;
   support
attitudes, dimensionality of 44–8, 402,
   406, 420, 423
attitudinal integration 20–1, 227, 344
Austria 312, 321, 330, 344–9, 351–2,
   355–6, 358, 360, 364–7, 378, 449,
   454
Austro-Hungarian Empire 368
authoritarianism 376

Bagehot 446
Balkan states 373, 395, 399
Baltic states 370–4, 376–9, 382–6, 388,
   397–8, 401, 450–1
Baltic World Values Study 383, 401
behaviour 45, 50, 304
Belgium 59–68, 80–99, 128–34, 143–7,
   152–5, 166–75, 178–87, 195–202,
   209–17, 232–43, 291, 295, 302, 305,
   326, 333–4, 407, 413, 416, 427, 441,
   443, 448, 452
beliefs 45–7
Berlin wall 344, 364, 407, 449
Bosnia-Hercegovina 369

boundaries 454
Britain 8, 59–69, 80–99, 128–34, 140–1,
   143–7, 152–5, 166–75, 178–87,
   195–202, 209–17, 232–43, 285, 291,
   293–4, 302, 306, 311, 314, 318, 321,
   326, 342–4, 347, 373, 376, 385, 407,
   413, 418–19, 427, 434–5, 440–3,
   447–8, 452, 456
British budget rebate 80, 318
Brussels 269, 354
budgetary transfers 80–2, 84, 86
Bulgaria 368–73, 375, 377–9, 382,
   388–90, 392–401, 450

CAP, *see* Common Agricultural Policy
capitalism 369, 377, 379, 397
Cascade model 137–8, 142–6, 161
Ceausescu, Nicolae 371
Central and Eastern Europe 312, 328,
   339, 343, 373, 376, 395, 398–9, 448,
   450–1, 454–6
centre–periphery, *see* core–periphery
CEVIPOF 427
Christian, religious parties 130–4, 152–5,
   158–9, 372
Christian Democrats, *see* Christian,
   religious parties
CIS, *see* Commonwealth of Independent
   States
citizenship, European, *see* identity,
   European
Civic Forum 372, 374
cleavages 355, 359–60, 363, 366, 370,
   372, 374–6, 383, 385, 397–8, 401,
   438
cognitions 33–6, 44–7
cognitive consistency model 124–6
cognitive mobilization 106, 139, 213–21,
   437
   see also opinion leaders
Cold War 365, 373, 404, 407